T0210564

Communications
in Computer and Information Science   581

Commenced Publication in 2007
Founding and Former Series Editors:
Alfredo Cuzzocrea, Dominik Ślęzak, and Xiaokang Yang

More information about this series at http://www.springer.com/series/7899

Markus Helfert · Víctor Méndez Muñoz
Donald Ferguson (Eds.)

Cloud Computing and Services Science

5th International Conference, CLOSER 2015
Lisbon, Portugal, May 20–22, 2015
Revised Selected Papers

 Springer

Editors
Markus Helfert
Dublin City University
Dublin 9
Ireland

Donald Ferguson
Dell
Round Rock
USA

Víctor Méndez Muñoz
Universitat Autònoma de Barcelona
Bellaterra
Spain

ISSN 1865-0929   ISSN 1865-0937 (electronic)
Communications in Computer and Information Science
ISBN 978-3-319-29581-7   ISBN 978-3-319-29582-4 (eBook)
DOI 10.1007/978-3-319-29582-4

Library of Congress Control Number: 2015961031

This Springer imprint is published by SpringerNature
The registered company is Springer International Publishing AG Switzerland

Preface

This book includes extended versions of a set of selected papers from CLOSER 2015 (the 5th International Conference on Cloud Computing and Services Science), held in Lisbon, Portugal, in 2015, organized and sponsored by the Institute for Systems and Technologies of Information, Control and Communication (INSTICC). This conference was held in cooperation with the Association for Computing Machinery - Special Interest Group on Management Information Systems and Turism of Lisbon. The papers were peer reviewed to the professional and scientific standards expected of a proceedings journal published by Springer. Papers were assessed according to the journal's peer review policy, which judges papers on aspects including scientific merit (notably scientific rigor, accuracy, and correctness), clarity of expression, and originality.

The technical program of CLOSER 2015 covered areas such as "Cloud Computing Fundamentals," "Services Science Foundation for Cloud Computing," "Cloud Computing Platforms and Applications," "Cloud Computing Enabling Technology," and "Mobile Cloud Computing and Services." We expect that these proceedings will appeal to a broad audience of engineers, scientists, and business people interested in cloud computing and service systems. We further believe that the papers in these proceedings demonstrate new and innovative solutions, and highlight technical problems in the aforementioned areas that are challenging and worthwhile.

The conference was also complemented with the second edition of the Emerging Software as a Service and Analytics Workshop — EsaaSA 2015 (co-chaired by Victor Chang, Muthu Ramachandran, Gary Wills, Robert Walters, Verena Kantere, and Chung-Sheng Li).

CLOSER 2015 received 146 paper submissions from all continents. From these, 23 papers were published and presented as full papers, 64 were accepted as short papers. These numbers, leading to a full-paper acceptance ratio of 15.8 % and an oral paper acceptance ratio of 60 %, show the intention of preserving a high-quality forum for the next editions of this conference.

The high quality of the CLOSER 2015 program was enhanced by five keynote lectures, delivered by experts in their fields, including: Victor Chang (Leeds Beckett University, UK), who delivered a keynote entitled "Cloud Computing and Big Data Can Improve the Quality of Our Life;" Paolo Traverso (Center for Information Technology - IRST (FBK-ICT), Italy) delivered a keynote on "Change Alone Is Unchanging - Continuous Context-Aware Adaptation of Service-Based Systems for Smart Cities and Communities;" Omer Rana (Cardiff University, UK) gave a keynote entitled "In-transit Analytics on Distributed Clouds - Applications and Architecture;" Chung-Sheng Li (IBM, USA) with a keynote entitled "At Scale Enterprise Computing;" and Cornel Klein (Siemens AG, Germany) with the keynote "Software and Systems Architecture for Smart Vehicles."

This book contains 15 papers from CLOSER 2015, which have been selected, extended, and thoroughly revised.

We wish to thank all those who supported and helped to organize the conference. On behalf of the conference Organizing Committee, we would like to thank the authors, whose work mostly contributed to a very successful conference, the keynote lecturers, and the members of the Program Committee, whose expertise and diligence were instrumental in ensuring the quality of the final contributions. We also wish to thank all the members of the Organizing Committee whose work and commitment were invaluable. Last but not least, we would like to thank Springer for their collaboration in getting this book to print.

May 2015

Markus Helfert
Donald Ferguson
Víctor Méndez Muñoz

Organization

Conference Chair

Markus Helfert   Dublin City University, Ireland

Program Co-chairs

Víctor Méndez Muñoz   Universitat Autònoma de Barcelona, UAB, Spain
Donald Ferguson   Columbia University, USA

Program Committee

Antonia Albani   University of St. Gallen, Switzerland
Vasilios Andrikopoulos   University of Stuttgart, Germany
Claudio Ardagna   Università degli Studi di Milano, Italy
Alvaro Arenas   Instituto de Empresa Business School, Spain
José Enrique   Universidad Pública de Navarra, Spain
 Armendáriz-Iñigo
Muhammad Atif   Australian National University, Australia
Amelia Badica   Faculty of Economics and Business Administration,
           University of Craiova, Romania
Costin Badica   University of Craiova, Romania
Costas Bekas   IBM Zurich Research Lab, Switzerland
Adam S.Z. Belloum   University of Amsterdam, The Netherlands
Simona Bernardi   Centro Universitario de la Defensa - Academia General
           Militar, Spain
Karin Bernsmed   SINTEF ICT, Norway
Nik Bessis   Edge Hill University, UK
Luiz F. Bittencourt   IC/UNICAMP, Brazil
Stefano Bocconi   TU Delft, The Netherlands
Anne Boyer   Loria - Inria Lorraine, France
Ivona Brandić   Vienna UT, Austria
Iris Braun   Dresden Technical University, Germany
Andrey Brito   Universidade Federal de Campina Grande, Brazil
John Brooke   University of Manchester, UK
Anna Brunstrom   Karlstad University, Sweden
Rebecca Bulander   Pforzheim University of Applied Science, Germany
Tomas Bures   Charles University in Prague, Czech Republic
Massimo Cafaro   University of Salento, Italy
Manuel Isidoro   University of Granada, Spain
 Capel-Tuñón

Keith Jeffery	Independent Consultant (previously Science and Technology Facilities Council), UK
Meiko Jensen	Unabhängiges Landeszentrum für Datenschutz SH, Germany
Yiming Ji	University of South Carolina Beaufort, USA
Ming Jiang	University of Sunderland, UK
Xiaolong Jin	Chinese Academy of Sciences, China
Carlos Juiz	Universitat de les Illes Balears, Spain
David R. Kaeli	Northeastern University, USA
Yücel Karabulut	VMware, USA
Gabor Kecskemeti	MTA SZTAKI, Hungary
Attila Kertesz	University of Szeged, Hungary
Claus-Peter Klas	GESIS Leibniz Institute for the Social Sciences, Germany
Carsten Kleiner	University of Applied Sciences and Arts Hannover, Germany
Geir M. Køien	University of Agder, Norway
Dimitri Konstantas	University of Geneva, Switzerland
George Kousiouris	National Technical University of Athens, Greece
László Kovács	MTA SZTAKI, Hungary
Marcel Kunze	Karlsruhe Institute of Technology, Germany
Young Choon Lee	Macquarie University, Australia
Miguel Leitão	ISEP, Portugal
Wilfried Lemahieu	KU Leuven, Belgium
Fei Li	Siemens AG, Austria, Austria
Donghui Lin	Kyoto University, Japan
Shijun Liu	School of Computer Science and Technology, Shandong University, China
Xumin Liu	Rochester Institute of Technology, USA
Francesco Longo	Università degli Studi di Messina, Italy
Pedro Garcia Lopez	University Rovira i Virgili, Spain
Suksant Sae Lor	HP Labs, UK
Joseph P. Loyall	BBN Technologies, USA
Simone Ludwig	North Dakota State University, USA
Glenn Luecke	Iowa State University, USA
Hanan Lutfiyya	University of Western Ontario, Canada
Theo Lynn	Dublin City University, Ireland
Shikharesh Majumdar	Carleton University, Canada
Elisa Marengo	Free University of Bozen-Bolzano, Italy
Ioannis Mavridis	University of Macedonia, Greece
Jose Ramon Gonzalez de Mendivil	Universidad Publica de Navarra, Spain
Mohamed Mohamed	IBM Research, Almaden, USA
Owen Molloy	National University of Ireland, Galway, Ireland
Marco Casassa Mont	Hewlett-Packard Laboratories, UK

Kamran Munir	University of the West of England (Bristol, UK), UK
Víctor Méndez Muñoz	Universitat Autònoma de Barcelona, UAB, Spain
Hidemoto Nakada	National Institute of Advanced Industrial Science and Technology (AIST), Japan
Philippe Navaux	UFRGS - Federal University of Rio Grande Do Sul, Brazil
Jean-Marc Nicod	Institut FEMTO-ST, France
Bogdan Nicolae	IBM Research, Ireland
Karsten Oberle	Alcatel-Lucent Bell Labs, Germany
Sebastian Obermeier	ABB Corporate Research, Switzerland
David Padua	University of Illinois at Urbana-Champaign, USA
Federica Paganelli	CNIT - National Interuniversity Consortium for Telecommunications, Italy
Claus Pahl	Dublin City University, Ireland
Michael A. Palis	Rutgers University, USA
Nikos Parlavantzas	IRISA, France
David Paul	The University of New England, Australia
Siani Pearson	HP Labs, Bristol, UK
Tomás Fernández Pena	University of Santiago de Compostela, Spain
Mikhail Perepletchikov	RMIT University, Australia
Juan Fernando Perez	Imperial College London, UK
Giovanna Petrone	University of Turin, Italy
Agostino Poggi	University of Parma, Italy
Antonio Puliafito	Università degli Studi di Messina, Italy
Francesco Quaglia	Sapienza Università di Roma, Italy
Cauligi (Raghu) Raghavendra	University of Southern California, Los Angeles, USA
Rajendra Raj	Rochester Institute of Technology, USA
Arcot Rajasekar	University of North Carolina at Chapel Hill, USA
Arkalgud Ramaprasad	University of Illinois at Chicago, USA
Manuel Ramos-Cabrer	University of Vigo, Spain
Nadia Ranaldo	University of Sannio, Italy
Andrew Rau-Chaplin	Dalhousie University, Canada
Christoph Reich	Hochschule Furtwangen University, Germany
Norbert Ritter	University of Hamburg, Germany
Luis Rodero-Merino	Spain
Jerome Rolia	Hewlett Packard Labs, Canada
Pedro Frosi Rosa	UFU - Federal University of Uberlandia, Brazil
Elena Sanchez-Nielsen	Universidad de La Laguna, Spain
Patrizia Scandurra	University of Bergamo, Italy
Erich Schikuta	Universität Wien, Austria
Lutz Schubert	Ulm University, Germany
Uwe Schwiegelshohn	TU Dortmund University, Germany
Wael Sellami	Faculty of Sciences Economics and management, Sfax, Tunisia
Giovanni Semeraro	University of Bari Aldo Moro, Italy

Carlos Serrao	ISCTE-IUL, Portugal
Armin Shams	Sharif University of Technology, Iran
Keiichi Shima	IIJ Innovation Institute, Japan
Marten van Sinderen	University of Twente, The Netherlands
Richard O. Sinnott	University of Melbourne, Australia
Frank Siqueira	Universidade Federal de Santa Catarina, Brazil
Cosmin Stoica Spahiu	University of Craiova, Romania
Josef Spillner	Zurich University of Applied Sciences, Switzerland
Ralf Steinmetz	Technische Universität Darmstadt, Germany
Burkhard Stiller	University of Zürich, Switzerland
Yasuyuki Tahara	The University of Electro-Communications, Japan
Cedric Tedeschi	IRISA - University of Rennes 1, France
Gilbert Tekli	Nobatek, France, Lebanon
Joe Tekli	Lebanese American University (LAU), Lebanon
Patricia J. Teller	University of Texas at El Paso, USA
Guy Tel-Zur	Ben-Gurion University of the Negev (BGU), Israel
Orazio Tomarchio	University of Catania, Italy
Johan Tordsson	Umea University and Elastisys, Sweden
Francesco Tusa	University College London, UK
Astrid Undheim	Telenor ASA, Norway
Geoffroy Vallee	Oak Ridge National Laboratory, USA
Luis M. Vaquero	HP Labs, UK
Sabrina de Capitani di Vimercati	Università degli Studi di Milano, Italy
Bruno Volckaert	Ghent University, Belgium
Hiroshi Wada	NICTA, Australia
Maria Emilia M.T. Walter	University of Brasilia, Brazil
Chen Wang	CSIRO ICT Centre, Australia
Dadong Wang	CSIRO, Australia
Martijn Warnier	Delft University of Technology, The Netherlands
Hany F. El Yamany	Suez Canal University, Egypt
Bo Yang	University of Electronic Science and Technology of China, China
Zhifeng Yun	University of Houston, USA
Michael Zapf	Georg Simon Ohm University of Applied Sciences, Germany
Wolfgang Ziegler	Fraunhofer Institute SCAI, Germany

Additional Reviewers

Márcio Assis	Unicamp, Brazil
Maria Estrela Ferreira da Cruz	Instituto Politécnico de Viana do Castelo, Portugal
Fernando Gómez-Folgar	Centro Singular de Investigación en Tecnoloxías da Información, Spain
Mehdi Khouja	University of Gabes, Tunisia

Amardeep Mehta   Umeå University, Sweden
Athina Provataki   University of Macedonia, Greece
Eduardo Roloff   UFRGS, Brazil

Invited Speakers

Victor Chang   Leeds Beckett University, UK
Paolo Traverso   Center for Information Technology - IRST (FBK-ICT),
                         Italy
Omer Rana   Cardiff University, UK
Chung-Sheng Li   IBM, USA
Cornel Klein   Siemens AG, Germany

Contents

Invited Paper

Cloud Computing at the *Edges* 3
    Luiz F. Bittencourt, Omer Rana, and Ioan Petri

Papers

Scalable and Cost-Efficient Algorithms for Reliable and Distributed
Cloud Storage. 15
    Makhlouf Hadji

Accountability Through Transparency for Cloud Customers 38
    Martin Gilje Jaatun, Daniela S. Cruzes, Julio Angulo,
    and Simone Fischer-Hübner

Towards a Standardized Quality Assessment Framework
for OCCI-Controlled Cloud Infrastructures 58
    Yongzheng Liang

Re-provisioning of Cloud-Based Execution Infrastructure Using the
Cloud-Aware Provenance to Facilitate Scientific Workflow Execution
Reproducibility 74
    Khawar Hasham, Kamran Munir, Richard McClatchey,
    and Jetendr Shamdasani

Security and Privacy Preservation of Evidence in Cloud
Accountability Audits 95
    Thomas Rübsamen, Tobias Pulls, and Christoph Reich

Using Model-Driven Development to Support Portable PaaS Applications . . . 115
    Elias Nogueira, Daniel Lucrédio, Ana Moreira, and Renata Fortes

LS-ADT: Lightweight and Scalable Anomaly Detection
for Cloud Datacentres 135
    Sakil Barbhuiya, Zafeirios Papazachos, Peter Kilpatrick,
    and Dimitrios S. Nikolopoulos

Performance and Cost Trade-Off in IaaS Environments: A Scientific
Workflow Simulation Environment Case Study. 153
    Santiago Gómez Sáez, Vasilios Andrikopoulos, Michael Hahn,
    Dimka Karastoyanova, Frank Leymann, Marigianna Skouradaki,
    and Karolina Vukojevic-Haupt

A Practical Evaluation of Searchable Encryption for Data Archives
in the Cloud 171
    Christian Neuhaus, Frank Feinbube, Daniel Janusz, and Andreas Polze

High Level Model Checker Based Testing of Electronic Contracts 193
    Ellis Solaiman, Ioannis Sfyrakis, and Carlos Molina-Jimenez

Streamlining APIfication by Generating APIs for Diverse Executables
Using Any2API 216
    Johannes Wettinger, Uwe Breitenbücher, and Frank Leymann

Hybrid TOSCA Provisioning Plans: Integrating Declarative and Imperative
Cloud Application Provisioning Technologies 239
    Uwe Breitenbücher, Tobias Binz, Oliver Kopp, Kálmán Képes,
    Frank Leymann, and Johannes Wettinger

An Analysis of Power Consumption in Mobile Cloud Computing 263
    Abdelmounaam Rezgui and Zaki Malik

Using Satellite Execution to Reduce Latency for Mobile/Cloud
Applications 279
    Robert Pettersen, Steffen Viken Valvåg, Åge Kvalnes, and Dag Johansen

Author Index 299

Invited Paper

Cloud Computing at the *Edges*

Luiz F. Bittencourt[1]([⊠]), Omer Rana[2], and Ioan Petri[2]

[1] Institute of Computing, University of Campinas, Campinas, Brazil
`bit@ic.unicamp.br`
[2] School of Computer Science and Informatics, Cardiff University, Cardiff, UK
`{ranaof,petrii}@cardiff.ac.uk`

Abstract. Currently, most cloud computing deployments are generally supported through the use of large scale data centres. There is a common perception that by developing scalable computation, storage, network, and by energy-acquisition at preferential prices, data centres are able to provide more efficient, reliable and cost effective hosting environments for user applications. However, although the network capacity within and in the proximity of such a data centre may be high – the connectivity of a user to their first hop network may not be. Understanding how a distributed cloud can be provisioned, enabling capability to be made available "closer" to a user (geographically or based on network metrics, such as number of hops or latency), remains an important challenge – aiming to provide the same benefits as a centralised cloud, but with better Quality of Service for mobile users. With increasing proliferation of mobile devices and sensor-based deployments, understanding how data from such devices can be processed in closer proximity to the device (ranging from capability directly available on the device or through first-hop network nodes from the device) also forms an important requirement of such distributed clouds. We review a number of technologies that could be useful enablers of distributed clouds – outlining common themes across them and identifying potential business models.

Keywords: Distributed clouds · Mobile computing · Edge device integration

1 Introduction and Overview

There has been a recent increase in the diversity, type and number of devices used to access cloud services – with such devices expected to reach 24 billion by 2020 [1] and generally part of the increasing interest in *Internet of Things* (IoT). IoT comprises any kind of objects that are able to generate a minimal piece of data and transmit it through the network, ranging from small fixed sensors to mobile, smart devices. The amount of data that can be generated by these devices and that need to be processed and/or stored has no precedents. Although the now established cloud computing paradigm could be utilised to store and process data generated by IoT devices, the expected amount of data can make this inefficient or even unpractical.

© Springer International Publishing Switzerland 2016
M. Helfert et al. (Eds.): CLOSER 2015, CCIS 581, pp. 3–12, 2016.
DOI: 10.1007/978-3-319-29582-4_1

One drawback of using a centralised data centre alone to process and store IoT data is related to constraints with existing network capacity and latency. Devices constantly generating and transferring data to the cloud can result in poor network conditions, yielding congestion and service disruption for many applications. Moreover, much of the data generated by IoT devices do not need to be stored in its raw form. There is now significant interest in combining cloud computing, offered at large scale data centres, with services that have been made available at regional data centres. With interest in providing cloud computing capability across different types of data centres, this often implies that there needs to be suitable coordination between distributed data centres that are able to receive and process data from such devices, which may be located at different geographical areas and operating with varying reliability criteria. The extent of this distributed cloud model also encompasses recent interest in supporting multiple micro and nano data centres, which may be connected over network links with varying bandwidth, availability profiles and latency.

The distributed cloud deployment model enables a variety of different types of market players to also engage and provision services and infrastructure, from telecom operators who may use their existing network infrastructure to offer cloud services, to a variety of businesses (such as coffee shops, supermarkets etc.), who can host cloud services to enable a better Quality of Experience (QoE) for a user. The benefits of this model are many and include: (i) improved resilience of cloud services; (ii) location specific contextualisation of provisioned services; (iii) ability to integrate regionally provisioned services in a seamless manner; (iv) latency hiding through automated service "hand-off"; (v) better coupling between cloud services and wireless access networks.

The distributed cloud model shares similarities with a number of emerging technologies and approaches – in all cases attempting to move data and processing closer to the user, thereby moving cloud provisioning from centralised data centres to *edge* servers with varying capability and connectivity. We briefly outline some of these in Sect. 2, to demonstrate common themes and outline a generalised architecture that attempts to combine features from these. Although each of these approaches have their own specific use scenarios, and have been developed by different communities, we notice a significant overlap in the underlying concepts being used. We characterise these in Sect. 3.

2   Related Approaches

The maturity of the cloud computing paradigm has contributed to a large number of distributed network applications that take advantage of cloud capacity to overcome computing and data storage requirements of a user. This centralised data centre architecture allows access to a large (potential) computing pool with unbounded[1] capacity. *Elasticity* is often a key enabler in such applications, allowing dynamic scale up/down based on instantaneous resource requirements [2,3].

---

[1] Unbounded here refers to the user perception of endless on-demand capacity.

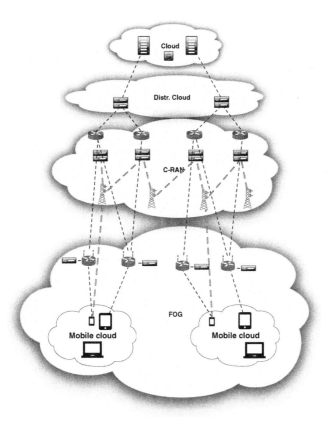

Fig. 1. Distributed Clouds – a conceptual perspective.

Data centres-based Cloud systems are able to fulfil many application requirements, needing limited upfront investment and easing the management of continuous change in requirements over time. Recently, however, there has been
interest in providing support for "distributed clouds", which provide similar
benefits but focus on cloud provisioning across multiple providers. We briefly
describe each of the approaches to support distributed clouds outlined in Fig. 1,
identifying their key characteristics and emphasising their similarities.

Distributed Data Centres: This approach involves the use of multiple types of
linked data centres, each type offering differing capabilities. Two general types are
often identified: (i) network data centres (NDC); (ii) cloud/enterprise data centres
(CDC). The first of these are generally owned and managed by network operators and able to provide a limited programmatic interface to external users. Existing efforts towards network function virtualisation and software defined networks
have enabled capability on network elements within an NDC, such as routers and
switches, to be directly accessed by external users – enabling a variety of in-network
operations to be made available (ranging from data encryption, data transcoding,
etc.). Techniques such as MiddleBox technologies (often also referred to as network

appliances) can be combined with such approaches to enable data streams arriving at NDCs to be aggregated in some way. Conversely, an enterprise data centre offers computational and data storage capability of a much greater capacity than an NDC, but often not situated at an intermediate point in the network. A CDC has much greater potential for infrastructure scalability and can be part of a much wider, global deployment (e.g. a CDC in Asia-Pacific, in Europe, etc.). A provider is able to use the combined capability of multiple CDCs to enable elastic provisioning to a user and to provide fault masking in one such CDC. There may be a variety of other types of data centres (some user owned) in addition to the two identified here, and significant recent research is attempting to identify potential types that could be use to support resource provisioning to a user [4,5].

Mobile Cloud and Cloud-Offloading: This approach involves moving computation (generally) and data stored on mobile devices to an enterprise/cloud data centre. The general motivation is to enable more computationally intensive processes to be carried out on large scale data centres (CDC) rather than on the device, enabling: (i) improved battery usage on the device; (ii) latency and network outage masking on the device – especially when a device user is moving across geographical areas with varying network coverage; (iii) handling wireless connectivity across highly heterogeneous networks (always-on connectivity, on-demand scalability and energy efficiency is a difficult problem across heterogeneous networks); (iv) improve (potential) availability when using a CDC – due to reduced capacity on radio/wireless networks. Approaches can range in complexity from providing a complete *copy* of a mobile device within a CDC, with periodic synchronisation of state between the processes on the device and the CDC-hosted copy (e.g. the CloneCloud system [6] to create a device clone on the Cloud and provide an application level Virtual Machine (VM) at the data centre). CloneCloud requires device to cloud connectivity for the clone to remain in sync. with the device. An alternative approach is to annotate program source code to identify what should run on the device and what should be cloud-hosted – e.g. the Maui system [7]. In this approach, two versions of a program are created, a local and a cloud version. The "reflection" technique from programming languages is then used to determine which part should run where and how the two copies should remain in sync. This approach generally requires source code annotation (and can tolerate disconnection from network). Other related approaches focus on annotating a program call graph (method calls) to determine which parts should be off loaded – making use of criteria such as data transfer costs and security/data privacy concerns (i.e. determining what should remain local to the device and what can be moved to a CDC) [8].

Cloudlets and Fog Computing: This approach considers that processing and storage can be performed on edge devices, as in the mobile cloud computing paradigm, whenever this brings optimisation to the system and better quality of service. Fog computing introduces the notion of *cloudlets* – "small clouds" which are geographically scattered across a network and acting as "small data centres" at the edge of the network [9,10]. Cloudlets aim to give support to IoT devices by providing increased processing and storage capacity as an extension of those devices, but without the need to move data/processing to a CDC. This leads to reduced communication delays and the overall size of data that needs to be migrated to a CDC. Data processing offered by cloudlets can employ a set of mechanisms to process data on behalf of the IoT device, effectively sending to the cloud only data that are aggregated results or that need data/processing that is not available at the cloudlet [11].

Cloud Radio Access Network (C-RAN): This approach provides an optimisation over an existing de-centralised Radio Access Network (RAN), due to a significant increase in mobile internet traffic over recent years and the cost associated with operating, building and upgrading such a network. The Cloud-RAN approach involves splitting the capability offered at a mobile base station into two: a Remote Radio Head (RRH) and a BaseBand Unit (BBU). In the C-RAN approach, the BBU is centralised and shared amongst multiple sites in a virtualised BBU pool – and often hosted at a data centre. This centralisation enables reduced operating costs, improves scalability and reduces potential energy consumption. As BBU's are virtualised and hosted on a single data centre, this enables multiple physical cells/sites to interact with lower delays leading additionally to increased spectral efficiency and throughput. The C-RAN approach also aligns well with recent interest in creating Heterogeneous and Small Cell networks (HetSNets), primarily leading to increased network capacity due to the additional cells now available. The C-RAN approach is particularly relevant in the context of distributed data centres as they enable improved handoff mechanisms for mobile users (due to the use of the same BBU hosting location) – being geographically closer the user and able to support partial processing [12].

3   Common Themes

There are conceptual similarities that arise in the paradigms listed in the previous section. In this section we discuss related concepts and general aspects on how these relate to cloud computing at network edges.

3.1   Architecture and Deployment

Enabling cloud computing at the edges involves, primarily, a decision on where processing/storage capacity should be placed in order to fulfil users' application requirements. This decision can depend on several factors, including how efficient and reliable the network is in connecting users to the edge processing/storage equipment, as well as connecting those equipment among themselves. Other criteria can also influence this decision – such as: (i) overall cost of undertaking computation; (ii) size of data that needs to be transferred from a local (proximity-based) device to a data centre; (iii) network reliability/availability, amongst others.

It is necessary to consider the trade off between the computational infrastructure needed to host services (such as cloudlet) and their proximity to the user. Locating a service closer to a user could potentially require a greater number of facilities to deploy such services. This incurs higher costs, but smaller latencies/delays for users accessing cloud data/applications. For example, a more geographically distributed architecture such as advocated in Fog Computing would be able to act as a real-time capacity extension for mobile devices, leading to a one-hop connection to processing/storage resources. On the other hand, deployment costs may require different business models to make it feasible.

The deployment of equipment to support such edge services leads to greater reliance on a dependable network. The straightforward approach is to let communication go through existing infrastructure, i.e., with traffic between distributed processing/storage equipment traversing the core network using ordinary TCP/IP communication – potentially leading to increased traffic in the core network. A second approach would be to provide a direct connection using a dedicated link (radio, fibre, or even ethernet), which increases cost but improves performance. This trade-off between cost and performance can be also a focus of study: distributed equipment "clusters" could be built using direct network connections in places where demand is significantly higher, preventing routing through the core network. Conversely, where communication requirement is lower (or sparse), the core network could be utilised.

An important aspect is a consideration of who would be responsible for deployment and maintenance of equipment when making use of distributed cloud computing resources. Feasible/ potential options include cloud providers, network (broadband) providers, mobile phone carriers, and/or local businesses. While cloud/broadband providers seem like the obvious choices, mobile phone carriers (especially in developing countries) and local businesses can utilise their intrinsic distributed presence to host equipment and provide computing services in addition to communication through 4G/LTE/5G and WiFi connections.

3.2   Virtualisation

Virtualisation enables sharing of infrastructure amongst users with software and, potentially, hardware isolation. The hypervisor (or virtual machine monitor – VMM) has the ability to replicate hardware interfaces and trap the necessary instructions in order to share the underlying hardware among multiple privileged tenants. Therefore, tenants generally have no knowledge they are running on a virtualised and shared hardware.

Efficient resource virtualisation is essential to enable various Quality of Service provisioning to be supported across a shared infrastructures – enabling different users (with varying service requirements and QoS needs) to be isolated from each other. In deploying cloud-based services, virtualisation is also important to ease management through the use of virtual machines (VMs), which can be migrated to different physical machines to fulfil an objective function, such as infrastructure cost reduction. What is virtualised can vary – for instance: (i) a physical machine or a mobile device can be virtualised (with CPU, memory and network interface); (ii) network function, e.g. routing and forwarding of packets can be virtualised; (iii) a base station capability (in C-RAN) can be virtualised, (iv) a physical sensor may be virtualised – enabling the same "virtual" sensor interface to communicate with different physical sensors at different times, or to enable data from multiple sensors to be aggregated and offered as a virtual sensor; (v) a firewall or security interface can be virtualised, etc. Over recent years, there has been interest in providing virtualisation at different levels of the computational infrastructure – with "enterprise" and "data centre" virtualisation enabling an aggregation of different levels of virtualisation to co-exist, leading to a much greater efficiency in how the physical infrastructure is used, providing isolation for users and enabling dynamic update of physical infrastructure that is accessed through a virtualised interface.

In a distributed cloud context, such virtualisation capability can now extend beyond a single data centre – along the different layers outlined above. Additionally, the isolation provided by virtualisation, the ability to replicate a user session across different VMs and support for VM migration can help in reducing latencies when the user moves from one geographical location to another. Services hosted within such a VM can be utilised to perform data/process migration along with user movement, aiming to reduce delays for specific applications. This could be specially interesting in the fog computing paradigm, where VMs can migrate among cloudlets to support users applications [13].

3.3   Data Migration and Management

When using a distributed cloud for mobility-based scenarios, support for efficient data migration is necessary, enabling data to be placed closer to the user (with a user location potentially changing several times during a single day). Nodes within a distributed cloud may be used for storing more "volatile" data that does not need to be kept for long periods of time, and such nodes can provide a pre-processing facility to reduce data transfer to the centralised cloud, where long-term data storage/processing can occur. To enable QoS-based provisioning, user data and applications should be placed as closest (in terms of number of hops or network latency) as possible to his/her device(s). The (potentially real-time) need for migration introduces new challenges in resource management. Data and processing should follow users, demanding mechanisms for mobility detection/prediction to anticipate migration and reduce the number of service disruptions seen by a user.

4   Business Models

Several business models may become relevant when considering virtualised distributed cloud environments. Nodes associated with a distributed cloud must be deployed and managed by an individual or organisation, and the costs of the infrastructure must be taken into account in the business model. Similar to current broad availability of WiFi access points and cell phone antennas, we envisage four general ways of funding cloud at the edge: (i) by cloud providers; (ii) by local businesses; (iii) by public funding; and (iv) by mobile carriers. Various trust models exist that may be associated with each of these four options.

Service Selection: in this model, the user would be able to choose a cloud at the edge provider on-the-go, according to his/her current activity or provider's availability and potential reputation within a market place. The use of a service-based approach enables loose coupling, enabling an eco-system of providers to co-exist. However, there is no guarantee that integrating externally provisioned services will lead to the fulfilment of the user objectives, since this would depend on providers' agreements to support data and process migration. Therefore, interoperability and trust issues are expected to dominate this selection decision.

Service Contracts: in this model, contracts are signed between the user and the provider, where criteria that adequately captures the circumstances that influence the performance of the externally provisioned services must be specified and pre-agreed. Contracts can be based on particular (monitorable) service-level objectives – where short-term contracts have proved to be more profitable options for service providers. Providers can also offer in-contract guarantees performance metrics (e.g. availability) to the customer, which is reflected in the associated price.

All-in-One Enterprise Cloud: this model is a more comprehensive approach, where a distributed node is actually hosted at a data centre. Therefore, large cloud providers could joining local businesses/ network providers in order to build a larger business ecosystem with greater financial stability, allowing users content/data/processing to freely travel across their boundaries.

Business models are important to make distributed clouds profitable, as well as to help users make informed decisions about providers. Each business model is associated with a set of cost models according to the provider's service strategies and business objectives, as for example:

– *Consumption-Based Cost Model*: clients only pay for the resources they use. For distributed clouds a user could be charged according to the size of his/her files or processing time utilised by applications that need edge computing.
– *Subscription-Cost Pricing Model*: clients pay a subscription charge for using a service for a period of time – typically on a monthly basis. This subscription cost typically provides unlimited usage (subject to some "fair use" constraints) during the subscription period. For example, local businesses can offer a subscription to their infrastructure that enables a user to have content/applications to be placed on that infrastructure.
– *Advertising-Based Cost Model*: clients get a no-charge or heavily-discounted service whereas the providers receive most of their revenue from advertisers. This model is quite common in cloud-based media services such as free TV providers (e.g. net2TV) and can also be adopted in distributed clouds.
– *Market-Based Cost Model*: clients are charged on a per-unit-time basis. When bringing computing to the edges, the user can have a configuration dashboard to establish the maximum usage quota/capacity and other relevant parameters, similarly to IaaS offerings such as Amazon EC2.
– *Group Buying Cost Model*: clients can acquire reduced cost services only if there are enough clients interested in a deal. This can be adapted for distributed clouds, enabling users to have access to a larger set of edge infrastructure but with limited concurrency among shared users, for example.

5   Application Scenarios

We describe two potential scenarios where the approach being proposed in this paper could be benefit:

- Crowd-sourced surveillance: this application would involve making use of user provisioned resources to capture local data, aggregated through the use of a Cloud-based platform. As increasing number of individuals posses mobile devices able to record (via photos, videos or text-based data) information about a scene locally, each of these devices could be used to record such information and tag this with the location of the user. Such information could then be submitted to a data centre for aggregation. While the information is in-transit from the capture source to the data centre, it could be aggregate enroute. Additional content related to crime rates within a geographical area, known crime reports within a particular time frame, etc. could be combined with such content to increase the potential veracity of information that is subsequently submitted to the data centre. The device owned by a user could connect to the nearest available "cloudlet" to offload some of the data recorded about the particular event being monitored. Cloudlets would interact with each other, based on the geographical proximity of other users to check if the same incident has been recorded by others.
- Real time streaming: this application would involve a user interacting with a real time information source, with a requirement tomaintain a persistent, high quality (low latency, high throughput) connection to the information source. In this scenario, the user would initially register their quality of service requirements to a cloudlet, and as the user moves from one region to another, there would need to be hand-off to other cloudlets. This hand-off could be supported through technologies such as C-RAN, where a common regional data centre may be used to host multiple cloudlets, with a potential predictive hand-off with user movement.

6   Conclusion

We describe a variety of emerging technologies that promote the integration of edge devices with Cloud computing, enabling both to be used in coordination. With increasing deployment and availability of sensing capability, there is a realisation that not all of this data needs to be migrated to a centralised data centre. Undertaking data processing and storage closer to a user allows masking of the *last mile* connectivity concerns that have been highlighted in Content Distribution Networks. Understanding how resources that have a more efficient (small number of hops or low latency) connection to a user, can be combined with large scale data centres remains an important challenge for many applications. This contribution attempts to highlight common issues that occur within multiple approaches addressing this concern.

Acknowledgements. We would like to acknowledge various individuals who have contributed to our views expressed in this article, these include: Manish Parashar, Javier Diaz-Montes, Mengsong Zou, Ali Reza Zemani (Rutgers University, USA), Rafael Tolosana-Calasanz, Jose Banares (University of Zaragoza, Spain), Congduc Pham (University of Pau, France), Yacine Rezgui, Tom Beach, Stuart Allen (Cardiff University).

References

1. Gubbi, J., Buyya, R., Marusic, S., Palaniswami, M.: Internet of things (IoT): a vision, architectural elements, and future directions. Future Gener. Comput. Syst. **29**, 1645–1660 (2013)
2. Bittencourt, L.F., Madeira, E.R.M., Da Fonseca, N.L.S.: Scheduling in hybrid clouds. IEEE Commun. Mag. **50**, 42–47 (2012)
3. Armbrust, M., Fox, A., Griffith, R., Joseph, A.D., Katz, R., Konwinski, A., Lee, G., Patterson, D., Rabkin, A., Stoica, I., et al.: A view of cloud computing. Comm. of the ACM **53**, 50–58 (2010)
4. Mazmanov, D., Curescu, C., Olsson, H., Ton, A., Kempf, J.: Handling performance sensitive native cloud applications with distributed cloud computing and SLA management. In: 2013 IEEE/ACM 6th International Conference on Utility and Cloud Computing (UCC), pp. 470–475 (2013)
5. Nygren, E., Sitaraman, R.K., Sun, J.: The akamai network: a platform for high-performance internet applications. SIGOPS Oper. Syst. Rev. **44**, 2–19 (2010)
6. Chun, B.G., Ihm, S., Maniatis, P., Naik, M., Patti, A.: Clonecloud: elastic execution between mobile device and cloud. In: Proceedings of the Sixth Conference on Computer Systems, EuroSys 2011, pp. 301–314. ACM, New York (2011)
7. Cuervo, E., Balasubramanian, A., Cho, D.K., Wolman, A., Saroiu, S., Chandra, R., Bahl, P.: Maui: making smartphones last longer with code offload. In: Proceedings of the 8th International Conference on Mobile Systems, Applications, and Services, MobiSys 2010, pp. 49–62. ACM, New York (2010)
8. Pedersen, M., Fitzek, F.: Mobile clouds: the new content distribution platform. Proc. IEEE **100**, 1400–1403 (2012)
9. Bonomi, F., Milito, R., Zhu, J., Addepalli, S.: Fog computing and its role in the internet of things. In: MCC Workshop on Mobile Cloud Computing, pp. 13–16. ACM (2012)
10. Bonomi, F., Milito, R., Natarajan, P., Zhu, J.: Fog computing: a platform for internet of things and analytics. In: Bessis, N., Dobre, C. (eds.) Big Data and Internet of Things: A Roadmap for Smart Environments. SCI, vol. 546, pp. 169–186. Springer, Heidelberg (2014)
11. Fesehaye, D., Gao, Y., Nahrstedt, K., Wang, G.: Impact of cloudlets on interactive mobile cloud applications. In: 2012 IEEE 16th International Enterprise Distributed Object Computing Conference (EDOC), pp. 123–132 (2012)
12. Checko, A., Christiansen, H., Yan, Y., Scolari, L., Kardaras, G., Berger, M., Dittmann, L.: Cloud ran for mobile networks - a technology overview. IEEE Commun. Surv. Tutorials **17**, 405–426 (2015)
13. Bittencourt, L.F., Lopes, M.M., Petri, I., Rana, O.F.: Towards virtual machine migration in fog computing. In: 10th International Conference on P2P, Parallel, Grid, Cloud and Internet Computing (2015)

Papers

Scalable and Cost-Efficient Algorithms for Reliable and Distributed Cloud Storage

Makhlouf Hadji[(✉)]

Technological Research Institute, SystemX,
8, Avenue de la Vauve, 91120 Palaiseau, France
makhlouf.hadji@irt-systemx.fr

Abstract. This paper focuses on minimizing jointly data storage and networking costs in a distributed cloud storage environment. We present two new efficient algorithms to place encrypted data chunks and enhance data availability when guaranteeing a minimum cost of storage and communication in the same time. The proposed underlying solutions, based on linear programming approach lead to an exact formulation with convergence times feasible for small and medium network sizes. A new polynomial time algorithm is presented and shown to scale to much larger network sizes. Performance assessment results, using simulations, show the scalability and cost-efficiency of the proposed distributed cloud storage solutions.

Keywords: Cloud computing · Distributed storage · Data replication · Commodity flow · Encryption · Broker · Optimization

1 Introduction

Cloud storage has emerged as a new paradigm to host user and enterprize data in cloud providers and data centers. Cloud storage providers (such as Amazon, Google, etc.) store large amounts of data and various distributed applications [21] with differentiated prices. Amazon provides for example storage services at a fraction of a dollar per Terabyte per month [21]. Cloud service providers propose also different SLAs in their storage offers. These SLAs reflect the different cost of proposed availability guarantees. End-users interested in more reliable SLAs, must pay more, and this leads to cause high costs when storing large amounts of data. The cloud storage providers to attract users do not charge for initial storage or put operations. Retrieval becomes unfortunately a hurdle, a costly process and users are likely to experience data availability problems. A way to avoid unavailability of data is to rely on multiple providers by replicating the data and actually chunk the data and distribute it across the providers so none of them can actually reconstruct the data to protect it from any misuse. This paper aims at improving this type of distributed storage across multiple

---

M. Hadji—A research fellow at the Technological Research Institute - IRT SystemX.

© Springer International Publishing Switzerland 2016
M. Helfert et al. (Eds.): CLOSER 2015, CCIS 581, pp. 15–37, 2016.
DOI: 10.1007/978-3-319-29582-4_2

providers to achieve high availability at reasonable (minimum) storage service costs by proposing new scalable and efficient algorithms to select providers for distributed storage. The objective is to optimally replicate data chunks and store the replicates in a distributed fashion across the providers. In order to protect the data even further, the chunks are encrypted.

1.1   Paper Contributions and Structure

We propose data chunk placement algorithms to tradeoff data availability and storage and communication cost and provide some guarantees on the performance of the distributed storage. We assume end-users involved in PUT (write) and GET (read) operations of data objects stored in an encrypted manner and distributed optimally in different data centers require a specified level of data availability during data retrieval. More specifically, after data encryption and partition operations which consist to split the data into encrypted chunks to be distributed across multiple data centers, our main work focuses on improving and optimizing two operations:

- **Data Chunks Placement Optimization:** through novel (b-matching and commodity flow techniques), efficient, scalable algorithms that minimize placement and networking cost and meet data availability requirements given probabilities of failure (or unavailability) of the storage systems and hence the stored data.
- **Chunk Replication:** to meet a required high level of availability of the data using optimal replication of chunks to reduce the risk of inaccessibility of the data due to data center failures (or storage service degradations).

To realize these objectives, we derive a number of mathematical models to be used by a broker to select the storage service providers leading to cost-efficient and reliable data storage. The proposed broker collaborates with the providers having different storage costs, minimum latency access and reliability (storage service availability), as depicted in detail in Fig. 1. We assume that the providers propose storage services to the broker and to end-users with same reliability but with different prices (prices for a real broker for instance will be lower than those proposed to end-users).

It is consequently assumed that there exist benefits for a storage service brokerage that optimally distributes encrypted data across the most appropriate providers. Thus, the aim of this paper consists to propose a scalable and polynomial algorithm spanning a cost efficient chunk placement model that can achieve optimal solutions, when guaranteeing high data availability to end-users.

Section 2 presents related work on cloud storage and optimization. In Sect. 3, we use the well known Advanced Encryption Standard (AES) algorithm [26] to encrypt end-user data and divide them into $|\mathcal{N}|$ chunks. In the same section, we propose mathematical models to deal with chunk placement and replication in an optimal manner for given server and networking costs and availabilities. Performance assessments and results are reported in Sect. 4. Conclusion and future work are reported in Sect. 5.

2   Related Work

Data storage and data replication has received a lot of attention at the data management, distribution and application level since the distribution of original data objects and their replicas is crucial to overall system performance, especially in the cloud environment where data are supposed to be protected and highly available in different data centers. The current literature concerns essentially the cloud storage problem in tandem with replication techniques to improve data availability, but to our knowledge, does not consider data transfer in/out costs, or migration costs, etc. We will nevertheless cite some of the related work even if it can not be directly compared to the proposed algorithms in this paper.

In [7], authors dealt with the problem of multi-cloud storage with a focus on availability and cost criteria. The authors proposed a first algorithm to minimize replication cost and maximize expected availability of objects. The second algorithm has the same objective subject to budget constraints. However, this paper did not embed security aspects apart from dividing the data into chunks or objects. In our work, we propose to divide data into encrypted chunks, that will be optimally stored and distributed through various data centers with minimum costs while satisfying the QoS required by end-users. Moreover, the proposed algorithm in [7] is a simple heuristic without any convergence guarantee to the optimal solution. Our proposed algorithm converges in few seconds to optimal solutions benchmarked by the Bin-Packing algorithm.

In [3], authors present Scalia, a system to deal with the problem of multi cloud data storage under availability and durability requirements and constraints. The authors note the NP-Hardness of the considered problem, and propose algorithms to solve small instances of the problem. In our work, we propose a new efficient and scalable solution capable of handling large instances in a few seconds. Clearly, the proposed solution in [3] suffers from scalability challenges to handle on with larger instances, when our algorithms are able to quickly solve large instances of the defined problem.

To avoid failure and achieve higher availability when storing data in the cloud, reference [5] proposes a distributed algorithm to better replicate data objects in different virtual nodes instantiated in physical servers. According to the traffic load of all considered nodes, the authors considered three decisions or actions as replicate, migrate, or suicide to better meet end-user requirements and requests. However, the proposed approach consists only in checking the feasibility of migrating a virtual node, performs suicide actions or replicating a copy of a virtual node, without optimizing the system. In our work, we propose optimization algorithms based on a complete description of the convexe hull of the defined problem, leading to reach optimal solutions even for large instances.

Reference [4] proposes a simple heuristic to give stored data greater protection and higher availability by splitting a file (data) into subfiles to be placed in different virtual machines belonging to the physical resources (data centers for example) of one provider or different providers. The paper dealt with PUT and GET operations to distribute and retrieve the required subfiles (data) without encrypting them. The proposed heuristic in [4] can only reach suboptimal solutions, leading to considerable gaps compared to the optimal solutions. We propose a new scalable and cost efficient solution to deal with the multi-cloud storage problem.

Aiming to provide cost-effective availability and improve performance and load balancing of cloud storage, the authors of reference [6] propose CDRM as a cost-effective dynamic replication management scheme. CDRM consists in maintaining a minimal number of replica for a given availability requirement, and proposes a replica placement based on the blocking probability of data nodes. Moreover, CDRM allows us to dynamically adjust the replica number according to changing workload and node capacities. However, the paper focuses only on the relationship between availability and replica number, and there is no proposal to deal with the optimal placement of replicas.

To achieve high performance and reduce data loss when we require storage services in the cloud, different papers in the literature propose various algorithms that are useful only for small instances due to the NP-Hardness of the problem. In [8], the authors propose a key-value store named Skute, which consists in dynamically allocating the resources of a data cloud to several applications in a cost effective and fair way using game theoretical models. To guarantee cloud object storage performance, the authors of [11] propose a dynamic replication scheme to enhance the workload distribution of cloud storage systems. The authors of [16] conduct a study based on a dynamic programming approach, to deal with the problem of selecting cloud providers offering storage services with different costs and failure probabilities.

Reference [12] proposes a distributed storage solution named RACS, to avoid vendor lock-in, reduce the cost of switching providers, and better tolerate provider outages. The authors applied erasure coding (see references [9, 10, 23]) to design the proposed solution RACS. In the same spirit, references [13–15, 18] addressed the cloud storage problem described above, under different constraints including energy consumption, budget limitation, limited storage capacities, and the availability of the stored data.

In [1], authors propose a new solution to guarantee the data integrity when stored in a cloud data center. The proposed solution is based on homomorphic verifiable response and hash index hierarchy. This kind of solutions can be integrated to our work to reenforce data security and privacy for reticent users. An other reference on secured multi cloud storage can be found in [2]. Authors presented a cryptographic data splitting with dynamic approach for securing information. The splitting approach of the proposed solution is not deeply studied. This may lead to not select cost efficient providers.

3   System Model

To store encrypted data in multiple DCs belonging to various cloud providers system, while optimizing storage and networking costs and failure probabilities, we separate the global problem into a number of combinatorial optimization sub-problems. To derive the model we make a simplifying assumption regarding the pricing scheme between cloud service providers, the broker and end-users. We assume that the proposed storage price by a service cloud provider to end-users is higher than that proposed to the broker. This can be explained by the large amount of demands that will be required by the broker aggregating the demands of a finite set of end-users seeking to avoid vendor lock-in and higher availability. One can assume that prices proposed by cloud providers are smaller as the volume of data is larger. Note that the broker will guarantee a minimum storage cost and minimum latency meeting end-users requirements, ensuring that the proposed cost to end-users can never exceed a certain threshold.

We first propose to use the well known AES (Advanced Encryption Standard) algorithm [26, 27] for efficient data encryption. This will generate different encrypted chunks to be distributed in the available storage nodes or data centers. This encryption ensures the confidentiality of the stored data. Moreover, the used solution permits to construct diverse chunks (with small sizes) to facilitate PUT and GET requests as is shown in Fig. 1.

We derive three algorithms to handle encrypted data chunk placement and replication to guarantee data high availability, network latency and storage cost efficiency. This can be summarized as follows:

- **Data Chunk Placement:** The first important objective of our paper consists in guaranteeing the availability of all chunks of stored data by optimally distributing them to a cost-efficient set of selected data centers (see Fig. 1). This avoids user lock-in, and reduces the total cost of the storage and networking service. This optimization is performed under end-user or data owner constraints and requirements such as the choice of a minimum number of data centers to be involved in storing the chunks of the data. This can reinforce the availability of data for given data centers failure probabilities.
- **Data Chunk Replication:** After optimally storing the encrypted chunks of a data according to network latency, we determine a replication algorithm based on bipartite graph theory, to derive optimal solutions of the problem of storing replica chunks. This ensures high data availability since content can be retrieved even if some servers or data centers are not available.

Once all data chunks are placed in different data centers, end-users may solicit the data by GET requests (download data). The broker needs to gather all the data chunks, sort them, decrypt them, and finally deliver the entire data to the end-user (see Fig. 1).

In the following, we suppose that each data object (chunk) has r replicas. Finding the optimal number of replicas of each chunk, is not in the scope of this paper. A well-known example on the choice of r is the Google storage solution based on $r = 3$ replicas of each stored data chunk [17].

3.1   Data Placement Cost Minimization: B-Matching Formulation

We start data chunks placement model by considering each data D of a user u, as a set of chunks (noted by $\mathcal{N}$), resulting from the AES algorithm. Let S

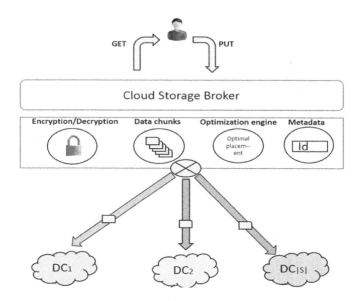

Fig. 1. The system model: PUT and GET requests.

be the set of all available data centers able to host and store end-user data. We investigate an optimal placement by storing all the chunks in the "best" available data centers. Each cloud provider with a data center $s \in S$ proposes a storage cost per Gigabyte and per month noted by μ_s. This price varies for different reasons: varying demands and workloads, data center reliability, geographical constraints, etc. End-user requests are submitted to the broker which will relay them to cloud service providers, in an encrypted form with optimized storage costs. The broker guarantees end-users high data availability with minimum cost by choosing a set of cloud providers (or DCs) meeting the requirements (see Fig. 1 for more details).

In the following, we will address chunks placement optimization model based on different constraints as the probability of failure of a data center or a provider, and a limited storage capacity. Each data center (or provider) has a probability of data availability (according to the number of nines in the proposed SLA), and a failure probability (f) is then equal to $1-$probability of data availability. Moreover, the limited storage capacity is given by a storage quota proposed by the provider to the broker according to a negotiated pricing menue.

Our optimization problem is similar to a classical Bin-Packing formulation, in which bins can be represented by the different Data Centers, and the items can be seen as the data chunks. Reference [24] has shown a while ago the NP-Hardness of the Bin-Packing problem. Thus, we deduce the complexity (NP-Hardness) of our chunks' placement problem.

For this reason, and the fact that workloads and requests to store date arrive overtime, the broker seeks a dynamic chunk placement solution that will be

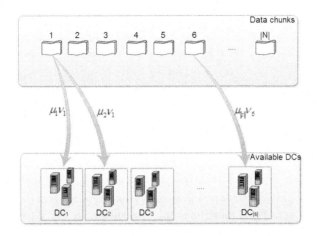

Fig. 2. Complete bipartite graph construction.

regularly and rapidly updated to remain cost-effective and ensure data high availability.

Each data chunk $i \in \mathcal{N}$ has a certain volume noted by ν_i. We graphically represent the storage of a chunk i in a data center k as an edge $e = (i, k)$ (with the initial extremity $(i = I(e))$ of e corresponding to a chunk, and the terminal extremity $(k = T(e))$ of e) representing the data center (see Fig. 2).

Based on this configuration, one can construct a new weighted bipartite graph $G = (\mathcal{N} \cup \mathcal{S}, E)$, where $\mathcal{N}$ is the set of vertices representing encrypted chunks to be stored, and $\mathcal{S}$ is the set of all available data centers (see Fig. 2). E is the set of weighted edges between $\mathcal{N}$ and $\mathcal{S}$ constructed as follows: there is an edge $e = (i, k)$ between each encrypted chunk i and each available data center k, and the weight of e is given by $\mu_k \nu_i$.

We now introduce the well known "minimum weight b-matching problem" to build a combinatorial optimization solution. The b-matching is a generalization of the minimum weight matching problem and can be defined as follows (see [24] for more details):

Definition 1. *Let G be an undirected graph with integral edge capacities: $u : E(G) \to \mathbb{N} \cup \infty$ and numbers $b : V(G) \to \mathbb{N}$. Then a b-matching in G is a function $f : E(G) \to \mathbb{N}$ with $f(e) \le u(e)$, $\forall e \in E(G)$, and $\sum_{e \in \delta(v)} f(e) \le b(v)$ for all $v \in \mathcal{V}(G)$.*

In the above, $\delta(v)$ represents the set of incident edges of v. To simplify notation, with no loss in generality, we use E and $\mathcal{V}$ for the edges and vertices of G. That is we drop the G in $E(G)$ and $\mathcal{V}(\mathcal{G})$.

From the definition, finding a minimum weight b-matching in a graph G consists in identifying f such that $\sum_{e \in E} \gamma_e f(e)$ is minimum, where γ_e is an associated cost to edge e. This problem can be solved in polynomial time since the full description of its convex hull is given in [24].

Proposition 1. *Let* $G = (\mathcal{N} \cup \mathcal{S}, E)$ *be a weighted complete bipartite graph built as described in Fig. 2. Then, finding an optimal chunk placement solution is equivalent to an uncapacitated* $(u \equiv \infty)$ *minimum weight b-matching solution, where* $b(v) = 1$ *if* $v \in \mathcal{N}$ *(v is a chunk) and for all vertices* $v \in \mathcal{S}$, *we put* $b(0) = 0$, *and for* $v \geq 1$, *we have*

$$b(v) = \left\lceil \frac{|\mathcal{N}| - \sum_{k=0}^{v-1} b(k)}{\beta} \right\rceil \tag{1}$$

where β is the minimum number of data centers to be used to store the data chunks. This parameter is required by end-users to avoid vendor lock-in.

To mathematically formulate our model, we associate a real decision variable x_e to each edge e in the bipartite graph. As shown in Fig. 2, each edge links a chunk to a data center. After optimization, if the decision is $x_e = 1$ then chunk i ($i = I(e)$ initial extremity) will be stored in data center j ($j = T(e)$ terminal extremity). Since the solution of a b-matching problem is based on solving a linear program, an integer solution of the minimum weight b-matching is found in polynomial time. This is equivalent to the optimal solution of the chunk placement problem described in this section.

According to the storage costs listed previously and by defining the probability of failure of a data center (or a provider) noted by f, we assign each chunk to the best data center with minimum cost. We note by $Cost_{plac}$ the total cost of placing $|\mathcal{N}|$ chunks in an optimal manner. We can formulate the objective function as follows:

$$\min Cost_{plac} = \sum_{e \in E, e=(i,j)} \left(\frac{\mu_j}{1 - f_j} \nu_i \right) x_e \tag{2}$$

where ν_i is the volume of chunk i, and $(1 - f)$ is the probability of data center availability (or provider availability).

This optimization is subject to a number of linear constraints. For instance, the broker has to consider the placement of all data chunks, and each chunk will be assigned to one and only one data center (the chunk replication problem will be discussed in the next section). This is represented by (3):

$$\sum_{e \in \delta(v)} x_e = 1, \forall v \in \mathcal{N} \tag{3}$$

Each data center s has a capacity Q_s. This leads to the following constraints:

$$\sum_{C=1}^{|\mathcal{N}|} \nu_C x_{Cs} \leq Q_s, \forall s \in \mathcal{S} \tag{4}$$

According to end-user requirements and to guarantee high data availability, chunks will be deployed in different data centers to avoid vendor lock-in. This is given by the following inequality:

$$\sum_{C=1}^{|\mathcal{N}|} x_{Cs} \leq b(s), \forall s \in \mathcal{S} \qquad (5)$$

Using the b-matching model with constraints (4), enables the use of the complete convex hull of b-matching and makes the problem easy in terms of combinatorial complexity theory.

Reference [24] gives a complete description of the b-matching convex hull expressed in constraints (3), (4) and (5). These families of constraints are reinforced by *blossom inequalities* to get integer optimal solutions with continuous variables:

$$\sum_{e \in E(G(A))} x_e + x(F) \leq \left\lfloor \frac{\sum_{v \in A} b_v + |F|}{2} \right\rfloor, \forall A \in \mathcal{N} \cup \mathcal{S}, \qquad (6)$$

where $F \subseteq \delta(A)$ and $\sum_{v \in A} b_v + |F|$ is odd, and $\delta(A) = \sum_{i \in A, j \in A} x_{(ij)}$. $E(G(A))$ represents a subset of edges of the subgraph $G(A)$ generated by a subset of vertices A. An in depth study of blossom constraints (6) is out of the scope of this paper, but more details can be found in [25].

Based on the bipartite graph G, we constructed a polynomial time approximation scheme of the data chunks placement problem by identifying the b-matching formulation. The blossom constraints (6) are added to our model to get *optimal integer solutions* of the *placement problem* whose model is finally given by:

$$\min Cost_{plac} = \sum_{s=1}^{|\mathcal{S}|} \sum_{C=1}^{|\mathcal{N}|} \frac{\mu_s}{1-f_s} \nu_C x_{Cs}$$
$$S.T. :$$
$$\begin{cases} \sum_{s=1}^{|\mathcal{S}|} x_{Cs} = 1, \forall C \in \mathcal{N} \\ \sum_{C=1}^{|\mathcal{N}|} \nu_C x_{Cs} \leq Q_s, \forall s \in \mathcal{S} \\ \sum_{C=1}^{|\mathcal{N}|} x_{Cs} \leq b(s), \forall s \in \mathcal{S} \\ \sum_{e \in E(G(A))} x_e + x(F) \leq \left\lfloor \frac{\sum_{v \in A} b_v + |F|}{2} \right\rfloor, \forall A \in \mathcal{N} \cup \mathcal{S} \\ F \subseteq \delta(A), \sum_{v \in A} b_v + |F| \text{ is odd} \\ x_{Cs} \in \mathbb{R}^+, \forall C \in \mathcal{N}, \ \forall s \in \mathcal{S} \end{cases} \qquad (7)$$

The variables and constants used in (7) are summarized in Table 1.

3.2 Data Placement and Network Latency Minimization: Commodity Flow Modeling

To derive the data storage system when taking into account hard constraints of network access to cloud data centers, we view the problem as a commodity flow. To derive the mathematical model for the commodity flow problem, we define the graph $G = (V, E)$ representing the network between the broker and all of the available providers or data centers. V is the set of vertices and E the set of arcs of G. Each arc e is weighted by a latency l_e. We consider a node b as the unique access point from the Broker to this network.

Table 1. Variables and constants of the model (7)

Variables	Meaning
$\mathcal{N}$	set of data chunks
$\mathcal{S}$	set of data centers
ν_C	volume of a data chunk C
μ_j	storage cost per Gigabyte/month of provider j
x_e	real variable indicating if e is solicited or not
b_v	upper bound of the degree of v
$\delta(A) =$	$\sum_{i \in A, j \in A} x_{(ij)}$
$\delta(v)$	set of incident edges to v
β	minimum number of providers

We investigate a commodity flow algorithm ensuring that all of the chunks ($|\mathcal{N}|$) are stored within data centers with efficient storage cost and minimal network latency. Thus, the commodity flow solution ensures the selection of the best storage providers proposing efficient access to the data for PUT and GET operations.

Since the objective is to minimize simultaneously the cost of storing data and the latency to access data centers, the objective function can be given as:

$$\min NetworkCost_{plac} = \sum_{e \in E} l_e x_e + \sum_{j=1}^{S} \mu_j y_j \qquad (8)$$

The first term in (8) consists to select arcs with minimum latency when accessing the data centers. The second term ensures that the storage providers (or data centers) with minimum storage cost are selected to access and manage the data.

The objective function described in (8) is subject to a number of constraints:

1. **Arc Capacity:** We note by x_e a continuous variable representing the fraction of commodity flow (data chunks) that goes through the arc e. Thus, the sum of all flows on an arc e can not exceed the arc capacity limit C_e. This is given by:
$$0 \le x_e \le C_e, \forall e \in E \qquad (9)$$

2. **Flow Conservation:** The following equation ensures flow conservation in nodes other than the source and sink nodes:
$$\sum_{w \in V} a_{wu} x_{wu} - \sum_{w \in V} a_{uw} x_{uw} = 0, \forall u \in V \qquad (10)$$

where a_{wu} is equal to 1 if the arc (w, u) exists, and 0 otherwise.

3. **Commodity Demand Satisfaction:** The demand of storing $|\mathcal{N}|$ data chunks from the source node b has to be equal to the cumulated outflow

from b, and in the same time equal to $|\mathcal{N}|$

$$\sum_{w \in V} a_{bw} x_{bw} = \sum_{v \in V} \sum_{s=1}^{S} a_{vs} x_{vs} = |\mathcal{N}| \qquad (11)$$

4. **Data Confidentiality:** To guarantee the data confidentiality when storing it through various providers, we seek for a solution to store a limited number of chunks within each provider. This is given as follows:

$$\sum_{t=1}^{T} a_{tj} x_{tj} \leq b(j) \qquad (12)$$

where $b(j)$ can be found in Proposition 1, and T is the number of nodes with direct access to data centers.

5. **Expected QoS:** Data owners can request for a certain QoS which consists to choose a minimum number of providers to be selected.

$$\sum_{j=1}^{S} y_j \geq \beta \qquad (13)$$

where y_j is a binary variable indicating if a data center j is used or not.

According to these constraints, we give the following mathematical model to cope with the problem of network access and storage cost optimization:

$$
\begin{aligned}
&\min NetworkCost_{plac} = \sum_{e \in E} l_e x_e + \sum_{j=1}^{S} \mu_j y_j \\
&S.T. : \\
&\begin{cases}
0 \leq x_e \leq C_e, \forall e \in E \\
\sum_{w \in V} a_{wu} x_{wu} - \sum_{w \in V} a_{uw} x_{uw} = 0, \forall u \in V \\
\sum_{w \in V} a_{bw} x_{bw} = \sum_{v \in V} \sum_{s=1}^{S} a_{vs} x_{vs} = N \\
\sum_{t=1}^{T} a_{tj} x_{tj} \leq b(j), \forall j = 1, \dots, S \\
\sum_{j=1}^{S} y_j \geq \beta \\
y_j \in \{0; 1\}, \forall j = 1, \dots, S
\end{cases}
\end{aligned} \qquad (14)
$$

3.3 Data Replication Algorithm

To enhance performance and availability of end-user stored data, we propose a replication model of data chunks depending on data center failure probabilities, and expected availability (noted by A_{expec}) required by each user. The objective consists in finding the optimal trade-off between data center availability and storage costs. This leads to avoiding expensive data centers with high failure probability.

We assume that each data chunk is replicated r times, and reconstituting a file data needs to get one copy of all chunks (i.e. $|\mathcal{N}|$ chunks among $r \times |\mathcal{N}|$ are necessary to reconstruct a data). Figure 3 gives more details and shows chunks replication procedure.

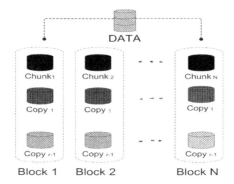

Fig. 3. Data replication.

It is important to note that initially, each encrypted chunk will be replicated by the selected hosting providers within their data centers, and the broker can reinforce this mechanism by proposing to add more replicas guaranteeing higher data availability.

In the following, we would like to replicate $|\mathcal{N}|$ chunks into $|\mathcal{S}|$ data centers according to various costs (storage costs) and performance requirements such as the data availability. We suppose that $S = \{s_1, s_2, \ldots, s_{|S|}\}$ and for the sake of simplicity (due to the problem NP-Hardness), we suppose w.l.o.g. each data center has a large amount of storage resources able to host data chunks and replicas. We associate each data center $s \in \mathcal{S}$ with a probability of failure f_s.

We suppose (as cited above) that each data chunk C $(C = \overline{1, |\mathcal{N}|})$ has r replicas to place in r data centers that do not contain the chunk C. Thus we ask the following question: *How do we replicate data chunks through available data centers so that the total cost of storage is optimal (minimal) and data availability is maximal?*

Thus, for each chunk C, the problem consists in selecting a subset φ_C of r available data centers that do not contain C, leading to a minimum storage cost and a high probability of data availability.

We note by $P(C)$ the probability of chunk C availability (respect. $P(\overline{C})$ is the probability of non-availability of a chunk C). $P(D)$ is the probability of data availability (respect. $P(\overline{D})$ is the probability of non-availability of data D). Note that a chunk C is not available if all of its copies are not available (see Fig. 3). In other words, a block in Fig. 3 with r replicas is non available if all of the data centers storing this block are non available. By supposing the data centers are independent, we get the following proposition:

Proposition 2. $P(\overline{C}) = \prod_{s \in \varphi_C} f_s$, and $P(D) = \prod_{C=1}^{|\mathcal{N}|} \left(1 - \prod_{s \in \varphi_C} f_s\right)$.

Proof.

$$P(\overline{C}) = P(\overline{C_1} \ and \ \overline{C_2} \ and \ \dots \ and \ \overline{C_r})$$
$$= P(\overline{C_1}) \times P(\overline{C_2}) \times \dots \times P(\overline{C_r})$$
$$= \prod_{s \in \varphi_C} f_s$$

A data D with $r \times |\mathcal{N}|$ chunks, is entirely available if all chunks are available. According to Proposition (2), the probability of data file availability (i.e. $P(D)$) is then given by:

$$P(D) = \prod_{C=1}^{|\mathcal{N}|} P(C)$$
$$= \prod_{C=1}^{|\mathcal{N}|} \left(1 - \prod_{s \in \varphi_C} f_s \right)$$

The QoS requirement for end-users is presented by the data availability. This is noted by A_{expect} (as used in [7] for example). Thus, to meet end-user QoS requirement, the broker should replicate each D in a selected sub-set of data centers that satisfies:

$$\prod_{C=1}^{|\mathcal{N}|} \left(1 - \prod_{s \in \varphi_C} f_s \right) \geq A_{expect} \tag{15}$$

We derive a mathematical model to efficiently reduce the replication costs noted by $Cost_{rep}$, under the QoS requirements described by the inequality (15). As the number of replicas of each chunk is supposed to be r, we seek an optimal sub-set of data centers of size r to store the replicas of each chunk. Moreover, our solution should not put all the chunks within the same data center to avoid vendor lock-in. Thus, in the following, we address a mathematical optimization model to efficiently replicate all the chunks of a data D.

$$\min_{\varphi_C} Cost_{rep} = \sum_{C=1}^{|\mathcal{N}|} \sum_{s \in \varphi_C} \mu_s \nu_C$$
$$S.T. :$$
$$\begin{cases} \prod_{C=1}^{|\mathcal{N}|} \left(1 - \prod_{s \in \varphi_C} f_s \right) \geq A_{expect}, ; \\ |\varphi_C| = r, & \forall C = \overline{1, |\mathcal{N}|}; \end{cases} \tag{16}$$

Solving the model (16) is equivalent to find a subset of data centers able to host chunks in a cost efficient manner, and that satisfies the requirement (15). We propose a simple and scalable algorithm to solve (16) in few seconds for large number of data centers and data chunks. Without loss of generality, we assume that minimizing a function Z is approximatively equivalent to minimize

$\ln(Z)$. Thus, for each chunk C, we seek a subset of data centers that minimizes $\ln(\prod_{s\in\varphi_C} f_s)$. This is equivalent to minimize $\sum_{s\in\varphi_C} \ln(f_s)$. Moreover, We construct a new bipartite graph $G_2 = (V_2 \cup S_2, E_2)$, where V_2 is the set of chunks to be stored and S_2 is the set of all available data centers (see Fig. 4). E_2 is the set of weighted edges between the two parts of vertices of G_2. There is an edge between each chunk C and each data center s (not containing a copy of chunk C) with a weight given by $\ln(f_s)$. If a data center s has already stored a copy of chunk C, then the weight of the edge (C, s) is equal to 2. Figure 4 gives more details.

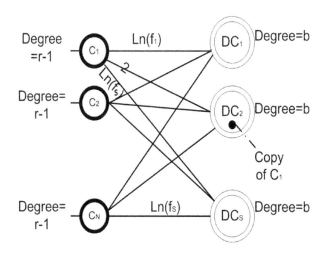

Fig. 4. New bipartite graph G_2 to replicate chunks.

From graph G_2, we identify a minimum weight b-matching with a given vector b as follows:

- for each $v \in V_2$, degree of v is equal to $b(v) = r - 1$,
- the degree of each vertex $v \in S_2$ is equal to $b(v)$ given by (1).

To summarize, we give the following algorithm, leading to find the best subset of data centers to replicate all the chunks in a cost efficient manner, verifying condition (15).

Algorithm 1. Data replication algorithm.

Step 0: Construct the bipartite graph G_2 (see Fig. 4);
Step 1: Compute a b-Matching with a minimum cost solution using the vector b;
Step 2: Check if (15) is satisfied;
Step 3: If (15) is not satisfied, GOTO Step 0, by incrementing the degrees of vertices in S_2;

The Algorithm 1 is deployed to replicate efficiently $r - 1$ copies of each chunk C of a data D.

3.4 Data Chunk Splitting

In this section, we discuss the rational number of chunks ($|\mathcal{N}^*|$) to be used to split the data according to data center failure probabilities (f_s for a DC s), number of replicas (r) of each chunk, and the data availability expected by end-users (A_{expect}).

According to Proposition (2), we seek a rational number of encrypted chunks to get after splitting the data when satisfying end-users QoS represented by data availability A_{expect}. We get the following inequality:

$$P_D = \prod_{C=1}^{|\mathcal{N}|} P_C = \prod_{C=1}^{|\mathcal{N}|} \left(1 - \prod_{s \in \varphi_C} f_s\right) \geq A_{expect} \tag{17}$$

As $A_{expect} < 1$ and $\prod_{C=1}^{|\mathcal{N}|} \left(1 - \prod_{s \in \varphi_C} f_s\right) < 1$, inequality (17) leads to the following one:

$$\ln \left(\prod_{C=1}^{|\mathcal{N}|} \left(1 - \prod_{s \in \varphi_C} f_s\right)\right) \leq \ln (A_{expect}) \tag{18}$$

We also note that for each chunk indexed by C, we have r replicas and then $|\varphi_C| = r$. For the sake of simplicity, we also suppose that the failure probability of each data center is close to the average failure probability given by $\overline{f}$. This allows us to deduce:

$$\prod_{s \in \varphi_C} f_s = \left(\overline{f}\right)^r \tag{19}$$

And following inequality (18), we get:

$$|\mathcal{N}| \times \ln \left(1 - \overline{f}^r\right) \leq \ln (A_{expect}) \tag{20}$$

According to (20), we deduce the number of data chunks as follows:

$$|\mathcal{N}^*| \geq \frac{\ln (A_{expect})}{\ln \left(1 - \overline{f}^r\right)} \tag{21}$$

4 Numerical Results

To evaluate and assess performance, our algorithms have been implemented and evaluated using simulations and an experimental platform managed by an instance of OpenStack [19]. The linear programming solver CPLEX [22] was used to derive the b-matching solution, the Commodity flow algorithm and the Bin-Packing solution used to benchmark our heuristic.

As our goal in this paper is to analyze and discuss the applicability and the interest of storage brokerage services in interaction with multiple data centers or cloud providers, we devote some numerical results to cross validating our proposed algorithms and assessing their cost efficiency and scalability for large data sizes. It is obvious to remark that the Bin-Packing model used to place data chunks invokes a branch and bound approach leading to explore the entire space of all the existing solutions. This leads to find "optimal" solutions for small data sizes serving as a benchmark for other approaches and algorithms. As the data size increases, the optimal solution for data chunk placement can only be found in exponential time. Thus, for large data, we resort to our heuristic solution based on graph theory (commodity flow) and the b-matching approach. In addition, our performance evaluation seeks to identify the limits of the discussed problem in terms of algorithmic complexity, and its suitability for optimizing real life instances. We will also determine the gap between the suboptimal heuristic solutions and the optimal solution provided by the Branch and Bound model when it can be reached in acceptable times.

4.1 Simulation Environment

The proposed algorithms in this paper were evaluated using a 1.70 GHz server with 6 GBytes of available RAM. We used data files with sizes ranging from 100 Megabytes to 4 Gigabytes. These data were stored in a distributed manner over a number of available data centers ranging from 10 to 50. We associate with each data center, a price per Gigabyte and per month, uniformly generated between 0 \$ and 1 \$. Each data is splitting multiple chunks and each chunk size is equal to 1 Megabyte. This configuration leads to construct a full mesh bipartite graph as described above. The number of generated bipartite graphs was set to 100 in our simulations yielding an average value reported in the following curves and tables. Without loss of generality, we suppose that each data center has an unlimited storage capacity. Moreover, we also used a platform of 20 servers running a Havana instance of OpenStack [19] in a multi-node architecture. Each server (assimilated to a data center in real life) proposes Swift containers [20] to store data chunks. We associate a storage cost to each container (or DC) as described above. It is important to note that we used Swift API only to guarantee PUT and GET operations from and to the broker by intercepting and hosting encrypted chunks, without considering Swift replication policy. To improve our broker functionalities, we will add an S3 compatible interface allowing end-users to request the broker storing their data within Amazon S3.

4.2 Performance Evaluation

The first experiment consists in comparing the Bin-Packing and b-Matching (heuristic) approaches in terms of delay to derive the optimal and suboptimal solutions, respectively. We report different scenarios in Table 2, varying the number of data centers able to store end-users data (from 12 to 700 DCs), and the number of chunks ranging from 50 chunks to 2000 chunks, which is equivalent to store data size of 50 Megabytes to 2000 Megabytes, as each chunk is of 1 Megabyte. The performance of the heuristic algorithm compared to the optimal solution is represented by a gap defined as the percentage difference between the cost of the optimal and the heuristic solutions:

$$Gap(\%) = 100 \times \frac{bM_{sol} - BP_{sol}}{BP_{sol}} \tag{22}$$

where BP_{sol} is the cost of the exact solution provided by the Bin-Packing algorithm (to use as a reference or benchmark) and bM_{sol} is the cost of the b-Matching solution.

Table 2 reports the results of the evaluation and clearly shows the difficulty to reach optimal solutions using the Bin-Packing (Branch and Bound) algorithm whose resolution times become prohibitive for the scenarios of a data file of 2 Gigabytes to be distributed on a selected set of data centers among 300, 500 and 700 providers or data centers. Our heuristic solution performs close to optimal with Gap not exceeding 6 % for the evaluated cases. More specifically the gap is in the interval [0.65 %; 5.93 %].

The results shown in Table 2 illustrate the difficulty to optimally solve the data chunks placement problem (see case of a data of 50 Mb with 25 DCs). At the same time, they demonstrate that the heuristic approach can find good and near-optimal solutions whose cost is quite close to the optimum (see case of data with 2000 MB and 700 DCs). Our algorithm provides an excellent trade-off between convergence time, optimality, scalability and cost. With respect to convergence time as seen in the third column of Table 2, it converges in a few seconds for the scenario with 2000 chunks and 700 DCs (54 secs compared to more than 3 hours for Bin-Packing).

To get a better grasp of the relative performance of the two algorithms used in this paper, a data file of 100 Megabytes is used and split into 100 encrypted chunks to be stored in a number of data centers ranging from 20 to 200. Figure 5 shows the characteristics of the algorithms. The b-matching algorithm achieves the best cost performance since it has consistently incurred the smallest cost, very close to the Bin-Packing which does not scale (as seen in Table 2). Exceptionally, one can remark in Fig. 5 (the scenario with 20 to 40 available DCs), the cost found by the b-Matching is slightly lower than the cost of the Bin-Packing leading to negligible SLA violations caused by the quality of the upper bound given by Eq. (1) which should be enhanced in a future work. This is explained by the difficulty to optimally store and place all the data chunks in different data centers.

Another experiment consists in evaluating the proposed heuristic solution to determine the trade-off between storage cost and data availability. We associate with each user a required percentage of its data availability, denoted by A_{expect}. We reformulate A_{expect} in terms of the number of nines required by a user. We simulated a cloud storage market of 15 data centers belonging to different providers having different failure rates. For example, Amazon S3 [21] offers two levels of services: "Standard Storage" witch has 11 nines of storage availability for 0.03\$ per Gigabyte per month, while "Amazon S3 Reduced Redundancy

Table 2. Encrypted data chunks placement: b-Matching algorithm performances.

$|\mathcal{N}|$	$|\mathcal{S}|$	b-Matching time (sec)	Bin-packing time (sec)	Gap (%)
50	12	0.15	0.16	2.24
	25	0.15	0.16	5.93
	40	0.17	0.18	2.06
100	25	0.17	0.20	3.08
	50	0.18	0.20	0.65
	75	0.20	0.22	2.98
500	100	1.10	2.11	1.94
	250	1.27	3.68	4.37
	350	1.33	4.20	0.97
1000	200	7.22	12.7	5.36
	400	8.5	17.5	1.37
	700	10.4	22.6	3.66
2000	300	30.7	>3 H	1.45
	500	45.2	>3 H	4.3
	700	54.8	>3 H	0.81

Storage (RRS)" has 4 nines of data availability for 0.024$ per GB per month. The simulated market is summarized in Table 3.

We consider a user data of 100 Gigabytes, and we investigate four methods to find the trade-off between a maximum data availability and a minimum price (cost). We use the following scenarios:

- **Minimum Price:** A user selects simply the cheapest provider in the market (Provider 15 proposing a price of $0.01 per Gigabyte and per month in Table 3) without concerns on data availability (3 nines). Following this approach, the data will be stored with a total minimum costs of 1$ and a weak data availability (3 nines in Fig. 6). Moreover, the user is locked-in within one cloud provider with a weak data availability. This can lead to disrupting services and loss of data.
- **Maximum Availability:** A user selects the provider with high availability in the simulated market (Provider 1 with 10 nines in Table 3). According to pricing proposal of Provider 2, the total storage cost is higher than the cost of the first scenario (10$ in Fig. 6). This may also lead to users' lock-in within the same provider.
- **Average Price:** In this case, we use the average price of the market, and we store the data within the provider with equivalent price (Provider 9 with 0.06$ per Gigabyte per month in Table 3). The total data cost in this case is equal to 6$ with 6 nines of data availability (according to the proposal of Provider 6). This scenario presents higher data availability than scenario 1

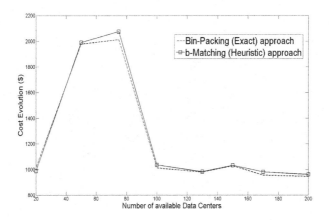

Fig. 5. Storage cost gap.

Table 3. Storage market costs and data availability.

Providers	Price ($/GB/month)	Data availability
Prov 1	0.1	99.99999999 %
Prov 2	0.095	99.99999995 %
Prov 3	0.09	99,9999999 %
Prov 4	0.085	99,9999995 %
Prov 5	0.08	99,999999 %
Prov 6	0.075	99,999995 %
Prov 7	0.07	99.99999 %
Prov 8	0.065	99,99995 %
Prov 9	0.06	99,9999 %
Prov 10	0.055	99,9995 %
Prov 11	0.05	99,999 %
Prov 12	0.04	99,995 %
Prov 13	0.03	99.99 %
Prov 14	0.02	99.95 %
Prov 15	0.01	99.9 %

with a considerable cost increase. In this case, we also solicited one provider to store the data, which may cause user lock-in.

- **Distributed Storage:** We used our proposed approach (Algorithm 1) to find the trade-off between data availability and price. As depicted in Fig. 6, our solution reaches a maximum availability of 8 nines with a minimum cost of 4$. This is due to data distribution over a set of selected providers with high availability and reasonable prices, avoiding user lock-in at the same time.

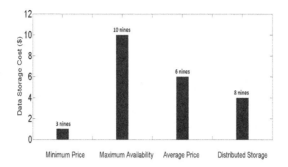

Fig. 6. Data storage cost and availability trade-off.

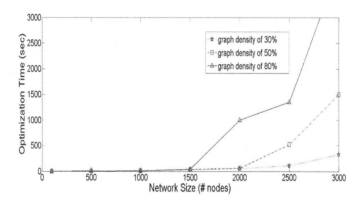

Fig. 7. Commodity flow time resolution.

The following experimentation evaluates the time resolution of the commodity flow algorithm to reach optimal solutions for small and large graph instances. Figure 7 depicts the behaviour of this solution for three types of graph density ranging in $\{30\,\%; 50\,\%; 80\,\%\}$.

The commodity flow algorithm optimizes network access cost and storage cost in tandem for different graph instances. We find that our approach reaches optimal solutions for graph instances (number of nodes less than 2500 for a density of 30 %), in acceptable times ($\approx 100\,\mathrm{s}$). When we increase the connectivity of the graph (50 % and 80 %), the commodity flow algorithm can reach optimal solutions in less than 100 s for graphs of less than 2000 nodes, but this time becomes prohibitively long past few thousands nodes (up than 2500 nodes). For this last case, we will investigate in a future work, new approaches (rounding techniques, for example) to accelerate solutions space exploration.

A last experiment consists in evaluating the behavior of the number of replicas (noted by r) of each chunk with the evolution of the number of data chunks ($|\mathcal{N}^*|$) identified in (21) for example. We supposed that the average value of data centers failure probability is equal to 10^{-3}, when the expected data availability required by cloud consumers is equal to 99.9999 %.

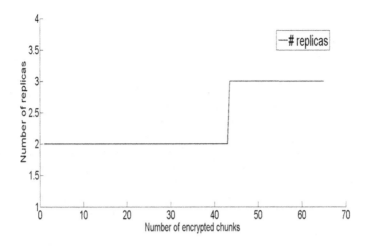

Fig. 8. Data chunks replication behavior.

Figure 8 depicts the evolution of r for different chunks number ranging from 1 to 60. Thus, we remark that for a number of chunks $|\mathcal{N}^*| \leq 43$, the number of required replicas is equal to 2, and for $|\mathcal{N}^*| \geq 44$ chunks, the number of replicas converges to 3 and there is no need to replicate more even for larger number of chunks. This may lead to store large data volumes with reduced costs when satisfying the required QoS (data availability). Note that this result is very similar than that determined by the Google File System solution [17].

5   Summary and Future Work

In this paper, we propose efficient and scalable algorithms to cope with the encrypted and distributed data storage problem in a multi-cloud environnement, when taking into account SLA requirements and network latency constraints. Our approaches are based on b-Matching and Commodity Flow theory to optimize the storage cost and the network latency in one shot, while considering data failure constraints. The b-Matching algorithm works in tandem with a replication solution allowing to efficiently increase the data availability of end-users. This replication algorithm is based on a simple and fast approach giving near optimal solutions even for large problem instances. The commodity flow algorithm leads to combine data storage and network latency in one stage to reduce total cost.

Our future research will extend the model of the commodity flow to address elasticity through predictions of dynamic incoming demands' variations or stochastic behavior. This can be done by proposing new polynomial algorithms based on rounding techniques to deal with large problem instances. This will lead to reinforce our broker's functionalities to give cloud consumers various means to consume proposed cloud resources in a more secure manner with reduced cost.

References

1. Varghese, L.A., Bose, S.: Integrity verification in multi cloud storage. In: Proceedings of International Conference on Advanced Computing (2013)
2. Balasaraswathi, V.R., Manikandan, S.: Enhanced security for multi-cloud storage using cryptographic data splitting with dynamic approach. In: Advanced Communication Control and Computing Technologies (ICACCCT) Conference, pp. 1190–1194 (2014)
3. Thanasis, P.G., Bonvin, N., Aberer, K.: Scalia: an adaptive scheme for efficient multi-cloud storage. In: Proceedings of the International Conference on High Performance Computing, Networking, Storage and Analysis, Los Alamitos, CA, USA, pp. 20: 1–20: 10 (2012)
4. Srivastava, S., Gupta, V., Yadav, R., Kant, K.: Enhanced distributed storage on the cloud. In: Computer and Communication Technology (ICCCT) Conference, pp. 321–325 (2012)
5. Yanzhen, Q., Naixue, X.: RFH: A resilient, fault-tolerant and high-efficient replication algorithm for distributed cloud storage. In: Parallel Processing (ICPP) Conference, pp. 520–529 (2012)
6. Qingsong, W., Veeravalli, B., Bozhao, G., Lingfang, Z., Dan, F.: CDRM: a cost-effective dynamic replication management scheme for cloud storage cluster. In: Cluster Computing (CLUSTER) IEEE Conference, pp. 188–196 (2010)
7. Mansouri, Y., Toosi, A.N., Buyya, R.: Brokering algorithms for optimizing the availability and cost of cloud storage services. In: Proceedings of the 2013 IEEE International Conference on Cloud Computing Technology and Science, Washington, DC, USA, vol. 01, pp. 581–589 (2013)
8. Bonvin, N., Papaioannou, T.G., Aberer, K.: A self-organized, fault-tolerant and scalable replication scheme for cloud storage. In: Proceedings of the 1st ACM Symposium on Cloud Computing, Indianapolis, Indiana, USA, pp. 205–216 (2010)
9. Rodrigues, R., Liskov, B.: High availability in DHTs: erasure coding vs. replication. In: van Renesse, R. (ed.) IPTPS 2005. LNCS, vol. 3640, pp. 226–239. Springer, Heidelberg (2005)
10. Li, J., Li, B.: Erasure coding for cloud storage systems: a survey. Tsinghua Sci. Technol. J. **18**, 259–272 (2013)
11. Jindarak, K., Uthayopas, P.: Enhancing cloud object storage performance using dynamic replication approach. In: Parallel and Distributed Systems (ICPADS) IEEE Conference, pp. 800–803 (2012)
12. Abu-Libdeh, H., Princehouse, L., Weatherspoon, H.: RACS: a case for cloud storage diversity. In: Proceedings of the 1st ACM Symposium on Cloud Computing, New York, NY, USA, pp. 229–240 (2010)
13. Ford, D., Labelle, F., Popovici, F., Stokely, M., Truong, V.A., Barroso, L., Grimes, C., Quinlan, S.: Availability in globally distributed storage systems. In: Proceedings of the 9th USENIX Symposium on Operating Systems Design and Implementation (2010)
14. Myint, J., Thinn Thu, N.: A data placement algorithm with binary weighted tree on PC cluster-based cloud storage system. In: Cloud and Service Computing (CSC) Conference, pp. 315–320 (2011)
15. Negru, C., Pop, F., Cristea, V., Bessisy, N., Jing, L.: Energy efficient cloud storage service: key issues and challenges. In: Emerging Intelligent Data and Web Technologies (EIDWT) Conference, pp. 763–766 (2013)

16. Chia-Wei, C., Pangfeng, L., Jan-Jan, W.: Probability-based cloud storage providers selection algorithms with maximum availability. In: Parallel Processing (ICPP) Conference, pp. 199–208 (2012)
17. Ghemawat, S., Gobioff, H., Leung, S.T.: The google file system. SIGOPS Oper. Syst. Rev. **37**, 29–43 (2003)
18. Zhang, Q.F., Xue-zeng, P., Yan, S., Wen-juan, L.: A novel scalable architecture of cloud storage system for small files based on P2P. In: Cluster Computing Workshops (CLUSTER WORKSHOPS) Conference, pp. 41–47 (2012)
19. Openstack. https://www.openstack.org/
20. Swift. http://docs.openstack.org/developer/swift/
21. Amazon Web Services. http://aws.amazon.com/fr/s3/pricing/
22. CPLEX Optimizer. http://www-01.ibm.com/software/commerce/optimization/cplex-optimizer/
23. Weatherspoon, H., Kubiatowicz, J.D.: Erasure coding vs. replication: a quantitative comparison. In: Druschel, P., Kaashoek, M.F., Rowstron, A. (eds.) IPTPS 2002. LNCS, vol. 2429, pp. 328–337. Springer, Heidelberg (2002)
24. Korte, B., Vygen, J.: Combinatorial Optimization: Theory and Algorithms. Springer, Heidelberg (2001)
25. Grotschel, M., Lovasz, L., Shrijver, A.: Geometric Algorithms and Combinatorial Optimization. Springer, Heidelberg (1985)
26. Kang, S., Veeravalli, B., Aung, K.M.M.: ESPRESSO: an encryption as a service for cloud storage systems. In: Sperotto, A., Doyen, G., Latré, S., Charalambides, M., Stiller, B. (eds.) AIMS 2014. LNCS, vol. 8508, pp. 15–28. Springer, Heidelberg (2014)
27. NIST: Announcing the Advanced Encryption Standard (AES) (2014)

Accountability Through Transparency for Cloud Customers

Martin Gilje Jaatun[1(✉)], Daniela S. Cruzes[1], Julio Angulo[2],
and Simone Fischer-Hübner[2]

[1] Department of Software Engineering, Safety and Security, SINTEF ICT,
7465 Trondheim, Norway
{martin.g.jaatun,danielac}@sintef.no
[2] Karlstad University, 65188 Karlstad, Sweden
{julio.angulo,simoner.fischer-huebner}@kau.se
http://infosec.sintef.no, http://www.kau.se/

Abstract. Public cloud providers process data on behalf of their customers in data centres that typically are physically remote from their
users. This context creates a number of challenges related to data privacy and security, and may hinder the adoption of cloud technology. One
of these challenges is how to maintain transparency of the processes and
procedures while at the same time providing services that are secure and
cost effective. This chapter presents results from an empirical study in
which the cloud customers identified a number of transparency requirements to the adoption of cloud providers. We have compared our results
with previous studies, and have found that in general, customers are in
synchrony with research criteria for cloud service provider transparency,
but there are also some extra pieces of information that customers are
looking for. We further explain how A4Cloud tools contribute to addressing the customers' requirements.

Keywords: Cloud computing · Accountability · Transparency · Privacy ·
Security

1 Introduction

Cloud computing, which allows for highly scalable computing and storage,
is increasing in importance throughout information technology (IT). Cloud
computing providers offer a variety of services to individuals, companies, and
government agencies, with users employing cloud computing for storing and
sharing information, database management and mining, and deploying web services, which can range from processing vast datasets for complicated scientific
problems to using clouds to manage and provide access to medical records [1].

Several existing studies emphasize the way technology plays a role in the adoption of cloud services, and most of these studies conclude that the most important
challenges are related to security, privacy and compliance [2–6]. Cloud service users

© Springer International Publishing Switzerland 2016
M. Helfert et al. (Eds.): CLOSER 2015, CCIS 581, pp. 38–57, 2016.
DOI: 10.1007/978-3-319-29582-4_3

may hand over valuable and sensitive information to cloud service providers without an awareness of what they are committing to or understanding of the risks, with no control over what the service does with the data, no knowledge of the potential consequences, or means for redress in the event of a problem. In the European A4Cloud research project[1], our focus is on accountability as the most critical prerequisite for effective governance and control of corporate and private data processed by cloud-based IT services. We want to make it possible to hold cloud service providers accountable for how they manage personal, sensitive and confidential information in the cloud, and for how they deliver services. This will be achieved by an orchestrated set of mechanisms: preventive (mitigating risk), detective (monitoring and identifying risk and policy violation) and corrective (managing incidents and providing redress). Used individually or collectively, they will make the cloud services in the short- and longer-term more transparent and trustworthy for:

- users of cloud services who are currently not convinced by the balance of risk against opportunity
- their customers, especially end-users who do not understand the need to control access to personal information
- suppliers within the cloud eco-system, who need to be able to differentiate themselves in the ultimate commodity market.

In this paper we report on the results of an elicitation activity related to transparency requirements from the perspective of cloud customers. A Cloud Customer in our context is an entity that (a) maintains a business relationship with, and (b) uses services from a Cloud Provider; correspondingly, a Cloud Provider is an entity responsible for making a [cloud] service available to Cloud Customers.

Transparency is the property of an accountable system that is capable of 'giving account' of, or providing visibility of, how it conforms to its governing rules and commitments [7]. Transparency involves operating in such a way as to maximize the amount of and ease-of-access to information which may be obtained about the structure and behavior of a system or process. An accountable organization is transparent in the sense that it makes the policies on treatment of personal and confidential data known to relevant stakeholders, can demonstrate how these are implemented, provides appropriate notifications in case of policy violation, and responds adequately to data subject access requests. In an ideal scenario, the user knows the information requirements and is able to communicate that clearly to the provider, and in return, the provider is transparent and thus willing to address the regulatory and legislative obligations required with regard to the assets.

The rest of the chapter is organized as follows. Section 2 presents some background from the literature. Section 3 explains the methods that we used to elicit the views of the stakeholders. In Sect. 4 we present the results, and in Sect. 5 we illustrate how the tools developed by the A4Cloud project contribute to meeting

---

[1] http://a4cloud.eu.

the customer transparency requirements. We discuss our findings compared to related work in Sect. 6, and draw our conclusions in Sect. 7.

2   Related Work

Transparency is closely connected to trust [8]. Onwubiko [9] affirms that trust is a major issue with cloud computing irrespective of the cloud model being deployed. He says that cloud users must be open-minded and must not whole-heartedly trust a provider just because of the written-down service offerings without carrying out appropriate due diligence on the provider; where certain policies are not explicit, users should ensure that missing policies are included in the service contract. By understanding the different trust boundaries, each cloud computing model assists users when making decision as to which cloud model they can adopt or deploy.

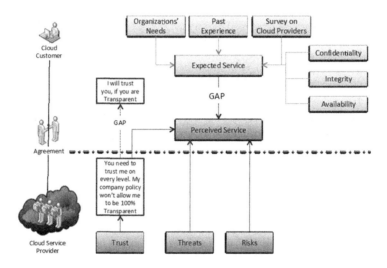

Fig. 1. Understanding cloud computing gaps.

Khorshed et al. [10] highlight the gaps between cloud customers' expectations and the actually delivered services, as shown in Fig. 1 (adapted from Khorshed et al. [10]). They affirm that cloud customers may form their expectations based on their past experiences and organizations' needs. They are likely to conduct some sort of survey before choosing a cloud service provider similar to what people do before choosing an Internet Service Provider (ISP). Customers are expected to also establish to what extent providers satisfy confidentiality, integrity and availability requirements. On the other hand, cloud service providers may promise a lot to entice a customer to sign a deal, but harsh reality is frequently accompanied by insurmountable barriers to keeping some of their promises. Many potential cloud customers are well aware of this, and are consequentially still sitting on the sidelines. They will not venture into cloud computing unless they get a clear indication that all gaps are within acceptable limits.

Durkee [11] says that transparency is one of the first steps to developing trust in a relationship, and that the end customer must have a quantitative model of

Table 1. Pauley's cloud provider transparency scorecard.

Aspect		Criteria	Mentioned in interviews?
Business factors	1	Length in years in business > 5?	No
	2	Published security or privacy breaches?	Yes
	3	Published outages?	Yes
	4	Published data loss?	Yes
	5	Similar customers?	Yes
	6	Member of ENISA, CSA, CloudAudit, OCCI, or other cloud standards groups?	No
	7	Profitable or public?	No
Security	8	Portal area for security information?	Yes
	9	Published security policy?	Yes
	10	White paper on security standards?	Yes
	11	Does the policy specifically address multi-tenancy issues?	Yes
	12	Email or online chat for questions?	No
	13	ISO/IEC 27000 certified?	Partially
	14	COBIT, NIST SP800-53 security certified?	Partially
	15	Offer security professional services (assessment)?	No
	16	Employees CISSP, CISM, or other security certified?	Partially
Privacy	17	Portal area for privacy information?	Yes
	18	Published privacy policy?	Yes
	19	White paper on privacy standards?	Yes
	20	Email or online chat for questions?	No
	21	Offer privacy professional services (assessment)?	No
	22	Employees CIPP or other privacy certified?	Partially
External audits or certifications	23	SAS 70 Type II	No
	24	PCI-DSS	No
	25	SOX	No
	26	HIPAA	No
Service-level agreements	27	Does it offer an SLA?	Yes
	28	Does the SLA apply to all services	No
	29	ITIL-certified employees?	No
	30	Publish outage and remediation?	Yes

the cloud's behavior. The cloud provider must provide details, under NDA if necessary, of the inner workings of their cloud architecture as part of developing a closer relationship with the customer. Durkee also says that this transparency can only be achieved if the billing models for the cloud clearly communicate the value (and avoided costs) of using the service. To achieve such clarity, the cloud vendor has to be able to measure the true cost of computing operations that the customer executes and bill for them.

Pauley [12] proposed an instrument for evaluating the transparency of a cloud provider. It is the only empirical evaluation that we found that focuses on transparency in the cloud as a subject of study. The study aims to help businesses assess the transparency of a cloud provider's security, privacy, auditability, and service-level agreements via self-service Web portals and publications. Pauley designed a scorecard (Table 1) to cover the assessment areas frequently raised in his research, and to begin to establish high-level criteria for assessing provider transparency. He concludes that further research is needed to determine the standard for measuring provider transparency. In our research we used a different strategy than Pauley; we have interviewed customers of cloud services to see what kind of information they would like to get from the cloud providers.

3   Method

As part of the project, we were responsible for running a set of stakeholder workshops for eliciting requirements for accountability tools. In total, our elicitation effort has involved more than 300 stakeholders, resulting in 149 stakeholder requirements. The first workshop dealt with eliciting initial accountability requirements, serving as a reality-check on the three selected business use cases we had constructed [13]. The second workshop dealt with risk perception. The aim was to focus on the notion of risk and trust assessment of cloud services, future Internet services and dynamic combinations of such services (mashups). After the first two workshops, we decided to organize multiple smaller, local workshops on each theme to ease participation of cloud customers and end users. The third set of workshops presented stakeholders with accountability mechanisms to gather their operational experiences and expectations about accountability in the cloud.

Of particular importance to this study was the risk workshop, where 15 tentative requirements related to transparency were identified. This workshop comprised 20 international stakeholders from the manufacturing industry, telecom, service providers, banking industry and academia, and the tentative transparency requirements were subsequently presented to our interviewees as a starting point for the discussion.

In addition to the stakeholder requirements, we have devised a set of high-level requirements which, from an organizational perspective, set out what it takes to be an accountable cloud provider [14]. These requirements intend to supplement the requirements elicitation process by providing a set of high-level "guiding light" requirements, formulated as requirements that accountable organizations should meet. In short, these requirements state that an accountable organization that processes personal and/or business confidential data must (1) demonstrate willingness and capacity to be responsible and answerable for its data practices (2) define policies regarding their data practices, (3) monitor their data practices, (4) correct policy violations, and (5) demonstrate policy compliance.

From these activities we have created a repository with requirements from all elicitation workshops, the guiding lights requirements as well as a number of more technical requirements that have originating from the conceptual work and technical packages in the project. These have been classified in terms of whether they are functional requirements, which are directly related to the actors involved in the cloud service delivery chain, or requirements for accountability mechanisms, which are related to the tools and technologies that are being developed in the project.

For refining and confirming the elicited requirements of transparency, we have performed an interview study with eight interviewees, followed by an in-depth analysis of the collected information.

Invitations were sent to our list of contacts in Norwegian software companies. Participation was voluntary. Eight people accepted to participate in the interviews. The participants were all IT security experts working with cloud related projects. The participants represented six different organizations: a consultancy, 2 cloud service providers (1 public, 1 private), an application service provider, a distribution service provider, and a tertiary education institution.

The interviews were performed on Skype and lasted about one hour. The main questions of the interview were:

1. What is the most important information you think should be provided to the cloud customer when buying services from cloud service providers? (Fig. 2)
2. In which parts would you like to be involved in making the decisions? In which parts would you like just to be informed of the decisions? (Fig. 3)
3. What would increase your trust that the data is secure in this scenario?
4. What do you want to know about how the provider corrects data security problems? (Fig. 4)

The eight interviews for this study were transcribed into text documents based on the audio recordings. For further analysis of the transcription, we followed the Thematic Synthesis recommended steps proposed by Cruzes and Dybå [15]. Thematic synthesis is a method for identifying, analyzing, and reporting patterns (themes) within data. It comprises the identification of the main, recurrent or most important (based on the specific question being answered or the theoretical position of the reviewer) issues or themes arising from a body of evidence. The level of sophistication achieved by this method can vary; ranging from simple description of all the themes identified, through to analyses of how the different themes relate to one another in a conceptual map. Five steps were performed in this research: initial reading of data/text (extraction), identification of specific segments of text, labeling of segments of text (coding), translation of codes into themes, creation of the model and assessment of the trustworthiness of the model.

4   Results

For the question "What is the most important information you think should be provided to the cloud customer in this scenario?" the participants talked mostly about nine themes (Fig. 2):

1. clear statements of what is possible to do with the data,
2. conformance to data agreements,
3. how the provider handles data,
4. location,
5. who else other than the provider is participant of the value chain,
6. multi-tenant situations,
7. what the provider does with the data,
8. procedures to leave the service,
9. assurance that the user still owns the right to the data.

One respondent commented that even though he would like to have clear statements of what is possible to do with the data: "100 pages document could be written about this, but for some non-technical people it would not help at all". Another one said: "I would like to have a [web] page where they could tell me about security mechanisms, for example, firewalls, backup etc."

On the conformance to data agreements, the respondents agree that having Data Agreements helps, but it is mainly for technicians, not for non-technical people. On how the provider handles data, the respondents said that they would like to have functional, technical and security related information about how the providers handle the data. On location, the respondents are concerned about where the data is physically stored, and the legal jurisdiction of the services. Another important piece of information is about sub-providers, if there are any; where they are located and whether they meet legal requirements of the customer's location. Multi-tenant situations are a concern of the customers, and they would like to have this information transparent. Also, information on how the providers ensure that data from one customer will not be accessed by another customer.

It is also important for transparency to know what the provider does to protect customers' data. One respondent said that he would like to have information on: "How to protect the information or how the information is protected; not much in detail for the end-user, but only for enterprises." It was also highlighted that they would like to have the procedures to leave the service and on how to move data from one service to another transparent. Besides, they would like to have the assurance that they still own the rights to their data. On the question "What would increase your trust that the data is secure in this scenario?" the participants mentioned eight different themes: (1) upfront transparency; (2) community discussions, (3) customer awareness; (4) way out; (5) reputation; (6) encryption; (7) data processor agreements; and (8) location.

Some answers were overlapping towards the answers from the first question: upfront transparency, location and conformance to data processor agreement.

Fig. 2. Important upfront information for transparent services.

Interesting answers for this question were related to community discussions, customer awareness and reputation. The respondents said that it increases their trust in a cloud provider if they know that the provider has an active security research team, or participates in security communities. The respondents also said that for security: "Customers should be proactive and make sure that all the documentation is there". And another one commented on the importance of having webpages telling what customers could do to keep the data safe. Two participants also

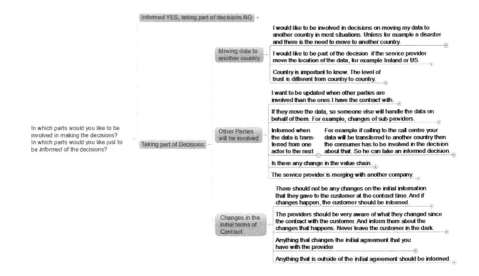

Fig. 3. Involvement on making decisions.

mentioned "Way out", meaning that they would like to have webpages telling them what to do to remove the data from the service provider.

On the questions: "In which parts would you like to be involved in making the decisions? In which parts would you like just to be informed of the decisions?" it was surprising that the participants mostly answered that they would like to be informed but not really taking part of every decision (Fig. 4); the exceptions were when the provider was moving data to another country, other parties are introduced in the service provider value chain, or there are significant changes in the initial terms of contract. One participant said: "Some customers sometimes have some requests, but in general they do not care about taking part in the decisions", and another one said: "there are some decisions that we don't need to explicitly know about, but it has to be regulated by some other agreement about the responsibility of each one towards the data". One respondent also said: "I would like to be involved in decisions on moving my data to another country in most situations. Unless for example a disaster and there is the need to move to another country." Some respondents said that they would like to be informed when the data is transferred from one actor to the next, one of them added: "For example if calling to the call center your data will be transferred to another country then the customers has to be involved in the decision about that. So he can take an informed decision." On changes in the initial terms of Contract, one respondent said: "the providers should be very aware of what they changed since the contract with the customer [was signed], and inform them about the changes that happen. Never leave the customer in the dark."

When asked on what they would want to know about how the provider corrects data security problems, it was again surprising to learn that the participants have not thought much on what they could expect from the providers if some

Fig. 4. Transparency on correction of data security problems.

security issue happens. Most of the respondents needed further elaboration of the question before they would start saying something. Then, the participants stated that they would like to know what is planned before something happens; when something happens they want to know how the providers are handling the situation, why the problem happened, and when will the services be back online. Interesting was also the fact that the participants wanted to know how the providers are improving their services after something happens, based on lessons learned. These responses are collated in the taxonomy shown in Fig. 4.

5 Transparency Tools

Many of the transparency mechanisms that customers expressed a desire for are actually being developed by the A4Cloud project [14]. Furthermore, a central theme of A4Cloud is the development of the Accountability PrimeLife Policy Language (A-PPL), which allows end users to specify a privacy policy that also covers accountability requirements, including transparency [16]. A4Cloud is developing an A-PPL Engine which will serve as a Policy Decision Point for the associated policies at each cloud provider. Other tools developed by A4Cloud include the Cloud Offerings Advisory Tool (COAT), which allow cloud customers to select an appropriate cloud provider based on relevant accountability requirements, including transparency [17]. This will eventually allow transparency requirements to be built into standard cloud service level agreements (SLAs), where transparency is just one of several security attributes [18].

In the following subsections, we will show in more detail how the A4Cloud DataTrack tool enhances transparency for end users by allowing users to visualize the personal data that have been disclosed to different online services.

5.1 The Data Track Tool

The Data Track transparency-enhancing tool was initially developed as part of the European FP6 and FP7 research projects PRIME[2] and PrimeLife[3]. Initially, the Data Track consisted of a history function for keeping a log of each transaction in

---

[2] EU FP6 project PRIME, https://www.prime-project.eu/.
[3] EU FP7 project PrimeLife http://primelife.ercim.eu/.

which a user discloses personal data. The log contained a record for the user on which personal data were disclosed to whom, for which purposes, which credentials and/or pseudonyms have been used in this context as well as the details of the agreed-upon privacy policy. These transaction records were stored at the user side in a secure manner. During the PrimeLife project and in the A4Cloud project, the Data Tack tool has been extended with online access functions, conceptually allowing users to exercise their data subjects' rights to access their data at the remote services sides and to request correction or deletion of their data (as far as this is permitted by the service side).

In its backend the architecture of the Data Track consists of four high-level components. First, the *user interface* (UI) component, which displays different visualizations of the data disclosures provided by the Data Track's *core*. Second, the *core* component is a backend to the UI with local encrypted storage. Through a RESTful API, the core is able to provide a uniform view to the UI of all users' data obtained from a service provider via so called *plugins*. Third, the *plugin* component provides the means for acquiring data disclosures from a given source (e.g., a service provider's database) and parsing them into the internal format readable by the core. Fourth, the Data Track specifies a generic *API* component that enables a service provider to support the Data Track by providing remote access, correction, and deletion of personal data. Based on solutions proposed by Pulls et al. [19], the transfer of data through a service's API can be done in a secure and privacy-friendly manner. By retrieving data from different services through their provided APIs users would be able to import their data immediately into the Data Track and visualize it in different ways, thus providing immediate value for end-users.

Detailed descriptions of the initial Data Track's proof-of-concept, user interfaces and results of its usability evaluations are given by Fischer-Hübner et al. [20], and further design process is described by Angulo et al. [21]. The security and privacy mechanisms of its software implementation have been documented by Hedbom, Pulls et al. [22–24].

5.2 Visualizing Data Disclosures

The design of the Data Track's UI considers different methods for visualizing a user's data disclosures in a way that is connected to this user's momentary intentions. Based on the ideas from previous studies suggesting ways to display data disclosures [25,26] and the creation of meaningful visualizations for large data sets [27–29], we have designed and prototyped two main visualizations for the Data Track as part of the A4Cloud project, we refer to them as the *trace view* and the *timeline view*

The main *trace view* interface, shown in Fig. 5, is separated into three main panels. The services to which the user has released information appear in the bottom panel and the information attributes that have been released by the user to these different services appear in the top panel. The user is represented by the panel in the middle, with the intention of giving users the feeling that this interface is a *place* that focuses on them (i.e., data about them and services that they have contacted). When the user clicks on one (or many) service(s) from the bottom panel, a trace is shown to the personal attributes (represented with graphical icons) that have been disclosed to the selected service(s). Similarly, if the user selects a personal attribute from the top panel, a trace is shown to the service(s) to which the selected attribute has been disclosed at some point in time. By its design, the trace view lets users answer the question of *"what information about me have I sent to which online services?"*

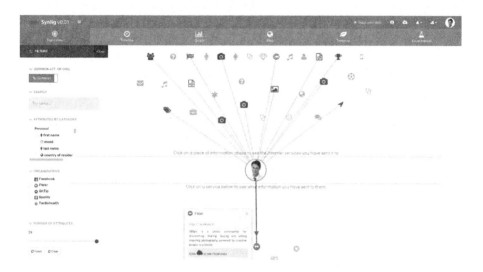

Fig. 5. The prototype of the *trace view* interface of the data track tool.

In order to cater for users perceptual capabilities and considering the screen real state, filtering mechanisms are put in place that would allow users to filter for information that is relevant to what they want to find out. In the trace view, users can search using free-text (i.e., by typing the name of a company, like Flickr or Spotify, or the name of a personal attribute, like 'credit card' or 'heart rate'), they can also select categories of data or individual pieces of data, as well as the number of entities to be displayed on the screen.

The other visualization presents each disclosure in chronological order, thus name the *timeline view*. In this view, shown in Fig. 6, each circle along the vertical line represents the service to which personal data has been disclosed at a specific point in time. Each box besides a circle contains the personal attributes that were sent with that particular disclosure. In order to keep the size of the boxes consistent and to not overwhelm users with visual information, the boxes only show four attributes initially, and users have the option to look at the rest of the attributes in that particular disclosure by clicking in the "Show more" button. Users can scroll vertically indefinitely, thus unveiling the disclosures of data that they have made over time, and allowing them to answer the question *"what information about me have I sent to which online services at a particular point in time?"*

Filters have also been considered for the timeline view, allowing users to search, for instance, for all disclosures made in a specified time interval, or all disclosures made to a particular service.

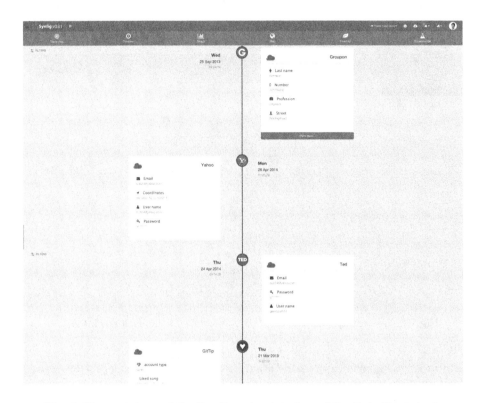

Fig. 6. The prototype of the *timeline view* interface of the Data Track tool.

Thanks to the envisioned architecture in the A4Cloud project, which considers the use of the A-PPL Engine mentioned earlier, the Data Track would allow its end-users to access personal data about them that is located in a service's side (i.e., stored in the service's databases). In both, the trace view and the timeline view, a button (in shape of a cloud) located besides a service providers logo, opens up a dialog showing users the data about them that is located on the services' side. This dialog, shown in Fig. 7, presents not only the personal attributes that have been explicitly collected by the service provider, but also data about the user that has been derived from analysis. Through this dialog users would also be able to request correction or deletion of personal attributes, thus being able to exercise their data access rights.

Fig. 7. The pop-up dialog showing the explicitly sent and derived data stored at the service's side.

5.3   User Evaluations of the Data Track's UI

Throughout the A4Cloud project, the user interface of the Data Track has gone through several iterative rounds of design and user evaluations. The evaluations had the purpose of testing the level of understanding of the interface, but also as a method for gathering end-user requirements on the needs and expectations that such a tool should provide to its users.

Usability testing of earlier designs of the Data Track revealed that lay users expressed feelings of surprise and discomfort with the knowledge that service providers analyze their disclosed data in order to derive additional insights about them, like their music preferences or religion. In general, evaluations have also shown that participants understand the purpose of the tool and ways to interact with it, identifying correctly the data that has been sent to particular service providers, and using the filtering functions to answer questions about their disclosed personal data. The tests also revealed users' difficulties when differentiating between data that is locally stored under their control on their computers and data that is accessed on the services' side (and shown through the pop-up dialog), as well as skepticism of the level of security of the data stored locally.

During an evaluation workshop, attendees discussed the advantages and possible risks of using such a tool, as well as the requirements to make such a tool not only user-friendly but also adopted in their routinary Internet activities. One participant, for instance, commented that the transparency that the Data Track provides, would encourage service providers to comply with their policies and be responsible stewards of their customers data, "*it would keep me informed and hold big companies in line.*". Another participant mentioned the benefit of becoming more aware of disclosures made to service providers, "*makes you aware of what information you put on the Internet, you probably would be more careful.*" On the other hand, a participant commented on the risk of accumulating large amounts of personal data in a single place, "if there is one tool collecting all the data, then it is a single point of failure...".

6   Discussion

After analyzing all the collected information we compiled a list of requirements elicited in the interviews, as shown in Appendix A. The main "topics" mentioned by the respondents were related to what is possible to do with the data, conformance to data agreements, data handling, value chain, multi-tenant situations, protection of the data, decisions and corrections of the data.

Pauley [12] designed a scorecard reproduced in Table 1 to cover the assessment areas frequently raised in the research, and to begin to establish high-level criteria for assessing provider transparency. When comparing our list of elicited requirements (see Appendix A) to Pauley's scorecard, we can see some slight differences in the criteria that Pauley described as information that should be provided by the cloud providers and the information that the customers are looking for. In the criteria about the business factors, the customers did not mention being concerned about the number of years in business, nor about membership of CSA, CloudAudit, OCCI, or other cloud standards groups, or if the providers are profitable or public. There is a possibility that the respondents did not mention these criteria because (a) companies in Norway are usually stable, and (b) membership of a group or association does not in itself guarantee good performance or compliance, even if the group or association promotes a certain standard.

On the security and privacy aspects, the customers mentioned all the criteria, but they did not mention directly the standards/certifying bodies, such as ISO/IEC 27000, COBIT and NIST, but they mentioned that it would be nice to know if the provider was certified somehow, based on some criteria. The customers also did not mention the need to know about "external" audits. One of the reasons for not mentioning security standards and certification bodies may be that companies that we have investigated are predominantly private companies in Norway, where there are not strong requirements from the certification bodies yet.

One important aspect not very much explored in Pauley's scorecard is that customers would like providers to be transparent about what is possible to do with the data. In addition, customers were quite concerned about transparency on exit procedures ("way out") and ownership of the data. The concern over data ownership is interesting seen in the light of Hon et al. [30], who found no evidence of cloud contracts leading to loss of Intellectual Property Rights.

Another aspect further mentioned by the customers is on the decisions made on "ongoing" services, where the customers would like that: "The cloud providers should get the consent of the cloud customer before moving the data to another country, in cases where new parties will be involved in the value chain and on changes on the initial terms of contract."

Physical location and legal jurisdiction, as well as specific information on the value chain was a very important aspect to be transparent about for the cloud customers, and it was not explicitly mentioned in Pauley's scorecard.

The interviewees did not show a desire for the kind of detailed information Durkee [11] deems necessary (the inner workings of their cloud architecture as part of developing a closer relationship with the customer), and as also pointed out by Durkee, some respondents were also aware that the costs of such clarity may be prohibitive, and we might add that this level of disclosure seems highly unlikely for ordinary customers of commodity cloud services.

The Data Track tool that we have described in Sect. 5 focuses more on end users (*data subjects*) than professional cloud users, but is clearly relevant for the customers of the cloud users. However, the tool can also be used to follow up on what a provider claims to be able to do with the data (Appendix A.1). It can be used to follow up on the geographical location of the customer's data (Appendix A.2), and can also help illustrating the existence of services from other parties (Appendix A.4).

7   Conclusions

Cloud computing has been receiving a great deal of attention, not only in the academic field, but also amongst the users and providers of IT services, regulators and government agencies. The results from our study focus on an important aspect of accountability of the cloud services to customers: transparency.

The customers made explicit all the information that they would like the providers to be transparent about. Much of this information can be easily provided at a provider's website. Our contention is that being transparent can be a business advantage, and that cloud customers who are concerned with, e.g., privacy of the data they put into the cloud, will choose providers who can demonstrate transparency over providers who cannot.

Our study increases the body of knowledge on the criteria needed for more accountable and transparent cloud services, and confirms the results from previous studies on these criteria. The list of requirements in Appendix A complements, in part, the existing criteria.

An area for future research is to further evaluate how cloud providers currently make the information required by cloud customers available. In addition, what are the effects of having transparent services in terms of costs and benefits to cloud customers and providers. Besides, we plan to increase the number of participants responding to our interview guide and adding strength to the evidence provided in this paper. Another aspect we would like to investigate, is if the results will be different for users of the different types of services (e.g., SaaS vs IaaS).

Acknowledgements. This paper is based on joint research in the EU FP7 A4CLOUD project, grant agreement no: 317550.

A   List of Requirements from Transparency Interviews

A.1   What is Possible to do with the Data

– The provider should show clear statements of what is possible to do with the data.
– The provider should allow the cloud customer to choose what is possible to do with his/her data.
– The provider should have a page that they could tell the cloud customer about security mechanisms, e.g., firewalls, backup etc.
– The provider should have some kind of standard certification level of description or standard language that they have to make the situation easier to the buyer to evaluate which security level do we need, what is required from us and what is the provider offering.
– The provider should have a document explaining what are the procedures to leave the service and take the data out of their servers.
– The provider should have a document in which they describe the ownership of the data.

A.2   Conformance to Data Agreement

– The provider should make available the technical documentation on how data is handled, how it is stored, and the procedures.
– There should be documentation of procedures in different levels of abstraction, for example for technical staff or for cloud subjects.
– The provider should show that they follow the data handling agreement to the type of data that is in question.
– The provider should provide geographical information of where the data is stored.

A.3   Data Handling

– The provider should provide functional, technical and security-related information about how they handle the data.
– The provider should provide very good information on how the data is stored and who has access to it.

A.4   Value Chain

– In case of using services from other parties, the provider should inform cloud customers on what the responsibilities of the parties involved in the agreement are.
– In case of using services from other parties, the provider should inform about the existence of sub providers, where they are located, and whether they meet legal requirements of the country of the cloud customer.

A.5   Multi-tenant Services

- The provider should inform the cloud customers on cases of multi-tenant services.
- In case of multi-tenant services, the provider should inform how the customers are separated from each other.
- In case of multi-tenant services, the provider should inform how they assure that data from one customer will not be accessed by another customer.

A.6   Protection of the Data

- The provider should inform the cloud customer on how to protect the information or how the information is protected not much in detail for the end-user, but only for enterprises.
- The provider should have a document describing the mechanisms that secure data not only for data loss but also for data privacy vulnerabilities.

A.7   Decisions

- The cloud providers should get the consent of the cloud customer before moving the data to another country, in cases where new parties will be involved in the value chain and on changes on the initial terms of contract.

A.8   Correction of the Data

- The cloud provider should have a document stating what are the procedures and mechanisms planned for cases of security breaches on customers' data.
- In case of security breaches, the cloud provider should inform the cloud customers on what happened, why did it happen, what are the procedures they are taking to correct the problem and when will services be normalized.

References

1. Paquette, S., Jaeger, P.T., Wilson, S.C.: Identifying the security risks associated with governmental use of cloud computing. Gov. Inf. Q. **27**, 245–253 (2010)
2. Kuo, A.M.: Opportunities and challenges of cloud computing to improve health care services. J. Med. Internet Res. **13**, e67 (2011)
3. Gavrilov, G., Trajkovik, V.: Security and privacy issues and requirements for healthcare cloud computing. In: Proceedings of the ICT Innovations (2012)
4. AbuKhousa, E., Mohamed, N., Al-Jaroodi, J.: e-health cloud: opportunities and challenges. Future Internet **4**, 621 (2012)
5. Rodrigues, J.J., de la Torre, I., Fernandez, G., Lopez-Coronado, M.: Analysis of the security and privacy requirements of cloud-based electronic health records systems. J. Med. Internet Res. **15**, e186 (2013)
6. Ahuja, S.P., Mani, S., Zambrano, J.: A survey of the state of cloud computing in healthcare. Netw. Commun. Technol. **1**, 12–19 (2012)

7. Felici, M., Koulouris, T., Pearson, S.: Accountability for data governance in cloud ecosystems. In: 2013 IEEE 5th International Conference on Cloud Computing Technology and Science (CloudCom), vol. 2, pp. 327–332 (2013)
8. Yang, H., Tate, M.: A descriptive literature review and classification of cloud computing research. Commun. Assoc. Inf. Syst. **31**, 35–60 (2012)
9. Onwubiko, C.: Security issues to cloud computing. In: Antonopoulos, N., Gillam, L. (eds.) Cloud Computing. Computer Communications and Networks, pp. 271–288. Springer, London (2010)
10. Khorshed, M.T., Ali, A.S., Wasimi, S.A.: A survey on gaps, threat remediation challenges and some thoughts for proactive attack detection in cloud computing. Future Gener. Comput. Syst. **28**, 833–851 (2012). Including Special sections SS: Volunteer Computing and Desktop Grids and SS: Mobile Ubiquitous Computing
11. Durkee, D.: Why cloud computing will never be free. Commun. ACM **53**, 62–69 (2010)
12. Pauley, W.: Cloud provider transparency: an empirical evaluation. IEEE Secur. Priv. **8**, 32–39 (2010)
13. Bernsmed, K., Tountopoulos, V., Brigden, P., Rübsamen, T., Felici, M., Wainwright, N., Santana De Oliveira, A., Sendor, J., Sellami, M., Royer, J.C.: Consolidated use case report. A4Cloud Deliverable D23.2 (2014)
14. Jaatun, M.G., Pearson, S., Gittler, F., Leenes, R.: Towards strong accountability for cloud service providers. In: 2014 IEEE 6th International Conference on Cloud Computing Technology and Science (CloudCom), pp. 1001–1006 (2014)
15. Cruzes, D.S., Dybå, T.: Recommended steps for thematic synthesis in software engineering. In: Proceedings of the ESEM 2011, pp. 275–284 (2011)
16. Azraoui, M., Elkhiyaoui, K., Önen, M., Bernsmed, K., De Oliveira, A.S., Sendor, J.: A-PPL: an accountability policy language. In: Garcia-Alfaro, J., Herrera-Joancomartí, J., Lupu, E., Posegga, J., Aldini, A., Martinelli, F., Suri, N. (eds.) DPM/SETOP/QASA 2014. LNCS, vol. 8872, pp. 319–326. Springer, Heidelberg (2015)
17. Alnemr, R., Pearson, S., Leenes, R., Mhungu, R.: Coat: cloud offerings advisory tool. In: 2014 IEEE 6th International Conference on Cloud Computing Technology and Science (CloudCom), pp. 95–100 (2014)
18. Jaatun, M.G., Bernsmed, K., Undheim, A.: Security SLAs – an idea whose time has come? In: Quirchmayr, G., Basl, J., You, I., Xu, L., Weippl, E. (eds.) CD-ARES 2012. LNCS, vol. 7465, pp. 123–130. Springer, Heidelberg (2012)
19. Pulls, T.: Preserving privacy in transparency logging. Ph.D. thesis, Karlstad University Studies, vol. 28 (2015)
20. Fischer-Hübner, S., Hedbom, H., Wästlund, E.: Trust and assurance HCI. In: Camenisch, J., Fischer-Hübner, S., Rannenberg, K. (eds.) Privacy and Identity Management for Life, pp. 245–260. Springer, Heidelberg (2011)
21. Angulo, J., Fischer-Hübner, S., Pulls, T., Wästlund, E.: Usable transparency with the data track: a tool for visualizing data disclosures. In: Extended Abstracts in the Proceedings of the Conference on Human Factors in Computing Systems, CHI 2015, Seoul, Republic of Korea, pp. 1803–1808. ACM (2015)
22. Hedbom, H., Pulls, T., Hjärtquist, P., Lavén, A.: Adding secure transparency logging to the PRIME core. In: Bezzi, M., Duquenoy, P., Fischer-Hübner, S., Hansen, M., Zhang, G. (eds.) IFIP AICT 320. IFIP AICT, vol. 320, pp. 299–314. Springer, Heidelberg (2010)
23. Hedbom, H.: A survey on transparency tools for enhancing privacy. In: Matyáš, V., Fischer-Hübner, S., Cvrček, D., Švenda, P. (eds.) The Future of Identity. IFIP AICT, vol. 298, pp. 67–82. Springer, Heidelberg (2009)

24. Pulls, T., Peeters, R., Wouters, K.: Distributed privacy-preserving transparency logging. In: Workshop on Privacy in the Electronic Society, WPES 2013, Berlin, Heidelberg, Germany, pp. 83–94 (2013)
25. Kani-Zabihi, E., Helmhout, M.: Increasing service users' privacy awareness by introducing on-line interactive privacy features. In: Laud, P. (ed.) NordSec 2011. LNCS, vol. 7161, pp. 131–148. Springer, Heidelberg (2012)
26. Kolter, J., Netter, M., Pernul, G.: Visualizing past personal data disclosures. In: ARES 2010 International Conference on Availability, Reliability, and Security. IEEE, pp. 131–139 (2010)
27. Becker, H., Naaman, M., Gravano, L.: Beyond trending topics: real-world event identification on twitter. In: Proceedings of the Fifth International AAAI Conference on Weblogs and Social Media, ICWSM 2011 (2011)
28. Freeman, L.C.: Visualizing social networks. J. Soc. Struct. **1**, 4 (2000)
29. Kairam, S., MacLean, D., Savva, M., Heer, J.: Graphprism: compact visualization of network structure. In: Proceedings of the International Working Conference on Advanced Visual Interfaces, ACM, pp. 498–505 (2012)
30. Hon, W., Millard, C., Walden, I.: Negotiating cloud contracts - looking at clouds from both sides now. Stan. Tech. L. Rev. **81** (2012). Queen Mary School of Law Legal Studies Research Paper No. 117/2012. https://journals.law.stanford.edu/stanford-technology-law-review/online/negotiating-cloud-contracts-looking-clouds-both-sides-now, http://papers.ssrn.com/sol3/papers.cfm?abstract_id=2055199

Towards a Standardized Quality Assessment Framework for OCCI-Controlled Cloud Infrastructures

Yongzheng Liang[(⊠)]

bwcon GmbH, Breitscheidstraße 4, 70174 Stuttgart, Germany
liang@bwcon.de
http://www.bwcon.de

Abstract. Considering standardized testing methodologies and related tool infrastructures as key elements of software quality assessment frameworks, for Clouds controlled by the Open Cloud Computing Interface OCCI this paper is going to present related first work based on the ETSI standardized test specification language TTCN-3. Initially motivated by studying the NIST Cloud Computing Program and the ETSI Cloud Standards Coordination (CSC) effort this approach is further stimulated by the recent evolution of the Cloud-oriented ETSI Network Functions Virtualization (NFV) and related projects such as the German Industrie 4.0.

Keywords: Cloud quality assessment · Standardized testing · TTCN-3 · Cloud Standards · OCCI · Software Defined Network · Network Functions Virtualization · Industrie 4.0

1 Introduction

Impacting basically all types of IT infrastructures "The Cloud" is one of the most important evolving IT paradigms. A standard-based Cloud quality and compliance assessment framework will be therefore of utmost importance. Bringing together the Open Cloud Computing Interface OCCI of the Open Grid Forum OGF and the ETSI standardized test specification language TTCN-3 and related test methodologies this paper is going to demonstrate initial steps towards such a framework. Taking into account the diversity of Cloud infrastructures, of service providers, and related architectural, harmonization and standardization effort our approach is initially motivated by studying the NIST Cloud Computing Program, NIST CC and the ETSI Cloud Standards Coordination (CSC). Reflecting the Cloud-orientation of the Software Defined Network (SDN) together with ETSI Network Functions Virtualization (NFV) and the recent Industrie 4.0 project in Germany [38, 39], this paper is also considering these initiatives within the scope of future standardized Cloud quality assessment framework.

The rest of the paper is organized as follows: Sect. 2 is introducing recent and ongoing work of NIST CC and ETSI CSC. The methodological look at NIST/ETSI will follow the triple "use cases – standards – testing" and corresponding mappings. Section 3 describes how, following the virtualization paradigm, the "Software Defined Network", SDN, and ETSI NFV have met the Cloud.

© Springer International Publishing Switzerland 2016
M. Helfert et al. (Eds.): CLOSER 2015, CCIS 581, pp. 58–73, 2016.
DOI: 10.1007/978-3-319-29582-4_4

Section 4 introduces the OGF OCCI standard. Section 5 describes some OCCI related effort of relevance in the given context. Section 6 introduces TTCN-3, the "Testing and Test Control Notation Version 3" the test specification language standardized by ETSI. Section 7 describes relevant TTCN-3 effort. Section 8 demonstrates "TTCN-3 on top of OCCI" for both a subset of the ETSI Interoperability test cases and for BonFIRE a large European Multi-Cloud project. Section 9 resumes the paper and gives an outlook on future work.

2 Toward a Standardized Cloud Quality Assessment Framework

In the context of this paper the term "quality assessment" is potentially very broad and related to testable attributes of Cloud systems such as conformance to protocol standards or regulations, performance metrics' or security measures etc. Such "assessment" may also be instrumental in the provision of "Cloud certification".

Both influenced by and possibly influencing the evolution of Cloud ecosystems potential Cloud adopters typically have developed related use cases of different abstraction levels above the basic technologies in question. At the same time and in a similar interdependency relation in numerous bodies Cloud standards have evolved and are still evolving. In such a situation mapping use cases to compatible or even "integrated" standards is one of the natural important steps. Eventually, addressing different test types such as conformance, performance etc. test cases will be specified. Such processes are assumed to be typical and necessary steps in the evolution towards a quality assessment framework.

Envisioning such a process and given the sheer weight of the US Government as a Cloud adopter and the important role of ETSI concerning high-quality standards and formal testing methodologies we are going to use the NIST Cloud Computing Program and the ETSI Cloud Standard Coordination effort in order to argue for a standardized Cloud quality assessment framework to be constructed "above" the two standards OCCI and TTCN-3.

2.1 NIST CC Program

The NIST (National Institute of Standards and Technology) designed its Cloud Computing Program, CC, "to support accelerated US government adoption, as well as leverage the strengths and resources of government, industry, academia, and standards organization stakeholders to support cloud computing technology innovation" [22]. The cited document "US Government Cloud Computing Technology Roadmap" comprising the Volume I "High-Priority Requirements to Further USG Agency Cloud Computing Adoption" and Volume II "Useful Information for Cloud Adopters" summarizes the results of the now finalized Phase I and defines and relates ten "high-level requirements" to the different NIST CC working groups for Phase II.

Key documents of Phase I are concerning Cloud taxonomy and vocabulary, reference architecture, standards and security; for references see [22].

The NIST projects and working groups apply a use case methodology to define business and technical operational scenarios and requirements. The NIST-chaired public Cloud Computing Business Use Case Working Group (CCBUCWG) has produced use cases at the functional mission level. Those "business use case are decomposed into a list of high-level requirements, then into successively more detailed requirements, until they can ultimately be mapped to technical requirements that are required to identify and executed" as "technical use cases". Dealt with by the group "Standards Acceleration to Jumpstart the Adoption of Cloud Computing" (SAJACC) the latter use cases are "designed to facilitate the qualitative testing of standards through the use of third-party APIs implemented in adherence to candidate specifications and emerging standards". SAJACC use cases represent single activities, such as the "deletion of data, and the actions needed to successfully execute that activity (receive the request, respond to the request, execute the request, etc.)".

Without any ambition towards formalization in terms of possible map-ability and automated processing, for the description of use cases two human-readable types of templates have been developed.

A particular set of standards in relation to a use cases was termed "compatible standards" – no specific exercise was undertaken to consider the "integration" of those specific standards in question – e.g. CDMI and OCCI; see also below [4]. However, concerning the "current state of conformity assessment in Cloud Computing", [24], Sect. 6.2.4 states: In some cases, such as the CDMI, OCCI, OVF, and CIMI standards ... industry-sponsored testing events and "plug-fests" are being advertised and conducted with participation from a variety of vendors and open source projects and community-based developers. In other cases, either the standards are not yet mature enough to permit such testing, or the participants have not yet exposed the conformity assessment processes to public view. – In this spirit NIST representatives gave presentations at the "First Cloud Interoperability Week" [34]; see also [17]. Finally, in order to cope with questions like "is the proposed quality assessment framework not overkill?" - it should be mentioned that the NIST is considering Cloud ecosystems as eventually big, complex and potentially endangered by "catastrophes" comparable to the famous Internet or global power grid breakdowns. Accordingly – with participation of the OGF Research Group on Grid Reliability and Robustness - NIST has started the "Complex Information Measurement Project - Koala" [23].

So far, NIST doesn't deal with SDN or NFV issues; see below.

2.2 ETSI CSC

Being part of the European Commission's Cloud related strategy the so-called key action "Cutting through the jungle of standards" was assigned by DG Connect to the specifically created ETSI working group "Cloud Standards Coordination", CSC. The latter created three "Specification identification gap analysis" working groups: SLAs, Security & Privacy, and Interoperability, Data port, Reversibility. Launched in December 2012, the CSC provided a final report [8]. This report stated that "the Cloud Standards landscape is complex but not chaotic and by no means a 'jungle'".

In this report ETSI CSC introduces vocabulary and taxonomies applicable to Cloud Actors and their Roles within Use Cases. The analysis of Use Cases comprises the following dimensions: "Phases and Activities", "Perspectives" (SLAs, Interoperability, and Security), and generic domains (e.g. "Applications in the Cloud", "Cloud Bursting" etc.). This schema is then used in a mapping of use cases to standards.

Gaps related to SLAs, security and privacy are dealt with in the final report.

Interoperability is specifically covered by the Technical Specification "CLOUD; Test Descriptions for Cloud Interoperability" [9]. The standards dealt with herein are OCCI, see below, and CDMI, CAMP, OVF and CIMI. In Sect. 8 we are going to demonstrate some initial work related to the OCCI-related test cases.

It should be mentioned that also ETSI CSC expresses a positive view concerning OCCI (together with CDMI and OVF): "OCCI as the universal and extensible interface description for the provisioning of virtualized computing resources."

Under the umbrella "user needs" (http://csc.etsi.org/phase2/UserNeeds.html) and in cooperation with NIST CC, ETSI CSC has started a second Phase of work to be completed towards the end of 2015. "Users" are mainly administrations and SMEs. The telecom sector as potentially important Cloud adopter is only indirectly mentioned, no other large scale effort such as e.g. Industrie 4.0 is considered. At present, August 2015, five ETSI CSC reports are out for public review. In the given context specifically "Interoperability and Security in Cloud Computing ...", "Cloud Computing Standards and Open Source ...", and "Cloud Computing Standards Maturity Assessment ..." are of interest: Based on high-level use cases, the first report [14], shows the conceptual relation between interoperability, portability and security and the state of related standards. While mentioning the OGF standards OCCI and WS-Agreement/Negotiation, this report is not a successor to Phase 1 "... Test Descriptions for Cloud Interoperability" [9]. No hints are given to the potential establishment of a testing framework in support of Cloud Certification authorities or similar bodies. Accordingly, there is also no mentioning of the ETSI TC MTS or the evolving Cloud related testing effort of ETSI NFV.

The second report, "... standards and Open Source in Cloud Computing" [13], is divided in a generic part and two specific Case Studies, the latter being (interestingly) only "ETSI NFV and OPNFV" and "OpenStack"; see the next Sect. 3 and [13], Sect. 7. There is no mentioning that – firstly – OpenStack is virtually the (only) Cloud platform in ETSI NFV PoC and OPNFV and – secondly – that neither the aforementioned efforts nor OpenStack as organization do support or use OCCI, specifically the "Core", or any other standard as unifying reference model for their evolving set of RESTful APIs; see e.g. [16] and below "MCN" [20].

The third report, "Cloud Computing Standards Maturity Assessment" [15], in addition to analyze the related progress since Phase 1, introduces the topic of "Cloud Certification". Again, there is no mentioning of the need and potential construction of a standards-based methodological test framework in support of Cloud certification processes.

3   ETSI NFV, SDN and the Cloud

Instrumental as a key concept and as enabler of many aspects of computing, storage and networking "Virtualization" lies at the ground of both the Cloud and concepts or initiatives such as the "Software Defined Network", SDN [32], and ETSI's "Network Function Virtualization", NFV [7].

SDN has evolved as a potential solution to both the growing management complexity of the overly successful Internet and, in turn, the growing "ossification" of the latter. Aiming at more flexibility and dynamicity of network services through programmability of network hardware boxes such as routers, switches, firewalls etc. the OpenFlow™ protocol and API is a key element in the context. Launched in 2011 by Deutsche Telekom, Facebook, Google, Microsoft, Verizon, and Yahoo!, the Open Networking Foundation (ONF) is a non-profit organization with more than 140 members whose mission is to accelerate the adoption of open, standardized OpenFlow-based SDN.

Used as generic term "software defined networking" is also addressed by the "Network Functions Virtualization - Industry Specification Group", NFV-ISG. Initiated in 2012 within ETSI by seven telecom operators the group was joined by over 200 companies including network operators, telecoms equipment vendors. Opposed to SDN, NFV was primarily driven by concerns related to CAPEX and OPEX of typical telecom hardware appliances and of service agility. NFV aims to use "advanced IT virtualization techniques" (aka Cloud plus Cloud enablers i.e. hypervisors etc.) in order to convert typical telecom appliances and service frameworks into "X as a Service" instances, the latter class being instantiated even into "IMS as a Service", IMSaaS.

SDN and NFV are highly complementary to and independent of each other.

In order to promote NFV trough OpenFlow-based SDN in March 2014 ONF and ETSI agreed on a related strategic partnership.

The NFV(ISG) has produced since five specifications covering NFV use cases, requirements, the architectural framework, and terminology. The fifth specification defines a framework for coordination and promotion of public demonstrations of Proofs of Concept, PoC [10]. The PoC demonstrate key aspects of NFV use cases – specifically the explicitly Cloud-related "NFV Infrastructure as a Service" (NFVIaaS), the "Virtual Network Functions as a Service" (VNFaaS), the "Service Chain Forwarding Graphs" (VNF FG), the "Virtual Network Platform as a Service" (VNPaaS) and the mobility–oriented "Virtualization of the Mobile Core Network and IMS". The first results of the NFV PoC have been showcased.

While aiming at vendor and product neutrality the Cloud "core" of the PoC was the OpenDaylight Hydrogen release of OpenStack comprising inter alia the OpenStack Neutron component as OpenFlow oriented SDN controller.

It should be noticed that this whole architecture is controlled by a (super-) set of the not standardized OpenStack RESTful APIs; see e.g. [16]. Emphasis in the OpenStack context is not on standardization or software technology issues of the existing or newly required interfaces. For a different approach see below the MCN project.

So far ETSI NFV doesn't refer to ETSI CSC or the ETSI TC MTS, the Technical Committee "Methods for Testing and Specification" [11]; specifically, there is no hint given to the ample, standardized TTCN-3-oriented test framework for IMS [12].

However, within its ongoing effort "Hot Topic 2: HT#2 (TST) Test Methodology for NFV" (http://nfvwiki.etsi.org/index.php?title=HT02_-_Test_Methodology_for_NFV; accessed August 17, 2015) NFV may eventually "meet" the aforementioned work via its formal cooperation partners, specifically ETSI EP E2NA and the ITU-T Study Groups 11 and 13.

4   OCCI

The Open Grid Forum's (OGF) 'Open Cloud Computing Interface' (OCCI) is a well-defined, RESTful Cloud management protocol and interface, which can be applied to and extended from its initial target IaaS to functional and non-functional aspects also of PaaS and SaaS – even in Multi-Cloud ecosystems [25].

The definition of OCCI comprises a "Core" and a meta-model aspect according to the following Fig. 1, see [26].

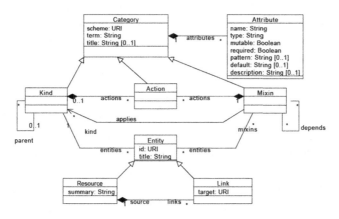

Fig. 1. The OCCI Core Model version 1.2.

The "Core" describes the foundation of the OCCI type system – "what types of resources can be out there". This is orthogonal and complementary to the "wire".

The meta-model aspect represents the descriptive part allowing for extensibility, hierarchies, and dynamic runtime modifications of resource instances and tagging via Mixins, and introspection via the mandatory discovery interface [5].

The Core document was complemented by two documents – the Infrastructure document [27], and the HTTP Rendering document [28].

The OCCI Working Group of the OGF is actively pursuing the further development of the OCCI standard. Representing "OCCI 1.2" (http://occi-wg.org/2015/05/04/occi-1-2-revision-in-public-comment/) a public review was just carried out till end of July 2015 of the following updated or new documents: Core, Infrastructure, Platform, HTTP-, JSON -, Text-Rendering, Monitoring, SLA, Compute-Resource-Template.

Members of the OCCI specification group also developed a related conformance platform in Python; see [29, 30]. This work was not continued after 2012. It is/was not directly targeting whole OCCI-controlled Cloud systems but the conformance of (language) specific OCCI implementations.

At the same time the WG is present at many related Cloud events such as the Cloud Interoperability Week mentioned above. Basically all WG members are also present in NIST CC or EGI [6] and MCN; see below.

5   OCCI-Related Effort

In order to further argue for the "robustness" of the OCCI case, in the following we are going to shortly mention effort covering technical and "market" aspects of OCCI applicability.

5.1   OCCI Technical Versatility

In [4] a standards conformant "integration scenario" of OCCI, CDMI and OVF is presented.

The "First Open Cloud Broker" developed in the CompatibleOne project and initiative is an early example for the extensibility of OCCI beyond IaaS [2].

The EU project MCN - Mobile Cloud Networking, 2012-2015, "is motivated primarily by an ongoing transformation that drives the convergence between the Mobile Communications and Cloud Computing industry enabled by the Internet" [20]. MCN's two scenarios are "Exploiting Cloud Computing for Mobile Network Operations" and "The End-To-End Mobile Cloud". While not fully concurrent with ETSI's NFV PoC architectural principles MSC is about to realize a comparable SDN/NFV framework wherein the Cloud component will be represented by OpenStack too. In contrast to ETSI's PoC non-standard set of related RESTful interfaces MCN is targeting OCCI. Referring to Core meta-model mechanisms [21], section "2.4.1 OCCI Extensions" and "2.4.2 OpenStack Extensions", the project has defined necessary extensions to both OCCI and OpenStack.

Finally, among the set of MCN's XaaS to be provided we are specifically mentioning MaaS, Monitoring as a Service (see also the OCCI Monitoring document and the BonFIRE project below) and IMSaaS, IMS as a Service.

The OCCI work in MCN is well aligned with the OCCI WG.

5.2   OCCI in Large Infrastructures

"The European Grid Infrastructure (EGI) is building a federated, standards-based IaaS Cloud platform, building on its decade-long experience in delivering a reliable, federated Grid infrastructure for scientific computing and e-Research across Europe and worldwide." "Federations are enabled by a set of core services such as seamless authentication and authorization of users, gathering of accounting information, information discovery, monitoring a VM management across multiple Cloud domains" [6].

In the given context it is of relevance that EGI Engage, the new project of the intiative, is targeting well defined OCCI extensions in order to increase functions and performance of its pan-European Cloud federation. This work is closely aligned with the OCCI WG; see also the OGF Compute-Resource-Template document mentioned above. The number of platforms supporting OCCI 1.2 is a formal activity parameter of the project (https://wiki.egi.eu/wiki/EGI-Engage:WP4).

Our tests below are using the so-called rOOCI, an OCCI implementation in ruby. The rOCCI is part of the EGI effort.

6   TTCN-3

TTCN-3, the "Testing and Test Control Notation Version 3" is a successful Test Specification Language standardized by ETSI [36]. Initially targeting protocol conformance testing e.g. for IPv6, or SIP, the coverage of TTCN-3 was extended to new technical domains such as the Web, embedded and real-time systems, and new sectors such as Health, Automotive and "Intelligent Transport Systems" (ITS). Related organizations are e.g. 3GPP, OMA and AUTOSAR. The ETSI TTCN-3 standards have also been adopted by International Telecommunication Union (ITU-T) in the Z.160 series.

The main characteristics of TTCN-3 are: Multi-Separation of Concerns by dividing a test system into an abstract but executable Test Specification Layer ("ATS" in Fig. 2), and Concrete Codec and System-Adaptation Layers; see again Fig. 2. From an effort point of view codec and adapter represent a major piece of (initial) work, paving the way towards a potential large testing framework at ATS level. This separation between concrete and abstract layer is also allowing for a high degree of reusability. Addressing testing by design TTCN-3 provides an elaborated mechanism for the construction of Templates the latter to be used as test oracles; see e.g. [33]. A related powerful Template matching mechanism then serves to validate output from the "System under Test" (SUT) on the level of the ATS; compare this e.g. with the language dependencies in [29].

Related global Verdicts are computed, possibly composed from local Verdicts.

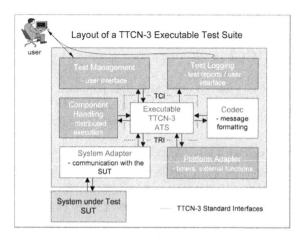

Fig. 2. Layout of a TTCN-3 executable test suite.

7   TTCN-3 Related Effort

In following, the Sect. 7.1 is shortly describing effort related to TTCN-3 language developments. Section 7.2 is showing TTCN-3 as an element of ETSI's effort towards model-based testing.

7.1   TTCN-3 Development

TTCN-3 related effort is devoted to both the development of the language as such (via well-defined formal procedures within the ETSI); an example of relevance in context is "MTS The Testing and Test Control Notation version 3; Part 11: Using JSON with TTCN-3" - and other aspects. Such work may be carried out e.g. in cooperation with tool providers. To improve the efficiency of the coding/decoding process in a Web service environment would be an example. For a recent overview see [35].

7.2   TTCN-3 in the ETSI TC MTS

TTCN-3 is not "just another standalone test specification language" but is part of an overall effort within ETSI to further the development of methodologies in the spirit of "model-based testing" [11].

Initially targeting communicating systems the ETSI MTS is addressing the formalization and mechanization/automation of a stack of processes and specifications ranging from requirements solicitation and "notation" over test and test purpose to test case specification. Herein TTCN-3 is placed at the bottom layer.

Looking at the test description in the human-readable table format by the NIST and ETSI CSC - the corresponding TC MTS historical effort is TPLan, ETSI ES 202 553. At present the TC MTS is pursuing with the TDL, Test Description Language, a more rigorous approach: integrating and unifying test description and test purpose specification layer above TTCN-3 TDL raises the abstraction layer of the latter and allows at the same time for down-mapping from the requirements layer [19].

8   TTCN-3 and OCCI

"TTCN-3 on top of OCCI" was, to our knowledge, presented for the first time at the "Cloud Interoperability Week Workshop" [17] and at the UCAAT 2013 [18]. This work was related to the initial version of ETSI "Test Descriptions for Cloud Interoperability" [9].

We improved and extended this effort in the following way:

– We wrote new versions of the Codec and the System Adapter allowing specifically for a complete treatment of all coding and systems requirements of the OCCI tests of [9]; see Figs. 2 and 3 again for the positioning these components.

– Using the current version of the ETSI document, so far we carried out all the OCCI Core and Infrastructure tests against a rOCCI-based EGI Cloud test infrastructure [6].
– We run initial tests of the BonFIRE Multi-Cloud project "Elasticity as a Service" (for "BonFIRE and OCCI" see below) [1].

8.1   TTCN-3 and OCCI Mapping

The Fig. 3 shows the functional components and potential mappings of a TTCN-3 test system and those of an OCCI controlled Cloud system.

Elements formatted according to the OCCI specification can be expressed in terms of a TTCN-3 Abstract Test Specification. The rendering of the different MIME types will be accomplished by the Codec. The OCCI transport via HTTP will be provided by the System Adaptor.

For example, the OCCI "Category" can be abstracted into the following TTCN-3 Data type:

```
Category {
     charstring category,
     CategoryValue category_value
}
type set CategoryValue {
     charstring term,
     charstring scheme,
     charstring class,
     charstring title optional,
     charstring rel optional,
     charstring location optional,
     charstring attributes optional,
     charstring actions optional
}
type set of Category CategoryList;
type record Category {
     charstring category,
     CategoryValue category_value
  }

  type set CategoryValue {
     charstring term,
     charstring scheme,
     charstring class,
     charstring title optional,
     charstring rel optional,
     charstring location optional,
     charstring attributes optional,
     charstring actions optional
}
type set of Category CategoryList;
```

In order to carry out the ETSI test case "TD/OCCI/INDRA/CREATE/004: Create an OCCI Compute Resource" one has to create the following TTCN-3 request template:

```
template OCCIReq  Req_TD_OCCI_INFRA_CREATE_004 :={
    url_req :={
    scheme := "http://",
    authority := "rocci.herokuapp.com",
    path := "/compute/"
},
category_list := {
    {
        category := "Category",
        category_value := {
            term    := "compute",
            scheme :=
"http://schemas.ogf.org/occi/infrastructure#",
            class   := "kind"
        }
    },
    {
     category := "Category",
     category_value := {
            term    := "small",
            scheme :=
"http://my.occi.service/occi/infrastructure/resource_tpl#",
            class   := "mixin"
     }
    },
    {
     category := "Category",
     category_value := {
            term    := "my_os",
            scheme :=
"http://my.occi.service/occi/infrastructure/os_tpl#",
            class   := "mixin"
     }
     }
    },
    link_list := omit,
    x_occi_attribute_list := omit

    }
```

This template represents the test oracle, i.e. the expected response of the SUT, for this conformance test.

The related HTTP verbs GET, POST, PUT and Delete and the OCCI rendering have to be parameterized as follows:

```
/* select HTTP verb */
modulepar boolean Create := true;
modulepar boolean Read := false;
modulepar boolean Update := false;
modulepar boolean Delete := false;

/* select OCCI Rendering */
modulepar charstring ContentType := "text/occi";
modulepar charstring AcceptValue := "text/occi";
```

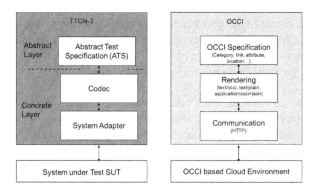

Fig. 3. Mapping TTCN-3 – OCCI.

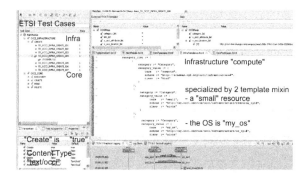

Fig. 4. Creating an Infrastructure OCCI Compute resource modified by two Mixins.

In the annotated Fig. 4 shows the corresponding result of the test in the tool-window [37]:

– the list of all the implemented ETSI tests - the currently executed is highlighted (left upper corner)
– the action "create" and the related content type "text/occi"

- a "compute" "kind" modified by the two "mixins" (large window, middle right; see Fig. 1 again for terminology); (the small window, upper corner right, is showing that the compute resource was created on a server of the PaaS provider HEROKU used by EGI for testing purposes).
- the OCCI Request/Response message exchange between the System_under_Test and the Test System (graphical window right bottom; the Verdict "pass" message is just not visible).

8.2   TTCN-3 and "Bonfire OCCI"

BonFIRE [1, 3], a recent EU project has realized and is providing a multi-site federated testbed on top of Cloud infrastructures operated by six project partners. BonFIRE IaaS offers heterogeneous compute, storage and network resources. In the given context, the main features of the BonFIRE (BF) architecture are the following:

- BF implements an "almost" OCCI-based resource manager on top of the participating IaaS testbed sites (no Categories etc., no MIXINS).
- The rendering uses the private type "application/vnd.bonfire+xml"
- BF provides a monitoring capability at both the VM and physical level. Under user control events generated by (Zabbix) monitoring agents are transported via AMQP to an "Aggregator". From a functional point of view, the BF monitoring fits well the "Focused Technical (security) Requirements" of [22] Part II, "Visibility/Control for Consumers".
- BF provides an experimental EaaS – Elasticity as a Service - across the test bed sides.

Formally, according to the BF data model, the BF user carries out "Experiments". In a full OCCI setting "Experiments" would be defined as a Category above the participating infrastructures. Except for the description part and the fixed allocation of monitoring agents to user created VMs the monitoring architecture is close to the proposal presently discussed within the OGF OCCI WG.

The annotated Fig. 5 shows

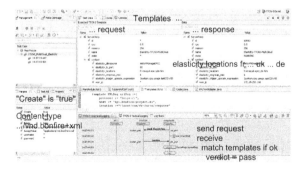

Fig. 5. Creating a BonFire elasticity group.

- the creation of a elasticity group distributed over several BonFIRE geographical sites in France, the UK and Germany - in response to the request template (upper part right)
- the related action is (naturally) "create"
- (left below) the rendering's private type "application/vnd.bonfire+xml"
- the verdict "pass" message (graphical window part).

Not considering the only "almost" OCCI compliance of the project BonFire is a clear and working example for the potential of OCCI beyond its initial specification.

9 Summary and Future Work

Using Cloud related work of NIST and ETSI we have proposed standards-oriented testing of standard-based Cloud infrastructures as a potential element of a Cloud quality assessment framework. We have shown that OCCI is well positioned to play a pivotal role within that context. And we have introduced the ETSI effort towards model-based testing, the latter comprising TTCN-3 at the lowest layer.

As a proof-of-concept we demonstrated "standardized" TTCN-3 test cases of ETSI CSC against OCCI controlled Cloud testbeds.

Assuming a key role of SDN/NFV in future Cloud provisioning for telecoms and efforts such as Industrie 4.0 we have discussed the ETSI NFV and also pointed to work using OCCI systematically in an SDN/NFV project.

We have seen possibilities to improve the coordination between ETSI CSC, ETSI TC MTS and ETSI NFV.

To further the vision "Standardized Cloud ecosystems as the next big application field of the well-established ETSI TTCN-3-related testing methodologies" future work should initiate TTCN-3-based test frameworks for OCCI controlled Cloud federations such as EGI ENGAGE and SDN/NFV-Systems such as MCN.

Acknowledgements. We would like to thank: Boris Parák of CESNET for support in using the rOCCI/EGI infrastructure, Andy Edmonds of ZHAW, former colleagues of BonFIRE for provision of the BonFIRE testbed, Ina Schieferdecker for guidance in the TTCN-3 world, and last but not least Testing Technologies for the friendly provision of their TTCN-3 tool TTworkbench.

This work was partially supported by the Cloud Socket project, Project number H2020-644690.

References

1. BonFIRE: www.bonfire-project.eu/. Accessed 06 January 2015
2. CompatibleOne: CompatibleOne The Open Source Cloud broker. http://www.compatibleone.org/. Accessed 06 January 2015
3. del Castillo, J.A.L., Mallichan, K., Al-Hazmi, Y.: OpenStack Federation in Experimentation Multi-cloud Testbeds. HP Laboratories. HPL-2013-58
4. Edmonds, A., Metsch, T., Luster, E.: An Open, Interoperable Cloud. http://www.infoq.com/articles/open-interoperable-cloud. Accessed 06 January 2015

5. Edmonds, A., et al.: Towards an Open Cloud Standards. IEEE Internet Comput. **16**, 15–25 (2012)
6. EGI: EGI European Grid Infrastructure. https://www.egi.eu/infrastructure/cloud/
7. ETSI: http://www.etsi.org/technologies-clusters/technologies/nfv. Accessed 06 January 2015
8. ETSI: Cloud Standards Coordination Final Report November 2013 VERSION 1.0, November 2013
9. ETSI: TS 103 142 V2.0.2 (2013-09) CLOUD; Test Descriptions for Cloud Interoperability
10. ETSI: NFV Proofs of Concept. http://www.etsi.org/technologies-clusters/technologies/nfv/nfv-poc. Accessed 06 January 2015
11. ETSI: TC Methods for Testing and Specification http://www.etsi.org/images/files/ETSITechnologyLealets/MethodsforTestingandSpecification.pdf. Accessed 06 January 2015
12. ETSI. http://www.etsi.org/technologies-clusters/technologies/testing/ims-testing. Accessed 27 January 2015
13. ETSI: Cloud Computing Standards and Open Source - Optimizing the relationship between standards and Open Source in Cloud Computing - Analysis, conclusions and recommendations from Cloud Standards Coordination Phase 2. For public comments - deadline for comments, 18 September 2015. ETSI SR 003 382 V1.0.0 (2015-07). http://csc.etsi.org/phase2/OpenSource.html. Accessed 06 August 2015
14. ETSI: Interoperability and Security in Cloud Computing. Analysis, conclusions and recommendations from Cloud Standards Coordination Phase 2. ETSI SR 003 382 V1.0.0 (2015-07). http://csc.etsi.org/phase2/OpenSource.html. Accessed 06 August 2015
15. ETSI: Cloud Computing Standards Maturity Assessment. A new snapshot of Cloud Computing Standards. Analysis, conclusions and recommendations from Cloud Standards Coordination Phase 2. For public comments SPECIAL REPORT ETSI SR 003 392 V1.0.0 (2015-08). Accessed 9 August 2015
16. Kavanagh, A.: OpenStack as the API framework for NFV: the benefits, and the extension needed. ERICSSON Review, 2 April 2015
17. Liang, Y.: Harnessing TTCN-3 test framework for OCCI-based cloud ecosystems. In: DMTF, ETSI, OASIS, OCEAN Project, OGF, OW2 and SNIA: First Cloud Interoperability Week Santa Clara, USA, 16–18 September and Madrid, Spain, 18–20 September 2013 (co-hosted with the EGI and SDC conferences) http://www.cloudplugfest.org/events/past-plugfest-agendas/cloud-interoperability-week/workshop. Accessed 14 December 2014
18. Liang, Y.: Towards a TTCN-3 test framework for OCCI-based cloud ecosystems. In: UCAAT, 1st User Conference on Advanced Automated Testing. Paris 22–24 October 2013. http://ucaat.etsi.org/2013/program_conf.html. Accessed 14 December 2014
19. Makedonski, P., et al.: Bringing TDL to Users: A Hands-on Tutorial. http://www.sweinformatik.uni-goettigen.de/sites/default/files/publications/TDL%20Ttorial.pdf. Accessed 06 January 2015
20. MCN: Mobile Cloud Networking project. http://www.mobile-cloud-networking.eu/site/
21. MCN: Future Communication Architecture for Mobile Cloud Services. FP7-ICT-2011-8 Project No: 318109. D3.1 Infrastructure Management Foundations – Specifications & Design for Mobile Cloud framework, 08 November 2013
22. NIST: Special Publication 500-293. Version 2. US Government Cloud Computing Technology Roadmap. Volume I. High-Priority Requirements to Further USG Agency Cloud Computing Adoption. Volume II. Useful Information for Cloud Adopters, October 2014. http://dx.doi.org/10.6028/NIST.SP.500-293
23. NIST, 2015. Koala. In "Measurement Science for Complex Information Systems". http://www.nist.gov/itl/antd/emergent_behavior.cfm. Accessed 06 January 2015

24. NIST: Special Publication 500-299. Draft. NIST Cloud Computing Security Reference Architecture
25. OCCI: http://occi-wg.org/about/. Accessed 06 January 2015
26. OCCI: Core Specification. http://ogf.org/documents/GFD.183.pdf
27. OCCI: Infrastructure. http://ogf.org/documents/GFD.184.pdf
28. OCCI: HTTP Rendering. http://ogf.org/documents/GFD.185.pdf
29. OGF: Grokking OCCI Syntax: OCCI ANTLR Grammar. http://occi-wg.org/2012/02/29/occi-antlr-grammar/. Accessed 06 January 2015
30. OGF: Do you Speak OCCI? http://occi-wg.org/2012/03/05/do-you-speak-occi/
31. OGF: OGF42 Updates from the Group. http://occi-wg.org/2014/09/15/updates_from_ogf42/. Accessed 06 January 2015
32. ONF: https://www.opennetworking.org/. Accessed 06 January 2015
33. Schieferdecker, I.: Oracles in TTCN-3 and UTP. In: CREST Workshop. 22nd May 2012, London. 35
34. Sill, A.: SAJACC: The NIST Cloud Use Case Test Definition Project. In: same as [17]
35. Stepien, B., Peyton, L.: Innovation and evolution in integrated web application testing with TTCN-3. Int. J. Softw. Tool Technol. Transf. **16**(3), 269–283 (2014)
36. TTCN-3: http://www.ttcn-3.org/. Accessed 06 January 2015
37. TTworkbench: http://www.testingtech.com/proucts/ttworkbench.php
38. Industrie 4.0 (2015). https://en.wikipedia.org/wiki/Industry_4.0. Accessed August 2019
39. Krojer, F., Furjanic, I.: NFV und SDN machen Produktionsnetze fit für Industrie 4.0. http://www.funkschau.de/datacenter/artikel/119192/2/. Accessed 19 August 2015

Re-provisioning of Cloud-Based Execution Infrastructure Using the Cloud-Aware Provenance to Facilitate Scientific Workflow Execution Reproducibility

Khawar Hasham$^{(\boxtimes)}$, Kamran Munir, Richard McClatchey,
and Jetendr Shamdasani

Centre for Complex Cooperative Systems (CCCS),
Department of Computer Science and Creative Technologies (CSCT),
University of the West of England (UWE), Frenchay Campus,
Coldharbour Lane, Bristol BS16 1QY, UK
{mian.ahmad,kamran2.munir,richard.mcclatchey,
jetendr2.shamdasani}@uwe.ac.uk

Abstract. Provenance has been considered as a means to achieve scientific workflow reproducibility to verify the workflow processes and results. Cloud computing provides a new computing paradigm for the workflow execution by offering a dynamic and scalable environment with on-demand resource provisioning. In the absence of Cloud infrastructure information, achieving workflow reproducibility on the Cloud becomes a challenge. This paper presents a framework, named ReCAP, to capture the Cloud infrastructure information and to interlink it with the workflow provenance to establish the Cloud-Aware Provenance (CAP). This paper identifies different scenarios of using the Cloud for workflow execution and presents different mapping approaches. The reproducibility of the workflow execution is performed by re-provisioning the similar Cloud resources using CAP and re-executing the workflow; and by comparing the outputs of workflows. Finally, this paper also presents the evaluation of ReCAP in terms of captured provenance, workflow execution time and workflow output comparison.

Keywords: Cloud computing · Scientific workflows · Cloud infrastructure · Provenance · Reproducibility · Repeatability

1 Introduction

Modern scientific experiments such as the Large Hadron Collider (LHC)[1], and projects such as neuGRID [1] and its follow-on neuGRIDforUsers [2] are producing huge amounts of data. This data is processed and analysed to extract meaningful information by employing scientific workflows that orchestrate the

---

[1] http://lhc.web.cern.ch.

© Springer International Publishing Switzerland 2016
M. Helfert et al. (Eds.): CLOSER 2015, CCIS 581, pp. 74–94, 2016.
DOI: 10.1007/978-3-319-29582-4_5

complex data analysis processes [3]. A large pool of compute and data resources is required to execute the workflows. These resources have been available through the Grid [4] and are now also being offered by the Cloud-based infrastructures.

Cloud computing [5] offers a new computing and storage paradigm, which is dynamically scalable and usually works on a pay-as-you-go cost model. Its ability to provide an on-demand computing infrastructure enables distributed processing of scientific workflows with increased complexity and data require-ments [6]. Research is under way to exploit the potential of Cloud infrastructure for workflow execution [7].

During the data processing, an important consideration is given to collect provenance [8] information. This can provide detailed information about both the inputs and the processed outputs, and the processes involved in a workflow execution. This information can be used to debug the workflow execution, to aid in error tracking and reproducibility. This vital information can enable scientists to verify the outputs and iterate on the scientific method, to evaluate the process and results of other experiments and to share their own experiments with other scientists [9]. The execution of scientific workflows in the Cloud brings to the fore the need to collect provenance information that is necessary to ensure the reproducibility of these experiments on the Cloud infrastructure.

A research study [10] conducted to evaluate the reproducibility of scientific workflows has shown that around 80 % of the workflows cannot be reproduced, and 12 % of them are due to the lack of information about the execution envi-ronment. This lack of information affects a workflow on two levels. It can affect a workflow's overall execution performance and also job failure rate. For instance, a data-intensive job can perform better on a resource with more available Ran-dom Access Memory (RAM) because it can accommodate more data in RAM, which is a faster medium to access data than hard disk. However, the job's performance will degrade if the allotted resource does not provide adequate RAM. Moreover, it is also possible that jobs will fail during execution if their required hardware dependencies are not met. This becomes a more challenging issue in the context of Cloud in which resources can be created or destroyed at runtime.

The dynamic nature of Cloud computing makes the capturing and process-ing of provenance information a major research challenge [11,12]. Since Cloud presents a transparent access to dynamic execution resources, the workflow para-meters including execution resource configuration should also be known to a scientist [13] i.e. what execution environment was used for a job in order to reproduce a workflow execution on the Cloud. Due to these reasons, there is a need to capture information about the Cloud infrastructure along with workflow provenance, to aid in the reproducibility of workflow experiments. There has been a lot of research related to provenance in the Grid (e.g. [14]) and a few ini-tiatives (e.g. [15,16]) for the Cloud. However, they lack the information that can be utilised for re-provisioning of resources on the Cloud, thus they cannot create the similar execution environment(s) for workflow reproducibility. In this paper, the terms Cloud infrastructure and virtualization layer are used interchangeably.

This paper presents a framework, named ReCAP, that augments workflow provenance with the Cloud infrastructure information; and uses it to provision similar execution environment(s) and reproduces the execution of a given workflow. Important areas discussed in this paper are as follows: Sect. 2 presents the related work in provenance related systems. Section 3 presents a set of requirements identified for workflow reproducibility on the Cloud after collecting guidelines used and discussed in literature. Section 4 presents an overview of ReCAP's architecture. Section 4 also discusses two scenarios of using Cloud resources and the provenance capturing approaches devised for these scenarios. Section 5 presents an evaluation of the developed prototype. And finally Sect. 6 presents some conclusions and directions for future work.

2   Related Work

Significant research [17,18] has been carried out in workflow provenance for Grid-based workflow management systems. Chimera [17] is designed to manage the data-intensive analysis for high-energy physics (GriPhyN)[2] and astronomy (SDSS) (http://www.sdss.org) communities. It captures process information, which includes the runtime parameters, input data and the produced data. It stores this provenance information in its schema, which is based on a relational database. Although the schema allows storing the physical location of a machine, it does not support the hardware configuration and software environment in which a job was executed. VisTrails [18] provides support for scientific data exploration and visualization. It not only captures the execution log of a workflow but also the changes a user makes to refine his workflow. However, it does not support the Cloud virtualization layer information. Similar is the case with Pegasus/Wings [19] that supports evolution of a workflow. However, this paper is focusing on the workflow execution provenance on the Cloud, rather than the provenance of a workflow itself (e.g. design changes).

There have been a few research studies (e.g. [15,16]) performed to capture provenance in the Cloud. However, they lack the support for workflow reproducibility. Some of the work in Cloud towards provenance is directed to the file system [20,21] or hypervisor level [22]. However, such work is not relatable to our approach because this paper focuses on virtualized layer information of the Cloud for workflow execution. Moreover, the collected provenance data provides information about the file access but it does not provide information about the resource configuration. The PRECIP [9] project provides an API to provision and execute workflows. However, it does not provide provenance information of a workflow.

There have been a few recent projects [23,24] and research studies e.g. [25] on collecting provenance and using it to reproduce an experiment. A semantic-based approach [25] has been proposed to improve reproducibility of workflows in the Cloud. This approach uses ontologies to extract information about the computational environment from the annotations provided by a user. This information

---

[2] http://www.phys.utb.edu/griphyn/.

is then used to recreate (install or configure) that environment to reproduce a workflow execution. On the contrary, our approach is not relying on annotations rather it directly interacts with the Cloud middleware at runtime to acquire resource configuration information and then establishes mapping between workflow jobs and Cloud resources. The ReproZip software [23] uses system call traces to provide provenance information for job reproducibility and portability. It can capture and organize files/libraries used by a job. The collected information along with all the used system files are zipped together for portability and reproducibility purposes. Similarly, a Linux-based tool, CARE [24], is designed to reproduce a job execution. It builds an archive that contains selected executable/binaries and files accessed by a given job during an observation run. Both these approach are useful at individual job level but are not applicable to an entire workflow, which is the focus of this paper. Moreover, they do not maintain the hardware configuration of the underlined execution machine. Furthermore, these approaches operate along with the job on the virtual machine (VM). On the contrary, out proposed approach works outside the virtual machine and therefore does not interfere with job execution.

3   Requirements for Workflow Reproducibility on Cloud

As per our understanding of the literature, there is not a standard reproducibility model proposed thus far for scientific workflows, especially in a Cloud environment. However, there are some guidelines or policies, which have been highlighted in literature to reproduce experiments. There is one good effort [26] in this regard, but it mainly talks about reproducible papers and it does not consider execution environment of workflows. In this section, we have highlighted a set of requirements for workflow reproducibility on Cloud that can provide guidelines for future work in this regard. These requirements are discussed as follows.

- **Data and Code Sharing:** In computational science, particularly for scientific workflow executions, it is emphasized that the data, code, and the workflow description should be available in order to reproduce an experiment [27]. Code must be available to be distributed, and data must be accessible in a readable format [28]. In the absence of such information, experiment reproducibility cannot be achieved because different result would be produced if the input data changes. It is also possible that the experiment cannot be successfully executed in the absence of the required code and its dependencies or configurations.
- **Execution Infrastructure:** The execution infrastructure is composed of a set of computational resources (e.g. execution nodes, storage devices, networking). The physical approach, where actual computational hardware are made available for long time periods to scientists, often conserves the computational environment including supercomputers, clusters, or Grids [25]. As a result, scientists are able to reproduce their experiments in the same hardware environment. However, this luxury is not available in the Cloud in which resources are virtual and dynamic. Therefore, it is important to collect the Cloud resource

information in such a manner that will assist in re-provisioning of similar resources on the Cloud for workflow re-execution.

From a resource provisioning as well as a performance point of view, various factors such as RAM, vCPU, Hard Disk and CPU speed (e.g. MIPS) are important in selecting appropriate resources especially on the Cloud. As discussed previously, the RAM can affect the job's execution performance as well as its failure rate. A job will fail if it is scheduled to a resource with less available RAM (as shown in Fig. 4). Similarly, vCPU (virtual CPUs meaning CPU cores) along with the MIPS (million instructions per second) value directly affect the job execution performance. In a study [29], it was found that the workflow task durations differ for each major Cloud, despite the identical setup.

Hard disk capacity also becomes an important factor in provisioning a new resource on the Cloud. It was argued [29] that building images for scientific applications requires adequate storage within a virtual machine (VM). In addition to the OS and the application software, this storage is used to hold job inputs and output that are consumed and produced by a workflow job executing on a VM [29].

- **Software Environment:** Apart from knowing the hardware infrastructure, it is also essential to collect information about the software environment. A software environment determines the operating system and the libraries used to execute a job. Without the access to required libraries information, a job execution will fail. For example, a job, relying on MATLAB library, will fail in case the required library is missing. One possible approach [30] to conserve software environment is thought to conserve VM that is used to execute a job and then reuse the same VM while re-executing the same job. One may argue that it would be easier to keep and share VM images with the research community through a common repository, however the high storage demand of VM images remains a challenging problem [31]. In the prototype presented in this paper, the OS image used to provision a VM is conserved and thought to present all the software dependencies required for a job execution in a workflow. Therefore, the proposed solution also retrieves the image information to build a virtual machine on which the workflow job was executed.

- **Provenance Comparison:** The provenance traces of two executed workflows should be compared to determine workflow reproducibility. The main idea is to evaluate the reproducibility of an entire execution of a given workflow, including the logical chaining of activities and the data. To provide the strict reproducibility functionality, a system must guarantee that the data are still accessible and that the corresponding activities are accessible [32]. Since the focus of this paper is on workflow reproducibility on the Cloud infrastructure, the execution infrastructure should also be part of the comparison. Therefore the provenance comparison should be made at following levels:

  1. Workflow structure should be compared to determine that both workflows are similar. Because it is possible that two workflows are having similar number of jobs but with different job execution order.
  2. Execution infrastructure (software environment, resource configuration) used on the Cloud for a workflow execution should also be compared.

3. Comparison of input and output should be made to evaluate workflow reproducibility. There could be a scenario that a user repeated a workflow but with different inputs, thus producing different outputs. It is also possible that changes in job or software library result into different workflow output. There are a few approaches [33], which perform workflow provenance comparison to determine differences in reproduced workflows. The proposed system in this paper incorporates the workflow output comparison to determine the reproducibility of a workflow.

– **Cloud Resource Pricing:** Cloud resource pricing can be important for experiments in which cost is also a main factor. However, this can also be argued that this information is not trivial for an experiment due to strong industry competition between big Cloud providers such as Amazon, Google, Microsoft etc., which can bring prices down. Having said this, one still cannot deny the fact that a cost is associated with each acquired resource on the Cloud, thus making this factor important to be focused on. The pricing factor has been used in various studies to conduct the feasibility of a Cloud environment for workflow execution [6]. In this study, the cost factor for various resources such as compute and storage has been evaluated for workflow execution. The pricing information has also been used in cost-effective scheduling and provisioning algorithms [34, 35]. Therefore, this pricing information, if collected as part of provenance, can help in reproducing an experiment within the similar cost as was incurred in earlier execution. However, one must keep this in mind that the prices are dynamic and subject to change and it depends entirely on the Cloud providers. For an environment, in which cost does not change rapidly, such information can be helpful. Therefore, this information is captured as part of the Cloud-Aware Provenance data.

Workflow versioning is another factor that aids in achieving workflow reproducibility [36]. Sandve et al. [26] also suggested archiving the exact versions of all processes and enabling version control on all scripts used in an experiment. With the help of workflow versioning, a user can track the evolution of a workflow itself. Since the focus of this research work is on the workflow execution provenance and not on the workflow evolution, this factor is outside the scope of the presented work. Based on the identified factors in this section, following section presents a framework, named ReCAP, to capture the Cloud infrastructure information and to interlink it with the workflow provenance to establish the Cloud-Aware Provenance (CAP). This information is used to re-provision similar execution infrastructure on the Cloud in order to reproduce the execution of a scientific workflow.

4   ReCAP: Workflow Reproducibility Using Cloud-Aware Provenance

An overview of the ReCAP's architecture, a proposed solution, is presented in this section. This architecture is inspired by the mechanism used in a paper [37] for executing workflows on the Cloud. Figure 1 illustrates the proposed architecture that collects the Cloud infrastructure information and interlinks it with the workflow provenance gathered from a workflow management system such as Pegasus. This augmented or extended provenance information compromising of workflow provenance and the Cloud infrastructure information is named as Cloud-Aware provenance (CAP). The components of this architecture are discussed as follow:

- **WMS Wrapper Service:** This component exposes the functionality of an underlining workflow management system (WMS) by providing a wrapper service. It is responsible for receiving various user and ReCAP's components requests in submitting a user provided workflow and monitoring its status. For instance, there is no suitable HTTP-based facility available that a user can use to submit a workflow and its associated files to Pegasus. Traditionally, a command-based approach is used in which Pegasus provided commands are invoked from a terminal. With such a service based component, a user can submit his workflow through an HTTP client. Another purpose of this component is to engage with a user from the very first step of workflow execution i.e. workflow submission. Although this paper is focusing on workflow execution, it still needs a mechanism to access the submitted workflow and its associated configuration files in order for it to reproduce and resubmit the same workflow. Therefore, such a mechanism was required that can act as an entry point for the system and also help in ensuring the access to the workflow source, which is one of the points of the reproducibility requirements identified for the Cloud (see Sect. 3).

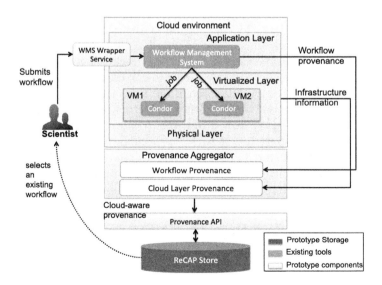

Fig. 1. General overview of the ReCAP architecture.

- **Workflow Provenance:** This component, named *WFProvenance*, is responsible for receiving provenance captured at the application level by the workflow management system e.g. Pegasus. Since workflow management systems may vary, a plugin-based approach is used for this component. Common interfaces are designed to develop plugins for different workflow management systems. The plugin also translates the workflow provenance according to the representation that is used to interlink the workflow provenance along with the information coming from the Cloud infrastructure.

- **Cloud Layer Provenance:** This component, *CloudLayerProvenance*, is responsible for capturing information collected from different layers of the Cloud. To achieve re-provisioning of resources on Cloud, this component focuses on the virtualization layer and retrieves information related to the Cloud infrastructure i.e. virtual machine configuration. This component interacts with the Cloud infrastructure as an outside client to obtain the resource configuration information. This component is discussed in detail in Sects. 4.2 and 4.3.

- **Provenance Aggregator:** This is the main component task to collect and interlink the provenance coming from different layers as shown in Fig. 1. It establishes interlinking connections between the workflow provenance and the Cloud infrastructure information. The provenance information is then represented in a single format that could be stored in the provenance store through the interfaces exposed by the *ProvenanceAPI*.

- **Provenance API:** This acts as a thin layer to expose the provenance storage capabilities to other components. Through its exposed interfaces, outside entities such as the *ProvenanceAggregator* would interact with it to store the workflow provenance information. This approach gives flexibility to implement authentication or authorization in accessing the provenance store.

- **ReCAP Store:** This data store is designed to keep record of the workflow and its related configuration files being used to submit a user analysis on the Cloud. It also keeps the mapping between workflow jobs and the virtual resources used for execution on the Cloud infrastructure. This information is later retrieved to reproduce the workflow execution.

4.1   Cloud Usage Scenarios

This section discusses the job to Cloud resource mapping, which will be used later for re-executing a workflow on similar Cloud resources, mechanisms devised in this research study. Before indulging into detailed discussion of these mechanisms, first it is important to understand two different resource usage scenarios on Cloud. These scenarios and their understanding provide a better picture of the requirements and the motivation behind devising different mechanisms to establish job to Cloud resource mapping for each discussed scenario.

- **Static Environment on Cloud.** In this environment, the virtual resources, once provisioned, remain in RUNNING state on Cloud for a longer time. This means that the resources will be accessible even after a workflows execution is finished. This environment is similar to creating a virtual cluster or Grid on top of Clouds resources. Such a Cloud environment is also in used in the N4U infrastructure. The Static Mapping approach devised for such environment has been discussed in Sect. 4.2.

- **Dynamic Environment on Cloud.** In this environment, resources are provisioned on demand and released when they are no more required. This means that the virtual machines are shutdown after the job is done. Therefore, a virtual resource, which was used to execute a job, will not be accessible once a job is finished. The Eager Mapping has been devised (see Sect. 4.3) to handle this scenario.

The mapping approaches discussed in following sections achieve the job to Cloud resource mapping using the workflow provenance information. One such information is an indication of execution host or its IP in the collected workflow provenance. Many a workflow management systems such as Pegasus, VisTrail or Chiron [38] do maintain either machine name or IP information. In Clouds infrastructure layer across one Cloud provider or for one user, no two virtual machines can have same IP at any given time. This means any running virtual machine should have unique IP or name. However, it is possible that a name or IP can be reused later for new virtual machines. All rest properties of a virtual machine accessible through the infrastructure layer can be used by multiple machines at a time. For instance, multiple machines can be provisioned with flavour m1.small or with OS image Ububtu 14.04 or Fedora etc.

4.2 Static Mapping Approach

As mentioned earlier, this information is used for reprovisioning the resources to provide a similar execution infrastructure to repeat a workflow execution. The Static Mapping approach has been devised for the Static environment on the Cloud. Once a workflow is executed, Pegasus collects the provenance and stores it in its own internal database. Pegasus also stores the IP address of the virtual machine (VM) where the job is executed. However, it lacks other VM specifications such as RAM, CPUs, hard disk etc. The CloudLayerProvenance component retrieves all the jobs of a workflow and their associated VM IP addresses from the Pegasus database. It then collects a list of virtual machines owned by a respective user from the Cloud middleware. Using the IP address, it establishes a mapping between the job and the resource configuration of the virtual machine used to execute the job. This information i.e. Cloud-Aware Provenance is then stored in the *ReCAPStore*. The flowchart of this mechanism is presented in Fig. 2. In this flowchart, the variable *wfJobs* representing a list of jobs of a given workflow is retrieved from the Pegasus database. The variable *vmList* represents a list of virtual machines in the Cloud infrastructure is collected from the Cloud. A mapping between jobs and VMs is established by matching the IP addresses (see in Fig. 2). Resource configuration parameters such as flavour and image are obtained once the mapping is established.

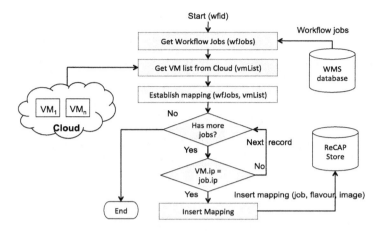

Fig. 2. Flowchart of the job to the Cloud resource mapping in the Static environment.

Flavour defines resource configuration such as RAM, Hard disk and CPUs, and image defines the operating system image used in that particular resource. By combining these two parameters together, one can provision a resource on the Cloud infrastructure. After retrieving these parameters and jobs, the mapping information is then stored in the Provenance Store (see in Fig. 2). This mapping information provides two important data (a) hardware configuration (b) software configuration using VM name. As discussed in Sect. 3, these two parameters are important in recreating a similar execution environment.

4.3   Eager Mapping Approach

This approach is devised to establish a job to Cloud resource mapping for the dynamic environment on Cloud. As discussed in Sect. 4.1, the resource on Cloud may not be accessible once a job is finished, thus making a job to resource mapping a challenge. This is why, this approach attempts to identify, as early as possible, the virtual machine on which a job is executing. In this mapping approach, the Cloud-aware provenance is acquired in two phases, which are discussed as follows.

Phase 1: Temporary Job to Resource Mapping: In this phase, the Eager approach monitors the underlying WMS database i.e. Pegasus for the implemented prototype. In Pegasus, along with the host name, its database also maintains the Condor's *schedd_ID*, which is assigned to each job by Condor [39]. The monitoring thread in *WFProvenance* retrieves the job's Condor ID and contacts the WMS Wrapper Service (WMS-WS) for information about the job. Since the WMS-WS works on top of the underlying workflow managment system, it has an access to the Condor cluster. Upon receiving the request, WMS-WS retrieves job information from the Condor. This information contains the

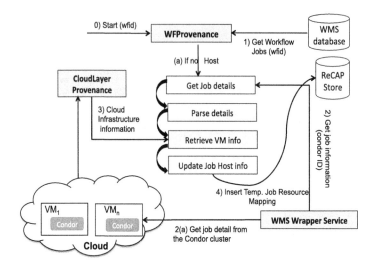

Fig. 3. Temporary resource mapping established in the phase 1 of the Eager approach.

machine IP on which the job is currently running. The *CloudLayerProvenance* component retrieves the virtual machine's configuration information from the Cloud middleware based on the machine IP (as discussed in the Sect. 4.2) and stores this information in the database. This information is treated as temporary because the job is not finished yet and there is a possibility that a job may be re-scheduled to another machine due to runtime failures [40]. This information is then used in the second phase for establishing the final mapping between the job and the Cloud resource. The flowchart of this mechanism is presented in Fig. 3.

Phase 2: Final Job to Resource Mapping: This phase starts when the workflow execution is finished. The *ProvenanceAggregator* component starts the job to resource mapping process. In doing so, it retrieves the list of workflows from the database and list of virtual machines from the Cloud middleware through the *CloudLayerProvenance* component. It starts the mapping between the jobs and the virtual machines based on the IP information, stored in the database, associated with the jobs. In the case of not finding any host information in the database, which is possible in the Dynamic use case, the *ProvenanceAggregator* retrieves the resource information for that job from the temporary repository that was created in the first phase (as discussed in the Sect. 4.2). Upon finding the Cloud resource information, the *Provenance Aggregator* component registers this Cloud-Aware Provenance information in the *ReCAPStore*. Once the mapping for a job is established and stored in the database, its corresponding temporary mapping is removed in order to reduce the disk storage overhead. The algorithm of the Eager mapping approach is shown in Algorithm 1.

Algorithm 1. Eager Approach.

Require: $wfJobs$: Set of jobs in the workflow.

1: *Phase 1*
2: **procedure** JOBMONITOR($wfJobs$)
3:     $cloudResources \leftarrow$ GETCLOUDRESOURCES$(())$}
4:     **for all** $job \in wfJobs$ **do**
5:         $condorid \leftarrow job.condor$ ▷ each job is assigned unique id
6:         $hostname \leftarrow'$ PEGASUSCLIENT.GETHOSTINFO($condorid$)
7:         $vm \leftarrow cloudResource[hostname]$
8:         **if** vm != None & VMMAPPINGEXISTS(vm, job) **then**
9:             $resourceFlavor \leftarrow$ vm.flavor
10:             $resourceImage \leftarrow$ vm.image
11:             CREATETEMPMAPPING($job, resourceFlavor, resourceImage$)

12: *Phase 2*
13: **procedure** ESTABLISHMAPPING($wfJobs$)
14:     **for all** $job \in wfJobs$ **do**
15:         $vm \leftarrow$ GETTEMPJOBMAPPING(job)
16:         **if** tempMap **then**
17:             $resourceImage \leftarrow$ vm.image
18:             $resourceFlavor \leftarrow$ vm.image
19:             STOREJOBRESOURCEMAPPING($job, resourceFlavor, resourceImage$)
20:             REMOVETEMPMAPPING($job, resourceFlavor, resourceImage$)

4.4 Workflow Reproducibility Using ReCAP

In Sect. 4, different mapping approaches have been discussed to interlink the job to Cloud resource information, which is stored in the database for workflow reproducibility purposes. In order to reproduce a workflow execution, researcher first needs to provide the wfID (workflow ID), which is assigned to every workflow in Pegasus, to ReCAP to re-execute the workflow using the Cloud-aware provenance. ReCAP retrieves the given workflow from the *ReCAPStore* along with the Cloud resource mapping stored against this workflow. Using this mapping information, it retrieves the resource flavour and image configurations, and provisions the resources on Cloud. Once resources are provisioned, it submits the workflow for execution. At this stage, a new workflow ID is assigned to this newly submitted workflow. This new wfID is passed over to the *ProvenanceAggregator* component to monitor the execution of the workflow and start collecting its Cloud-aware provenance information. Recapturing the provenance of the repeated workflow is important, as this will enable us to verify the provisioned resources by comparing their resource configurations with the old resource configuration.

4.5 Workflow Output Comparison

Another aspect of workflow reproducibility is to verify that it has produced the same output that was produced in its earlier execution (as discussed in Sect. 3). In order to evaluate workflow repeatability, an algorithm has been proposed that compares the outputs produced by two given workflows. It uses the MD5 hashing algorithm [41] on the outputs and compares the hash value to verify the produced outputs. The two main reasons of using a hash function to verify the produced outputs are; (a) simple to implement and (b) the hash value changes with a single bit change in the file. If the hash values of two given files are same, this means that the given files contain same content.

Algorithm 2. Pseudocode to compare outputs produced by two given workflows.

Require: $srcWfID$: Source Workflow ID.
       $destWfID$: Destination Workflow ID

```
 1: procedure COMPAREWORKFLOWOUTPUTS(srcWfID, destWfID)
 2:     srcWorkflowJobs ← GETWORKFLOWJOBS(srcWfID)
 3:     destWorkflowJobs ← GETWORKFLOWJOBS(destWfID)
 4:     FileCounter ← 0
 5:     ComparisonCounter ← 0
 6:     for all jobfiles ∈ srcWorkflowJobs do
 7:         src_container ← jobfiles.container_name
 8:         src_filename ← jobfiles.file_name
 9:         dest_container ← destWorkflowJobs[jobfiles.jobname]
10:         dest_filename← destWorkflowJobs[jobname].file_name
11:         src_cloud_file ← GETCLOUDFILE(src_container  src_filename )
12:         dest_cloud_file ← GETCLOUDFILE(dest_container  dest_filename )
13:         FileCounter ← FileCounter + 1
14:         if src_cloud_file.hash = dest_cloud_file.hash then
15:             ComparisonCounter ← ComparisonCounter + 1
16:     if FileCounter = ComparisonCounter then
17:         return True
18:     return False
```

The proposed algorithm (as shown in Algorithm 2) operates over the two given workflows identified by $srcWfID$ and $destWfID$, and compares their outputs. It first retrieves the list of jobs and their produced output files from the Provenance Store for each given workflow. It then iterates over the files and compares the source file, belonging to $srcWfID$, with the destination file, belonging to $destWfID$. Since the files are stored on the Cloud, the algorithm retrieves the files from the Cloud (see lines 11 and 12). Cloud storage services such as OpenStack Swift (http://swift.openstack.org), Amazon S3 (http://aws.amazon.com/s3) use the concept of a bucket or a container to store a file. This is why $src\_container$ and $dest\_container$ along with $src\_filename$ and $dest\_filename$ are given in the $GetCloudFile$ function to identify a specific file in the Cloud. The algorithm then compares the hash value of both files and increments $ComparisonCounter$. If all the files in both workflows are the same, $ComparisonCounter$ should be equal to $FileCounter$, which counts the number of files produced by a workflow. Thus, it confirms that the workflows are repeated successfully. Otherwise, the algorithms returns false if both these counters are not equal.

5   Results and Discussion

To demonstrate the effect of Cloud resource configuration such as RAM on job failure rate, a basic memory-consuming job is written in Java. The job attempts to construct an alphabet string of given size (in MB), which is provided at runtime. To execute this experiment, three resource configurations, (a) m1.tiny, (b) m1.small and (c) m1.medium, each with 512 MB, 2048 MB and 4096 MB RAM respectively were used. Each job is executed at least 5 times with a given memory requirement on each resource configuration. The result in Fig. 5 shows that jobs fail if required RAM (hardware) requirement is not fulfilled. All jobs with RAM requirement less than 500 MB executed successfully on all resource configurations. However, the jobs start to fail on Cloud resources with m1.tiny configuration (as shown in Fig. 4) as soon as the jobs memory requirement approaches 500 MB because the jobs could not find enough available memory on the given resource. This result confirms the presented argument (discussed in Sect. 1 and also in Sect. 3) regarding the need for collecting Cloud resource configuration and its impact on job failure. Since a workflow is composed of many jobs, which are executed in a given order, a single job failure can result in a workflow execution failure. Therefore, collecting Cloud-aware provenance is essential for reproducing a scientific workflow execution on the Cloud.

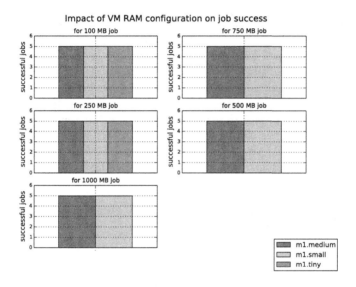

Fig. 4. The effect of the Cloud resource's RAM configuration on the job's success rate.

To evaluate the presented mapping algorithm, which collects the Cloud infrastructure information and interlinks it with the workflow provenance, a Python based prototype has been developed using Apache Libcloud[3], a library to interact with the Cloud middleware. The presented evaluation of the prototype is very basic currently. However, as this work progresses further a full evaluation will be conducted. To evaluate this prototype, a 20 cores Cloud infrastructure is acquired from the Open Science Data Cloud (OSDC) (opensciencedatacloud.org). This Cloud infrastructure uses the OpenStack middleware (openstack.org) to provide Infrastructure-as-a-Service (IaaS) capability. A small Condor cluster of three virtual machines is also configured. In this cluster, one machine is a master node, which is used to submit workflows, and the

---

[3] http://libcloud.apache.org.

remaining two are compute nodes. These compute nodes are used to execute workflow jobs. Using the Pegasus APIs, a wordcount workflow application composed of four jobs is written. This workflow has both control and data dependencies [42] among its jobs along with the split and merge characteristics, which are common characteristics in scientific workflows. The first job (Split job) takes a text file and splits it into two files of almost equal length. Later, two jobs (Analysis jobs), each take one file as input, and then calculate the number of words in the given file. The fourth job (merge job) takes the outputs of earlier analysis jobs and calculates the final result i.e. total number of words in both files.

This workflow is submitted using Pegasus. The wfID assigned to this workflow is 114. The collected Cloud resource information is stored in database. Table 1 shows the provenance mapping records in the *ReCAPStore* for this workflow. The collected information includes the flavour and image (image name and Image id) configuration parameters. The Image id uniquely identifies an OS image hosted on the Cloud and this image contains all the software or libraries used during the job execution (as discussed earlier in Sect. 3). As an image contains all the required libraries of a job, this prototype does not extract the installed libraries information from the virtual machine at the moment for workflow reproducibility purpose. However, this can be done in future iterations to enable the proposed approach to reconfigure a resource at runtime on the Cloud. The reproducibility of the workflow using the proposed approach (discussed in Sect. 4.2) has also been tested. The prototype is requested to repeat the workflow with wfID 114. Upon receiving the request, it first collects the resource

Table 1. Cloud-Aware Provenance captured for a given workflow.

WfID	Host IP	nodename	Flavour Id	minRAM	minHD	vCPU	image name	image Id
114	174.16.1.49	osdc-vm3	2	2048	20 GB	1	wf_peg_repeat	f102960c-557c-4253-8277-2df5ffe3c169
114	174.16.1.98	mynode	2	2048	20 GB	1	wf_peg_repeat	f102960c-557c-4253-8277-2df5ffe3c169

Table 2. Provenance data of the reproduced workflow showing that ReCAP successfully re-provisioned similar resources on the Cloud.

WfID	Host IP	nodename	Flavour Id	minRAM	minHD	vCPU	image name	image Id
117	172.16.1.183	osdc-vm3-rep	2	2048	20 GB	1	wf_peg_repeat	f102960c-557c-4253-8277-2df5ffe3c169
117	172.16.1.187	mynode-rep	2	2048	20 GB	1	wf_peg_repea	f102960c-557c-4253-8277-2df5ffe3c169
122	172.16.1.114	osdc-vm3-rep	2	2048	20 GB	1	wf_peg_repeat	f102960c-557c-4253-8277-2df5ffe3c169
122	172.16.1.112	mynode-rep	2	2048	20 GB	1	wf_peg_repea	f102960c-557c-4253-8277-2df5ffe3c169

configurations, captured from earlier execution, from the database and provisions the resources on the Cloud infrastructure. The name of re-provisioned resource(s) for the repeated workflow has a postfix -rep e.g. mynova-rep as shown in Table 2. It was named 'mynova' in original workflow execution as shown in Table 1. From Table 2, one can assess that similar resources have been re-provisioned using the ReCAP system to reproduce the workflow execution because the RAM, Hard disk, vCPUs and image configurations are similar to the resources used for workflow with wfID 114 (as shown in Table 1). This result confirms that the similar resources on the Cloud can be re-provisioned with the Cloud-Aware Provenance (CAP) collected using the proposed approach (discussed in Sect. 4). Table 2 shows two repeated workflow instances of original workflow 114. In order to measure the execution time of the original workflow and the re-produced workflow on the similar execution infrastructure on the Cloud, the same workflow was executed multiple times on the Cloud infrastructure. An average execution time is calculated for these workflow executions and treated as the average execution time of the original workflow. The ReCAP approach is then used to reproduce the workflow execution by re-provisioning the similar execution infrastructure using the Cloud-Aware Provenance (CAP). The same workflow was re-executed on the re-provisioned resources to measure the execution time of the reproduced workflow. Figure 5 shows the average workflow execution times for both the original and reproduced workflows respectively. In the case of original execution, the average workflow execution is 434.84 ± 6.52 s and the workflow execution time for the reproduced workflow is 434.76 ± 7.3657 s. This result shows that there is no significance difference (i.e. 0.08 s) in workflow execution time because of the similar execution infrastructure used for workflow re-execution. This result confirms that workflow can be reproduced with similar execution performance provided a similar execution infrastructure is available on the Cloud.

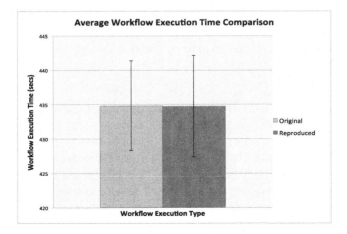

Fig. 5. Comparing the average workflow execution time of the original and the reproduced workflow execution.

The other aspect to evaluate the workflow reproducibility (as discussed in Sect. 3) is to compare the outputs produced by both workflows. This has been achieved using the algorithm discussed in Sect. 4.5. Four jobs in both the given workflows i.e. 114 and 117 produce the same number of output files (see Table 3). The Split job produces two output files i.e. wordlist1 and wordlist2. Two analysis jobs, Analysis1 and Analysis2, consume the wordlist1 and wordlist2 files, and produce the analysis1 and analysis2 files respectively. The merge job consumes the analysis1 and analysis2 files and produces the *merge_output* file. The hash values of these files are shown in the MD5 Hash column of the Table 3, here both given workflows are compared with each other. For instance, the hash value of wordlist1 produced by the Split job of workflow 117 is compared with the hash value of wordlist1 produced by the Split job of workflow 114. If both the hash values are same, the algorithm returns true. This process is repeated for all the files produced by both workflows. The algorithm confirms the verification of workflow outputs if the corresponding files in both workflows have the same hash values. Table 3 shows that both workflows have produced the identical files because the hash values are same. In order to measure the impact of provenance mapping approaches (as discussed in Sects. 4.2 and 4.3) on the workflow execution performance, the workflow jobs were modified to eliminate the effect of the data transfer time on the workflow execution. The jobs in the workflow mimic the job processing by introducing a sleep interval for a given time period, which is passed as an argument. Figure 6 shows that the average workflow execution time in the absence of any provenance approach (i.e. No Mapping) is 434.69 ± 6.52 s. The average workflow execution time is 434.71 ± 4.49 and 434.74 ± 4.28 s for the Static and Eager Mapping approaches respectively. The difference between the execution times is 0.02 and 0.05 s for the Static and Eager approaches respectively. This slight difference in execution time is mainly caused by the delays a job faces during its execution. The overall workflow execution time remains almost the same in the presence of the proposed provenance capturing approaches. The main reason for these mapping approaches to not having a major impact on the

Table 3. Provenance data of the reproduced workflow showing that ReCAP successfully re-provisioned similar resources on the Cloud.

Job	WfID	Container Name	File Name	MD5 Hash
Split	114	wfoutput123011	wordlist1	0d934584cbc124eed93c4464ab178a5d
	117	wfoutput125819	wordlist1	0d934584cbc124eed93c4464ab178a5d
	114	wfoutput123011	wordlist2	0d934584cbc124eed93c4464ab178a5d
	117	wfoutput125819	wordlist2	0d934584cbc124eed93c4464ab178a5d
Analysis1	117	wfoutput125819	analysis1	494f24e426dba5cc1ce9a132d50ccbda
	114	wfoutput123011	analysis2	127e8dbd6beffdd2e9dfed79d46e1ebc
Analysis2	114	wfoutput123011	analysis2	127e8dbd6beffdd2e9dfed79d46e1ebc
	117	wfoutput125819	analysis2	127e8dbd6beffdd2e9dfed79d46e1ebc
Merge	114	wfoutput123011	merge_output	d0bd408843b90e36eb8126b397c6efed
	117	wfoutput125819	merge_output	d0bd408843b90e36eb8126b397c6efed

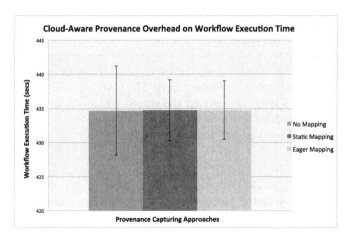

Fig. 6. Cloud-Aware Provenance capturing overhead on the workflow execution time.

workflow execution time is because they work outside the virtual machines, thus they don't interfere with the job execution.

6   Conclusion and Future Direction

The dynamic nature of the Cloud makes provenance capturing of workflow(s) with the underlying execution environment(s) and their reproducibility a difficult challenge. In this regard, a list of workflow reproducibility requirements has been presented after analysing the literature and workflow execution scenario on the Cloud infrastructure. The proposed ReCAP's framework can augment the existing workflow provenance with the Cloud infrastructure information. Based on the identified Cloud usage scenarios i.e. Static and Dynamic, the proposed mapping approaches iterate over the workflow jobs and establishes mappings with the resource information available on the Cloud. The results show that the proposed approaches can capture the Cloud-Aware Provenance (CAP) by capturing the information related to Cloud infrastructure (virtual machines) used during a workflow execution. It can then re-provision a similar execution infrastructure with same resource configurations on the Cloud using CAP to reproduce a workflow execution. Figure 5 shows that the workflow execution time remains the same for reproduced workflow because similar execution infrastructure was provisioned using the Cloud-Aware Provenance. The workflow reproducibility is verified by comparing the outputs produced by the workflows. In this regard, the proposed algorithm (see Algorithm 2) compares the outputs produced by two given workflows. Furthermore, this paper also presents the impact of the devised mapping approaches on the workflow execution time. The result in Fig. 6 shows that the presented mapping approaches do not significantly affect the workflow execution time because they work outside the virtual machine and do not interfere with the job execution. In future, the proposed approach will be extended and a detailed evaluation of the ReCAP framework will be conducted. Different performance matrices such as the impact of different resource configuration on workflow execution performance, and total resource provisioning time will also be measured. In this paper, only workflow outputs have been used to compare two workflows' provenance traces. In future, the comparison algorithm will also incorporate workflow structure and execution infrastructure (as discussed in Sect. 3) to verify workflow reproducibility. Moreover, the ReCAP framework has not addressed the issue of securing the stored Cloud-Aware Provenance. In future, the presented architecture will be extended by adding a security layer on top of the collected Cloud-Aware Provenance.

Acknowledgements. This research work has been funded by a European Union FP-7 project, N4U neuGrid4Users (grant agreement n. 283562, 2011-2014). Besides this, the support provided by OSDC by offering a free Cloud infrastructure of 20 cores is highly appreciated.

References

1. Mehmood, Y., Habib, I., Bloodsworth, P., Anjum, A., Lansdale, T., McClatchey, R.: A middleware agnostic infrastructure for neuro-imaging analysis. In: 22nd IEEE International Symposium on Computer-Based Medical Systems, CBMS 2009, pp. 1–4, August 2009
2. Munir, K., Kiani, S.L., Hasham, K., McClatchey, R., Branson, A., Shamdasani, J.: Provision of an integrated data analysis platform for computational neuroscience experiments. J. Syst. Inf. Technol. **16**(3), 150–169 (2014)
3. Deelman, E., Gannon, D., Shields, M., Taylor, I.: Workflows and e-science: An overview of workflow system features and capabilities. Future Gener. Comput. Syst. **25**(5), 528–540 (2009)
4. Foster, I., Kesselman, C. (eds.): The Grid: Blueprint for a New Computing Infrastructure. Morgan Kaufmann Publishers Inc., San Francisco (1999)
5. Mell, P. M., Grance, T.: Sp 800–145. The nist definition of cloud computing. Technical report, Gaithersburg, MD, United States (2011)
6. Deelman, E., Singh, G., Livny, M., Berriman, B., Good, J.: The cost of doing science on the cloud: the montage example. In: Proceedings of the 2008 ACM/IEEE Conference on Supercomputing, SC 2008. pp. 50:1–50:12. IEEE Press, USA (2008)
7. Juve, G., Deelman, E.: Scientific workflows and clouds. Crossroads **16**(3), 14–18 (2010)
8. Simmhan, Y.L., Plale, B., Gannon, D.: A survey of data provenance in e-science. SIGMOD Rec. **34**(3), 31–36 (2005)
9. Azarnoosh, S., Rynge, M., Juve, G., Deelman, E., Niec, M., Malawski, M., da Silva, R.: Introducing PRECIP: an API for managing repeatable experiments in the cloud. In: 2013 IEEE 5th International Conference on Cloud Computing Technology and Science (CloudCom), vol. 2, pp. 19–26, December 2013
10. Belhajjame, K., Roos, M., Garcia-Cuesta, E., Klyne, G., Zhao, J., De Roure, D., Goble, C., Gomez-Perez, J.M., Hettne, K., Garrido, A.: Why workflows break - understanding and combating decay in taverna workflows. In: Proceedings of the 2012 IEEE 8th International Conference on E-Science (e-Science), E-SCIENCE 2012, pp. 1–9. IEEE Computer Society, USA (2012)
11. Vouk, M.: Cloud computing - issues, research and implementations. In: 30th International Conference on Information Technology Interfaces, ITI 2008, pp. 31–40, June 2008

12. Zhao, Y., Fei, X., Raicu, I., Lu, S.: Opportunities and challenges in running scientific workflows on the cloud. In: 2011 International Conference on Cyber-Enabled Distributed Computing and Knowledge Discovery (CyberC), pp. 455–462, October 2011
13. Shamdasani, J., Branson, A., McClatchey, R.: Towards semantic provenance in cristal. In: Third International Workshop on the Role of Semantic Web in Provenance Management (SWPM 2012) (2012)
14. Stevens, R.D., Robinson, A.J., Goble, C.A.: myGrid: personalised bioinformatics on the information grid. Bioinformatics **19**, i302–i304 (2003)
15. de Oliveira, D., Ogasawara, E., Baiao, F., Mattoso, M.: Scicumulus: a lightweight cloud middleware to explore many task computing paradigm in scientific workflows. In: 2010 IEEE 3rd International Conference on Cloud Computing (CLOUD), pp. 378–385, July 2010
16. Ko, R.K.L., Lee, B.S., Pearson, S.: Towards achieving accountability, auditability and trust in cloud computing. In: Abraham, A., Mauri, J.L., Buford, J.F., Suzuki, J., Thampi, S.M. (eds.) ACC 2011, Part IV. CCIS, vol. 193, pp. 432–444. Springer, Heidelberg (2011)
17. Foster, I., Vöckler, J., Wilde, M., Zhao, Y.: Chimera: a virtual data system for representing, querying, and automating data derivation. In: Proceedings of the 14th International Conference on Scientific and Statistical Database Management, pp. 37–46 (2002)
18. Scheidegger, C., Koop, D., Santos, E., Vo, H., Callahan, S., Freire, J., Silva, C.: Tackling the provenance challenge one layer at a time. Concurr. Comput.: Pract. Exper. **20**(5), 473–483 (2008)
19. Kim, J., Deelman, E., Gil, Y., Mehta, G., Ratnakar, V.: Provenance trails in the wings-pegasus system. Concurr. Comput.: Pract. Exper. **20**(5), 587–597 (2008)
20. Zhang, O.Q., Kirchberg, M., Ko, R.K., Lee, B.S.: How to track your data: the case for cloud computing provenance. In: 2011 IEEE Third International Conference on Cloud Computing Technology and Science (CloudCom), pp. 446–453. IEEE (2011)
21. Tan, Y.S., Ko, R.K., Jagadpramana, P., Suen, C.H., Kirchberg, M., Lim, T.H., Lee, B.S., Singla, A., Mermoud, K., Keller, D., Duc, H.: Tracking of data leaving the cloud. In: 2013 12th IEEE International Conference on Trust, Security and Privacy in Computing and Communications, pp. 137–144 (2012)
22. Macko, P., Chiarini, M., Seltzer, M.: Collecting provenance via the xen hypervisor. In: 3rd USENIX Workshop on the Theory and Practice of Provenance (TAPP) (2011)
23. Chirigati, F., Shasha, D., Freire, J.: Reprozip: using provenance to support computational reproducibility. In: Proceedings of the 5th USENIX Workshop on the Theory and Practice of Provenance, TaPP 2013, pp. 1:1–1:4. USENIX Association, Berkeley (2013)
24. Janin, Y., Vincent, C., Duraffort, R.: Care, the comprehensive archiver for reproducible execution. In: Proceedings of the 1st ACM SIGPLAN Workshop on Reproducible Research Methodologies and New Publication Models in Computer Engineering, TRUST 2014, pp. 1:1–1:7. ACM, New York (2014)
25. Santana-Perez, I., Ferreira da Silva, R., Rynge, M., Deelman, E., Pérez-Hernández, M.S., Corcho, O.: A semantic-based approach to attain reproducibility of computational environments in scientific workflows: a case study. In: Lopes, L., et al. (eds.) Euro-Par 2014, Part I. LNCS, vol. 8805, pp. 452–463. Springer, Heidelberg (2014)
26. Sandve, G.K., Nekrutenko, A., Taylor, J., Hovig, E.: Ten simple rules for reproducible computational research. PLoS Comput. Biol. **9**(10), e1003285 (2013)

27. Stodden, V.C.: Reproducible research: addressing the need for data and code sharing in computational science. Comput. Sci. Eng. **12**, 8–12 (2010)
28. Santana-Perez, I., Ferreira da Silva, R., Rynge, M., Deelman, E., Perez-Hernandez, M.S., Corcho, O.: Leveraging semantics to improve reproducibility in scientific workflows. In: The Reproducibility at XSEDE Workshop (2014)
29. Vöckler, J.S., Juve, G., Deelman, E., Rynge, M., Berriman, B.: Experiences using cloud computing for a scientific workflow application. In: Proceedings of the 2nd International Workshop on Scientific Cloud Computing, ScienceCloud 2011, pp. 15–24. ACM, USA (2011)
30. Howe, B.: Virtual appliances, cloud computing, and reproducible research. Comput. Sci. Eng. **14**(4), 36–41 (2012)
31. Zhao, Y., Li, Y., Raicu, I., Lu, S., Tian, W., Liu, H.: Enabling scalable scientific workflow management in the cloud. Future Gener. Comput. Syst. **46**, 3–16 (2014)
32. Lifschitz, S., Gomes, L., Rehen, S. K.: Dealing with reusability and reproducibility for scientific workflows. In: 2011 IEEE International Conference on Bioinformatics and Biomedicine Workshops (BIBMW), pp. 625–632. IEEE (2011)
33. Missier, P., Woodman, S., Hiden, H., Watson, P.: Provenance and data differencing for workflow reproducibility analysis. Concurr. Comput.: Pract. Exp. (2013)
34. Abrishami, S., Naghibzadeh, M., Epema, D.H.: Deadline-constrained workflow scheduling algorithms for infrastructure as a service clouds. Future Gener. Comput. Syst. **29**(1), 158–169 (2013). Including Special section: AIRCC-NetCoM 2009 and Special section: Clouds and Service-Oriented Architectures
35. Malawski, M., Juve, G., Deelman, E., Nabrzyski, J.: Algorithms for cost- and deadline-constrained provisioning for scientific workflow ensembles in iaas clouds. Future Gener. Comput. Syst. **48**, 1–18 (2015). Special Section, Business and Industry Specific Cloud
36. Woodman, S., Hiden, H., Watson, P., Missier, P.: Achieving reproducibility by combining provenance with service and workflow versioning. In: Proceedings of the 6th Workshop on Workflows in Support of Large-scale Science, WORKS 2011, pp. 127–136. ACM, USA (2011)
37. Groth, P., Deelman, E., Juve, G., Mehta, G., Berriman, B.: Pipeline-centric provenance model. In: Proceedings of the 4th Workshop on Workflows in Support of Large-Scale Science, WORKS 2009, pp. 4:1–4:8. ACM, USA (2009)
38. Horta, F., Silva, V., Costa, F., de Oliveira, D., Ocaña, K., Ogasawara, E., Dias, J., Mattoso, M.: Provenance traces from chiron parallel workflow engine. In: Proceedings of the Joint EDBT/ICDT 2013 Workshops, EDBT 2013, pp. 337–338. ACM, New York (2013)
39. Tannenbaum, T., Wright, D., Miller, K., Livny, M.: Beowulf Cluster Computing with Linux, pp. 307–350. MIT Press, Cambridge (2002)
40. Latchoumy, P., Khader, P.S.A.: Survey on fault tolerance in grid computing. Int. J. Comput. Sci. & Eng. Surv. (IJCSES) **2** (2011)
41. Stallings, W.: Cryptography and Network Security: Principles and Practice, 5th edn. Prentice Hall Press, Upper Saddle River (2010)
42. Ramakrishnan, L., Plale, B.: A multi-dimensional classification model for scientific workflow characteristics. In: Proceedings of the 1st International Workshop on Workflow Approaches to New Data-Centric Science, Wands 2010, pp. 4:1–4:12. ACM, USA (2010)

Security and Privacy Preservation of Evidence in Cloud Accountability Audits

Thomas Rübsamen[1]([✉]), Tobias Pulls[2], and Christoph Reich[1]

[1] Cloud Research Lab, Furtwangen University, Furtwangen, Germany
{thomas.ruebsamen,christoph.reich}@hs-furtwangen.de
[2] Department of Mathematics and Computer Science, Karlstad University,
Karlstad, Sweden
tobias.pulls@kau.se

Abstract. Cloud accountability audits are promising to strengthen trust in cloud computing by providing reassurance about the processing data in the cloud according to data handling and privacy policies. To effectively automate cloud accountability audits, various distributed evidence sources need to be considered during evaluation. The types of information range from authentication and data access logging to location information, information on security controls and incident detection. Securing that information quickly becomes a challenge in the system design, when the evidence that is needed for the audit is deemed sensitive or confidential information. This means that securing the evidence at-rest as well as in-transit is of utmost importance. In this paper, we present a system that is based on distributed software agents which enables secure evidence collection with the purpose of automated evaluation during cloud accountability audits. We thereby present the integration of Insynd as a suitable cryptographic mechanism for securing evidence. We present our reasoning for choosing Insynd by showing a comparison of Insynd properties with requirements imposed by accountability evidence collection as well as an analysis how security threats are being mitigated by Insynd. We put special emphasis on security and privacy protection in our system analysis.

1 Introduction

Cloud Computing is known for its on demand computing resource provisioning and has now become mainstream. Many businesses as well as private individuals are using cloud services on a daily basis. The nature of these services varies heavily in terms of what kind of information is being out-sourced to the cloud provider. Often, that data is sensitive, for instance when Personal Identifiable Information (PII) is being shared by an individual. Also, businesses that move (parts of) their processes to the cloud, for instance by using Customer Relationship Management Software as a Service, are actively participating in a major paradigm shift from having all data on-premise to moving data to the cloud.

However, many new challenges come along with this trend. Two of the most important issues are customer trust and compliance [14,22]. These issues are

M. Helfert et al. (Eds.): CLOSER 2015, CCIS 581, pp. 95–114, 2016.
DOI: 10.1007/978-3-319-29582-4_6

closely tied to the loss of control over data. When moving to the cloud, direct control over (i) where data is stored, (ii) who has access to it and (iii) how it is shared and processed is given up. Because of this loss of control, cloud customers have to trust cloud providers that they treat their data in an appropriate and responsible way. One way to enable that trust is by strengthening transparency and accountability [12,30] of the cloud provider and services. This includes providing information about data locality, isolation, privacy controls and data processing in general.

Cloud audits can be used to check how data has been processed in the cloud (i.e., by whom, for what purpose) and whether or not this happened in compliance with what has been defined in previously agreed-upon privacy and data handling policies. This way, a cloud customer can regain some of the information he has given up control of by moving to the cloud. A central responsibility of cloud audits is the collection of data that can be used as evidence. Depending on the data processing policies in place, various sources of evidence need to be considered. For instance, logs are a very important source of evidence, when it comes to auditing the cloud operation (e.g., access logs and error logs). However, other sources of information are also important, such as files (e.g., process documentation) or events registered in the cloud management system (e.g., access control decisions, infrastructure changes, data transfers).

To capture evidence from this variety of sources, centralized logging mechanisms are not enough. We therefore propose a system for accountability evidence collection and audit. With this system, cloud providers are enabled to demonstrate their compliance with data handling policies to their customers and to third-party auditors in an automated way.

In our previous work, we proposed a concept [28] for cloud accountability audits, that enables automated collection of evidential data in the cloud ecosystem with the goal of performing accountability audits. A key mechanism of this system is the secure and privacy-friendly collection and storage of evidence. In our previous work we also explored the use of a somewhat homomorphic encryption scheme to secure evidence collected in the evidence store [17], which has proven practical but very limited in terms of performance and functionality.

In this paper, we present a more practical alternative that imposes less restrictions on evidence collection.

The contributions of this paper are:

- An architecture for automated evidence collection for the purpose of cloud accountability audits
- A process for secure and privacy-protecting evidence collection and storage

The remainder of this paper is structured as follows: in Sect. 2 we present related work in the area of secure evidence collection and cloud auditing. The core principles of Insynd are introduced in Sect. 3. Section 4 introduces the Audit Agent System (AAS) and its architecture. Following that, we present in Sect. 5 a mapping of typical characteristics of digital evidence and secure evidence collection in the cloud to how these are addressed by integrating Insynd in our audit agent system. In Sect. 6 we describe the architectural details of the

Insynd integration. We also present a scenario-based evaluation of our system in Sect. 7 and conclude this paper in Sect. 8.

2 Related Work

Redfield and Date propose a system called Gringotts [27] that enables secure evidence collection, where evidence data is signed at the system that produces it, before it is sent to a central server for archival using the Evidence Record Syntax. It is similar to our system with respect to the automatic collection of evidential data from multiple sources. However, their focus is on the archival of evidence, whereas we propose a system that also enables automated evidence processing for audits. Additionally, our system also addresses privacy concerns of evidence collection in a multi-tenant environment such as the cloud by introducing evidence encryption, whereas Redfield and Date focus on archival and preservation of evidence integrity.

Zhang et al. [31] identify potential problems when storing massive amounts of evidential data. They specifically address possible information leaks. To solve these issues, they propose an efficient encrypted database model that is supposed to minimize potential data leaks as well as data redundancy. However, they focus solely on the storage backend and do not provide a workflow that addresses secure evidence collection as a whole.

Gupta [11] identifies privacy issues in the digital forensics process, when it comes to data storage devices that typically do not only contain investigation related data, but may also hold sensitive information that may breach privacy. He also identifies a lack of automation in the digital investigation process. To address these issues, Gupta proposes the Privacy Preserving Efficient Digital Forensic Investigation (PPEDFI) framework. PPEDFI automates the investigation process by including knowledge about previous investigation cases, and which kinds of files were relevant then. With that additional information, evidence search on data storage devices is faster. However, while Gupta acknowledges privacy issues, the PPEDFI framework is focused on classic digital forensics and may not be applicable to a cloud ecosystem, where there is typically no way of mapping specific data objects to storage devices, in full.

The Security Audit as a Service (SAaaS) system proposed by Dölitzscher et al. [9,10] is used to monitor cloud environments and to detect security incidents. SAaaS is specifically designed to detect incidents in the cloud and thereby consider the dynamic nature of such ecosystems, where resources are rapidly provisioned and removed. However, the main focus of SAaaS is not to provide auditors with a comprehensive way of auditing the cloud provider's compliance with accountability policies, which requires additional security and privacy measures to be considered in the data collection process.

3 Insynd

Insynd is a cryptographic scheme where a forward-secure *author* sends messages intended for *clients* through an untrusted *server* [23,24]. The author is forward-secure in the sense that the author is initially trusted but assumed to turn into an active adversary at some point in time [5]. Insynd protects messages sent prior to author compromise. The server is untrusted, which is possible thanks to the use of Balloon, a forward-secure append-only persistent authenticated data structure [23]. This means that the server storing all messages can safely be outsourced, e.g., to traditional cloud services. Clients are assumed trusted to read messages sent to them by authors. Insynd contains support for clients to also be in the forward-security model, by discarding key-material as messages are read. For sake of ease of implementation, Insynd is designed around the use of NaCl [6], an easy-to-use high-speed cryptography software library.

Insynd provides the following properties:

Forward Integrity and Deletion Detection. Nobody can modify or delete messages sent prior to author compromise, as defined by Pulls et al. [25]. This property holds independently for Balloon (the data structure) and the Insynd scheme. For Balloon, anyone can verify the consistency of the data structure, i.e., it is publicly verifiable [23].

Secrecy. Insynd provides authenticated encryption [2].

Forward Unlinkability of Events. For each run by the author of the protocol to send new messages, all the events sent in that run are unlinkable. This implies that, e.g., an attacker (or the server) cannot tell which events belong to which client [24]. When clients receive their events by querying the server, if they take appropriate actions including but not limited to accessing the server over an anonymity network like Tor [8], their events remain unlinkable.

Publicly Verifiable Proofs. Both the author and client receiving a message can create publicly verifiable proofs of the message sender (the author), the receiving client (by registered identity), and the time the message was sent relative to e.g. a time-stamping authority [24]. The proof-of-concept implementation of Insynd uses Bitcoin transactions [20] as a distributed time-stamping server.

Distributed Settings. Insynd supports distributed authors, where one author can enable other authors to send messages to clients it knows of without requiring any interaction with clients. Client identifiers (public keys) are blinded in the protocol, ensuring forward-unlinkable client identifiers between different authors [24].

Pulls and Peters show that Insynd provide the above cryptographic properties under the assumptions of the decisional Diffie-Hellman (DDH) assumption on Curve25519, an unforgeable signature algorithm, an unforgeable one-time MAC, a collision and pre-image resistant hash function, a IND-CCA2 secure public-key encryption scheme, and the security of the time-stamping mechanism (in our case, the Bitcoin block-chain) [24]. The prototype implementation of Insynd shows performance comparable to state-of-the-art secure logging schemes, like PillarBox [7], securing syslog-sized messages (max 1 KiB) in the order of hundreds of microseconds on average on a commodity laptop. We stress that Insynd is subject to its own review and evaluation; in this paper, we use Insynd as a building block to facilitate secure evidence collection and storage for cloud accountability audits.

4   Audit Agent System

In the following, the main actors, components and the general flow of information from the evidence-producing source to the audit report in our Audit Agent System (AAS) are described.

4.1   Privacy and Accountability Cloud Audit System Actors

The main actor using the AAS is the *Cloud Auditor*. According to NIST, a cloud auditor is a "A party that can conduct independent assessment of cloud services, information system operations, performance and security of the cloud implementation." [16] In general, a cloud consumer, cloud provider or an independent third-party can act as a cloud auditor. Depending on the actual stakeholder that assumes the role of the auditor, isolation issues can arise:

- A *data protection authority (DPA)* typically acts in good faith as a third-party and assesses privacy policies. Therefore, they typically have broad access to a provider's internal documentation, infrastructure and potentially customer's data.
- A *commercial third-party auditor* is usually a specialized service provider (e.g., a penetration or security testing specialist) acting on behalf of the cloud provider. Their access to information is similar to that available to the DPA.
- A *customer* can also assume the role of an auditor, however with a much more limited scope of available information. We consider two major sub-types, businesses as customers and individuals as customers.

In our proposed system, we consider business customers (e.g., companies using cloud services to replace their IT) to be potential auditors but exclude private individuals. Additionally, providers use the AAS internally for self-auditing to regularly and continuously assess their policy compliance and detect potential violations in a timely manner. Depending on the view on an organization (i.e., depending on who assumes the role of cloud auditor), data protection is an issue to consider, when potential confidential information is processed during an audit. This means data confidentiality, integrity and isolation have to be preserved during an automated audit.

4.2   Architectural Components Audit Agent System

The architecture of the Audit Agent System (see Fig. 1) is based on the use of software agents. This allows for improved flexibility by allowing to rapidly react on infrastructure changes, and improved extensibility especially with respect to data collectors that are used to gather information that is evaluated during an audit. The collectors are adapters for the various heterogeneous sources of evidence in a cloud environment. In Sect. 6.1, we describe more details of how the collectors work. The architecture of the AAS comprises of the following components: *Audit Policy Module (APM), Audit Agent Controller (AAC), Evidence*

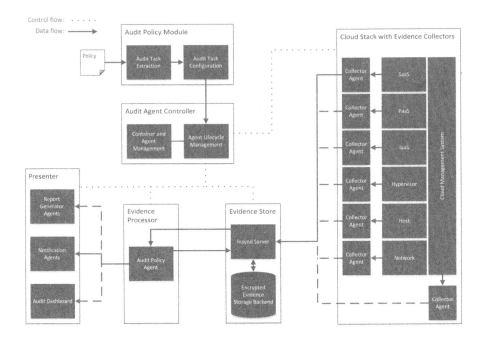

Fig. 1. Privacy and accountability cloud audit system architecture.

Processor and Presenter (EPP) and *Evidence Store (ES)*. Especially the Evidence Store and the aforementioned collection agents make heavy use of Insynd to assure that data protection requirements are being met. To a lesser extent, the AAC and EPP also utilize Insynd for securely transporting evidence.

All components are implemented as software agents based on the Java Agent DEveleopment framework (JADE) [13] and make heavy use of the JADE Agent Communication Language (ACL) for agent interaction. In the following, we describe the architecture components:

Audit Policy Module. The main input to the AAS are machine-readable policies that describe data handling obligations (e.g., access control), security controls (e.g., service configuration) and data protection mechanisms (e.g., encryption). From such policies, tasks for collecting evidence, and rules for evaluation of the evidence with the goal of producing a compliance statement are extracted. Additional input to the APM is provided by the auditor. We assume, that there is always a need for at least some manual input for defining an automated audit because the input policy might not be complete with respect to all the parameters that are required for an automated audit. Such parameters include the audit type (periodic or event-driven), the frequency (e.g., daily, monthly...) but also more task-specific information that is not provided by the input policy. Depending on the actual audit task, the input comprises of policies and auditor-supplied information:

1. Policies, which define obligations that have to be fulfilled by the cloud provider, such as data access restrictions and usage policies, requirements for the implementation of privacy controls, data retention requirements and general security requirements. The A4Cloud [1] research project develops a machine-readable policy language based on the Primelife Policy Language [3] called Accountability PPL [4]. The A-PPL is capable of describing obligations providers have to adhere to, such access control rules and data handling (e.g., data location, purpose etc.). A-PPL serves as the main input to the Audit Agent System and for defining audits.
2. It is possible that an input policy does not necessarily include all information required for mapping policy requirements to specific evidence sources, collectors (e.g., evidence source specific REST client or log parser) and evaluators (e.g., API endpoints, access credentials). That information is provided by the auditor.

With the above mentioned data, the APM builds audit tasks - a combination of evidence collector, processor and presenter agents - and passes that task on to the Audit Agent Controller for instantiation.

Audit Agent Controller. The AAC is the core component of the Audit Agent System. Its main responsibility is the management (i.e., instantiation, configuration, deployment) of any type of agent in the AAS. The main input comes from the APM, which effectively instructs the AAC on how to setup specific audit tasks. A typical audit task deployment in AAS is called an audit workflow. The typical audit workflow (depicted in Fig. 2) is as follows:

1. *Preparation*: The APM extracts audit task configuration from the policy, combines it with input provided by the auditor and passes it on to the AAC.
2. *Configuration*: According to the input provided by the APM, the AAC configures audit policies, its tasks and corresponding collection and evaluation agents.
3. *Instantiation*: the AAC instantiates the previously configured agents as well as the associated evidence store.
4. *Migration*: Agents are migrated from the core platform where the AAC is running to the target platforms (agent runtime environments as close as possible to the evidence source).
5. *Monitoring*: During the agents' lifetime, the AAC monitors registered platforms and registered agents, handles exceptions, and manages the creation, archival and deletion of evidence stores
6. *Termination*: The AAC disposes of the collector and evaluation agents when they are not needed anymore. It also handles archival and / or deletion of the corresponding evidence store in that case.

Evidence Processor and Presenter. After the collector agents have gathered evidence data and stored it in the evidence store, the evaluation agent(s) of an audit task retrieve that data and analyze it according to the rules that have been

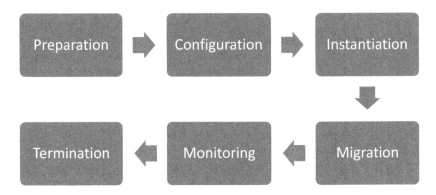

Fig. 2. Audit Agent System Architecture - Audit Workflow.

extracted from the policies in the preparation phase by the APM. The results that are produced by the evaluation agents are written back to the evidence store. A result can either positive (e.g., a message of proven compliance or the absence of a violation) or negative (e.g., a violation that is detected by the evaluation agent). Additionally the result is passed on to presenter agents that inform the auditor about the audit results. Currently the presenter agents can either display the audit result in a web-based dashboard or pass on the violation in a machine-readable format to other tools or services via a REST API. The whole of processor and presenter agents logically forms the EPP component. It is thereby irrelevant, where these agents are running as long as they are able communicate via a network, which helps in balancing the load that can be introduced with complex analysis mechanisms or the sheer amount of evidence data that needs to be analyzed. According to the complexity of task, due to the amount of obligations, or the volume of evidence to analyse, different verification processes may need to be considered for the evaluation agents, ranging from log mining, checking for predefined tokens or patterns, to automated analysers and automated reasoning upon the audit trail.

The processing or analysis of evidence consists of two steps:

1. Retrieve the appropriate information from Evidence store.
2. A verification process, which checks the correctness of recorded events according to defined obligations and authorizations.

Evidence Store. The ES is the central repository for storing evidence. Some of the more important characteristics of evidence are that they are associated with a policy for which they were collected and contain supporting information such as log entries collected by an agent, which points out a potential policy violation or incident. For each cloud tenant, there is a separate ES to ensure basic data protection principles are being adhered to by isolating tenants and their data. This addresses some of the confidentiality and privacy issues associated with a share data pool for potentially sensitive information.

There are several approaches to harmonizing the storage format for digital evidence that can be reused in the ES such as [15, 26, 29]. AAS uses a custom evidence format that is based on concepts described in [26, 29].

Securing the transport and storage of evidence is a considerable challenge. The remainder of this paper focusses on how this is achieved in AAS by utilizing Insynd.

5 Audit Evidence Storage Requirements

In this Section, we present a comparison of general evidence attributes, how they apply in the context of evidence collection for cloud accountability audits and how the integration of Insynd solves key issues in evidence storage.

5.1 Requirements of Digital Evidence

In [19] the core principles of any evidence are described as:

Admissibility. Evidence must conform to certain legal rules, before it can be put before a jury.
Authenticity. Evidence must be tieable to the incident and may not be manipulated.
Completeness. Evidence must be viewpoint agnostic and tell the whole story.
Reliability. There cannot be any doubts about the evidence collection process and its correctness.
Believability. Evidence must be understandable by a jury.

These principles apply to common evidence as well as digital evidence. Therefore, the evidence collection process for audits has to consider special requirements, which help in addressing these attributes and ensure best possible validity in audits and applicability in court.

In Table 1 we present a mapping of the previously described evidence attributes and how they are supported by the integration of Insynd as a means of storing evidence records. We thereby focus on the key properties of Insynd as described in Sect. 3.

Table 1. Mapping the Impact of Insynd Properties to Evidence Attributes.

		Insynd	
		Forward Integrity and Deletion Detection	Publicly Verifiable Proofs
Evidence Store	Admissibility		
	Authenticity	✓	✓
	Completeness	✓	✓
	Reliability	✓	✓
	Believability		

Admissibility of digital evidence is influenced by the transparency of the collection process and data protection regulation. Digital evidence can be any kind of data (e.g., e-mail messages, social network messages, files, logs etc.). Insynd does not have any direct influence on the admissibility of the evidence stored in it.

Authenticity of digital evidence before court is closely related to the integrity requirement put on evidence records. Evidence may not be manipulated in any way and must be protected against any kind of tampering (willingly and accidentally). Insynd ensures that data cannot be tampered with once it is stored.

Completeness is not directly ensured by Insynd, but rather needs to be ensured by the evidence collection process as a whole. Especially important are the definition of which evidence sources provide relevant evidence that need to be considered during the collection phase. Insynd can complement the evidence collection process by providing assurance of that all data stored in the evidence store are made available as evidence, and not cherry-picked.

Reliability is indirectly supported by integrating necessary mechanisms into the evidence collection process, such as Insynd.

Believability of the collected evidence is not influenced by implemented mechanisms, but rather by the interpretation and presentation by an expert in court. This is due to judges and juries usually being non-technical, which requires an abstracted presentation of evidence. Insynd does not influence the believability in that sense.

5.2 Privacy Requirements

Not all requirements that a secure evidence storage has to fulfill can be captured by analyzing the attributes of digital evidence. Other aspects have to be taken into account to address privacy concerns. Protecting privacy in the process of evidence collection is utmost importance, since the collected data is likely to contain personal data. For cloud computing, one limiting factor may be whether or not the cloud provider is willing to provide deep insight into its infrastructure. Table 2 presents a mapping of privacy principles and properties of our evidence process.

Below we summarise some key privacy principles:

Confidentiality. of data evolves around mechanisms for the protection from unwanted and unauthorized access. Typically, cryptographic concepts, such as encryption, are use to ensure confidentiality of data.

Table 2. Mapping of Insynd properties to Evidence Collection Requirements.

		Insynd		
		Secrecy	Forward Unlinkability of Events	Forward Unlinkability of Recipients
Evidence Store	Confidentiality	✓	✓	✓
	Data Minimisation		✓	✓
	Purpose Binding			
	Data Retention	✓		

Data Minimization. states that the collection of personal data should be minimized and limited to only what is strictly necessary.

Purpose Binding. of personal data entails that personal data should only be used for the purposes it was collected for.

Retention Time. is concerned with how long personal data may be stored and used, before it needs to be deleted. These periods are usually defined by legal and business requirements.

Insynd and our evidence process provides various mechanisms that support these privacy principles.

Confidentiality. A central property of Insynd is that it is always encrypting data using public-key cryptography. By encrypting the evidence store, compromising the privacy of cloud customer data that has been collected in the evidence collection processes becomes almost impossible by attacking the evidence store directly. This goes as far as being able to safely outsource the evidence store to an untrusted third-party, a key property of Insynd [24].

Data Minimisation. Furthermore, Insynd provides forward unlinkability of events and client identifiers, as described in Sect. 3, which helps prevent several types of information leaks related to storing and accessing data. Collection agents are always configured for a specific audit task, which is very limited in scope of what needs to be collected. Agents are never configured to arbitrarily collect data, but are alway limited to a specific source (e.g., a server log) and data objects (e.g., a type of log events).

Purpose Binding. Neither Insynd nor our evidence process can directly influence the purpose for which collected data is used. Indirectly, the use of an evidence process like ours, incorporating secure evidence collection and storage, may serve to differentiate data collected for auditing purposes with other data collected e.g., for marketing purposes.

Retention time poses a real challenge. In cloud computing, the precise location of a data object is usually not directly available, i.e., the actual storage medium used to store a particular block is unknown, making data deletion hard. However, if data has been encrypted before storage, a reasonably safe way to ensure "deletion" is to discarding the key material required for decryption. Insynd supports forward-secure clients, where key material to decrypt messages are discarded as messages are read.

In Sect. 7, we also describe the threat model for the system described in this paper and present an evaluation of how Insynd is used to mitigate these threats.

6   Secure Evidence Storage Architecture

In this Section, we provide an architectural overview of the integration of Insynd into a secure evidence collection and storage process. We describe the overall architecture and its components, how the components of Insynd are mapped into the Audit Agent System and which setup process is required to use Insynd for securing evidence collection and storage.

6.1   Architecture

In this Section we discuss the architectural integration of Insynd as an evidence store in our audit system. There are basically three different components required to perform secure evidence collection. Figure 3 shows an overview of these components - *Evidence Source*, *Evidence Store* and *Evidence Processing* (see Sect. 4 and Fig. 1 for reference) - as well as the flow of data between them. From the various sources of evidence in the cloud, evidence records are collected that will be stored in the evidence store on a per-tenant basis. The evidence store is thereby located on a separate server. As previously mentioned, the server may be an untrusted third-party cloud storage provider. This is important to ensure so that this approach scales well with a growing number of tenants, evidence sources and evidence records.

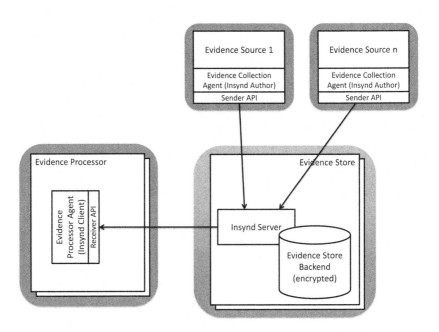

Fig. 3. Evidence Collection, Storage and Processing Workflow.

Evidence Collection. There are various evidence sources to be considered, such as logs, cryptographical proofs, documentation and many more. For each, there needs to be a suitable collection mechanism. For instance, a log parser for logs, a tool for cryptographical proofs or a file retriever for documentation. This is done by a software agent called *Evidence Collection Agent* that is specifically developed for the data collection from the corresponding evidence source. The collection agent acts as an *Insynd Author* meaning it uses the *Sender API* to store evidence into the Evidence Store. The encryption happens in the Sender

API. Typically, this agent incorporates or interfaces with a tool to collect evidential data, for instance forensic tools, such as file carvers, log parsers or simple search tools. Another type of collection agent have client APIs implemented to interface with more complex tools, such as Cloud Management Systems (CMS). Generally, these agents receive or collect information as input and translate that information into an evidence record, before storing it in the Evidence Store.

Evidence Storage. From the Evidence Collection Agent, evidence records are sent to the Evidence Store. The Evidence Store is implemented by the *Insynd Server*. Since Insynd functions as a key-value store for storing evidence records (encrypted messages identified by a key) NoSQL or RDBMS-based backend for persisting evidence records can be used. All data contained in the Evidence Store is encrypted. Each record is addressed to a specific receiver (e.g., an Evidence Processing Agent). The receiver's public key is used in the Sender API to encrypt the record on the Evidence Store. This means that only the receiver is able to access the evidence data from the Evidence Store. Isolation between tenants in a single Evidence Store is achieved by providing one container for each tenant where his evidence records are stored. However, even stronger isolation is also possible by providing a separate Evidence Store hosted on a separate VM. Additionally, Evidence records require a unique identifier in the Evidence Store to enable selective retrieval of records. In our implementation, we use a combination of a policy identifier and a rule identifier (where a rule is part of a policy) to enable the receiver to reduce the amount of records to receive to a manageable size.

Evidence Processing. Evidence Processing components are located at the receiving end of this workflow. The Receiver API is used by the processing agent (Insynd Client) to retrieve evidence records from the Evidence Store. The receiver can request multiple records from a period of time at once. The Client is also in possession of the corresponding private key to decrypt evidence records, which means records can only be decrypted at the Client.

6.2   Identity Management and Key Distribution

Since asymmetric encryption is such an important part of our system, we describe the encryption key distribution sequence next. In this software agent-based system, the automated setup of key material and registration with Insynd is particularly important. Figure 4 depicts the initialization sequence of collection and processing agents with a focus on key distribution.

In Fig. 4, we introduce an additional component beyond those already described in the general architecture: the *Controller*. The Controller serves as an entry point that controls the agent setup and distribution process in the audit system. It is an important part of the lifecycle management of the system's agents (e.g., creating and destroying of agents or migration between platforms).

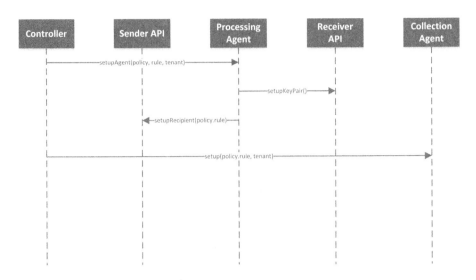

Fig. 4. Evidence Collection Setup Sequence.

In Fig. 4, we describe the initialization sequence for a simple scenario, where a particular tenant wishes to audit compliance with a policy and one rule included in that policy in particular. The following steps have to be performed to setup the evidence collection and storage process for that particular rule:

1. In the first step, a Processing Agent is created and configured according to the input policy and rule respectively for the tenant.
2. During the setup phase, the Processing Agent sets up a key pair at the Receiver API. The Receiver API is a RESTful service that holds private key material and is therefore located at the same servers hosting the Processing Agents (i.e., a trusted environment).
3. After the key material has been generated, the Processing Agent registers itself as a recipient at the Sender API. For this, it uses a unique identifier generated from the policy ID and the rule ID (i.e., *policyID.ruleID*).
4. In the last step, the Controller sets up the required Collection Agents and connects them with the corresponding Processing Agents by using the unique recipient identifier.

Now, it is possible for the Collection Agents to send evidence records to their corresponding Processing Agents. The messages will be encrypted at the Sender API service before storage, using the provided recipient's public key. The Processing Agent then pulls the evidence records from the Evidence Store using the Receiver API the records are decrypted using the receiver's private key.

7   Evaluation

In this Section we present an informal security evaluation of the system we have implemented for secure evidence collection. We describe the evidence collection work flow using a fictitious scenario. By applying the evidence collection and storage process to the setting described in this scenario, we demonstrate how the requirements stated in Sect. 5 are addressed. Additionally, we provide a model that states threats and adversaries to the process as well as the mitigation functions introduced by Insynd.

In this scenario, the CCOMP company is a customer of the Infrastructure as a Service provider CloudIA. In particular, we analyze the security properties of the evidence collection process by looking at the data at rest as well as the data in transit protection at any time during the flow from the evidence source to its processor. We thereby assume that CloudIA is using OpenStack [21] as a its Cloud Management System (CMS), since this a widely popular open source CMS, which we use for developing our audit agent system. However, any other CMS could be used as well as long as it provides the needed monitoring interfaces.

7.1   Scenario

CloudIA is specialized in providing its customers with virtualized resources in the form of virtual machines, networks and storage. CCOMP has outsourced most of its IT services to CloudIA. Among them is a service that processes data of CCOMP's customers. For that data, CCOMP has to guarantee data retention. CCOMP has identified snapshots to be one major problem with respect to the data retention policy, since the virtual machine's storage is duplicated in the process. This means for CCOMP that in order to be compliant with the data retention policy, a snapshot of that virtual machine may have a maximum lifetime of one day, which limits its usefulness to e.g., backing up before patching. Now, we assume a trustworthy but sloppy administrator at CCOMP who creates a snapshot before patching software on the virtual machine, but then omits deleting the snapshot after he is done. However, an automated daily audit of its cloud resources was put in place by CCOMP to detect such compliance violations.

7.2   Implementation

The collection agent required for the above scenario communicates with our OpenStack CMS to gather evidence of the CMS behavior regarding virtual machine snapshots. The processing agent contains the logic for detecting snapshot violations (i.e., base virtual machine and a maximum age of the snapshot derived from the retention policy). The collection agent is deployed at the CMS controller node and has access to OpenStack's RESTful API. The processing agent is located on the same trusted host as the controller agent (see Fig. 3 for reference). The evidence store is located on a separate, untrusted virtual machine. Now, the following steps are performed:

1. The collection agent opens a connection to the OpenStack RESTful API on the same host and requests a history of snapshot events for CCOMP's virtual machine. Despite there being no communication over the network, HTTPS is

used to secure the communication between the collection agent and the CMS. Since the policy only requires information about snapshots to be collected, the CMS agent limits evidence record generation to exactly that information, nothing more.

2. The collection agent sets up the receiver of the evidence according to the process depicted in Fig. 4 and sends the collected records to the evidence store (Insynd). The communication channel is encrypted using HTTPS and the payload (evidence records) is encrypted with the receiving agent's public key.

3. The processing agent pulls records from the evidence store in regular intervals (e.g., every 24 h), analyses them and triggers a notification of a detected violation. The communication between the processing agent and the evidence store is secured using HTTPS.

4. In the last step, evidence records are deleted because their retention limit has been reached. This is done by discarding the keys required for decryption.

7.3   Threat Model

To demonstrate which security threats exist for the evidence collection process and Insynd is used to mitigate them, we describe the threat model for this system categorized according to the STRIDE [18] threat categorization:

– **S**poofing Identity
– **T**ampering with Data
– **R**epudiation
– **I**nformation disclosure
– **D**enial of Service
– **E**levation of Privilege

We have identified the following major threats to the evidence collection and storage process:

– *Unauthorized access to evidence (S,I)*: the protection of evidence from being accessed by unauthorized persons. Possible adversaries are a malicious third-party evidence storage provider (cloud service provider), another tenant (isolation failure) or an external attacker. Using Insynd for evidence collection and storage addresses this threat since recipients of messages are authenticated using appropriate mechanisms such as user credentials for API authentication and public keys for encryption.

– *Data leakage (S,I)*: the protection from unintentional data leakage. This could be caused by misconfiguration (e.g., unencrypted evidence being publicly available). Using Insynd for evidence collection and storage addresses this threat by encrypting data by default.

– *Eavesdropping, (T,I)*: the protection of evidence during the collection phase, especially in transit. Possibly adversaries are another tenant (isolation failure) or external attackers in case evidence is transported to an external storage provider or auditor. Using Insynd for evidence collection and storage addresses this threat by using transport layer as well as message encryption.

– *Denial of Service (D)*: the protection of the evidence collection and storage process from being attacked directly with the goal of disabling or shutting it down completely (e.g., to cover-up simultaneous attacks on another service). Possible adversaries are external attackers. This is a very generic threat that cannot be addressed by a single tool or control but rather requires a set a measures (on the network and application layer) to enhance denial of service resilience.

– *Evidence manipulation (T,R,I)*: the protection of evidence from intentional manipulation (e.g., deletion of records, changing of contents, manipulation of timestamps). Possible adversaries are malicious insiders and external attackers. Using Insynd for evidence collection and storage addresses this threat, since Insynd provides tampering and deletion detection.

Some of these threats can be mitigated by implementing appropriate security controls (i.e., using Insynd for evidence transport and storage). It provides effective protection by employing security techniques described in Sect. 3.

7.4 Requirements Evaluation

In this section, we evaluate the integration of Insynd against the requirements described in Sect. 5. In step 1 of the fictitious scenario, the data minimization principle is being followed because the specialized agent only collects evidence on the existence of snapshots.

This workflow is secure as soon as the collection agent inserts data into the evidence store in step 2. More precisely, evidence records are tamper-evident and encrypted. This is true, even though the evidence is actually stored on an untrusted virtual machine. The only way to compromise evidence now, is to attack the availability of the server hosting the Insynd server.

When the processing agent in step 3 retrieves records for evaluation, it can be assured of the authenticity of the data and that it has been provably collected by a collection agent. Since evidence records may be subject to maximum data retention regulation, records that are not needed anymore are deleted.

As previously mentioned in Sect. 6 we use JADE as an agent runtime. To secure our system against non-authorized agents, we use the TrustedAgents add-on for the JADE platform. This ensures that only validated agents are able to join our runtime environment. This effectively prevents agent injection attacks, where malicious agents could be inserted at either the collection or processing side to compromise our system.

As can be seen, the evidence records are protected all the way from the evidence source to the processing agent using only encrypted communication channels and having an additional layer of security (message encryption) provided by Insynd. Additionally, while the evidence is being stored, it remains encrypted.

7.5   Scalability

Obviously, since there is a vast amount of evidence sources and therefore a potentially equal number of collection agents, ensuring the scalability of the process and the implementation is very important. This has been considered very early in the design process by choosing an software agent-based approach for the system architecture. Software agents are inherently distributable and allow for complex message flow modeling in an infrastructure. Therefore, the core components evidence collection, storage and processing become distributable as well. In our future work, we'll focus on the scalability aspects. We will follow a methodology where we focus on the following technical key scalability indicators:

- Data transfer volume: amount of evidence data being transferred over the network
- Message volume: amount of evidence message transmissions over the network
- Storage volume: amount of storage required for evidence
- Encryption overhead: performance impact introduced by encryption and decryption

Based on the identified performance impact of each of these indicators, in the second step, we model different message flow optimization strategies to alleviate their impact and ensure scalability.

8   Conclusion and Future Work

In this paper, we presented our system design and implementation for secure evidence collection in cloud computing. The evidence provides the general basis for performing cloud accountability audits. Accountability audits take a large variety of evidence sources and data processing requirements into account.

We showed what the requirements for a secure evidence collection process are and demonstrated how these issues are addressed by incorporating Insynd into our system. We described how the core principles of digital evidence are addressed by our system. Additionally, we considered data protection principles for the evidence collection process, how they influence our approach and how they are addressed in our system by integrating Insynd. For this, we presented the relevant architectural parts of our prototype. Additionally, we provided an overview of how the evidence collection is integrated in our system for automated cloud audits.

In our future work, we will focus on the scalability of our audit system in general and the scalability of the components involved in evidence collection in particular. For that reason, we will focus on the distribution of the audit system and evidence collection not only in the same domain (i.e., in the same infrastructure), but also taking into account outsourcing and multi-provider collection scenarios.

Acknowledgements. This work has been partly funded from the European Commission's Seventh Framework Programme (FP7/2007–2013), grant agreement 317550, Cloud Accountability Project - http://www.a4cloud.eu/ - (A4CLOUD).

References

1. A4Cloud FP7 Project (2015). http://www.a4cloud.eu/
2. An, J.H.: Authenticated encryption in the public-key setting: security notions and analyses. IACR Cryptology ePrint Archive 2001, 79 (2001). http://eprint.iacr.org/2001/079
3. Ardagna, C.A., Bussard, L., Vimercati, S.D.C.D., Neven, G., Paraboschi, S., Pedrini, E., Preiss, S., Raggett, D., Samarati, P., Trabelsi, S., Verdicchio, M.: Primelife policy language (2009). http://www.w3.org/2009/policy-ws/papers/Trabelisi.pdf
4. Azraoui, M., Elkhiyaoui, K., Önen, M., Bernsmed, K., De Oliveira, A.S., Sendor, J.: A-PPL: an accountability policy language. In: Garcia-Alfaro, J., Herrera-Joancomartí, J., Lupu, E., Posegga, J., Aldini, A., Martinelli, F., Suri, N. (eds.) DPM/SETOP/QASA 2014. LNCS, vol. 8872, pp. 319–326. Springer, Heidelberg (2015). http://www.eurecom.fr/publication/4381
5. Bellare, M., Yee, B.: Forward-security in private-key cryptography. In: Joye, M. (ed.) CT-RSA 2003. LNCS, vol. 2612, pp. 1–18. Springer, Heidelberg (2003)
6. Bernstein, D.J., Lange, T., Schwabe, P.: The security impact of a new cryptographic library. In: Hevia, A., Neven, G. (eds.) Latin-Crypt 2012. LNCS, vol. 7533, pp. 159–176. Springer, Heidelberg (2012). http://dx.doi.org/10.1007/978-3-642-33481-8_9
7. Bowers, K.D., Hart, C., Juels, A., Triandopoulos, N.: PillarBox: combating next-generation malware with fast forward-secure logging. In: Stavrou, A., Bos, H., Portokalidis, G. (eds.) RAID 2014. LNCS, vol. 8688, pp. 46–67. Springer, Heidelberg (2014). http://dx.doi.org/10.1007/978-3-319-11379-1_3
8. Dingledine, R., Mathewson, N., Syverson, P.F.: Tor: The second-generation onion router. In: Blaze, M. (ed.) Proceedings of the 13th USENIX Security Symposium, 9–13 August 2004, San Diego, CA, USA, pp. 303–320. USENIX (2004), http://www.usenix.org/publications/library/proceedings/sec04/tech/dingledine.html
9. Doelitzscher, F., Reich, C., Knahl, M., Passfall, A., Clarke, N.: An agent based business aware incident detection system for cloud environments. J. Cloud Comput. Adv. Syst. Appl. **1**(1), 9 (2012)
10. Doelitzscher, F., Ruebsamen, T., Karbe, T., Reich, C., Clarke, N.: Sun behind clouds - on automatic cloud security audits and a cloud audit policy language. Int. J. Adv. Netw. Serv. **6**(1,2), 1–16 (2013)
11. Gupta, A.: Privacy preserving efficient digital forensic investigation framework. In: 2013 Sixth International Conference on Contemporary Computing (IC3), pp. 387–392, August 2013
12. Haeberlen, A.: A case for the accountable cloud. In: Proceedings of the 3rd ACM SIGOPS International Workshop on Large-Scale Distributed Systems and Middleware (LADIS 2009), October 2009
13. JADE: Java Agent Developement framework (2015). http://jade.tilab.com
14. Jansen, W., Grance, T.: Sp 800–144. guidelines on security and privacy in public cloud computing. Technical report, National Institute of Standards and Technology, Gaithersburg, MD, United States (2011)
15. Jerman Blaič, A., Klobučar, T., Jerman, B.D.: Long-term trusted preservation service using service interaction protocol and evidence records. Comput. Stand. Interfaces **29**(3), 398–412 (2007). http://dx.doi.org/10.1016/j.csi.2006.06.004
16. Liu, F., Tong, J., Mao, J., Bohn, R., Messina, J., Badger, L., Leaf, D.: Nist cloud computing reference architecture (2011). http://www.nist.gov/customcf/get_pdf.cfm?pub_id=909505

17. Lopez, J., Ruebsamen, T., Westhoff, D.: Privacy-friendly cloud audits with somewhat homomorphic and searchable encryption. In: 2014 14th International Conference on Innovations for Community Services (I4CS), pp. 95–103, June 2014
18. Microsoft Developer Network: The Stride Threat Model (2015). https://msdn.microsoft.com/en-US/library/ee823878(v=cs.20).aspx
19. Mohay, G.M., Anderson, A.M., Collie, B., de Vel, O., McKemmish, R.D.: Computer and Intrusion Forensics. Artech House, Boston (2003). http://eprints.qut.edu.au/10849/. For more information about this book please refer to the publisher's website (see link) or contact the authors
20. Nakamoto, S.: Bitcoin: a peer-to-peer electronic cash system. Consulted **1**(2012), 28 (2008)
21. OpenStack: Openstack (2015). http://www.openstack.org/
22. Pearson, S.: Toward accountability in the cloud. IEEE Internet Comput. **15**(4), 64–69 (2011)
23. Pulls, T., Peeters, R.: Balloon: a forward-secure append-only persistent authenticated data structure. In: Pernul, G., Y A Ryan, P., Weippl, E., Torres, C.F., Jonker, H., Mauw, S., Diao, W., Liu, X., et al. (eds.) ESORICS. LNCS, vol. 9327, pp. 622–641. Springer, Heidelberg (2015). doi:10.1007/978-3-319-24177-7_31
24. Pulls, T., Peeters, R.: Insynd: secure one-way messaging through Balloons. Cryptology ePrint Archive, Report 2015/150 (2015)
25. Pulls, T., Peeters, R., Wouters, K.: Distributed privacy-preserving transparency logging. In: Sadeghi, A.R., Foresti, S. (eds.) WPES, pp. 83–94. ACM (2013)
26. R. Brandner, U.P., Gondrom, T.: Evidence record syntax (ERS) (2014). http://tools.ietf.org/html/rfc4998
27. Redfield, C. M., Date, H.: Gringotts: securing data for digital evidence. In: 2014 IEEE Security and Privacy Workshops (SPW), pp. 10–17, May 2014
28. Ruebsamen, T., Reich, C.: Supporting cloud accountability by collecting evidence using audit agents. In: 2013 IEEE 5th International Conference on Cloud Computing Technology and Science (CloudCom), vol. 1, pp. 185–190, December 2013
29. Turner, P.: Unification of digital evidence from disparate sources (digital evidence bags). Digit. Investig. **2**(3), 223–228 (2005). http://dx.doi.org/10.1016/j.diin.2005.07.001
30. Weitzner, D.J., Abelson, H., Berners-Lee, T., Feigenbaum, J., Hendler, J., Sussman, G.J.: Information accountability. Commun. ACM **51**(6), 82–87 (2008). http://doi.acm.org/10.1145/1349026.1349043
31. Zhang, R., Li, Z., Yang, Y., Li, Z.: An efficient massive evidence storage and retrieval scheme in encrypted database. In: 2013 International Conference on Information and Network Security (ICINS 2013), pp. 1–6, November 2013

Using Model-Driven Development to Support Portable PaaS Applications

Elias Nogueira[1,2,3]([envelope]), Daniel Lucrédio[1,2,3], Ana Moreira[1,2,3], and Renata Fortes[1,2,3]

[1] University of São Paulo (ICMC-USP), São Paulo, Brazil
[2] Federal University of São Carlos (UFSCar), São Carlos, Brazil
[3] NOVA LINCS, Universidade NOVA de Lisboa, Lisbon, Portugal
{eliasnog,renata}@icmc.usp.br, daniel@dc.ufscar.br, amm@fct.unl.pt

Abstract. Context: In cloud computing, lock-in refers to the difficulty of porting an application and/or data from one cloud platform to another. Current attempts to address this problem revolve around standardization of APIs and frameworks. We propose a different path, using model-driven engineering (MDE).
Objective: Our goal is to build a repository of MDE transformations and use code generation to reduce the development effort for each platform, thus reducing repetitive programing tasks, increasing portability and minimizing lock-in side-effects.
Method: To attain this objective, we developed an MDE approach to handle persistence for Google App Engine and Azure, and discuss how MDE can reconcile the differences between features of each platform persistence model. A controlled experiment has been performed to evaluate the proposal, in which subjects were asked to use two versions of the same application implemented using our MDE approach. Both versions, one for each platform, were generated from the same domain model.
Results: According to the subjects, no differences in functionality were perceptible between the two versions. Indeed, applications were more easily ported between the two chosen cloud providers without noticeable differences in terms of persistence functionality.
Conclusion: The main contribution of our work is to show that there is an alternative path to the standardization of cloud technologies. MDE can increase the portability of the applications by reducing the negative impacts of lock-in. A limitation of our approach, that is inherent to most MDE approaches, is that if the generated code needs to be adapted or modified, the MDE life-cycle can be broken. Changes in the generated code have to be replicated, either in the models or in the transformations, which is not a trivial task.

Keywords: Cloud computing · Model-Driven Engineering · Platform-as-a-Service · Portability · Persistence

© Springer International Publishing Switzerland 2016
M. Helfert et al. (Eds.): CLOSER 2015, CCIS 581, pp. 115–134, 2016.
DOI: 10.1007/978-3-319-29582-4_7

1   Introduction

Cloud computing is not a new technological model, but the integration of technologies from the past [1]. What is new though, is the different ways in which it is used to provide computing power as-a-service through the Internet. According to Armbrust et al. [2], cloud computing permits acquiring computing resources on demand, enables payment according to the utilization volume, and allows a company to ignore the sources of the resources.

In previous work [3] we identified ten cloud computing research opportunities for software engineers. Lock-In and lack of portability between cloud platforms are two of the opportunities that stand out. Several technological requirements are needed for the cloud model to operate properly. The most common are virtualization technologies, standards and interfaces that allow shared access, facilitated instantiation and management of virtual servers, the so-called IaaS (Infrastructure-as-a-Service). Additionally, different kinds of cloud resources are available, such as load balancing, data persistence and analytics. Given this variety, and depending on its field of expertise, each cloud provider offers a different set of services. Some even provide a complete development platform (PaaS — Platform-as-a-Service) that puts together many different resources, all under the control of the cloud provider.

The heterogeneity and diversity of cloud services result in increased complexity and reduced reuse and portability of the applications [4]. In practice, some applications need to be highly specialized with respect to a particular type of resource (e.g., hardware, platform and/or set of services), yielding the *lock-in* problem [2]. For example, when choosing a particular PaaS provider, the application developer usually has to follow a specific data management system and programming style. This typically reduces portability, resulting in applications "locked-in" to that particular environment.

Some strategies based on standardization have been proposed to address this issue [5]. However, standards take time to define and approve and acceptance by the community is very slow. Currently, there are so many different standards being proposed [25] that even choosing one may be a difficult task. Another difficulty is that cloud providers may not want to follow a standard and instead use specific technologies to create solutions that are better-aligned with their own business goals. Thus, until standardization becomes a fact, portability, and lock-in in particular, remains a problem.

We have been exploring how Model-Driven Engineering (MDE) (see Sect. 2) can be used to increase portability. Approaches based on MDE [6] have been investigated in several other contexts and may constitute an interesting alternative to address the problem. The choice for MDE over standardization is justified by the additional benefits offered by this development paradigm. In particular, MDE claimed increase on quality and productivity [7] could leverage cloud adoption while simultaneously reducing Lock-In.

We have investigated how to build a simple textual domain-specific language (DSL) that allows the specification of applications at a high abstraction level [4]. Also, we built a code generation prototype to support *Google's App Engine*

(GAE) and *Microsoft Azure* platforms. The prototype demonstrates that the developed language, despite simple, can be used as input to a full code generation process targeting a cloud platform. In previous work [5] we show how differences between persistence models can be hidden using a single conceptual model, and discuss a set of MDE artifacts to support this idea. This can be seen as an abstraction layer that allows specifying entities and a set of code generators to build similar persistence models for different storage mechanisms. The result is applications that are more easily ported between the two cloud providers.

The contribution of this paper is to extend that previous work [4,5] and discuss the experiment we performed, presenting more details and results about this evaluation. As mentioned before, our long-term goal is to build a repository of MDE transformations and use code generation to reduce the development effort for each platform, consequently reducing repetitive programing tasks, increasing portability, and minimizing the lock-in effects. The two central points of the idea are: (i) using a DSL for modeling entities; (ii) building a set of transformations that, from the same set of source models, generate code for different targets. Such code-generation approach allows developers focus on platform-independent models, thus achieving portability by reducing the lock-in effects. Both, the models created using DSLs and the transformations using those models to generate implementations for different platforms constitute two fundamental reusable artifacts that can be made available in a repository.

As our approach is generic, transformations considering standards may also be added to the repository later. Although the typical claimed MDE-benefits are expected (e.g., facilitated maintenance and increased productivity), an analysis of the economic viability of creating and maintaining a repository of transformations is out of the scope of this paper[1].

The rest of this paper is organized as follows. Section 2 presents some conceptual background, including a more detailed definition of the lock-in problem, the different types of cloud portability, concepts of MDE and an overview of the previously proposed MDE approach. Section 3 discusses the two platforms that were the subject of this study (GAE and Azure), focusing on the differences in their persistence models. Section 4 presents our proposed solution using MDE and Sect. 5 discusses the evaluation performed. Section 6 presents related work and, finally, Sect. 7 concludes with some final remarks and future work.

2   Background

This section starts with a discussion of lock-in and known types of portability. It then introduces model-driven engineering, and finishes with a summary of our vision on the use of MDE to support PaaS portability.

---

[1] Mohaghegi and Dehlen present a summary of experiences from applying MDE in industry [8].

2.1   The Lock-in Problem

Lock-in is the difficulty faced to move data and programs from one cloud platform to run on another one [2]. This is a major issue in the PaaS scenario: in
order to take advantage of a very flexible cloud architecture, the applications
are developed conforming to the specificity of the chosen platform. For example,
to offer great elasticity, the GAE PaaS provider imposes a specific programming
style and specific data management policies. Thus, an application developed for
it may not be easily ported to a different PaaS provider, nor can its data. Even
if the developer wants to host the application in his own private cloud later, considerable effort may be necessary to rebuild the code, redeploy it, and migrate
all the data. This lack of portability causes the so-called lock-in effect.

The possibility of becoming "locked in" to a particular platform, not being
able to choose a different one later (customer lock-in), leaves developers in a
difficult position. They mostly fear being charged abusive fees later, or having
their applications unavailable due to lack of service quality [2].

2.2   Types of Portability

Prior to deciding on the adoption of a cloud model, an organization should
take into account the viability of the one that better fits its business. It must
carefully analyze the constraints related to cloud platforms, both technical and
organizational [4], as well as its business requirements [9]. The main problem
caused by the lack of portability is that the work committed to platform-specific
tasks cannot be reused in a different platform. Ideally, software development
should be more conceptual and less focused on repetitive tasks [10].

The ISO 9126 standard [11], developed to identify software quality attributes,
defines portability in terms of how easy it is to migrate software from one environment to another. It has the following sub-attributes: **Adaptability**: the software's ability to adapt to different environments without the need for additional
actions (settings); **Capacity to be installed**: identifies the ease with which the
system can be installed into a new environment; **Coexistence**: measures how
easily a software coexists with other software installed in the same environment;
Ability to replace: measures how easily the system is replaced by another.

In the context of this research, portability is a key attribute for the improvement and dissemination of the cloud model, and four main types can be distinguished [4]:

Portability of Virtual Machines between Cloud Providers: the IaaS
model normally uses server virtualization[2] to provide computing resources to
customers. Typically, the virtual machines are managed by the customers themselves. Migrating a virtual machine from one provider to another causes little
impact on the systems being virtualized, as all that is needed is a copy of the

---

[2] Server Virtualization is the technique of running one or more virtual servers on one
physical server [12].

virtual disk. The Open Virtualization Format (OVF[3]) makes this task even easier; it provides a standard format, reducing the effort required to port a virtual machine from one provider to another (as long as both support this format).

Portability of Applications in the Context of IaaS: instead of virtual machines (VM), some providers offer hosting plans that support only a specific technology. Many propose plans for hosting Java, Ruby, PHP, among others. In this case, users have no control over the VM, i.e., the provider manages the entire infrastructure. Once applications are deployed, and depending on how much configuration is needed, a big effort is necessary to change the provider, because each provider offers plans according to different business goals. Many providers offer specific plans, and the user has the option to buy only the package according to the technologies he needs. If a user chooses to change the provider, he must check if the destination provider supports the same technologies.

Portability of PaaS Applications: users of the PaaS service model must follow a specific programming style and use libraries and technologies offered by the providers. The migration of applications between two platforms often requires a total re-engineering process [3]. The developer must know the libraries and details of each platform, what makes migration difficult and expensive.

Data Portability between Cloud Providers: similarly to the previous case, there is not a standard for using traditional database management systems (DBMS) in the cloud [2]. Therefore, data portability between providers is another detail to consider. In the IaaS case, the user may choose to install his own instance of a DBMS, and use it in a single, virtual machine. If elasticity is necessary, the user is responsible for setting multiple, interconnected servers and define some kind of distribution scheme. Another possibility is to hire a provider that supports a particular DBMS. Thus, just as for applications' portability, it is important to ensure that the new provider supports the DBMS. Shirazi et al. [13] present a solution based on design standards to allow data portability among some cloud databases. However, the solution is still in the research phase and more studies are required.

This paper focuses on portability of PaaS applications. However, the code generators and repository proposed here can be used in other contexts. Petcu et al. present a list of initiatives to handle portability [25]. They also discuss the reasons, scenarios, taxonomies, measurements, and requirements for portability. Several other authors are also looking at the problem and proposing alternative solutions (see Sect. 6). One such alternative is the use of MDE.

2.3   Model-Driven Engineering (MDE)

Despite the advances of software development techniques, concerns about reuse, productivity, maintenance, documentation, validation, optimization, portability and interoperability are still under discussion. Model-Driven Engineering,

---

[3] OVF: http://www.dmtf.org/standards/ovf.

or MDE, aims at solving some of those issues [7], shifting the focus of modern development methodologies from implementation to conceptual modeling. Models are then first-class citizens, and transformation mechanisms are used to generate code from them, reducing developers' effort [7] and increasing portability and productivity [4]. The vision is that MDE will reduce the accidental complexity by increasing the level of abstraction used to develop software.

According to Schmidt, MDE technologies" offer a promising approach to address the inability of third-generation languages to alleviate the complexity of platforms and express domain concepts effectively" [21]. That is exactly our goal: use MDE to abstract away platform-specific details, building conceptual domain models that express the essence and logic of the domain. From these models, applications can then be generated through automatic transformations, thus reducing the development effort for implementations on different platforms.

Such models are abstract descriptions or specifications of the system and are usually represented as a combination of graphical (Domain-Specific Modeling Languages – DSML) and textual elements (Domain-Specific Languages – DSL) [14]. DSLs are small languages focused on a particular problem/domain, and are normally declarative [15]. The language definition usually requires a metamodel capable of capturing the common and variable elements of a specific domain [14,15].

2.4   A Model-Driven Approach for Cloud PaaS Portability

Previous study [4] discusses a vision for using MDE to increase cloud PaaS portability, and shows how to build a DSL and a set of code transformations, based on the Model-View-Controller (MVC) architecture, to reduce the effort of developing cloud applications. We also presented a DSL metamodel, samples of code transformations, the grammar of the DSL and a quasi-experiment [16,17] showing that MDE helps both reducing the development effort and achieving portability. Figure 1 summarizes the methodology followed.

Adopting a typical MDE life-cycle, this methodology obeyed to the following strategy:

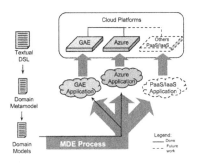

Fig. 1. A MDE approach for cloud PaaS portability.

1. Case studies were developed to identify the main concepts of PaaS. These studies involved a careful analysis of the different providers' documentation, as well as the development of sample applications for different platforms.
2. These concepts were used to prototype a specification language. This language serves to support the creation of platform-independent models that developers will use to specify the applications' structure and logic. This step involves developing a domain metamodel and a concrete syntax.
3. Based on the case studies and on the specification language, transformations were defined to automatically generate code for cloud platforms.
4. Tests were performed to verify the conformance between the generated code and the platforms' requirements.

3   Persistence in PaaS

The PaaS model leverages the flexibility of the cloud model, by providing a complete platform for software development. A cloud platform hides many of the complexities of developing cloud software, therefore increasing scalability and elasticity. In the PaaS model, the development platform is provided as-a-service. Applications that are developed for this particular platform can benefit from a specific programming model that can be fully, fine grained, managed by the platform provider.

Among the existing platforms, we selected two well-known ones for developing our prototype: the Google App Engine[4] (GAE) and the Windows Azure. However, as the developed DSL is platform independent (although domain dependent), it can be used to generate code for any other platform.

One of the services managed by cloud providers is data persistence. By defining its own way to store data, a provider may incorporate services such as load balancing, automatic data distribution and optimized querying. This is so for the two selected platforms for our study. Both GAE and Azure offer PaaS solutions incorporating NoSQL storage. This service is provided to applications through simple configuration steps. Actually, Azure offers two types of cloud services: IaaS and PaaS. It is not hard porting an IaaS application because this offer is based on virtual machines (VM). Just migrating a VM from one provider to another causes little impact on the systems being virtualized, as all that is needed for them to run is a copy of the virtual disk. The Open Virtualization Format (OVF[5]) makes this task even easier, by providing a standard format so that there is little effort to port a virtual machine from one provider to another, as long as both support this format. The main issue in this case is to choose a different provider that accepts the same VM format[6].

However, in terms of PaaS, both Azure and GAE offer solutions based on Java servlets and JSP with NoSQL storage. Even if they allow the same set of

---

[4] https://cloud.google.com/appengine.

[5] OVF: http://www.dmtf.org/standards/ovf.

[6] Paasify may be an interesting solution to select compatible PaaS: http://www.paasify.it/vendors.

technologies (Java based), applications implemented for them are not portable. This happens mainly because of the differences between their persistence models. (Section 3 discusses these models in detail.) Indeed, Gorton in a post[7] at Software Engineering Institute's blog and Armbrust et al. [18] highlight that the differences in data management technologies make applications less reusable by different providers.

The next subsections present specific details of each platform persistence model, and finish with a discussion of the main issues found.

3.1   Google App Engine

Google App Engine DataStore is typically one of the first choices for big data applications. The DataStore is GAE's native API and its scalability is managed by the platform itself, which means that the user does not need to worry about the actual storage details.

GAE's DataStore offers two mechanisms to specify persistent entities: Java Data Objects[8] (JDO) and Java Persistence API[9] (JPA). The JDO and JPA interfaces are implemented using the Datanucleus[10] platform, which is an open-source implementation of JDO and JPA. With JDO/JPA, GAE allows the definition of simple entity relationships. As a result, even without direct relational support from the actual database system, applications can use GAE's DataStore to manage related entities.

For simplicity reasons, we chose JDO for this study. To persist an entity in GAE's DataStore, all that is necessary is to annotate a class according to the JDO specification. Related entities (one-to-one and one-to-many) are also managed by GAE automatically through proper annotations.

Let us consider a simple example: a clinical laboratory system must maintain a record of customers, doctors and examinations; each customer has one doctor, and each doctor may choose among a set of examinations to be performed.

The first step is to annotate the classes that represent persistent entities according to the JDO specification. After this, calls to JDO's CRUD[11] methods can be used directly. In summary, all that is needed to make an entity persistent are some annotations. The actual storage of the entity and its related entities is performed by the platform.

It is important to stress that even with the possibility to define simple relationships through annotations, the GAE DataStore service is a NoSQL solution. If a relational solution is needed, a fully-fledged SQL solution, such as the MySQL-based service offered by GAE (Google Cloud SQL), is recommended. A tradeoff between scalability and robustness is necessary in these cases.

---

[7] http://blog.sei.cmu.edu/post.cfm/importance-software-architecture-big-data-syste ms-013.

[8] http://www.oracle.com/technetwork/java/index-jsp-135919.html.

[9] http://www.oracle.com/technetwork/java/javaee/tech/persistence-jsp-140049. html.

[10] http://www.datanucleus.org/.

[11] CRUD: Create, Retrieve, Update and Delete.

3.2   Windows Azure

Windows Azure is the Microsoft's cloud platform, which offers different services, such as virtualization, storage and web hosting. Similarly to GAE, Azure's PaaS solution supports regular web-based applications (pages, controllers and other classes/libraries), but with a wider choice of languages (.Net, Node.js, PHP, Java, etc.).

Azure offers persistence through four main storage options:

- **Table Storage:** this is Azure's NoSQL persistence solution. It is a simple persistence model that allows applications to store basic data types (e.g., integer, string, boolean). It is a highly scalable solution, but with three major restrictions. First, Azure's Table Storage structures do not directly support relationships between entities. Second, there is a limit of 255 properties per entity, and every entity must define at least two properties for identification, which leaves 253 properties for general use. Third, data in a single entity cannot exceed one MByte.
- **SQL Database:** formerly known as SQL Azure, this is a fully managed relational database service. Being a relational database, it is not as scalable as the NoSQL service.
- **SQL Server in Windows Azure VM:** if the developer wants more control over the DBMS, he may opt to deploy his own instance of SQL Server in a virtual machine. This renders more control, but also requires more effort to setup, and to manage the database server and the virtual machine.
- **Blob Storage:** this service supports the storage of large, non-structured data. It has great scalability, but it is focused on files like audio and video.

As Azure also allows NoSQL services, which offer a good combination between storage and scalability for big data applications, we also chose to study this model in Azure. However, unlike GAE JDO/JPA-based implementation, Azure does not have an official support for JPA/JDO. As a result, the developer has to deal with relationships manually. Additionally, there are many restrictions in Azure, for example: persistence is defined through inheritance, and not annotations as in GAE; the identification field (primary key) has to be manually managed.

In Azure Table Storage, entities are stored in table structures called partitions. One partition can store multiple entities, which may be of different types. An entity has a unique identification field. Partition names and identification fields are both strings, and are inherited by the entity classes.

To perform CRUD operations, the Table Storage API has some predefined methods. Listing 1.1 shows an example of how an entity can be persisted. The method "saveOrUpdate" (line 1) is used to either create or update an entity. First, a table client object is obtained ("tableClient"), based on some predefined connection string (line 2). Next, a table operation is created, in this case, to insert or replace an entity (line 3). Then, the table (partition) is created, if it does not exist already (line 5). Finally, the operation is executed (line 6). In this example, for simplicity, the name of the partition and of the entity class will be the same.

Listing 1.1. Persisting an entity in Azure.

```
1 public void saveOrUpdate(TableServiceEntity tse) {
2     CloudTableClient tableClient = CloudStorageAccount.parse(
          storageConnectionString).createCloudTableClient();
3     TableOperation tableOperation = TableOperation.
          insertOrReplace(tse);
4     try {
5         tableClient.getTableReference(tse.getClass().
              getSimpleName()).createIfNotExist();
6         tableClient.execute(tse.getClass().getSimpleName(),
              tableOperation);
7     } catch (StorageException e) { ... }
8 }
```

Dealing with relationships requires manual management of the id fields. For one-to-one relationships, it is possible to simply store the id of the related (dependent) entity as a property in the container entity. For example, in the customer-has-a-doctor one-to-one relationship, to obtain the doctor for a given customer, first we obtain its id, and then we perform a query in the Doctor table.

For one-to-many or many-to-many relationships, the strategy is to maintain a separate entity for relationships. Listing 1.2 illustrates the idea. In this example, "Relationship" (line 1) is a persistent entity that merely stores two string values: the "end1" and the "end2" (lines 2 and 3), each representing an end of the relationship. This entity will be stored in a partition of its own, called "Relationship" (line 5).

Listing 1.2. Persistent relationship in Azure.

```
1 public class Relationship extends TableServiceEntity {
2     private String end1;
3     private String end2;
4     public Relationship() {
5         this.partitionKey ="Relationship";
6     }
7     ... setters and getters ...
8 }
```

The "Relationship" entity from Listing 1.2 can be used to establish a relationship between any two entities. A Method "saveRelationship" realises a relationship between two entities, instantiating the "Relationship" entity and persisting it using calls to Azure's API.

Once the relationship is established, retrieving all related entities can be done by searching through the "Relationship" partition. The example of Listing 1.3 shows a way to implement this strategy. The method "getAllRelatedEntities" (line 1) gets all entities related to a given entity. The id of the containing entity and the class of the related entity are provided as arguments. First, all relationships are retrieved (line 2) through the "getAll" method, which is not shown here but should be trivial to imagine. Then, the resulting list is iterated in search for instances that have a matching "end1" property (lines 4–5). For those matching relationships, the instance corresponding to the "end2" is retrieved and added to the result (line 6). A method "retrieve", which is not shown here, looks into the partition of the corresponding entity class and returns the instance itself.

Listing 1.3. Retrieving related entities in Azure.

```
1 public List getAllRelatedEntities(String end1Id, Class end2Class
      ) {
2     List<Relationship> temp = getAll(Relationship.class);
3     List result = new ArrayList();
4     for (Relationship r : temp) {
5         if (r.getEnd1().equals(end1Id)) {
6             result.add(retrieve(end2Class, c.getEnd2()));
7         }
8     }
9     return result;
10 }
```

The implementation of Listing 1.3 is not very efficient, as it examines all relationships every time. However, it is not difficult to optimize this code with more refined structures such as trees or hash functions.

3.3   Difficulties in Conciliating both Persistence Models

Although both GAE and Azure offer NoSQL services, GAE adds a layer that facilitates the management of relationships between persistent entities, while Azure demands some additional effort to be able to deliver similar functionality. The problem, however, is not the extra effort required by Azure. In fact, the jpa4azure[12] third-party API, adds an object-relational mapping layer to Azure, similar to what is natively available in GAE. (At the time we started our research, this API was not stable, at least according to our tests; so we decided to implement our own layer.) The problem, really, is that even allowing the use of the same set of technologies, the differences between the platforms impose specific programming styles when developing for each one. For this reason, the effort spent on specific programing tasks cannot be reused. Even considering the existence of a common API, the problem remains, due to the differences between the implementations and storage philosophies. Standardization could be an alternative, but, as we discussed before, it is not the path followed in this work.

Hence, despite the apparent similarities of the platforms (which use the same set of technologies: Java back-end, web-based front-end, and NoSQL persistence), the resulting applications have considerable differences. If for a small application like the one presented here the differences are so substantial, in a real case, managing thousands of persistent entities, the effort of developing such a system can increase quickly. If we consider other platforms, supporting different technologies such as Redis[13] or memcacheDB[14], the problem becomes even worse.

---

[12] https://jpa4azure.codeplex.com/.

[13] http://redis.io/.

[14] http://memcachedb.org/.

We argue that MDE can solve the portability problem in a more fundamental way, reaching flexibility levels that no API or standard can provide. The following section describes our proposal, based on a single platform-independent development model that hides the details of the platforms. This proposal also helps to reduce the extra effort needed by Azure, or any other platform that uses different technology.

4 Supporting Multiple Persistence Models Using MDE

This section presents a model implemented using the previously developed DSL, discusses the specific details of the generated code for GAE and Azure, gives a synthesis of the whole generation process, and offers some highlights on the work done.

Listing 1.4 presents the model for the clinical laboratory system. This example uses the language presented in a previous work [4], which is summarized next. First, the model defines some basic configuration properties, such as the application name (line 1), visual theme (line 2), version (line 3), title (line 4), and a set of tabs to be displayed in the main interface (lines 5–10). Next are the entities and their relationships. The syntax is straightforward. Two points worth mentioning are the definition of the primary keys (lines 14, 27 and 34), which are inspired by JDO's annotations, and the possibility to define custom labels to be displayed in the main interface (line 36).

Listing 1.4. Model of the clinical laboratory system.

```
1  ...
2  entity Customer {
3    pk { id:Key(strategy=IDENTITY) readOnly=true }
4    property name : String
5    property address : String
6    property email : String
7    property phone1 : String
8    property birth : Date
9    property doctor : Doctor
10   property gender : String
11   property examinations : Examination[]
12 }
13
14 entity Examination {
15   pk { id:Key(strategy=IDENTITY) readOnly = true }
16   property name : String
17   property material : String
18   property price : Double
19 }
20 ...
```

Listing 1.4 also shows the relationships established for this system. One customer has one doctor (line 21) and many examinations (line 23 - the [] suffix indicates that a property may have multiple instances). These appear in the model as properties mapped to other entities.

We developed two sets of transformations, one for GAE and another for Azure. A more generic view of this process can be seen in our previous works [4,5].

4.1 Generating Persistence Code for GAE

Since GAE has JDO support, the transformations are not too difficult to define. One JDO-annotated Java class is generated for each persistent entity, including its properties and relationships. There is a single, generic, non-generated data-access object (DAO) that performs basic CRUD operations. The invocations of the CRUD operations for each entity are generated in specific controller classes. One controller class is generated for each entity. For further information on the code generation strategy the reader is directed to [5].

4.2 Generating Persistence Code for Azure

For Azure, one class per persistent entity is generated. For basic CRUD operations, as well as for dealing with relationships manually, there is a single, generic, non-generated data-access object (DAO). Details the code generation strategy for this case can also be found in [5].

5 Evaluation

In an evidence-based view [16,17,19], the case study presented in [5] already constitutes some evidence that it is possible to deal with different database models at high abstraction level and port applications between different cloud providers using our approach. But to reinforce such evidence, we performed a more careful evaluation (see Sect. 7).

We defined a set of test cases, which subjects executed on the same application generated for the two platforms (GAE and Azure). After executing the tests, the subjects perceived no difference in terms of functionality, which indicates that portability can indeed be achieved through our approach. We also observed considerable gains in productivity, due to the automation power of MDE transformations.

Following the experimental phases suggested by Wohlin et al. [16], we started with the planning, then proceeded to the execution and ended with the data analysis.

5.1 Planning

The main idea of the evaluation was to have two versions of the same application, one running on Google App Engine, and the other running on Windows Azure. Subjects were then asked to use both versions, and tell if they could perceive any difference. Since both versions are generated from a single model, if there are no perceivable differences, we consider that portability is successful. With this in mind, the planning involved the following four phases:

Context Selection: the experiment occurred in the academic environment. It was performed at the Software Engineering Laboratory at Federal University of São Carlos.

Research Question: is it possible to use MDE to port an application between cloud platforms so that the final users do not perceive any differences between the original and the ported applications?

Selection of Subjects: the subjects were selected through convenience sampling, i.e., the nearest and most convenient people [16].

Design: Inspired by other reports from the literature [20], we defined a set of black box test cases to serve as a script for the subjects. The idea was to ensure they would use both versions in a similar way, and also exercise all functions of the application. These are conventional test cases, with a description, preconditions, a set of steps to be performed, and the expected results.

For this evaluation, we used the clinical laboratory domain described in Sect. 3. A total of eleven test cases were defined, as shown in Table 1.

Table 1. Description of the test cases.

Id	Description	Entities involved	Type	Relationship
1	Insert a doctor	Doctor	Create	none
2	Insert an examination	Examination	Create	none
3	Insert a customer	Doctor, customer	Retrieve, create	one-to-one
4	Register an examination	Customer, examination	Retrieve, create	one-to-many
5	Update a customer's address	Customer	Update	none
6	Change a doctor	Doctor, customer	Retrieve, update	one-to-one
7	Update a doctor's registration number	Doctor	Update	none
8	Update an examination's price	Examination	Update	none
9	Remove an examination	Examination	Delete	none
10	Unregister an examination	Customer, examination	Retrieve, delete	one-to-many
11	Remove a doctor	Doctor	Delete	none

Since our focus was on persistence, these test cases were designed to cover all CRUD operations and involve different kinds of entities and relationships. In this sense, the following criteria were adopted:

- **All CRUD Operations:** test cases 1 through 4 involve "create" operations, test cases 5 through 8 involve "update" operations, and test cases 9 through 11 involve "delete" operations. "Retrieve" operations are implicitly involved in all test cases, since the main user interface starts with a listing of all entities of a particular type. But test cases 3, 4 and 6 add more refined "retrieve" operations. For example, in test case 3, to insert a customer, the user must first retrieve the corresponding doctor. In test case 4, to register an examination for a customer, the user must first retrieve it from a list. In test case 10, to unregister an examination, the user must first obtain a list of registered examinations, and choose one to unregister.
- **All Domain Entities:** the test cases also attempt to exercise the different entities of the domain. All four entities are present in at least five test cases, as it can be seen in Table 1. We also attempted to perform all possible CRUD operations in all entities. Test cases 1, 3, 6, 7 and 11 are responsible for creating, retrieving, updating and deleting doctors. Test cases 2, 4, 8, 9 and 10 involve the examination entity. And test cases 3, 4, 5, 6 and 10 involve the customer entity.
- **Both Kinds of Relationships:** the test cases also involve the two types of relationships that are supported by our approach: one-to-one and one-to-many. They also attempt to perform all possible CRUD operations in these two kinds of relationships. In this sense, test case 3 creates a one-to-one relationship. Test case 6 updates a one-to-one relationship. Test case 4 creates a one-to-many relationship, and test case 10 deletes a one-to-many relationship. Retrieving relationships is implicit in all related test cases, because a listing of related entities is shown whenever some entity is being edited. But they appear more explicitly in test cases 4 and 10 (retrieving examinations), and in test case 6 (retrieving a doctor). Some combinations are missing, as follows: in this domain it is not possible to delete a one-to-one relationship, because a customer must have at least one associated doctor. It also makes no sense to update a one-to-many relationship, because examinations are either added or removed from the customer's list.

5.2 Execution

Continuing with the experimental phases suggested by Wohlin et al. [16], we moved on to the execution. The tests were executed in 2 steps:

Step 1: Preparation. In this step the following two instrumentation elements were elaborated:

- **Guidelines** — this material consisted of one document with the description of the tasks and instructions the subject should follow and one document with the application description and support material;
- **Data Collection Instruments** — data collection was performed in two moments. The first moment was during test case execution, where after each test case description, in the task description document, the subjects would need to respond if they considered the test case successful. In a second

moment, after the execution of all test cases, a questionnaire was given to each subject to ask about his perception on portability. This questionnaire was based on the ISO standard 9126 [11], which defines portability as a set of attributes that bear on the ability of software to be transferred from one environment to another. Among its four attributes (e.g., adaptability, installability, co-existence and replaceability), we focused on replaceability, as we believe that it is the most adequate to the goal of this research.

Step 2: Execution. Here we used our approach to generate the two versions of the application, for the two supported platforms (GAE and Azure). As described earlier, we used the laboratory analysis example. The subjects were then asked to execute the test cases. This study had ten participants The execution took one day, strating with an initial training and finishing with answering the questionnaire.

5.3   Data Analysis

All ten subjects were able to use both versions of the application and perform all test cases successfully. Regarding the questionnaire, the results of each question are discussed next.

Question 1. Do you consider that the two versions of the application are equivalent in terms of functionality? For two applications A and B to be equivalent in terms of persistence operations, the set of CRUD functions implemented in A must be equal to the set of functions implemented in B. All the subjects answered that the two versions of the application were equivalent in terms of persistence operations.

Question 2. Do you consider that the two versions of the application are equivalent in terms of the interface? Two applications can be equivalent in terms of functionality but have different interfaces. All the subjects answered that the two versions of the application were equivalent in terms of the interface, i.e., the interfaces allow equivalent access to persistence operations.

Question 3. Do you consider that for the same input on each version of the application, the outputs were equal? This question evaluates if the systems are equivalent in terms of input and output. All the subjects answered that the two versions of the application were equivalent in terms of input/output, i.e., persistence works in the same way in both versions.

Question 4. Do you consider that the Azure version can be replaced by the GAE version, and vice-versa? All the subjects answered that the two versions could be replaced by each other.

From this evaluation, we can conclude that our approach supports porting an application between cloud platforms in such a way that the final users do not perceive the differences when using the two versions. This is particularly interesting if we consider that the underlying data management mechanisms are different, as discussed in Sect. 3. This effectively puts MDE as a possible alternative to port applications between cloud providers.

5.4   Threats to Validity

Low Number of Subjects: a small set of users participated in the tests. A larger number of people using the system can lead to the discovery of some fails and differences.

Simple Domain: the application built for the case study is relatively small and represents a small problem domain. These elements may have facilitated the analysis, and it is possible that we did not test all situations, although we attempted to cover all combinations between CRUD operations, entities and relationships.

Statistical Treatment: the collected data did not allow a formal, complete statistical treatment, which could lead to more solid results. But we believe the qualitative analysis has lead to important insights regarding the approach.

6   Related Work

There are several different proposals for developing portable cloud applications, being standardization and open source software the more popular in the industry. In academia, many authors also attempt to use MDE to solve to lock-in problem.

Miranda et al. present their vision on how MDE can support the development of adaptive multi-cloud applications, thus integrating MDE and Software Adaptation techniques [22]. Developers are requested to tag the components indicating in which cloud they will be deployed. MDE techniques are then applied to generate an XML-based cloud deployment plan. The source code and the XML deployment plan are processed to generate cloud compliant artifacts to access the underlying cloud services. This work aims at generating the deployment plan while our targets the design and development time. MODAClouds[15] (MOdelDriven Approach for the design and execution of applications on multiple Clouds) aims at supporting system developers and operators in exploiting multiple clouds and in migrating their applications from cloud to cloud as needed [23]. Its main objective is to provide methods, a decision support system, an open source IDE and runtime environment for the high-level design, early prototyping, semi-automatic code generation, and automatic deployment of applications on multiple clouds. It also helps administrators to monitor the services and measure their quality. While the project is developing a post-fact adoption standard [24] with CloudML, a domain-specific modeling language and runtime environment that facilitates the specification of cloud application provisioning, deployment, and adaptation, we argue that each enterprise can build its own language or generation strategy more aligned with their business.

A strategy to solve the portability without MDE is described in [26]. Giove et al. propose a library called CPIM (Cloud Provider Independent Model), that encapsulates PaaS-level services such as message queues, noSQL, and caching. Instead of relying on the providers following a standard, they add a mediation

---

[15] http://www.modaclouds.eu/.

layer that hides the details of the underlying PaaS provider and exposes a common API that allows platform-independent code to be developed on top of it.

Both our approach and the CPIM library attempt to deal with the differences between PaaS services. Both agree that standardization may not be the only solution. And both allow platform-independent applications to be specified. Our proposal has the advantage of allowing developers to work on a higher abstraction level. Therefore, we can collect additional benefits in terms of productivity and maintenance. On the other hand, CPIM requires no effort to setup a modeling and code generation environment, resulting in less upfront investment and being easier to adopt. In fact, an hybrid solution, combining MDE and a mediation layer, could bring benefits from both approaches.

More research issues and approaches related to the development of systems to the cloud model can be found in Armbrust et al. [2] and our previous works [4,5]. Cloud computing is still evolving, and research opportunities are still being identified. More research and evaluations are still necessary.

7   Concluding Remarks and Future Work

This paper shows how the differences in cloud persistence models can make an application difficult to reuse and/or be ported to a different provider. It extends our previous works on exploring the use of MDE to overcome portability in cloud computing, and shows how that previous approach can be used to solve the persistence related lock-in issue. The main contribution of our work is to show that there is an alternative path to the standardization of cloud technologies. MDE can increase the portability of the applications, but it can also lead to additional benefits inherently associated with it, consequently, reducing the impacts of lock-in.

In the near future we plan to include more platforms to implement the repository of models and transformations, and to perform some more evaluations, which includes applying our approach to other case studies.

Acknowledgements. We would like to thank FAPESP (processes 2012/24487-3 and 2012/04549-4), Coordination of Superior Level Staff Improvement - CAPES and Brazil-Europe Erasmus Mundus project (process BM13DM0002) for partially funding this research.

References

1. Chen, Y., Li, X., Chen, F.: Overview and analysis of cloud computing research and application. In: 2011 International Conference on E-Business and E-Government (ICEE), pp. 1–4 (2011)
2. Armbrust, M., Fox, A., Griffith, R., Joseph, A.D., Katz, R., Konwinski, A., Lee, G., Patterson, D., Rabkin, A., Stoica, I., Zaharia, M.: Above the clouds: a Berkeley view of cloud computing. Dept. Electrical Eng. and Comput. Sciences, University of California, Berkeley, Report UCB/EECS 28 (2009)

3. da Silva, E.A.N., Lucredio, D.: Software engineering for the cloud: a research roadmap. In: 2012 26th Brazilian Symposium on Software Engineering, pp. 71–80 (2012)
4. da Silva, E.A.N., Fortes, R.P.M., Lucrédio, D.: A model-driven approach for promoting cloud paas portability. In: Proceedings of the 2013 Conference of the Center for Advanced Studies on Collaborative Research, CASCON 2013, Riverton, NJ, USA, pp. 92–105. IBM Corp. (2013)
5. da Silva, E.A.N., Moreira, A., Lucrrédio, D., andFortes, R.P.M.: Supporting multiple persistence models for PaaS applications using model-driven engineering. In: Proceedings of the 5th International Conference on Cloud Computing and Services Science, CLOSER 2015, Lisbon, Portugal. INSTICC (2015)
6. France, R., Rumpe, B.: Model-driven development of complex software: a research roadmap. In: Future of Software Engineering, FOSE 2007, pp. 37–54. IEEE Computer Society, Washington, DC (2007)
7. Kleppe, A., Jos, W., Wim, B.: MDA Explained, the Model-Driven Architecture: Practice and Promise. Addison-Wesley, Boston (2003)
8. Mohagheghi, P., Dehlen, V.: Where is the proof? - a review of experiences from applying MDE in industry. In: Schieferdecker, I., Hartman, A. (eds.) ECMDA-FA 2008. LNCS, vol. 5095, pp. 432–443. Springer, Heidelberg (2008)
9. Khajeh-Hosseini, A., Sommerville, I., Bogaerts, J., Teregowda, P.: Decision support tools for cloud migration in the enterprise. In: 2011 IEEE International Conference on Cloud Computing (CLOUD), pp. 541–548 (2011)
10. Lucrédio, D., Almeida, E.S., Fortes, R.P.M.: An investigation on the impact of MDE on software reuse. In: 2012 Sixth Brazilian Symposium on Software Components Architectures and Reuse (SBCARS), pp. 101–110. IEEE (2012)
11. ISO/IEC9126: Software product evaluation - Quality characteristics and guidelines for their use. ISO Norm. (1991)
12. Daniels, J.: Server virtualization architecture and implementation. Crossroads **16**, 8–12 (2009)
13. Shirazi, M.N., Kuan, H.C., Dolatabadi, H.: Design patterns to enable data portability between clouds' databases. In: 2012 12th International Conference on Computational Science and Its Applications (ICCSA), pp. 117–120 (2012)
14. Brambilla, M., Cabot, J., Wimmer, M.: Model-driven software engineering in practice. Synth. Lect. Softw. Eng. **1**, 1–182 (2012)
15. Van Deursen, A., Klint, P., Visser, J.: Domain-specific languages: an annotated bibliography. ACM Sigplan Not. **35**, 26–36 (2000)
16. Wohlin, C., Runeson, P., Host, M., Ohlsson, C., Regnell, B., Wesslén, A.: Experimentation in Software Engineering: An Introduction. Springer, Heidelberg (2000)
17. Juristo, N., Moreno, A.M.: Basics of Software Engineering Experimentation. Springer, Heidelberg (2010)
18. Armbrust, M., Fox, A., Griffith, R., Joseph, A.D., Katz, R., Konwinski, A., Lee, G., Patterson, D., Rabkin, A., Stoica, I., Zaharia, M.: A view of cloud computing. Commun. ACM **53**, 50–58 (2010)
19. Tichy, W.F.: Should computer scientists experiment more? Computer **31**, 32–40 (1998)
20. Silva, L., Soares, S.: Analyzing structure-based techniques for test coverage on a J2ME software product line. In: 10th Latin American Test Workshop, LATW 2009, pp. 1–6. IEEE (2009)
21. Schmidt, D.C.: Model-driven engineering. Comput.-IEEE Comput. Soc. **39**(2), 25 (2006)

22. Miranda, J., Guillén, J., Murillo, J.M., Canal, C.: Development of adaptive multi-cloud applications a model-driven approach. In: MODELSWARD (2013)
23. Ardagna, D., Di Nitto, E., Mohagheghi, P., Mosser, S., Ballagny, C., D'Andria, F., Casale, G., Matthews, P., Nechifor, C.S., Petcu, D., et al.: Modaclouds: a model-driven approach for the design and execution of applications on multiple clouds. In: 2012 ICSE Workshop on Modeling in Software Engineering (MISE), pp. 50–56. IEEE (2012)
24. Petcu, D.: Portability and interoperability between clouds: challenges and case study. In: Abramowicz, W., Llorente, I.M., Surridge, M., Zisman, A., Vayssière, J. (eds.) ServiceWave 2011. LNCS, vol. 6994, pp. 62–74. Springer, Heidelberg (2011)
25. Petcu, D., Vasilakos, A.V.: Portability in clouds: approaches and research opportunities. Scalable Comput. Pract. Experience 15(3) (2014)
26. Giove, F., Longoni, D., Yancheshmeh, M.S., Ardagna, D., Di Nitto, E.: An approach for the development of portable applications on paas clouds. In: Proceedings of CLOSER, pp. 591–601 (2013)

LS-ADT: Lightweight and Scalable Anomaly Detection for Cloud Datacentres

Sakil Barbhuiya, Zafeirios Papazachos[(✉)], Peter Kilpatrick, and Dimitrios S. Nikolopoulos

School of Electronics, Electrical Engineering and Computer Science, Queens University Belfast, Belfast BT7 1NN, UK
{sbarbhuiya03,z.papazachos,p.kilpatrick,d.nikolopoulo}@qub.ac.uk

Abstract. Cloud data centres are implemented as large-scale clusters with demanding requirements for service performance, availability and cost of operation. As a result of scale and complexity, data centres typically exhibit large numbers of system anomalies resulting from operator error, resource over/under provisioning, hardware or software failures and security issus anomalies are inherently difficult to identify and resolve promptly via human inspection. Therefore, it is vital in a cloud system to have automatic system monitoring that detects potential anomalies and identifies their source. In this paper we present a lightweight anomaly detection tool for Cloud data centres which combines extended log analysis and rigorous correlation of system metrics, implemented by an efficient correlation algorithm which does not require training or complex infrastructure set up. The LADT algorithm is based on the premise that there is a strong correlation between node level and VM level metrics in a cloud system. This correlation will drop significantly in the event of any performance anomaly at the node-level and a continuous drop in the correlation can indicate the presence of a true anomaly in the node. The log analysis of LADT assists in determining whether the correlation drop could be caused by naturally occurring cloud management activity such as VM migration, creation, suspension, termination or resizing. In this way, any potential anomaly alerts are reasoned about to prevent false positives that could be caused by the cloud operator's activity. We demonstrate LADT with log analysis in a Cloud environment to show how the log analysis is combined with the correlation of systems metrics to achieve accurate anomaly detection.

Keywords: Data analysis · Cloud computing · SPARK · Distributed data processing · Monitoring

1 Introduction

A cloud data centre comprises of large pools of compute, storage, and networking resources. The VMs in a cloud are hosted on compute nodes which manage the VMs with the help of the hypervisor. The major task of these nodes is to host the VMs, hence the largest part of the workload of these nodes consists of the VM

© Springer International Publishing Switzerland 2016
M. Helfert et al. (Eds.): CLOSER 2015, CCIS 581, pp. 135–152, 2016.
DOI: 10.1007/978-3-319-29582-4_8

execution. In an anomaly-free compute node most of the supporting services are designed so as not to interfere with the execution of the VMs. However, an anomaly on the hosting services could cause the node to utilise resources which are not justified by the VMs workload. Moreover, a malicious attack could compromise the system security and let the intruder access the compute nodes' resources. Security breaches of this kind have been recorded in the past and they have been always addressed with high priority. An example of these breaches is the Blue Pill attack which manipulates kernel mode memory paging and the instructions that control the interaction between the host and guest (virtual machine). This permits undetected, on-the-fly placement of the host operating system in its own secure virtual machine allowing for complete control of the system including manipulation by other malware. Accessing the host resources in this way could interfere with workload of the registered VMs.

Modern analytic tools are capable of extracting information from logs [1,2] and use statistical learning techniques to build models that detect and diagnose system anomalies in data centres. The complexity of these models imposes several difficulties both on their interpretation by human operators and on their efficient implementation in large scale cloud platforms. As an alternative to using console logs, a number of anomaly detection tools use system metrics [3–7]. Such metrics can be collected with minimum overhead and without requiring access to the source code of hosted applications. EbAT [4] analyses metric distributions and measures the dispersal or concentration of the distributions. The metrics are aggregated by entropy distributions across the cloud stack in order to form entropy time series. EbAT uses online tools like spike detection, signal processing and subspace methods to detect anomalies in the entropy time series. The tool incurs the complexity of analysing the metric distributions and also requires third party tools to detect anomalies.

In previous work [8] we introduced a Lightweight Anomaly Detection Tool (LADT) which monitors system-level and virtual machine (VM)-level metrics in Cloud data centres to detect node-level anomalies using simple metrics and correlation analysis with Apache Pig [9]. In this study we combine system metric information with console logs analysis. In this way we perform a diagnosis on the alert to determine whether it could be a false positive that is derived from usual cloud management activities on the hosting node such as the migration or creation of new VM. We also present the performance of the correlation analysis on the collected data using Apache Spark. The major contribution of LADT over other tools in this context is the ability to efficiently detect anomalies in a Cloud data centre by combining in an effective way monitoring information from logs, VM metric measurements and host node metric measurements without requiring complex algorithms, application source code availability, or complex infrastructure set up.

The evaluation of the LADT tool is done in an OpenStack testbed, where it continuously collects and stores system metrics from all nodes and VMs. The tool shows that the cpu and disk I/O metrics in each hosted node are strongly correlated with the aggregate VM cpu and disk I/O metrics, but this correlation vanishes when a cpu or disk-stressing application is introduced in a node, indicating a node-level anomaly. We also demonstrate how the VM actions on the hosting node can affect the correlation analysis and the way the log analysis can prevent a false positive alert.

The remainder of the paper is organised as follows. Section 2 presents background and related work in anomaly detection. Sects. 3 and 4 provide detail of the LADT architecture and algorithm, respectively. Experimental results are presented and discussed in Sect. 5. Section 6 concludes the paper and discusses future work.

2 Background and Related Work

In this section we describe the challenges of detecting anomalies in Cloud data centres. A number of different tools and methods are considered and placed into separate categories based on the input they analyse. We consider two cases for monitoring and detecting anomalies: console log based anomaly detection and anomaly detection based on system metrics.

2.1 Anomaly Detection Challenges

Cloud data centres are implemented as large-scale clusters with demanding requirements for service performance, availability and cost of operation. As a result of scale and complexity, data centres exhibit large numbers of system anomalies caused by operator error [10], resource over/under provisioning [11], and hardware or software failures [12]. These anomalies are inherently difficult to identify and resolve promptly via human inspection [13]. Thus, automatic system monitoring that captures system state, behaviour and performance becomes vital. Computer system logs are the main source of information for anomaly detection. Logs can be of two types: structured or unstructured. Unstructured logs are free-form text strings, such as console logs, which record events or states of interest and capture the intent of service developers [1], whereas structured logs are numerical logs, such as logs of system metrics, which capture workload and system performance attributes, such as CPU utilisation, memory usage, network traffic and I/O.

2.2 Console Log Based Anomaly Detection

Analytic tools for anomaly detection based on console logs, such as SEC [14], Logsurfer [15] and Swatch [16] check logs against a set of rules which define normal system behaviour. These rules are manually set by developers based on their knowledge of system design and implementation. However, rule-based log analysis is complex and expensive because it requires significant effort from system developers to manually set and tune the rules. Moreover, modern systems consisting of multiple components developed by different vendors and the frequent upgrades of those components make it difficult for a single expert to have complete knowledge of the total system and to set the rules effectively.

This complexity has given rise to statistical learning based log analytic tools such as the works of Lou et al. [1] and Xu et al. [2], which extract features from console logs and then use statistical techniques to automatically build models for system anomaly identification.

Lou et al. [1] propose a statistical learning technique which consists of a learning process and a detection process. The learning process groups the log message parameters and then discovers the invariants among the different parameters within the groups. For new input logs, the detection process matches their invariants among the parameters with learned invariants from the learning process. Each mismatch in the invariants is considered to be anomalous. Xu et al. [2] propose a new methodology to mine console logs to automatically detect system problems. This first creates feature vectors from the logs and then applies the PCA (Principal Component Analysis) algorithm on the feature vectors to detect anomalies. However, the learning based tools require a custom log parser for mining the console logs in order to create the features for the learned model. The log parsers require source code of the hosted applications to recover the inherent structure of the logs.

2.3   System Metric Based Anomaly Detection

A number of anomaly detection tools use system metrics [3–7], which can be collected with minimum overhead and without requiring any access to the source code of hosted applications. Using system metrics for detecting anomalies has advantages over traditional log-based anomaly detection tools due to consideration of elasticity and workload evolution in Cloud computing, but also due to provisioning, scaling, and termination of services in short periods of time. Some of these tools are based on feature selection and machine learning outlier detection to flag anomalies [17].

EbAT [4] is a tool that uses entropy based anomaly detection. EbAT analyses metric distributions and measures the dispersal or concentration of the distributions. The metrics are aggregated by entropy distributions across the Cloud stack in order to form entropy time-series. EbAT uses online tools like spike detection, signal processing and subspace methods to detect anomalies in the entropy time-series. The tool incurs the complexity of analysing the metric distributions and also requires third party tools to detect anomalies.

PeerWatch [6] uses canonical correlation analysis (CCA) to extract the correlations between multiple application instances, where attributes of the instances are system resource metrics such as CPU utilisation, memory utilisation, network traffic etc. PeerWatch raises an alarm for an anomaly whenever some correlations drop significantly. As a result of analysing the application instance behaviours and correlating them, this tool is capable of detecting application-level or VM-level anomalies. However, this approach requires statistical metrics analysis and knowledge of the hosted applications, which is a limitation in large-scale Clouds, where hundreds of different types of applications run on the VMs.

Varanus [5] uses a gossip protocol, which is layered into Clouds, groups and VMs in order to collect system metrics from the VMs and analyse them for anomalies. This approach allows in-situ collection and analysis of metrics data without requiring any dedicated monitoring servers to store the data. However, setting up a dedicated gossip protocol across thousands of VMs in a large-scale Cloud environment and maintaining the gossip based overlay network over each of the VMs is a challenging task.

The metric-based black box detection technique presented in [3] uses the LFD (Light-Weight Failure Detection) algorithm to detect system anomalies. LFD raises an alarm when there is a lack of correlation between two specific system metrics. The anomaly indicates a system problem and each such problem is associated with a specific system metrics pair. LFD is a lightweight algorithm with lower complexity than EbAT, PeerWatch and Varanus. Furthermore, LFD does not require any training or source code and understanding of hosted applications. The LFD follows a decentralised detection approach, where each node analyses its own system metrics in order to achieve higher scalability. However, this may also limit LFD in large-scale Cloud data centres, where it may not be feasible to implement LFD on each node individually, due to overhead.

In this paper we address the limitations of existing system anomaly detection tools by introducing LADT. LADT uses Apache Chukwa [18] for collecting metrics data from all nodes and VMs in a data centre, and HBase [19] for storing the data in servers to allow centralised monitoring of Cloud systems. LADT implements a new correlation algorithm to perform the correlation analysis on the centrally stored metrics data. The LADT algorithm correlates node-level and VM-level metrics, which is a new approach to correlation analysis in detecting Cloud system anomalies. Furthermore, the LADT algorithm deals with the synchronisation problem between the node and VM generated metrics timestamp. This problem arises due to latency in storing the VM-level metrics in the monitoring server and results in poor correlation analysis. LADT is lightweight as it uses a simplified infrastructure set-up for metrics data monitoring and the LADT algorithm uses the simple Pearson correlation coefficient for analysing the metrics data. We program the algorithm using Apache Spark [9] to leverage MapReduce jobs in order to achieve higher throughput. We use disk I/O metrics from both nodes and VMs in an actual Cloud set-up to detect I/O performance anomalies.

3   LADT Architecture

The following sub-sections describe the architecture of the LADT tool and its functionality.

3.1   Metrics Data Monitoring

LADT utilises an agent-based monitoring architecture to retrieve system metrics from the hosting nodes and VMs in a Cloud data centre. The monitoring agent extracts system metrics from the nodes and VMs at regular time intervals. The collector gathers the data extracted by the agents. LADT uses the agents and

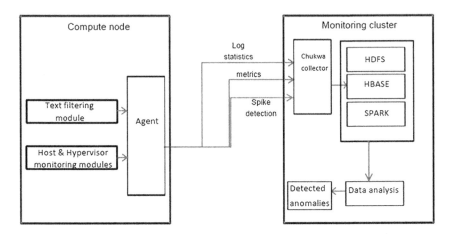

Fig. 1. LADT Architecture.

collectors provided by Apache Chukwa's [18] runtime monitoring. The Chukwa agent collects CPU, memory, disk, and network information from the hosting nodes using sigar [20] and from the VMs using Virt-Top [21]. The Chukwa collector then collects the output generated by the agents. The collector processes the data and registers the input to HBase, which is installed in the monitoring node.

Figure 1 illustrates the architecture of LS-ADT. The tool installs one Chukwa agent for collecting both node-level and VM-level metrics on each monitored node in the data centre. LS-ADT uses Chukwa collectors running on data analysis servers for collecting node-level and VM-level metrics into HBase. The correlation analysis on the stored metrics is performed by Spark. Each Chukwa agent consists of adaptors which are dynamically loadable modules that run inside the agent process. LS-ADT sends the metrics from the agents to the Chukwa collectors via HTTP. The primary task of the collector is to parse the collected data from the agent and store the extracted information in an HBase database. HBase runs on top of the Hadoop Distributed File System (HDFS) [22].

3.2   Metrics Data Analysis

The LS-ADT framework has been extended as compared with LADT with the necessary modules to allow for parallel trace analysis. This includes in-situ modules which run locally in each compute node and perform pre-processing and analysis of local data before storing them in the monitoring database. The advantage of this technique is that part of the analysis workload is off loaded to the compute nodes which provide an additional level of real-time processing much closer to the data source. The log filtering module enables LADT to detect VM operations on the node such as creation of a new VM or migration of a VM. It also allows detection of erroneous entries inside the log files. The filtering module is assessing the number of these occurrences over a selected time period and registers to the database a statistical number of them along with a timestamp. In this way, only a few entries are required to be recorded in the database, instead of a full log record. To analyse the stored information in HBase, we use a Lightweight Anomaly Detection Tool (LADT) which is currently based on the apache Spark framework. The Spark framework has an advanced DAG execution engine that supports cyclic data flow and in-memory computing. It is a fast and general engine for large-scale data processing. LADT runs the metrics correlation analysis on the stored metrics between the node-level and VM-level metrics to detect anomalies. It then takes the mean values of the metric samples in 15-s windows. The program groups the mean values into 5-min windows and calculates the Pearson Correlation Coefficient between the node-level and VM-level metrics in each group. Finally, the program compares the correlation coefficient value with the threshold value and generates an anomaly alarm if it finds the coefficient value is below an adjustable threshold level. Any potential alerts are then validated by checking for any log entries coming from VM activities such as new VM creation. A VM action could consume host resources which are not yet registered as VM utilisation and therefore indicate a false alarm. However, the log analysis can provides us with valuable information about any ongoing VM activities.

4   LADT Hypothesis and Algorithm

The underlying approach of LADT is based on the premise of the LFD technique, which identifies two metrics that are correlated during normal operation but diverge in the presence of an anomaly.

4.1   LFD: The Baseline Method

LFD is a lightweight technique for anomaly detection proposed by Tan et al. [3]. The hypothesis of LFD is that in an anomaly-free system, whenever an application requests service, the processing alternates between two phases: the communication phase and the compute phase. In the communication phase, the application responds to requests received from the user, reads data from the disk, or writes data to the disk. In the compute phase, the application operates on the received inputs or requests. At the operational level, the compute phase is characterised by user-space CPU activity, whereas the communication phase is characterised by the behaviour of one or more types of system-level resource consumption, including kernel-space CPU time, disk I/O or network I/O. Behavioural change between the two phases results in a correlation between user-space CPU utilisation and system resource consumption. The LFD also hypothesises that in the case of an anomaly, there will be a significant change in the relationship between the compute phase and the communication phase. Hence, there will be lack of correlation between user-space CPU utilisation and system resource consumption, based on which anomalies can be detected in the system.

4.2 LADT Hypothesis

LADT formulates a new hypothesis, according to which there is strong correlation between the node-level and VM-level metrics in a Cloud system. Also, that this correlation will drop significantly in the event of any performance anomaly at the node-level and a continuous drop in the correlation can indicate the presence of a true anomaly in the node.

4.3 LADT Algorithm

We propose a new algorithm based on LFD, to correlate node-level and VM-level metrics. We use disk I/O metrics as a running example. The algorithm correlates disk I/O between the hosting node and the VMs in order to detect anomalies in IaaS Cloud environments. LADT computes the Pearson correlation coefficient (ρ) between the hosting node disk IOPS and the aggregated VM disk IOPS. Pearson's correlation coefficient is the ratio of the covariance between the two metrics to the product of their standard deviations as described in Eq. 1 and ranges between -1.0 and 1.0.

$$\rho_{N,V} = \frac{covariance(N,V)}{\sigma_N \sigma_V} \qquad (1)$$

where

$N =$ time-series of node disk IOPS
$V =$ time-series of VM disk IOPS

Similar to the LFD algorithm, there are five tunable parameters in the LADT algorithm, which are summarised in Table 1. LADT collects raw disk I/O metrics with a 3 s period from both the nodes and VMs. The metrics collection period is set to more than a second in order to mitigate the timestamp synchronisation problem between the node-level and VM-level metrics, which arises as a result of latency in storing VM-level metrics in the LADT monitoring server. Before calculating the correlation coefficient between the metrics, their mean values are taken in small windows ($LW = 5$) in order to reduce noise. An anomaly alarm is raised when the average of D consecutive values of the correlation coefficient drops below the threshold T in order to detect the true anomalies by considering a larger range of system behaviour.

Table 1. Tunable parameters in LADT Algorithm.

LW, low-pass window width	Raw samples to take mean
LS, low-pass window slide	Raw samples to slide
W, correlation window width	Samples to correlate
S, correlation window slide	Samples to slide detection window
D, diagnosis window	Correlation coefficients to consider

We keep the same parameter values as the LFD algorithm for four parameters ($LW = 5, LS = 5, W = 60, D = 10$) [3], which we experimentally found to achieve best performance. However, the correlation window slide, S is changed from 12 to 60 as this amortises better the overhead of a Spark program, which is used to execute the LADT algorithm. Therefore, each correlation coefficient value considers the last $LW \times W = 300\,s$ (5 min) of system behaviour.

4.4 Console Log Analysis

In a cloud data centre which supports automatic management of the resources, there is a series of different actions happening on the background in order to achieve different goals set by the operator, some of the most important goals are to keep the workload balanced, maintain Service Level Agreements (SLAs) and optimise energy consumption. These macroscopic targets imply certain VM actions happening on each node of the cloud. The following are some examples of a VM action on a node: migration, new VM creation, suspend, terminate, resize. The VM actions and any potential errors on a node are registered into different log files. The amount of information on the log file and the large number of nodes included in a cloud platform makes it difficult for cloud operators to track important events.

Tracking VM actions efficiently is important for the analysis of the system performance and allows cloud data centre operators to manage their platform. In order for a VM action to complete, it requires different amount of resources before it boots up. For example, creating a new instance on a node would require claiming memory, disk and VCPUs from the node by the VM. It would also create a temporal network and disk I/O bandwidth consumption on the node for the VM image to be transferred. All the aforementioned resource demands could cause an analysis on the node to lead to faulty results if they are not taken into account. For this reason we examine coupling the parallel correlation analysis of LADT with the functionality of a cloud log tracking mechanism to reduce any false positives by the detection mechanism (Fig. 2).

The procedure of log processing is displayed in Fig. 16. The process starts from each compute node of the cloud data centre where the log file is generated. A text analysis module is triggered periodically by an agent resided in each node. The module is tailing the file for the logs of the most recent time interval. Then it searches for a set of specific patterns of words and phrases that indicated certain

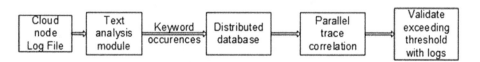

Fig. 2. One kernel at x_s (*dotted kernel*) or two kernels at x_i and x_j (*left and right*) lead to the same summed estimate at x_s. This shows a figure consisting of different types of lines. Elements of the figure described in the caption should be set in italics, in parentheses, as shown in this sample caption.

VM actions or errors. For example, the phrase Attempting claim: memory X MB, disk Y GB, VCPUs Z indicates that a new VM allocation is in progress on the current node. Other examples of interesting occurrences are: Instance destroyed successfully, Migrating instance to X finished successfully, QEMU: error. These occurrences are then organised into an HBase row-key with the key time_period-node and a column family VMActions which has different columns such as Placement and migration. Each of these columns has a value equal to the number of occurrences that placement and migration related keywords/phrases appeared during the period and by the node marked by the row-key. In this way the actual log files are filtered and only a statistical row-key is recorded in the datastore. Part of the information in the log file is unique and contains information relevant to the service that produced the log. This means that it is difficult to retrieve this information by another way, since this information might not be available elsewhere. The LADT tool performs the correlation analysis using Spark and in the case of detected anomalies it tries to validate them by looking on the entries of the related period to see if these alarms are justified by other VM management activities on the current node.

5   Experimental Evaluation

This section describes the workload and the experimental set-up used to evaluate LADT. The section also analyses our experimental results and the functionality of the LADT tool.

5.1   Experimental Set-Up

To test the functionality of our tool we used a compute node from an OpenStack cloud testbed. The host is a Dell PowerEdge R420 server which runs CentOS 6.6 and has 6 cores, 2-way hyper-threaded, clocked at 2.20 GHz with 12 GB DRAM clocked at 1600 MHz. The node includes two 7.2K RPM hard drives with 1 TB of SATA in RAID 0 and a single 1GBE port. KVM is the default hypervisor of the node. The sampling rate of the performance metrics from the node is one measurement every 3 s. The node level metrics are generated using Sigar (Sigar, 2015) and the vm-level metrics are generated from Virt-Top (Virt-Top, 2015).

Four active instances on the node are running the Data Serving and the Graph Analytics benchmark from Cloud-Suite [23]. The Data Serving benchmark relies on the use of Cassandra, an open-source NoSQL datastore, stimulated by the Yahoo! Cloud Serving Benchmark. YCSB is a framework to benchmark data store systems. This framework comes with the interfaces to populate and stress many popular data serving systems. The second benchmark from Cloud-Suite is the Graph Analytics benchmark which uses the GraphLab machine learning and data mining software. Graph Analytics performs data analysis on large-scale graphs, using a distributed graph-processing system. Graph Analytics becomes increasingly important with the emergence of social networks such as Facebook and Twitter. The graph analytics benchmark implements TunkRank on GraphLab, which provides the influence of a Twitter user based on the number of that user's followers.

The experiment runs over a time period of 60 min, where we inject an anomaly in the node at the end of the first 30 min using a disk and CPU stressing application, which periodically increases the disk read/write operations and CPU load runs for the remaining 30 min. This anomaly reflects a Blue Pill or a Virtual Machine Based Rootkit (VMBR) attack on a Cloud system, where the attacker introduces fake VMs via a hidden hypervisor on the victim hosting node to get access to the hardware resources such as CPU, memory, network or disk [24]. Research such as [25] has already used system resource-level anomaly analysis to deal with such attacks. That research analyses system resource utilisation to explore the normal system behaviour and builds a model, based on which it detects the abnormal behaviours in the system, and subsequently, the attacks. However, this approach of detecting the attacks requires a large amount of historical data and use of machine learning techniques. LADT can detect the attacks using the correlation analysis between the node-level and the VM-level metrics. LADT is implemented in the testbed, which uses Chukwa agents in each of the hosting nodes to collect both the hosting node and VM disk read/write metrics. The tool stores the collected metrics in the HBase running in the monitoring node, which is a dual AMD Opteron 6272 server. Finally, in the monitoring node, LADT analyses the stored metrics by running the algorithm, which calculates the correlation between the individual hosting node metrics and the aggregated performance measurements of all the VMs in that node, to detect the injected anomaly. Current implementation of LADT is based on Spark, which has an advanced DAG execution engine that supports cyclic data flow and in-memory computing. It is a fast and general engine for large-scale data processing. Spark uses the concept of resilient distributed datasets (RDD), which represent a read-only collection of objects partitioned across a set of machines that can be rebuilt if a partition is lost. Users can explicitly cache an RDD in memory across machines and reuse it in multiple MapReduce-like parallel operations.

5.2 Results and Discussion

In Figs. 6 and 7 we illustrate the data collected for the CPU utilisation and Input/Output Operations Per Second(IOPS) of the hosting node (blue line) and the aggregated VM CPU utilisation and IOPS (red line) respectively. We present the normalised values of the IOPS, which are the mean values in small windows of 15 s, including 5 samples of metrics data (the frequency of metrics collection is 3 s). The correlation coefficient values are calculated in correlation windows of 5 min, covering 5 min of metrics data. Hence, there are 12 correlation intervals in the 60 min of experiment. The fault injection in both cases appears after 30 min. In the case of IOPS, the node IOPS appear to be higher than the aggregated VM IOPS because of the overhead that is inflicted by the extra software layer of the hypervisor, which is interposed between guest operating systems and hardware [26]. The hypervisor multiplexes I/O devices by requiring guest operating systems to access the real hardware indirectly and hence induces an overhead in the I/O context. The IOPS measurements are also taken with a different tool in each case (virt-top and Sigar), which means that the accuracy of each tool might differ. However, the correlation trace analysis is not significantly affected by these factors, since the major factor is the pattern and the relation of the two measurements.

The correlation analysis for CPU utilisation and IOPS in Figs. 8 and 9 respectively, clearly shows that there is a strong correlation between the hosting node metrics and the aggregated metrics of the VMs for the first half of the experiment, where the correlation coefficient values are above 0.5. However the correlation value drops below 0.0 suddenly at the tenth interval when the fault injection starts. The coefficient value remains very low during the injected anomaly. We consider correlation coefficient values above 0.5 (marked with red line) to indicate a strong correlation in this case. This is a clear reflection of the injected anomaly in the host node, which distorts the correlation in both cases of CPU utilisation and IOPS.

The time taken to process one hour of collected data with a different number of assigned cores is presented in Figs. 10 and 11. We observed experimentally that different runs did not yield any significant difference in execution time. The first figure is giving us the execution time that is needed for the section of the program that does the analysis on the collected data. This section does not include loading the values from HBase into proper structures that can be processed by Hadoop or Spark. The reason we exclude this part in the first figure is that it cannot be simply parallelised by just adding more working cores to the node and the procedure can be limited by having to access the data from the nodes disk. This becomes clearer when we do a comparison with Fig. 11 where we realise that there is a fixed difference between the graphs of the two figures which remains the same for different number of cores. Another observation based on the number of assigned cores is that the performance of the tool is improving while adding up to 8 cores, but remains the same for 16 cores. The throughput of LADT is depicted in Figs. 13 and 14. In the first case we calculate the throughput in terms of total HBase rowkeys processed per second when we consider only the data processing part of the application. The second case is showing the number of records processed per second if we include loading the data from HBase into structures which can be processed by Spark.

5.3   Textual Log Analysis

In the following section we examine the effect of a new VM placement on the node. We identify any correlation drops and examine if these are justified by any activities that are recorded by the text analysis tool. We also analyse any overhead that the text analysis adds to the LADT tool (Figs. 3, 4 and 5).

The graphs in Figs. 17 and 18 present the CPU utilisation and IOPS for the node and the VMs. In the case of the VMs the measurements are aggregated for all the active VMs. In this scenario, we examine the correlation analysis using the Spark implementation of the extended LADT under the influence of a new VM allocation and an injected anomaly occurring at two different time frames.

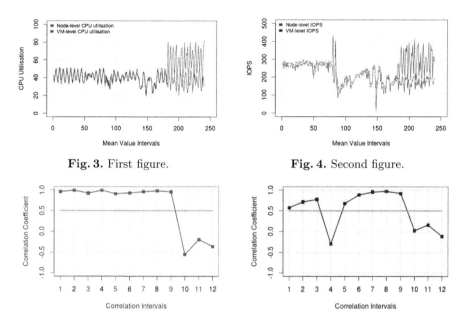

Fig. 3. First figure.   **Fig. 4.** Second figure.

Fig. 5. First figure (Color figure online).

Fig. 6. Second figure (Color figure online).

The VM allocation is taking place after 15 min and the fault injection is happening on the 45th min. The VM allocation requires only a few minutes (approximately 5 min) to be fulfilled in this case. The parallel trace analysis tool is examining the correlation results (Figs. 19 and 20) along with the HBase records of the VM placement. We notice that the first occasion where the correlation values for the IOPs (Fig. 20) drops is when the VM placement takes place (at the 4rth time interval of Fig. 21). The correlation drop is explained if we consider that the VM allocation required a significant amount of disk to store the new VM instance. In the case of the correlation analysis of the CPU utilisation in Fig. 19, we observe that the correlation values remain above the 0.5 threshold during the allocation of the new VM on the node. The reason is that the process of allocating the new VM does not require significant amount of CPU utilisation. Therefore, the correlation analysis of the CPU utilisation remains unaffected. The second drop in Fig. 20 is matching the appearance of the injected fault. The same fault also affects the CPU correlation in Fig. 19 and there is no indicated VM action in Fig. 21. Furthermore, the duration of the fault is longer that the VM allocation correlation drop and also affects both IOPS and CPU utilisation. All these factors are indicating that this is an actual anomaly instead of a false positive generated by normal cloud operation activity. We conclude that the analysis of textual log files plays an important role in deciding whether an anomaly alert is true or just a false positive.

148   S. Barbhuiya et al.

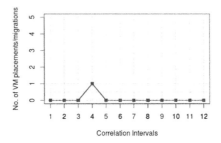

Fig. 7. One kernel at x_s (*dotted kernel*) or two kernels at x_i and x_j (*left and right*) lead to the same summed estimate at x_s. This shows a figure consisting of different types of lines. Elements of the figure described in the caption should be set in italics, in parentheses, as shown in this sample caption (Color figure online).

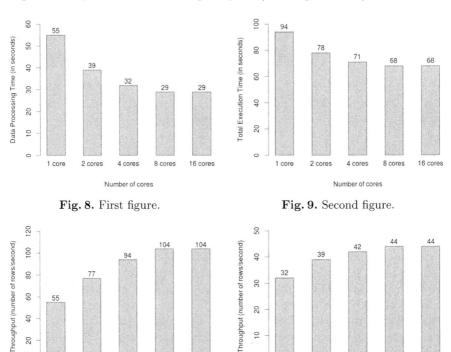

Fig. 8. First figure.

Fig. 9. Second figure.

Fig. 10. First figure.

Fig. 11. Second figure.

5.4 LADT Overhead

Our next experiment assesses LADT in terms of the overhead that it introduces on hosted application VMs, because of the LADT agents that collect metrics simultaneously with the execution of application workloads. To investigate this we executed a test where a single VM runs a data serving benchmark for the duration of 10000 data operations with a rate of 200 operations/sec. With an agent running concurrently with the data serving benchmark, and during an execution interval of 50 s, the average update and read latencies of the benchmark were 0.21 ms and 8.28 ms, respectively. With no agent running and during the same 50 s execution interval, the average update and read latencies were 0.21 ms and 6.97 ms, respectively. In both cases we observed the expected response time from the benchmark and any differences observed in the average latencies of the update and read operations were justified by the variability introduced by the storage medium.

5.5   Further Analysis

We observe that during normal operation there is a strong correlation between the node disk IOPS and aggregated disk IOPS of the VMs. However, the correlation becomes weaker during some intervals for short periods. This happens because in these intervals the overhead on the VM I/O operations resulting from accessing the disk indirectly via the hypervisor [26] rises unpredictably and degrades the VM IOPS with respect to the corresponding node IOPS. Although the correlation coefficient value drops in some intervals even when the hosts are in a stable expected state, this drop is not as significant as it is in the case of an anomaly. Moreover, the correlation coefficient average drops below 0 when an anomaly occurs, whereas the average coefficient value ranges between 0.5 and 1 when the hosts are anomaly-free.

   We conclude that the correlation coefficient values require normalisation in order to avoid false alarms for anomaly, which could arise because of a fluctuation in the overhead on VM IOPS. We detect the true anomalies by considering a larger period of system behaviour and this is done by taking the average of D consecutive coefficient values and checking if it is below the threshold value, T. The values of T and D depend on how often the user wishes to get an alarm for the anomalies. From the results, we observe the anomaly as the security attack when the correlation coefficient value drops significantly and stays low for a longer period of time.

6   Conclusion and Future Work

We presented LADT, a lightweight anomaly detection tool for Cloud data centres. LADT is based on the hypothesis that, in an anomaly-free Cloud data centre, there is a strong correlation between the node-level and VM-level performance metrics and that this correlation diminishes significantly in the case of abnormal behaviour at the node-level. The LADT algorithm raises an anomaly alarm when the correlation coefficient value between the node-level and VM-level metrics drops below a threshold level. We have demonstrated a lightweight distributed implementation of LADT using Chukwa and also demonstrated that the tool can detect node-level disk performance anomalies by correlating the hosting node IOPS with the aggregated hosted VM IOPS. Such anomalies may arise as a result of security attacks such as distributed denial-of-service (DDoS). We also demonstrated that LADT introduces acceptably low overhead, while recognizing that the implementation is amenable to optimisation along the entire path of metrics collection, data aggregation and analysis.

We intend to conduct a detailed analysis of possible attack models of the system. LADT can also detect CPU/memory/network related performance anomalies, due to the performance implications of virtualisation and resource management software stacks. We wish to explore these anomalies in more detail, using both controlled and uncontrolled set-ups (i.e. production-level set-ups with unseen anomalies) in our Cloud testbed. We plan to conduct a more thorough analysis of LADT performance, scalability and intrusion minimisation with respect to the hosted VMs. We are particularly interested in co-executing VMs with diverse characteristics (e.g. CPU-intensive, I/O-intensive), and latency sensitivity. Our aim is to understand whether adapting parameters such as the number of agent adaptors in the hosts, the frequency of data collection per VM in the hosts and the number of data aggregation tasks and cores used by collectors is necessary to keep the monitoring overhead low.

References

1. Lou, J.G., Fu, Q., Yang, S., Xu, Y., Li, J.: Mining invariants from console logs for system problem detection. In: Proceedings of the 2010 USENIX Conference on USENIX Annual Technical Conference, USENIXATC 2010, pp. 24–24. USENIX Association, Berkeley, CA, USA (2010)
2. Xu, W., Huang, L., Fox, A., Patterson, D., Jordan, M.I.: Detecting large-scale system problems by mining console logs. In: Proceedings of the ACM SIGOPS 22nd Symposium on Operating Systems Principles, SOSP 2009, pp. 117–132. ACM, New York, NY, USA (2009)
3. Tan, J., Kavulya, S., Gandhi, R., Narasimhan, P.: Light-weight black-box failure detection for distributed systems. In: Proceedings of the 2012 Workshop on Management of Big Data Systems, MBDS 2012, pp. 13–18. ACM, New York (2012)
4. Wang, C.: Ebat: Online methods for detecting utility cloud anomalies. In: Proceedings of the 6th Middleware Doctoral Symposium, MDS 2009, pp. 4:1–4:6. ACM, New York (2009)
5. Ward, J.S., Barker, A.: Varanus: In situ monitoring for large scale cloud systems. In: Proceedings of the 2013 IEEE International Conference on Cloud Computing Technology and Science, CLOUDCOM 2013, Computer Society, vol. 02, pp. 341–344. IEEE, Washington, DC (2013)
6. Kang, H., Chen, H., Jiang, G.: Peerwatch: a fault detection and diagnosis tool for virtualized consolidation systems. In: Proceedings of the 7th International Conference on Autonomic Computing, ICAC 2010, pp. 119–128. ACM, New York (2010)
7. Jiang, M., Munawar, M.A., Reidemeister, T., Ward, P.A.: System monitoring with metric-correlation models: problems and solutions. In: Proceedings of the 6th International Conference on Autonomic Computing, ICAC 2009, pp. 13–22. ACM, New York (2009)

8. Barbhuiya, S., Papazachos, Z., Kilpatrick, P., Nikolopoulos, D.: In: A Lightweight Tool for Anomaly Detection in Cloud Data Centres, SCITEPRESS Digital Library, pp. 343–351 (2015)
9. Olston, C., Reed, B., Srivastava, U., Kumar, R., Tomkins, A.: Pig latin: a not-so-foreign language for data processing. In: Proceedings of the 2008 ACM SIGMOD International Conference on Management of Data, SIGMOD 2008, pp. 1099–1110. ACM, New York (2008)
10. Oppenheimer, D., Ganapathi, A., Patterson, D.A.: Why do internet services fail, and what can be done about it? In: Proceedings of the 4th Conference on USENIX Symposium on Internet Technologies and Systems, USITS 2003, vol. 4, p. 1. USENIX Association, Berkeley, CA, USA (2003)
11. Kumar, V., Cooper, B.F., Eisenhauer, G., Schwan, K.: iManage: policy-driven self-management for enterprise-scale systems. In: Cerqueira, R., Campbell, R.H. (eds.) Middleware 2007. LNCS, vol. 4834, pp. 287–307. Springer, Heidelberg (2007)
12. Pertet, S., Narasimhan, P.: Causes of failure in web applications. Technical report, CMU-PDL-05-109 (2005)
13. Kephart, J.O., Chess, D.M.: The vision of autonomic computing. Computer **36**, 41–50 (2003)
14. Rouillard, J.P.: Refereed papers: real-time log file analysis using the simple event correlator (sec). In: Proceedings of the 18th USENIX Conference on System Administration, LISA 2004, pp. 133–150. USENIX Association, Berkeley, CA, USA (2004)
15. Prewett, J.E.: Analyzing cluster log files using logsurfer. In: in Proceedings of the 4th Annual Conference on Linux Clusters (2003)
16. Hansen, S.E., Atkins, E.T.: Automated system monitoring and notification with swatch. In: Proceedings of the 7th USENIX Conference on System Administration, LISA 1993, pp. 145–152. USENIX Association, Berkeley, CA, USA (1993)
17. Azmandian, F., Moffie, M., Alshawabkeh, M., Dy, J., Aslam, J., Kaeli, D.: Virtual machine monitor-based lightweight intrusion detection. ACM SIGOPS Operating Syst. Rev. **45**, 38–53 (2011)
18. Rabkin, A., Katz, R.: Chukwa: a system for reliable large-scale log collection. In: Proceedings of the 24th International Conference on Large Installation System Administration, LISA 2010, pp. 1–15. USENIX Association, Berkeley, CA, USA (2010)
19. Vora, M.: Hadoop-hbase for large-scale data. In: 2011 International Conference on Computer Science and Network Technology (ICCSNT), vol. 1, pp. 601–605 (2011)
20. Sigar: https://support.hyperic.com/display/sigar (2014)
21. Virt-Top: http://virt-tools.org/about/ (2014)
22. Shvachko, K., Kuang, H., Radia, S., Chansler, R.: The hadoop distributed file system. In: Proceedings of the 2010 IEEE 26th Symposium on Mass Storage Systems and Technologies (MSST), MSST 2010, Computer Society, pp. 1–10. IEEE, Washington, DC (2010)
23. Ferdman, M., Adileh, A., Kocberber, O., Volos, S., Alisafaee, M., Jevdjic, D., Kaynak, C., Popescu, A.D., Ailamaki, A., Falsafi, B.: Clearing the clouds: a study of emerging scale-out workloads on modern hardware. In: Proceedings of the Seventeenth International Conference on Architectural Support for Programming Languages and Operating Systems, ASPLOS 2012, pp. 37–48. ACM, New York (2012)
24. Dahbur, K., Mohammad, B., Tarakji, A.B.: A survey of risks, threats and vulnerabilities in cloud computing. In: Proceedings of the 2011 International Conference on Intelligent Semantic Web-Services and Applications, ISWSA 2011, pp. 12:1–12:6. ACM, New York (2011)

25. Antunes, J., Neves, N., Verissimo, P.: Detection and prediction of resource-exhaustion vulnerabilities. In: 19th International Symposium on Software Reliability Engineering, ISSRE 2008, pp. 87–96 (2008)
26. Li, D., Jin, H., Liao, X., Zhang, Y., Zhou, B.: Improving disk i/o performance in a virtualized system. J. Comput. Syst. Sci. **79**, 187–200 (2013)

Performance and Cost Trade-Off in IaaS Environments: A Scientific Workflow Simulation Environment Case Study

Santiago Gómez Sáez[✉], Vasilios Andrikopoulos, Michael Hahn,
Dimka Karastoyanova, Frank Leymann, Marigianna Skouradaki,
and Karolina Vukojevic-Haupt

Institute of Architecture of Application Systems, University of Stuttgart,
Stuttgart, Germany
{gomez-saez,andrikopoulos,hahn,karastoyanova,leymann,skouradaki,
vukojevic}@iaas.uni-stuttgart.de

Abstract. The adoption of the workflow technology in the eScience domain has contributed to the increase of simulation-based applications orchestrating different services in a flexible and error-free manner. The nature of the provisioning and execution of such simulations makes them potential candidates to be migrated and executed in Cloud environments. The wide availability of Infrastructure-as-a-Service (IaaS) Cloud offerings and service providers has contributed to a raise in the number of supporters of partially or completely migrating and running their scientific experiments in the Cloud. Focusing on Scientific Workflow-based Simulation Environments (SWfSE) applications and their corresponding underlying runtime support, in this research work we aim at empirically analyzing and evaluating the impact of migrating such an environment to multiple IaaS infrastructures. More specifically, we focus on the investigation of multiple Cloud providers and their corresponding optimized and non-optimized IaaS offerings with respect to their offered performance, and its impact on the incurred monetary costs when migrating and executing a SWfSE. The experiments show significant performance improvements and reduced monetary costs when executing the simulation environment in off-premise Clouds.

Keywords: Workflow simulation · eScience · Iaas · Performance evaluation · Cost evaluation · Cloud migration

1 Introduction

The introduction and adoption of the workflow technology has been widely noticed in the last years in several domains, such as business or eScience. Reasons that contributed towards such direction are its offered high level abstraction, design, and runtime flexibility, and the continuous development of the necessary middleware support for enabling its execution [1]. Such a technology has

© Springer International Publishing Switzerland 2016
M. Helfert et al. (Eds.): CLOSER 2015, CCIS 581, pp. 153–170, 2016.
DOI: 10.1007/978-3-319-29582-4_9

encompassed the fulfillment of different domain-specific requirements in terms of enforced functionalities and expected behavior of the underlying infrastructure for different types of applications. Focusing on eScience applications as the foundations for the case study evaluation driving this work, simulation workflows are a well-known research area, as they provide scientists with the means to model, provision, and execute automated and flexible long running simulation-based experiments [2]. Ordinary simulation-based experiments typically enclose the following characteristics: (i) the gathering and processing of large amounts of data, (ii) the transfer and consumption at irregular time intervals of multiple distributed simulation services during (iii) long periods of time. Due to the access and resource consumption behaviour exhibited by such services, previous works have targeted the migration and adaptation of such environments. These environments can be deployed, provisioned, and executed in Cloud infrastructures in order to optimize the provisioning and usage of computational resources, while minimizing incurred monetary costs [3–6].

The introduction and adoption of Cloud computing in different domains has contributed in the creation and expansion of existing and new Cloud services and providers. Nowadays, the number of applications partially or completely running in different *Everything*-as-a-Service Cloud offerings has substantially increased. The existence of a wide variety of Cloud services offering different and frequently optimized Quality of Service (QoS) characteristics has introduced a broadened landscape of alternatives for selecting, configuring, and provisioning Cloud resources. These offer the possibility to host the different application components with special resources consumption patterns in a distributed manner, e.g. computationally or memory intensive ones in compute optimized or memory optimized virtualized resources, respectively. However, such a wide spectrum of possibilities has become a challenge for application developers for deciding among the different Cloud providers and their corresponding services.

Previous works targeted such a challenge by assisting application developers in the tasks related to selecting, configuring, and adapting the distribution of their application among multiple services [4,7]. Previous findings identify the existence of multiple decision points that can influence the distribution of an application, e.g. cost, performance, security concerns, etc. [8]. This work incorporates such findings towards the development of the necessary support for assessing application developers in the selection and configuration of Infrastructure-as-a-Service (IaaS) offerings for migrating scientific applications to the Cloud. More specifically, the focus of this research work is to provide an overview, evaluate, and analyze the trade-off between the performance and cost when migrating a Scientific Workflow-based Simulation Environment (SWfSE) to different Cloud providers and their corresponding IaaS offerings.

The contributions of this work build upon the research work presented in [9], and can be summarized as follows:

- the selection of a set of viable and optimized IaaS offerings for migrating a previously developed simulation environment,
- a price analysis of the previously selected IaaS offerings,

- an empirical evaluation focusing on the performance and the incurred monetary costs, and
- an analysis of the performance and cost trade-off when scaling the simulation environment workload.

The rest of this work is structured as follows: Sect. 2 motivates this work and frame the challenges that will be addressed. The case study simulation environment used for evaluating this work is introduced in Sect. 3. Section 4 presents the experiments on evaluating the performance and incurred costs when migrating the simulation environment to different IaaS offerings, and discusses our findings. Finally, Sect. 5 summarizes related work, and Sect. 6 concludes and presents our plans for future work.

2   Motivation and Problem Statement

Simulation workflows, a well-known topic in the field of eScience, describe the automated and flexible execution of simulation-based experiments. Common characteristics of such simulation workflows are that they are long-running as well as being executed in an irregular manner. However, during their execution a wide amount of resources are typically provisioned, consumed, and released. Considering these characteristics, previous works focused on migrating and executing simulation environments in the Cloud, as Cloud infrastructures significantly reduce infrastructure costs while coping with an irregular but heavy demand of resources for running such experiments [5].

Nowadays there exists a vast amount of configurable Cloud offerings among multiple Cloud providers. However, such a wide landscape has become a challenge for deciding among (i) the different Cloud providers and (ii) the multiple Cloud offering configurations offered by such providers. We focus in this work on IaaS solutions, as there exists a lack of Platform-as-a-service (PaaS) offerings that enable the deployment and execution of scientific workflows in the Cloud. IaaS offerings describe the amount and type of allocated resources, e.g. CPUs, memory, or storage, and define different VM instance types within different categories. For example, the Amazon EC2[1] service does not only offer VM instances of different size, but also provides different VM categories which are optimized for different use cases, e.g. computation intensive, memory intensive, or I/O intensive. Similar offerings are available also by other providers, such as Windows Azure[2] or Rackspace[3]. The offered performance and incurred cost significantly vary among the different Cloud services, and depend on the simulation environment resource usage requirements and workload. In this work, we aim to analyze the performance and cost trade-off when migrating to different Cloud offerings a simulation environment developed and used as case study, as discussed in the following section.

---

[1] Amazon EC2: http://aws.amazon.com/ec2/instance-types/.

[2] Windows Azure: http://azure.microsoft.com/en-us/.

[3] Rackspace: http://www.rackspace.com/.

3   The OPAL Simulation Environment

A Scientific Workflow Management System (SimTech SWfMS) is being developed by the Cluster of Excellence in Simulation Technology (SimTech[4]), enabling scientists to model and execute their simulation experiments using workflows [2,10]. The SimTech SWfMS is based on conventional workflow technology which offers several non-functional requirements like robustness, scalability, reusability, and sophisticated fault and exception handling [11]. The system has been adapted and extended to the special needs of the scientists in the eScience domain [10]. During the execution of a workflow instance the system supports the modification of the corresponding workflow model, which is then propagated to the running instances. This allows running simulation experiments in a trial-and-error manner.

The main components of the SimTech SWfMS shown in Fig. 1 are a modeling and monitoring tool, a workflow engine, a messaging system, several databases, an auditing system, and an application server running simulation services. The workflow engine provides an execution environment for the workflows. The messaging system serves as communication layer between the modeling- and monitoring tool, the workflow engine, and the auditing system. The auditing system stores data related to the workflow execution for analytical and provenance purposes.

The SimTech SWfMS has been successfully applied in different scenarios in the eScience domain; one example is the automation of a Kinetic Monte-Carlo (KMC) simulation of solid bodies by orchestrating several Web services being implemented by modules of the OPAL application [13]. The OPAL Simulation Environment is constituted by a set of services which are

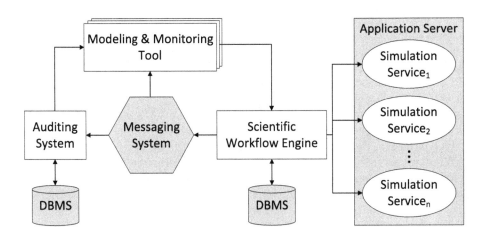

Fig. 1. System overview of the SimTech Scientific Workflow Management System (SWfMS).

---

[4] SimTech: http://www.iaas.uni-stuttgart.de/forschung/projects/simtech/.

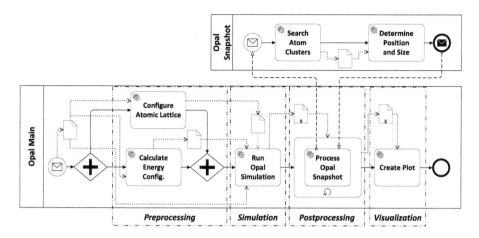

Fig. 2. Simplified simulation workflows constituting the OPAL simulation environment [12].

controlled and orchestrated through a main OPAL workflow (the *Opal Main* process depicted in Fig. 2). The simulation services are implemented as Web services and divided into two main categories: (i) resource management, e.g. distributing the workload among the different servers, and (ii) wrapped simulation packages depicted in [14,15]. The main workflow can be divided in four phases as shown in Fig. 2: preprocessing, simulation, postprocessing, and visualization. During the preprocessing phase all data needed for the simulation is prepared. In the simulation phase the workflow starts the Opal simulation by invoking the corresponding Web service. In regular intervals, the Opal simulation creates intermediate results (snapshots). For each of these snapshots the main workflow initiates the postprocessing which is realized as a separate workflow (*Opal Snapshot* process in Fig. 2). When the simulation is finished and all intermediate results are postprocessed, the results of the simulation are visualized.

4   Experiments

4.1   Methodology

As shown in Fig. 2, the OPAL Simulation Environment is comprised of multiple services and workflows that compose the simulation and resource management services. The environment can be concurrently used by multiple users, as the simulation data isolation is guaranteed through the creation of independent instances (workflows, services, and temporal storage units) for each user's simulation request. The experiments must therefore consider and emulate the usage of the environment by multiple users concurrently.

The migration of the simulation environment to the Cloud opens a wide set of viable possibilities for selecting and configuring different Cloud services for the different components of the OPAL environment. However, in this first set of

Table 1. IaaS Ubuntu Linux On-demand instances categories per provider (in January 2015) for the European (Germany - DE, and Ireland - IRL) and USA regions.

Instance Category	Cloud Provider	Instance Type	vCPU	Memory (GB)	Region	Price (US$/h)
Micro	on-premise	micro	1	1	EU (DE)	0.13
	AWS EC2	t2.micro	1	1	EU (IRL)	0.014
	Windows Azure	A1	1	1.75	EU (IRL)	0.06
	Rackspace	General 1	1	1	USA	0.06
General Purpose	on-premise	large	2	4	EU (DE)	0.26
	AWS EC2	m3.large	2	7.5	EU (IR)	0.154
	Windows Azure	A2	2	3.5	EU (IR)	0.12
	Rackspace	General 2	2	2	USA	0.074
Compute Optimized	on-premise	compute3.large	4	4	EU (DE)	0.52
	AWS EC2	c3.large	2	3.75	EU (IRL)	0.120
	Windows Azure	D2	2	7	EU (IRL)	0.23
	Rackspace	Compute 1-3.75	2	3.75	USA	0.1332
Memory Optimized	on-premise	memory4.large	2	15	EU (DE)	0.26
	AWS EC2	r3.large	2	15.25	EU (IRL)	0.195
	Windows Azure	D3	4	14	EU (IRL)	0.46
	Rackspace	Memory 1-15	2	15	USA	0.2522

experiments we restrict the distribution of the simulation environment components by hosting the complete simulation application stack in one VM, which is made accessible to multiple users. Future investigations plan to distribute such environment using different Cloud offerings, e.g. Database-as-a-Service (DBaaS) for hosting the auditing databases. We therefore focus this work on *driving a performance and cost analysis when executing the OPAL Simulation Environment in on- and off-premise infrastructures, and using different IaaS offerings and optimized configurations.*

Table 1 shows the different VM categories, based on their characteristics and offered prices by three major Cloud providers: Amazon AWS, Windows Azure, and Rackspace. In addition to the off-premise VM instances types, multiple on-premise VM instances types were created in our virtualized environment, configured in a similar manner to the ones evaluated in the off-premise scenarios, and included in such categories. The on-premise VM instances configurations are based on the closest equivalent to the off-premise VM configurations within each instance category. The encountered providers and offerings showed two levels of VM categories, i.e. based on the optimization for custom use cases (*Micro, General Use, Compute Optimized,* and *Memory optimized*), and based on a quantitative assignment of virtualized resources. This fact must be taken into consideration in our evaluation due to the variation in the performance, and its impact on the final incurred costs for running simulations in different Cloud offerings. The pricing model for the on-premise scenarios was adopted from [16] as discussed in the following section, while for the off-premise scenarios the publicly available information from the providers was used [17], taking into account on-demand pricing models only.

4.2 Setup

The scientific workflow simulation environment is constituted by two main systems: the SimTech SWfMS [2,10], and a set of Web services grouping the resource management and the KMC simulation tasks depicted in [14,15]. The former comprises the following middleware stack:

- an Apache Orchestration Director Engine (ODE) 1.3.5 (Axis2 distribution) deployed on
- an Apache Tomcat 7.0.54 server with Axis2 support.
- The scientific workflow engine (Apache ODE) utilizes a MySQL server 5.5 for workflow administration, management, and reliability purposes, and
- provides monitoring and auditing information through an Apache ActiveMQ 5.3.2 messaging server.

The resource management and KMC simulation services are deployed as Axis2 services in an Apache Tomcat 7.0.54 server. The underlying on- and off-premise infrastructure configurations selected for the experiments are shown in Table 1. The on-premise infrastructure aggregates an IBM System x3755 M3 server[5] with an AMD Opteron Processor 6134 exposing 16 CPU of speed 2.30 GHz and 65 GB RAM. In all scenarios the previously depicted middleware components are deployed on an Ubuntu server 14.04 LTS with 60 % of the total OS memory dedicated to the SWfMS. Figure 3 depicts the topological representation of the migrated to the Cloud Opal Simulation Environment. As previously introduced, the evaluation in this work is geared towards the analysis of the performance and cost when using different instance categories among different providers. Consequently, we provisioned for the driven experiments a total of 16 Ubuntu 14.04 virtual machines, each one hosting an Apache Servlet Container, an ActiveMQ Message Broker, and a MySQL Database Server, as the fundamental middleware components of the Opal Simulation Environment. Such middleware components host the different simulation Web services, JMS-based[6] message events, and auditing and engine databases, respectively (see Fig. 3).

For all evaluation scenarios a system's load of 10 concurrent users sequentially sending 10 random and uniformly distributed simulation requests/user was created using Apache JMeter 2.9 as the load driver. Such a load aims at emulating

---

[5] IBM System x3755 M3: http://www-03.ibm.com/systems/xbc/cog/x3755m3_7164/x3755m3_7164aag.html.

[6] Java Message Service Specification (JMS): http://www.oracle.com/technetwork/java/docs-136352.html.

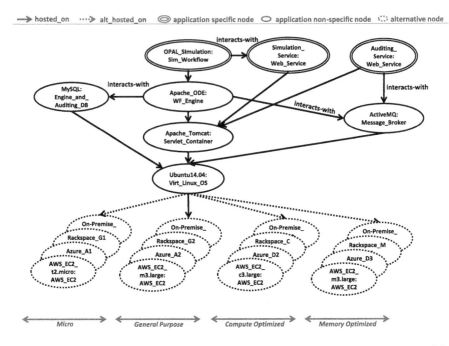

Fig. 3. Opal simulation infrastructure cloud topology - specified as depicted in [8].

a shared utilization of the simulation infrastructure. Due to the asynchronous nature of the OPAL simulation workflow, a custom plugin in JMeter was realized towards receiving and correlating the asynchronous simulation responses. The latency perceived by the user for each simulation was measured in milliseconds (ms). Towards minimizing the network latency, in all scenarios the load driver was deployed in the same region as the simulation environment.

On-Premise Cost Model. The incurred monetary costs for hosting the simulation environment on-premise are calculated considering firstly the purchase, maintenance, and depreciation of the server cluster, and secondly by calculating the price of each CPU time. [16] proposes pricing models for analyzing the cost of purchasing vs. leasing CPU time on-premise and off-premise, respectively. The real cost of a CPU/hour when purchasing a server cluster, can be derived using the following equations:

$$\frac{(1 - 1/\sqrt{2}) \times \sum_{T=0}^{Y-1} \frac{C_T}{(1+k)^T}}{(1 - (1/\sqrt{2})^Y) \times TC} \qquad (1)$$

where C_T is the acquisition (C_0) and maintenance ($C_{1..N}$) costs over the Y years of the server cluster, k is the cost of the invested capital, and

$$TC = TCPU \times H \times \mu \qquad (2)$$

where $TCPU$ depicts the total number of CPU cores in the server cluster, H is the expected number of operational hours, and μ describes the expected utilization. The utilized on-premise infrastructure total cost breaks down into an initial cost (C_0) of approximately 8500\$ in July 2012 and an annual maintenance cost $(C_{1..N})$ of 7500\$, including personnel costs, power and cooling consumption, etc. The utilization rate of such cluster is of approximately 80 %, and offers a reliability of 99 %. Moreover, the server cluster runs six days per week, as one day is dedicated for maintenance operations. Such a configuration provides 960K CPU hours annually. As discussed in [16], we also assumed in this work a cost of 5 % on the invested capital. The cost for the off-premise scenarios was gathered from the different Cloud providers' Web sites.

Table 1 depicts the hourly cost for the CPUs consumed in the different on-premise VM configurations. In order to get a better sense of the scope of the accrued costs, the total cost calculation performed as part of the experiments consisted of predicting the necessary time to run 1 K concurrent experiments. Such estimation was then used to calculate the incurred costs of hosting the simulation environment in the previously evaluated on- and off-premise scenarios. The monetary cost calculation was performed by linearly extrapolating the obtained results for the 100 requests to a total of 1 K requests. The scientific library Numpy of Python 2.7.5 was used for performing the prediction of 1 K simulation requests. The results of this calculation, as well as the observed performance measurements are discussed in the following section.

4.3 Evaluation Results

Performance Evaluation. Figure 5 shows the average observed latency for the different VM categories depicted in Table 1 for the different Cloud providers. The latency perceived in the scenarios comprising the selection of *Micro* instances have been excluded from the comparison due to the impossibility to finalize the execution of the experiments. More specifically, the on-premise micro-instance was capable of stably running approximately 80 requests (see Fig. 4(a)), while in the off-premise scenarios the load saturated the system with 10 requests approximately in the AWS EC2 and Windows Azure scenarios (see Fig. 4(b) and (c), respectively). For the scenario utilizing Rackspace, the VM micro instance was saturated immediately after sending the first set of 10 concurrent simulation requests.

With respect to the remaining instance categories (*General Purpose, Compute Optimized*, and *Memory Optimized*), the following performance variation behaviors can be observed:

1. The on-premise scenario shows in average a latency of 320 K ms. over all categories, which is 40 % higher in average than the perceived latency in the off-premise scenarios.
2. However, the performance is not constantly improved when migrating the simulation environment off-premise. For example, the *General Purpose* Windows Azure VM instance shows a degraded performance of 11 %, while the

162   S. Gómez Sáez et al.

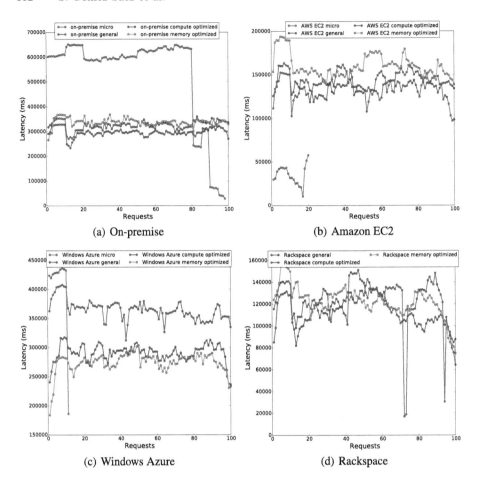

Fig. 4. Performance analysis per provider and VM category.

Windows Azure *Compute Optimize* VM instance shows only a slightly performance improvement of 2 %, when compared with the on-premise scenario.

3. The performance when migrating the simulation environment to the Cloud improves by approximately 56 % and 62 % for the AWS EC2 and Rackspace *General Purpose* VM instances, respectively,
4. 54 %, 2 %, and 61 % for the AWS EC2, Windows Azure, and Rackspace *Compute Optimized* VM instances, respectively, and
5. 52 %, 19 %, and 63 % for the AWS EC2, Windows Azure, and Rackspace *Memory Optimized* VM instances, respectively.

When comparing the average performance improvement among the different optimized VM instances, the *Compute Optimized* and *Memory Optimized* instances enhance the performance by 12 % and 6 %, respectively.

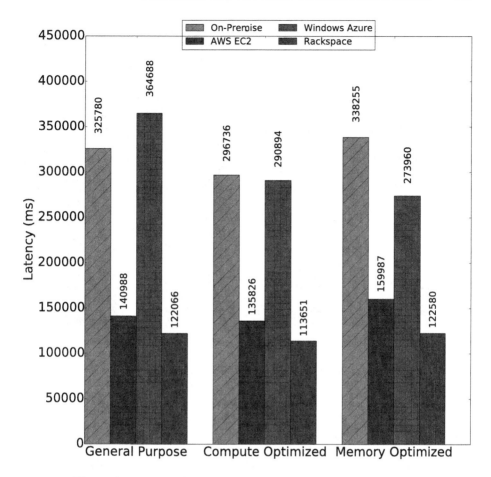

Fig. 5. Average simulation latency per provider and VM category.

Figure 4 shows the perceived latency for the different requests. During the execution of the simulation environment in the Rackspace infrastructure that the performance highly varies when increasing the number of requests (see Fig. 4(d)). Such performance variation decreases in the on-premise, AWS EC2, and Windows Azure infrastructures (see Fig. 4(a), (b) and (c), respectively). In all scenarios, the network latency does not have an impact in the performance due to the nature of our experimental setup described in the previous section.

When comparing the performance improvement among the different VM instances categories, the Windows Azure infrastructure shows the greatest when selecting a *Compute Optimized* or *Memory Optimized* VM instance over a *General Purpose* VM instance (see Fig. 4(c)).

Cost Comparison. Figures 6 and 7 present an overview of the costs per hour of usage published by the Cloud providers (referring to Table 1), and the expected costs for running 1 K experiments among 10 users. The following pricing variations can be observed:

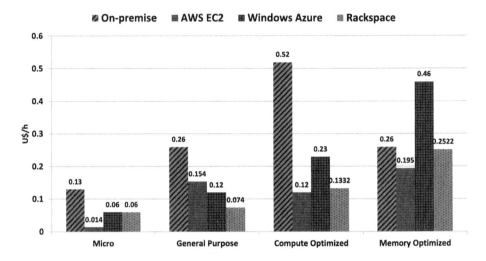

Fig. 6. Cost comparison (in January 2015 prices).

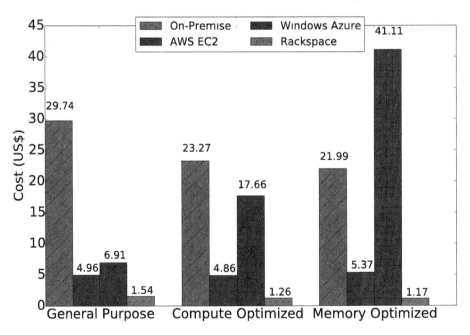

Fig. 7. Cost comparison extrapolated to 1 K simulation requests (in January 2015 prices).

1. The provisioning of on-premise resources shows in average an increase of 65 %, 55 %, 69 % of the price, for the micro, general purpose, and compute optimized VM instances, respectively. However,
2. the provisioning of on-premise memory optimized instances incurs in average a 16 % less monetary costs.
3. Amazon EC2 instances are in average 36 % low-priced, when comparing it to the on-premise costs and the remaining of the public Cloud services considered in this work.
4. The incurred costs of hosting the simulation environment on-premise is 25\$ in average.
5. When migrating the simulation infrastructure off-premise, the cost descends in average 80 %, 12 %, and 94 % when utilizing the AWS EC2, Windows Azure, and Rackspace IaaS services, respectively.
6. When comparing the incurred costs among the different VM categories, the *Memory Optimized* categories are in average 61 % and 47 % more expensive when compared to the *Compute Optimized* and *General Purpose* VM categories, respectively.
7. Among the different off-premise providers, Windows Azure is in average 900 % more expensive for running the simulation environment.

4.4   Discussion

The experiments driven as part of this work have contributed to derive and report a bi-dimensional analysis focusing on the selection among multiple IaaS offerings to deploy and run the OPAL Simulation Environment. With respect to performance, it can be concluded that:

1. The migration of the simulation environment to off-premise Cloud services has an impact on the system's performance, which is beneficial or detrimental depending on the VM provider and category.
2. The selection of *Micro* VM instances did not offer an adequate availability to the simulation environment in the off-premise scenarios. Such a negative impact was produced by the non-automatic allocation of swap space for the system's virtual memory.
3. When individually observing the performance within each VM category, the majority of the selected off-premise IaaS services improved the performance of the simulation environment. However, the *General Purpose* Windows Azure VM instances showed a degradation of the performance when compared to the other IaaS services in the same category.
4. The perceived by the user latency was in average reduced when utilizing *Compute Optimized* VM instances. Such an improvement is in line with the compute intensity requirements of the simulation environment.

The cost analysis derived the following conclusions:

1. There exists a significant monetary cost reduction when migrating the simulation environment to off-premise IaaS Cloud services.

2. Despite of the improved performance observed when running the simulation environment in the *Compute Optimized* and *Memory Optimized* VM instances, scaling the experiments to 1 K simulation requests produces in an average increase of 9 % and 61 % with respect to the *General Purpose* VM instances cost, respectively.
3. The incurred monetary costs due to the usage of Windows Azure services tend to increase when using optimized VM instances, i.e. *Compute Optimized* and *Memory Optimized*. Such behavior is reversed for the remaining off-premise and on-premise scenarios.
4. Due to the low costs demanded for the usage of Rackspace IaaS services (nearly 40 % less in average), the final price for running 1 K simulations is considerably lower than the other off-premise providers and hosting the environment on-premise.

The previous observations showed that the IaaS services provided by Rackspace are the most suitable for migrating our OPAL Simulation Environment. However, additional requirements may conflict with the migration decision of further simulation environments, e.g. related to data privacy and transfer between EU and USA regions, as Rackspace offers a limited set of optimized VMs in their European region.

5   Related Works

We consider our work related to the following major research areas: performance evaluation of workflow engines, workflow execution in the Cloud, and migration and execution of scientific workflows in the Cloud.

When it comes to evaluating the performance of common or scientific workflow engines, a standardized benchmark is not yet available. A first step towards this direction is discussed in [18], but propose approach is premature and could not be used as the basis for this work. Beyond this work, performance evaluations are usually custom to specific project needs. Specifically for BPEL engines not much work is currently available. For example [19] summarize nine approaches that evaluate the performance of BPEL engines. In most of the cases, workflow engines are benchmarked with load tests with a workload consisting of 1–4 workflows. Throughput and latency are the metrics most frequently used.

There are only few Cloud providers supporting the deployment and execution of workflows in a Platform-as-a-Service (PaaS) solution. The WSO2 Stratos Business Process Server [20] and Business Processes on the Cloud is offered by IBM Business Process Manager[7]. These offer the necessary tools and abstraction levels for developing, deploying and monitoring workflows in the Cloud. However, such services are optimized for business tasks, rather than for supporting simulation operations.

Scientific Workflow Management Systems are exploiting business workflows concepts and technologies for supporting scientists towards the use of scientific

---

[7] http://www-03.ibm.com/software/products/en/business-process-manager-cloud.

applications [2,21]. Zhao et al. [6] develop a service framework for integrating Scientific Workflow Management Systems in the Cloud to leverage from the scalability and on-demand resource allocation capabilities. The evaluation of their approach mostly focuses on examining the efficiency of their proposed PaaS based framework.

Simulation experiments are driven in the scope of different works [14,15]. Later research efforts focused on the migration of simulations to the Cloud. Due to the diverse benefits of Cloud environments the approaches evaluate the migration with respect to different scopes. The approaches that study the impact of migration to the performance and incurred monetary costs is considered more relevant to our work. In [4] the authors examine the performance of X-Ray Crystalography workflows executed on the SciCumulus middleware deployed in Amazon EC2. Such workflows are CPU-intensive and require the execution of high parallel techniques. Likewise, in [3] the authors compare the performance of scientific workflows migrated from Amazon EC2 to a typical High Performance Computing system (NCSA's Abe). In both approaches the authors conclude that migration to the Cloud can be viable but not equally efficient to High Performance Computing environments. However, Cloud environments allow the provisioning of specific resources configurations irregularly during the execution of simulation experiments [22]. Moreover, the performance improvement observed in Cloud services provide the necessary flexibility for reserving and releasing resources on-demand while reducing the capital expenditures [23]. Research towards this direction is a fertile field. Juve et al. [24] execute nontrivial scientific workflow applications on grid, public, and private Cloud infrastructures to evaluate the deployments of workflows in the Cloud in terms of setup, usability, cost, resource availability, and performance. This work can be considered complementary to our approach, although we focused on investigating further public Cloud providers and took into account the different VM optimization categories.

Further Cloud application migration assessment frameworks, such as the CloudSim [25] or CloudMIG [26], focus on estimating the benefit of using Cloud resources under different configurations. However, the vast majority rely on the usage of simulation techniques, which require the definition of the corresponding behavioral model for each Cloud. Moreover, such approaches solely target the application's QoS dimension, while in our work we aim at bridging and comparing the trade-off between the observed performance and the incurred monetary costs.

6   Conclusion and Future Work

Simulation workflows have been widely used in the eScience domain due to their easiness to model, and because of their flexible and automated runtime properties. The characteristics of such workflows together with the usage patterns of simulation environments have made these type of systems suitable to profit from the advantages brought by the Cloud computing paradigm. The existence of a vast amount of Cloud services together with the complexity introduced by the different pricing models have become a challenge to efficiently select which Cloud service to host the simulation environment. The main goal of this investigation is to report the performance and incurred monetary cost findings when migrating the previously realized OPAL simulation environment to different IaaS solutions.

A first step in this experimental work consisted of selecting a set of potential IaaS offerings suitable for our simulation environment. The result of such selection covered four major deployment scenarios: (i) in our on-premise infrastructure, and in (ii) three off-premise infrastructures (AWS EC2, Windows Azure, and Rackspace). The selection of the IaaS offerings consisted of evaluating the different providers and their corresponding optimized VM instances (*Micro*, *General Purpose*, *Compute Optimized*, and *Memory Optimized*). The simulation environment was migrated and its performance was evaluated using an artificial workload. A second step in our analysis consisted on extrapolating the obtained results towards estimating the incurred costs for running the simulation environment on- and off-premise. The analyses showed a beneficial impact in the performance and a significant reduction of monetary costs when migrating the simulation environment to the majority of off-premise Cloud offerings.

The efforts in this work build towards the assessment for the migration of Cloud applications to the Cloud, as defined in [27]. More specifically, in this work we cover the subset of tasks relevant to the selection and configuration of Cloud resources to distribute the application, w.r.t. their performance and the incurred monetary costs. Despite our efforts towards analyzing and finding the most efficient Cloud provider and service to deploy and run our simulation environment, our experiments solely focused on IaaS offerings.

Future works focus on analyzing further service models, i.e. Platform-as-a-Service (PaaS) or Database-as-a-Service (DBaaS), as well as evaluating the distribution of the different components that constitute the simulation environment among multiple Cloud offerings. Investigating different autoscaling techniques and resources configuration possibilities is also part of future work, e.g. feeding the application distribution system proposed in [28] with such empirical observations.

Acknowledgements. The research leading to these results has received funding from the FP7 EU project ALLOW Ensembles (600792), the German Research Foundation (DFG) within the Cluster of Excellence in Simulation Technology (EXC310), and the German DFG project BenchFlow (DACH Grant Nr. 200021E-145062/1).

References

1. Leymann, F., Roller, D.: Production Workflow: Concepts and Techniques. Prentice Hall, Upper Saddle River (2000)
2. Sonntag, M., Karastoyanova, D.: Next generation interactive scientific experimenting based on the workflow technology. In: Alhajj, R., Leung, V., Saif, M., Thring, R. (eds.) Proceedings of the 21st IASTED International Conference on Modelling and Simulation (MS 2010). ACTA Press (2010)

3. Juve, G., Deelman, E., Vahi, K., Mehta, G., Berriman, B., Berman, B., Maechling, P.: Scientific workflow applications on Amazon EC2. In: 2009 5th IEEE International Conference on E-Science Workshops, pp. 59–66 (2009)
4. de Oliveira, D., Ocaña, K., Ogasawara, E.S., Dias, J., Baião, F.A., Mattoso, M.: A performance evaluation of X-Ray crystallography scientific workflow using Sci-Cumulus. In: Liu, L., Parashar, M. (eds.) IEEE CLOUD, pp. 708–715. IEEE
5. Vukojevic-Haupt, K., Karastoyanova, D., Leymann, F.: On-demand provisioning of infrastructure, middleware and services for simulation workflows. In: 2013 IEEE 6th International Conference on Service-Oriented Computing and Applications (SOCA), pp. 91–98. IEEE (2013)
6. Zhao, Y., Li, Y., Raicu, I., Lu, S., Lin, C., Zhang, Y., Tian, W., Xue, R.: A service framework for scientific workflow management in the cloud. In: IEEE Transactions on Services Computing, p. 1 (2014)
7. Gómez Sáez, S., Andrikopoulos, V., Leymann, F., Strauch, S.: Design support for performance aware dynamic application (Re-) distribution in the cloud. IEEE Trans. Serv. Comput. 8, 225–239 (2014)
8. Andrikopoulos, V., Gómez Sáez, S., Leymann, F., Wettinger, J.: Optimal distribution of applications in the cloud. In: Jarke, M., Mylopoulos, J., Quix, C., Rolland, C., Manolopoulos, Y., Mouratidis, H., Horkoff, J. (eds.) CAiSE 2014. LNCS, vol. 8484, pp. 75–90. Springer, Heidelberg (2014)
9. Gómez Sáez, S., Andrikopoulos, V., Hahn, M., Karastoyanova, D., Leymann, F., Skouradaki, M., Vukojevic-Haupt, K.: Performance and cost evaluation for the migration of a scientific workflow infrastructure to the cloud. In: Proceedings of the 5th International Conference on Cloud Computing and Service Science (CLOSER 2015), pp. 1–10. SciTePress (2015)
10. Sonntag, M., Hahn, M., Karastoyanova, D.: Mayflower - explorative modeling of scientific workflows with BPEL. In: Proceedings of the Demo Track of the 10th International Conference on Business Process Management (BPM 2012), CEUR Workshop Proceedings, 2012, pp. 1–5. CEUR Workshop Proceedings (2012)
11. Görlach, K., Sonntag, M., Karastoyanova, D., Leymann, F., Reiter, M.: Conventional workflow technology for scientific simulation. In: Yang, X., Wang, L., Jie, W. (eds.) Guide to e-Science, pp. 323–352. Springer, London (2011)
12. Sonntag, M., Karastoyanova, D.: Model-as-you-go: an approach for an advanced infrastructure for scientific workflows. J. Grid Comput. 11, 553–583 (2013)
13. Sonntag, M., Hotta, S., Karastoyanova, D., Molnar, D., Schmauder, S.: Using services and service compositions to enable the distributed execution of legacy simulation applications. In: Abramowicz, W., Llorente, I.M., Surridge, M., Zisman, A., Vayssière, J. (eds.) ServiceWave 2011. LNCS, vol. 6994, pp. 242–253. Springer, Heidelberg (2011)
14. Binkele, P., Schmauder, S.: An atomistic monte carlo simulation of precipitation in a binary system. Zeitschrift für Metallkunde 94, 858–863 (2003)
15. Molnar, D., Binkele, P., Hocker, S., Schmauder, S.: Multiscale modelling of nano tensile tests for different Cu-precipitation states in α-Fe. In: Proceedings of the 5th International Conference on Multiscale Materials Modelling, pp. 235–239 (2010)
16. Walker, E.: The real cost of a CPU hour. IEEE Comput. 42, 35–41 (2009)
17. Andrikopoulos, V., Song, Z., Leymann, F.: Supporting the migration of applications to the cloud through a decision support system. In: 2013 IEEE Sixth International Conference on Cloud Computing (CLOUD), pp. 565–572. IEEE (2013)

18. Skouradaki, M., Roller, D.H., Frank, L., Ferme, V., Pautasso, C.: On the road to benchmarking BPMN 2.0 workflow engines. In: Proceedings of the 6th ACM/SPEC International Conference on Performance Engineering ICPE 2015, pp. 1–4. ACM (2015)
19. Röck, C., Harrer, S., Wirtz, G.: Performance benchmarking of BPEL engines: a comparison framework, status quo evaluation and challenges. In: 26th International Conference on Software Engineering and Knowledge Engineering (SEKE), Vancouver, Canada, pp. 31–34 (2014)
20. Pathirage, M., Perera, S., Kumara, I., Weerawarana, S.: A multi-tenant architecture for business process executions. In: Proceedings of the 2011 IEEE International Conference on Web Services, ICWS 2011, pp. 121–128. IEEE Computer Society, Washington, DC, USA (2011)
21. Sonntag, M., Hotta, S., Karastoyanova, D., Molnar, D., Schmauder, S.: Workflow-based distributed environment for legacy simulation applications. In: ICSOFT, vol. 1, pp. 91–94 (2011)
22. Strauch, S., Andrikopoulos, V., Bachmann, T., Karastoyanova, D., Passow, S., Vukojevic-Haupt, K.: Decision support for the migration of the application database layer to the cloud. In: 2013 IEEE 5th International Conference on Cloud Computing Technology and Science (CloudCom), vol. 1, pp. 639–646. IEEE (2013)
23. Ostermann, S., Iosup, A., Yigitbasi, N., Prodan, R., Fahringer, T., Epema, D.: A performance analysis of EC2 cloud computing services for scientific computing. In: Avresky, D.R., Diaz, M., Bode, A., Ciciani, B., Dekel, E. (eds.) Cloud Computing. LNICST, vol. 34, pp. 115–134. Springer, Heidelberg (2010)
24. Juve, G., Chervenak, A., Deelman, E., Bharathi, S., Mehta, G., Vahi, K.: Characterizing and profiling scientific workflows. Future Gener. Comput. Syst. 29, 682–692 (2013)
25. Calheiros, R.N., Ranjan, R., Beloglazov, A., De Rose, C.A., Buyya, R.: Cloudsim: a toolkit for modeling and simulation of cloud computing environments and evaluation of resource provisioning algorithms. Softw. Pract. Experience 41, 23–50 (2011)
26. Frey, S., Hasselbring, W.: The cloudmig approach: model-based migration of software systems to cloud-optimized applications. Int. J. Adv. Softw. 4, 342–353 (2011)
27. Darsow, A., Karastoyanova, D., Andrikopoulos, V., Leymann, F.: CloudDSF – the cloud decision support framework for application migration. In: Villari, M., Zimmermann, W., Lau, K.-K. (eds.) ESOCC 2014. LNCS, vol. 8745, pp. 1–16. Springer, Heidelberg (2014)
28. Gómez Sáez, S., Andrikopoulos, V., Wessling, F., Marquezan, C.C.: Cloud adaptation and application (Re-) distribution: bridging the two perspectives. In: Proceedings of the First International Workshop on Engineering Cloud Applications and Services (EnCASE 2014), pp. 163–172. IEEE Computer Society Press (2014)

A Practical Evaluation of Searchable Encryption for Data Archives in the Cloud

Christian Neuhaus[1]([⊠]), Frank Feinbube[1], Daniel Janusz[2], and Andreas Polze[1]

[1] Operating Systems and Middleware Group, Hasso Plattner Institut,
Potsdam, Germany
{christian.neuhaus,frank.feinbube,andreas.polze}@hpi.de
[2] DBIS Group, Humboldt-Universität Zu Berlin, Berlin, Germany
janusz@informatik.hu-berlin.de

Abstract. Traditional encryption schemes can effectively ensure the confidentiality of sensitive data stored on cloud infrastructures. Unfortunately, they also prevent most operations on the data such as search by design. As a solution, searchable encryption schemes have been proposed that provide keyword-search capability on encrypted content. In this paper, we evaluate the practical usability of searchable encryption schemes and analyze the tradeoff between performance, functionality and security. We present a prototypical implementation of such a scheme embedded in a document-oriented database, report on performance benchmarks under realistic conditions and analyze the threats to data confidentiality and corresponding countermeasures.

Keywords: Keyword search · Searchable encryption · Cloud computing · Performance · Security · Data confidentiality

1 Introduction

Data sharing is essential to companies and government services alike. A striking example is healthcare, where doctor's offices, hospitals, and administrative institutions rely on exchange of information to offer the best level of care and optimizing cost efficiency at the same time. For scenarios like these, moving to the cloud solves many problems: The scalability of the cloud makes resources simple to provision and extend and centralization of data improves the availability and helps to avoid information silos. Most importantly, cloud computing helps to reduce IT expenses – an effect most welcome in healthcare. However, concerns about data confidentiality still prevent the use of cloud in many domains. Traditional encryption is of little help: It effectively protects the privacy of data but also prevents important operations such as search. While efficient encryption schemes that enable generic operations on encrypted data are still elusive, searching over encrypted data is possible: searchable encryption schemes enable keyword search without disclosing these keywords to the cloud operator. The query performance of such schemes cannot match unencrypted operation, but

© Springer International Publishing Switzerland 2016
M. Helfert et al. (Eds.): CLOSER 2015, CCIS 581, pp. 171–192, 2016.
DOI: 10.1007/978-3-319-29582-4_10

may well be suitable for areas of application such as electronic health records, where data has to be retrieved from a cloud-hosted archive.

In this paper[1], we investigate the trade-off between performance and security when using searchable encryption schemes for data archives in the cloud. We make the following contributions:

(1) We report on an architecture for integrating Gohs Z-IDX searchable encryption scheme [1] into a database and present a practical implementation by the example of MongoDB.
(2) We discuss the overhead introduced by encrypted search and provide benchmark results on the performance of using Gohs scheme for encrypted search with MongoDB. These benchmarks give a meaningful account of the practical performance and usability of searchable encryption in databases.
(3) We give a qualitative assessment of the security implications of using searchable encryption schemes for cloud data archives using attack-defense-tree models. This assessment is generic to searchable encryption and not limited to Goh's scheme. We also discuss mitigation strategies to manage threats by statistical inference attacks.

2   Related Work

In this section, we review related work in the field of private database outsourcing and searchable encryption.

Private Database Outsourcing. Outsourcing private data to a remote database inherently bears the risk of exposure of confidential information – through eavesdropping, data theft or malfunctions. The key challenge is to protect private data from being accessed by potentially untrusted cloud providers. In this paper, we focus on technologies that protect data within a database. While encryption is the basic mechanism to ensure data confidentiality, providing an efficient database-as-a-service that can run on encrypted data is a challenging task. Several recent approaches try to offer solutions for outsourcing private databases.

TrustedDB [2] and Cipherbase [3] offer SQL database functionalities that support the full generality of a database system while providing high data confidentiality. Both systems use a secure co-processor for performing operations on the cloud server side. The drawbacks of such approaches are at least twofold: On one hand all clients have to trust the secure co-processor with their private data. On the other hand it is not clear how the co-processor scales up in the number of clients connected and the amount of data processed. In CryptDB [6], the authors apply an layered approach that makes use of several cryptographic schemes, where values are only decrypted to a level that is required to complete the query.

---

[1] This paper is an extended version of the article *Secure Keyword Search over Data Archives in the Cloud* presented at the *5th International Conference on Cloud Computing and Services Science* in Lisbon, Portugal in 2015.

Another class of approaches aims at processing encrypted data directly without any decryption. To this day, there are no efficient encryption schemes that enable fully encrypted operation of a DBMS (database management system) without loss of functionality. An early approach for keyword search on encrypted data was published by [4]. An approach for securely processing exact match queries on database cells was proposed by [5]. However, most DBMS rely on other common operations such as range and aggregation queries as well as updates, inserts and deletes. Existing approaches cannot efficiently process this type of queries on encrypted data. A common solution is to reduce data confidentiality to gain query efficiency, e.g., order preserving encryption [7] may reveal the underlying data order. Most methods can be attacked by statistical analysis of the encrypted data or the access patterns. Another solution is to lose some query efficiency in order to guarantee confidentiality. While *(fully) homomorphic encryption schemes* as proposed by Rivest et al. [8] in fact allow the encrypted computation of any circuit (and therefore computer program), current constructions (see [9,10]) are yet too inefficient for practical application.

Traditional databases use indices for efficient record search. The existing methods have been adapted to work on encrypted data [11]. Private indexing [12] enable an untrusted server to evaluate obfuscated range queries with limited information leakage. Wang et al. [13] propose a secure B^+-Tree to efficiently process any type of database query. Encrypted index-based approaches do not rely on any trusted third parties or trusted hardware. This seems to be a practical and secure method to search in encrypted databases. The next section discusses searchable encryption.

Searchable Encryption. Searchable encryption schemes provide one or many cryptographic data structures called *search indices* that allow encrypted keyword search for exact keyword matches. A good overview of searchable encryption schemes is given in [14]. In general, searchable encryption schemes do not replace symmetric encryption schemes but provide the search capability through additional data structures – the *index* (see Fig. 1). To provide keyword search

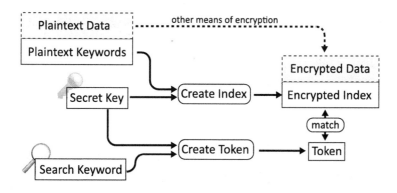

Fig. 1. Searchable encryption: conceptual view.

on data, a list of keywords is extracted from the plaintext. This keyword list is used to create a secure index using a dedicated secret key for the searchable encryption scheme. The data is encrypted separately (usually symmetric block ciphers such as *AES*) and uploaded stored alongside the encrypted index in a remote location. To search over the uploaded data in the remote location, a *search token* is generated for a search keyword using the secret key. This token is sent to the remote server. The remote sever can now determine whether the token matches a search index without being able to learn the keyword.

Searchable encryption schemes can be distinguished between *Symmetric Searchable Encryption* (SSE) and *Asymmetric Searchable Encryption* (ASE) schemes. SSE schemes use the same secret key both for insertion and searching of data. In general, they are more efficient than ASE schemes and provide stronger security guarantees. They were first introduced by [4], where the authors provide a linear search capability over ciphertext – one of the few schemes that does not make use of indices. To speed up search, the scheme of Goh [1] uses indices that are created separately for every searchable data item, which enables efficient update. Improved search time can achieved by using an inverted index (see e.g. [15]). A scheme that enables both efficient updates and optimal search time (linear in the number of documents that contain the keyword) is offered in a recent construction by Kamara et al. [16].

In contrast, ASE schemes use different keys for insertion and searching of data, which provides greater flexibility. However, the constructions of ASE schemes are generally less efficient than those of SSE schemes and provide weaker security guarantees. The first construction was given by Boneh et al. [17] and is based on elliptic curve cryptography. Improved constructions were introduced in [18]. Unfortunately, ASE are generally susceptible to dictionary attacks against search tokens (see [19]). This limits the application of ASE schemes to use case where keywords are either hard to guess or the keyword attack is tolerable.

3   The Z-IDX Scheme

For our implementation, we chose the Z-IDX searchable encryption scheme by [1]. As a symmetric scheme, it is not susceptible to dictionary attacks on search tokens like ASE schemes (see Sect. 2). This scheme offers several desirable properties:

- **Maturity:** While the field of research in searchable encryption schemes is rather young, Goh's scheme was one of the earliest proposed. In contrast to more recent constructions, the scheme passed several years without the discovery of security flaws.
- **Per-document Indexing:** The Z-IDX scheme creates per-document indices. This property facilitates integration into existing DBMS.
- **Standard Cryptographic Primitives:** The cryptographic mechanisms used by Z-IDX are widely available in software libraries for most platforms.

In this section, we give an overview of *Bloom Filters* and how they are used to construct Gohs Z-IDX scheme.

3.1 Bloom Filters

The encrypted indices in Z-IDX make use of space-efficient probabilistic data structures called *bloom filters* [20]. For a set of elements $E = \{e_1, ..., e_n\}$, the set membership information is encoded in a bit array of length l. A number of r hash functions $h_1, ..., h_r$ is selected that map every element of E to a number $\in [1; l]$. To store the set membership of an element e_x in the filter, its hash value from every hash function $h_1, ..h_r$ is calculated. These hash values $h_1(e_x), ..., h_r(e_x)$ are used as index positions in the filter bit array. At every referenced index position, the bit in the array is set to 1. To test the set membership for an element e_y, the procedure is similar: All hash values $h_1(e_y), ..., h_r(e_y)$ are calculated and used as index positions in the filter bit array. If all positions in the array pointed to by the hash function values are set to 1, the element is assumed to be in the set.

This design of bloom filters can produce false positives: If all corresponding array positions of an element e_z were set to 1 by insertion of other elements, the bloom filter produces a false positive for e_z. On the other hand, false negatives do not occur. The false positive rate of a bloom filter can be influenced by adjusting the size of the bit array and the number of hash functions used.

3.2 Gohs Secure Indexes

Based on bloom filters, Goh constructs a secure index scheme called *Z-IDX* [1] that allows encrypted keyword search. Like similar schemes, it does not replace other means of encryption but provides additional data structures for its functionality (see Fig. 1). The scheme builds upon the abstraction of *documents*, which are the units of granularity for keyword search. Every document $d_i \in D$ can contain a number of keywords $w \in W$ and is identified by a unique ID $i \in I$. Authorized clients hold a secret key K_{priv}. The scheme is then defined by the following operations:

- **Keygen**(s) outputs a secret key K_{priv}, where s is a variable security parameter.
- **Trapdoor**(K_{priv}, w) outputs a trapdoor T_w for keyword w using the secret key K_{priv}.

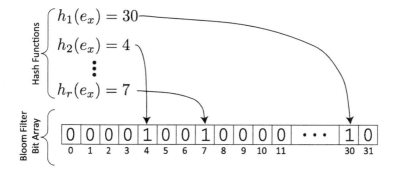

Fig. 2. Example of a Bloom Filter with a 32-bit array.

- BuildIndex(d, K_{priv}) outputs an encrypted index for document d using the secret key K_{priv}.
- SearchIndex(T_w, d) takes a trapdoor for keyword w and tests for a match in the index of document d. If d contains w it outputs 1 and 0 otherwise.

Additionally, a pseudorandom function $f : \{0,1\}^* \times \{0,1\}^s \rightarrow \{0,1\}^m$ is required.

For a precise formal definition, e.g. with respect to bit string lengths, please see the original publication [1]. In this presentation of the scheme, we also omit the step of adding *blinding bits* to the filter.

To set up the scheme, security parameter s, a number of hash functions r and a index size m are chosen (for choice of m and r, see Sect. 5.2). Then, a secret key is generated by the Keygen operation, so that $K_{priv} = (k1, ..., k_r) \leftarrow \{0,1\}^{sr}$.

To create a search index for a document d with a set of keywords $W_d = \{w_1, ..., w_x\} \subset W$, BuildIndex operation first creates an empty bloom filter with a bit array of length m. First, a trapdoor T_w is calculated for every keyword w using the Trapdoor operation, so that $T_w = (t_{w_1}, ..., t_{w_r}) = (f(w, k_1), ..., f(w, k_r))$. This results in a set of trapdoors: Using the set of trapdoors $T_{w_1}, ..., T_{w_x}$ and the *id* of the document d, the set of codewords $C_{w_1}, ..., C_{w_x}$ is calculated. For every trapdoor T_w the codeword C_w is calculated so that $C_w = (c_{w_1}, ..., c_{w_r}) = (f(id, t_{w_1}), ..., f(id, t_{w_r}))$. Then, the filter of the document is populated by setting every bit position ti 1 that is referenced by the trapdoors: For every trapdoor C_w, the bits at positions $c_{w_1}, ..., c_{w_r}$ are set to 1 (see Fig. 2).

To query a collection of documents for a keyword w, the trapdoor T_w is calculated using the Trapdoor operation and sent to the server. To test whether a document contains the keyword, the server calculates the codeword C_w using the trapdoor T_w and the document *id*. Using the trapdoor C_w the server tests whether all bit at positions $c_{w_1}, ..., c_{w_r}$ are set to 1. If so, the document is sent back to the client as a match. This process is applied to all documents in the collection. In the Z-IDX scheme, a separate index data structure is created per document. This accounts for a search time that is linear over the number of documents, but facilitates the administration of secure indices, as they can be created stored alongside the documents. This makes the addition or removal of documents a simple operation.

From a more technical perspective, the above steps can be described and implemented using a keyed hash function such as HMAC-SHA1 [21], which is also used in our implementation (see Sect. 4). In a first step, a keyword w is hashed with all elements of the secret key $k_1, ..., k_r$ to obtain the trapdoor vector. The elements of the trapdoor vector are each hashed again together with the document identifier *id* to obtain the codeword vector. Each of the codeword vector elements is used as an index position to set a bit in the bloom filter bit array to 1.

4   Searchable Encryption in MongoDB

To evaluate the practical usability of searchable encryption, we created a prototypical implementation of Z-IDX scheme and integrated it into the document oriented database *MongoDB*. In this section, we explain why we chose MongoDB, present the architecture of our prototype, introduce new commands for secure keyword search and present implementation details.

4.1   Selection of a Database System

While the searchable encryption scheme Z-IDX can be used standalone, its practical usability and performance under realistic workloads can only be evaluated if the scheme is used in conjunction with other means of encryption and data handling. To do this, we integrated Z-IDX into an existing DBMS. The choice of a DBMS has to correspond to the basic properties of the Z-IDX scheme – exact keyword matching as a search mechanism and the notion of *documents* as the basic units of granularity for searching.

To select a DBMS, we considered different database paradigms: The most widespread type of databases are **relational databases** – most of them supporting the *Structured Query Language* (SQL). This type of database has a long development history and offers features such as transactional security, clustering techniques and master-slave-configurations to ensure availability. The SQL language allows detailed queries, where specific data fields in the database can be selected and returned using complex search criteria based on structure or data field values and logical combinations thereof. The expressive power of the SQL language goes far beyond simple keyword search. It is therefore difficult to isolate queries that can make use of searchable encryption. Additionally, the fine-grained selection of data fields does not correspond well to the document-oriented approach of searchable encryption.

Besides relational databases, other database types have been developed under the umbrella term of NoSQL databases. A very minimalistic approach are *key-value stores* (e.g. *Redis, Dynamo*): They omit many of the features known from SQL databases in favor of simplicity and performance. However, the complexity of data structures is severely limited. This makes storing documents and associated indices difficult or impossible.

Document-oriented databases, however, are well-suited to implement searchable encryption. As the name suggests, data is organized in containers called *documents* as opposed to tables in relational databases. These documents are the units of granularity for search operations and can contain complex data structures without adhering to a schema definition. As this approach corresponds well to the properties of searchable encryption schemes, we chose to add searchable encryption features to the open-source document-oriented database *MongoDB*.

Floratou et al. [22] compare MongoDB to Microsoft SQL Server. They show that relational databases may have better query performance. However, MongoDB is optimized for storing data records across multiple machines and offers efficient load balancing, which makes it more suitable for cloud-based applications. Furthermore, the increasing use of NoSQL databases in real world applications lead to an increasing demand for enhancing these databases with privacy technologies such as searchable encryption.

4.2   Extended MongoDB Commands

As MongoDB is a document-oriented database, a *document* is the primary unit of abstraction for organization of data. A document does not adhere to a fixed schema and can store data in a JSON-like fashion of field-value pairs. Like in JSON, documents support a number of primitive data types (e.g. `integer`, `String`) and a data structures like arrays. All of these data structures can be nested. In addition to standard JSON, MongoDB can also store binary data in fields. Documents in MongoDB are stored in *collections*, these, in turn, are stored in a *database*. The prime commands for data handling in collections are `insert()` and `find()`. They accept a document as a parameter. To make searchable encryption explicitly available, we introduced two additional commands:

- The `insertSecure()` can be used to insert documents into a collection using searchable encryption. Using this command, every array of strings in the document is removed and its content used as keywords. The contained strings are inserted into a Z-IDX filter or encrypted search. Every other datatype remains untouched.
- The `findSecure()` command triggers encrypted search over all documents of a collection. As a parameter, it takes a keyword embedded in a document, e.g.: `findSecure({keyword: 'foo'})`

4.3   Architecture and Implementation

We created a prototypical implementation of the Z-IDX scheme as a separate C++ translation unit that can easily be integrated with the existing code of MongoDB. The C++ module contains methods for the computation of trapdoors, codewords and the resulting filters as well as helper code to load cryptographic key information for the scheme from files. In our implementation, we omitted the step of adding blinding bits to the filter data structures of Z-IDX for better performance of the scheme. The security implications of the step are discussed in Sect. 5.1.

To integrate the implementation of Z-IDX with MongoDB, modifications were made to booth the server and the command line client. An overview of the architecture of MongoDB server and client is given in Fig. 3. In theory, it is possible to add searchable encryption to MongoDB modifying only the client but not the server. However, this leads to a disproportionately high increase in communication overhead as per-document operations would have to be carried out on the client, each requiring the transmission of the documents Z-IDX data structures.

The MongoDB command line client is comprised of a JavaScript shell that uses a core driver written in C++. The client connects to the server, which is also written in C++. To provide searchable encryption functionality, we implemented the Z-IDX scheme (see Sect. 3) and additional helper functions in a separate module that is compiled both into the server and the C++ driver of the client (*Z-IDX Module*, see Fig. 3). As suggested by Goh, we apply data compression

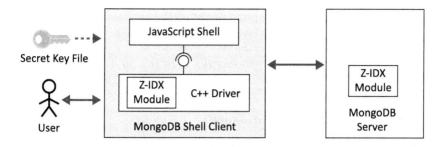

Fig. 3. Architecture of MongoDB server and client.

(zlib) to the index data structures before transmission over the network. As these data structures are very sparse, the compression works very effectively and the additional compute overhead is easily outweighed by reduced transmission times in most settings.

To integrate the functionality, we made the following modifications: The **JavaScript shell** is modified to read the secret key information from a file, which has to be passed as a parameter at startup. If a secure search or insert request is identified, the request is modified to include the secret key information. This information is stored in a dedicated `_zidx` field in the query. After this, the request is passed to the clients' C++ driver. The **C++ driver** is modified to recognize queries that contain Z-IDX key information injected by the JavaScript shell. For inserts, a Z-IDX filter is built and populated with the contained strings of every string array in the document. Subsequently, the string arrays and the key information are removed and the command is passed on to the server. For a search query, the C++ driver uses the key to compute trapdoors for every search keyword. The trapdoors are inserted, the key is removed and the query is passed on to the server. The **MongoDB server** is modified to process the search queries. For the trapdoors of a search query, the server generates the corresponding codewords using the *document id*. These codewords are then checked against the bloom filters of a document to test for a match. This architecture and implementation makes searchable encryption available without affecting non-encrypted use of the database, as regular MongoDB commands are processed as expected.

5   Performance Evaluation

The use of encrypted search functionality introduces an overhead in computation, storage and data transmission. Since speed and throughout are critical factors for databases, we present performance measurements of our approach in this section. The figures allow to evaluate the practicability of searchable encryption in databases for real-life scenarios.

To assess the performance impact of our approach, we ran insert and search queries in encrypted and unencrypted settings under various parameters settings (dictionary size, false positive rate) and analyzed the performance as well as the memory footprint of the additional data structures of Z-IDX. To avoid synthetic test data, we chose the publicly available *Enron corpus* – a collection of emails which we use as documents. All benchmarks were run on a Intel Core i5-3470 machine with 8GB main memory, running Ubuntu 12.04 LTS.

5.1 Filter Blinding vs. Performance

The original specification of the Z-IDX scheme includes a step of *blinding bits* to the filter data structures after the insertion of the codewords. In this step, a number of random 1's are added to the filter so that the density of 1's is approximately equal in all filter data structures. This noise insertion technique prevents an attacker from drawing conclusions on the number of represented keywords from a given index. It serves to fulfill the original IND-CKA security guarantee of the scheme in which an attacker, given a Z-IDX index and two documents, should not be able to deduce which document is encoded in the index with a probability better than $\frac{1}{2}$.

In our implementation, we chose to omit the step of adding blinding bits to the filters to investigate a tradeoff between performance and security. On the one hand, the omission of the blinding step enables attackers to estimate the number of keywords represented by a filter. This information could be used for statistical inference attacks (see Sect. 6). However, statistical attacks are only possible using background knowledge. On the other hand, the omission of blinding significantly improves the efficiency of the scheme, as the less densely populated filters enable higher compression rates and lead to fewer false negatives on search operations.

5.2 Memory Footprint of Z-IDX Filters

As the encrypted filters are added to every document, they add overhead to communication and storage footprint. They are therefore a crucial factor that influences the performance of a database using this scheme.

The size of these data structures is determined by the desired false positive rate f_p and the number of unique keywords to be represented by the filters n. From the false positive rate f_p, the number of hash functions r is determined by calculating $r = -log_2(f_p)$. From r, the number of bits m in the filter can be determined by calculating $m = nr/ln2$. In practice, these data structures can become quite large. This is especially unfavourable in settings with large numbers n of distinct keywords and small document sizes, as the filter sizes can easily exceed the size of the original documents.

To improve the efficiency of the scheme, data compression can be used on the filters (as suggested by Goh). While filter compression decreases storage and communication overhead, it also introduces additional steps of computation on the client and server side: Upon document insertion, filters have to be compressed and decompressed for every search operation. This represents a tradeoff between data size and computational overhead.

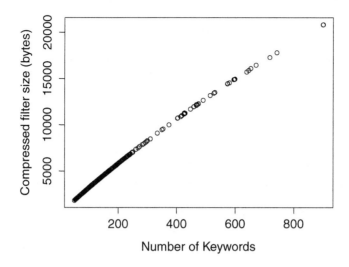

Fig. 4. Relationship between number of document keywords and compressed filter size.

To investigate this issue, we first tested the effectiveness of compression on indexes. In practice, these filters are bit array that contain mostly 0's and sparsely distributed 1's (depending on the number of contained keywords). To determine the achievable compression ratio, we used a set of 1000 documents from the Enron corpus containing 127.5 keywords on average. Assuming a set of 100000 distinct keywords and a false positive rate of 0.0001 % leads to an uncompressed filter size of 252472 bytes. We implemented the compression of filters using the free *zlib*[2] compression library. Using the *zlib* standard compression strategy, the average compression ratio achieved is 0.02 with the given parameters. Using a run-length encoding strategy that exploits the sparse property of the filters, compression becomes even more effective with an average compression ratio of 0.0154. This means that using compression, filter sizes can be considerably reduced in size (here: to 1.54 % of their original size, average size of compressed filters 3889 bytes).

Our benchmarking results show that using filter compression dramatically speeds up database operations even over fast network connections (100 Mbit/s speed). This means that the overhead for data compression is by far outweighed by the advantage in network transmission speed due to smaller filters. Therefore, we use RLE-based filter compression as a default in all subsequent measurements.

It can be observed that the size of compressed filters is closely correlated with the number of represented keywords (see Fig. 4): Documents with few keywords have small compressed filters while more keywords produce larger sizes. This means that a trade-off of the Z-IDX scheme is mitigated: To accommodate large sets of distinct keywords without false-positives, large filter sizes are required. These large filters take up of large amounts of memory – even for small

---

[2] http://zlib.net/.

documents with few or no keywords at all. However, using compression, filter sizes can be generously chosen as compressed filters remain compact, depending on the number of keywords in the document. In fact, using the settings above, compressed filter sizes are 3389 bytes on average. When increasing the number of unique keywords from 100000 to a million (tenfold), the average size is only 6648 bytes on average (only a twofold increase).

5.3   Query Performance

To assess the performance of the scheme, we evaluated insert and search performance of our Z-IDX implementation embedded in MongoDB. To obtain realistic results, we tested our setup under two different network profiles: The LAN profile corresponds to the typical properties of a wired local network (2 ms ping, 100 Mbit/s), the WAN profile corresponds to the properties of a domestic internet connection in Germany (20 ms ping, 10 Mbit/s). For reference, the same benchmarks were also conducted with a Localhost profile, where the network delays are essentially non-existent. The LAN and WAN profiles were generated by using network link conditioning on the machines' loopback network device, using Linux' tc command. All benchmarks were conducted using a false positive rate of 0.001 and a maximum dictionary size of 10000.

Insert Query Performance. To assess the performance of insert queries, we inserted a collection of 10000 documents from the Enron corpus in batches of 100. We ran every insert query 100 times and took the mean as our measurement value. The results for these queries in the Localhost, LAN and WAN profiles for encrypted and unencrypted operation are shown in Fig. 5.

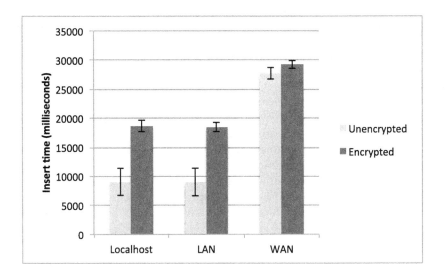

Fig. 5. Benchmark: insert of 10000 documents.

The longer duration of encrypted operation is explained by the additional steps required on the client: Before submission of a document, a Z-IDX filter has to be created using the document's keywords and the document content has to be encrypted. The Z-IDX filter introduces data which slightly increases the time of data transmission. On the server, no additional steps have to be executed on insert. Our experiments show that the performance penalty for encryption in insert queries is indeed moderate: In the Localhost- and LAN-settings, the insert time is about doubled compared to the unencrypted setting. In the WAN setting, where network performance has a larger effect, the duration of encrypted and unencrypted insert queries are nearly the same.

Search Query Performance. To determine the performance of search queries, we issued a search query with a randomly chosen keyword on the same document collection as used in the insert queries. We ran every search query 100 times and took the mean as our measurement value. The results for these queries in the Localhost, LAN and WAN profiles for encrypted and unencrypted operation are shown in Fig. 6. Unencrypted search time is very small (0,13 ms in the Localhost setting, 2,32 ms LAN, 20,37 ms WAN) when compared to encrypted operation and mainly determined by the network latency. In contrast, encrypted searches took around half a second (≈ 530 ms), with little variation depending on network performance, as only little data had to be transmitted.

This discrepancy is caused by the fundamental properties of the Z-IDX scheme: Searching in an unencrypted database is usually carried out using an inverted index, where the matching documents for a given keyword can be looked up with linear complexity ($\mathcal{O}(1)$). In encrypted operation using the Z-IDX-scheme, search complexity is linear in the number of documents in the collection

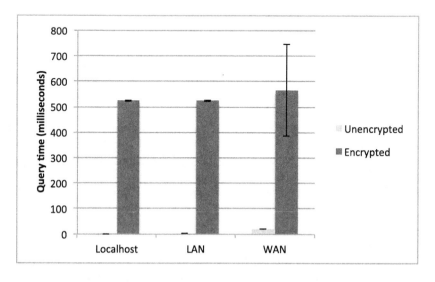

Fig. 6. Benchmark: search query over 10000 documents.

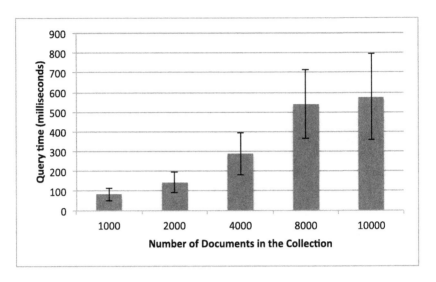

Fig. 7. Benchmark: search query over collections of different sizes (WAN setting).

($\mathcal{O}(n)$, n = number of documents). Therefore, the duration of search operations is expected to scale in proportion to the number of documents in the collection. This behavior was confirmed by running search queries on collections of different sizes in WAN setting. The results are presented in Fig. 7 show a clear dependency between query time and size of the collection, where queries over smaller collections are slightly less efficient due to communication overhead.

5.4 Implications for Practical Use

Our measurements have shown that the performance penalty for using the Z-IDX searchable encryption scheme in a database is very unevenly distributed: While the performance penalty for insert queries is almost negligible in under realistic conditions (WAN profile), the penalty for search queries is tremendous by comparison. At the same time, the query performance varies greatly depending on collection size (linear effort) and filter parameters: A search query on a 10000-documents-collection in our experiments took between 219 ms ($f_p = 0.01$, $n = 1000$) and 4612 ms ($f_p = 0.0001$, $n = 100000$). It should be noted that these figures were obtained using a single threaded implementation of Z-IDX. As the search operations over a document collection of documents are embarrassingly parallel, an almost ideal speedup can be expected for parallel implementations.

6   Security

The motivation for using searchable encryption schemes such as Z-IDX is to protect the confidentiality of information that is stored on untrusted infrastructures (e.g. cloud providers). In this section, we give a qualitative evaluation of

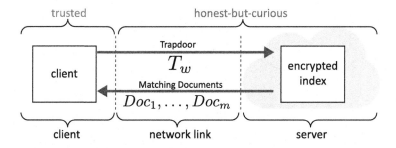

Fig. 8. Encrypted search on a remote system: abstract model.

the security implications when searchable encryption schemes are used to search over encrypted data stored on a remote server. This security evaluation is generally applicable to searchable encryption schemes that correspond to the abstract model given in Sect. 6 and therefore not specific to Goh's Z-IDX scheme [1], unless explicitly noted otherwise.

The *security* of computer systems constituted by the attributes of confidentiality, integrity and availability (as defined in the ITSEC criteria [23], see also [24]). As the purpose of searchable encryption is to protect the searched keywords from being disclosed to unauthorized parties, we focus our evaluation on the property of data confidentiality of search keywords.

Abstract System Model. For the security evaluation, we assume a setup as shown in Fig. 8 (see also [25]). A server holds a set of n documents $Doc_1, \ldots, Doc_n$. It also holds an encrypted data structure which contains a mapping for every keyword $w \in W$ to all documents containing w. To query the encrypted index, the client generates a trapdoor T_w and sends it to the server over the network. Using this trapdoor, the server can determine all documents that contain keyword w and sends them back to the client over the network. The mapping between keywords and trapdoors $w \mapsto T_w$ is deterministic, i.e. under the same encryption key there exists exactly one trapdoor T_w for every keyword w. These properties apply to most symmetric searchable encryption schemes.

Attacker Model. Attacks to learn the plaintext of keywords and their association with encrypted documents can generally be undertaken in any part of the architecture. Attacks on the client are the most dangerous, as clients hold the cryptographic key and handle unencrypted information. We assume authorized users on these clients to be trustworthy. For the operator of the network link and the server we assume a honest-but-curious attacker model (see e.g. [26]): These operators will generally execute programs and transmit information correctly and faithfully, but can record arbitrary information and perform additional calculations on it. Under this adversarial model, data confidentiality is challenged while integrity and availability are not affected.

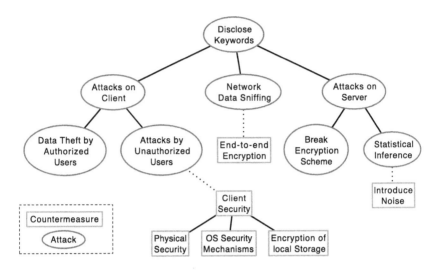

Fig. 9. Attack-defense-tree: threats for confidentiality of keywords.

6.1   Threats to Keyword Confidentiality

To illustrate the threats to the confidentiality of keywords in the system we use the ADTree model (Attack-Defense-Trees, see [27,28]), which build upon the concept of attack trees [29]. Attack trees are used to model the threats to a specific security property of a system and their logical interdependencies. Individual threats are represented as leaves of the tree and are connected by AND and OR operators to the root of the tree, which represents a specific security property. The attack of the system that corresponds to a specific threat is indicated in the model by assigning a boolean TRUE value of the node in the tree. If a combination of attacks results in a propagation of a TRUE value to the root node the security property is considered to be breached. By evaluating the attack tree, sets of possible attacks can be derived. The ADTree model extends attack trees by introducing and explicitly modeling countermeasures, which can be employed to mitigate or prevent attacks. In Fig. 9, an ADTree shows threats for keywords confidentiality in searchable encryption schemes and according countermeasures. Attacks to learn keywords can be undertaken on the client, on the network and the server which holds the encrypted index. In the following sections, we discuss the relevance and implications of the shown threats and their countermeasures.

6.2   Attacks on the Client

Attacks on the client are potentially severe as the client handles plaintext data and holds the cryptographic key for the searchable encryption scheme. By obtaining the key, an attacker can uncover document-keyword associations by generating valid queries and launching a dictionary attack against either the server or against intercepted trapdoors. Theft of data or keys cannot by authorized users cannot be prevented. However, in our attacker model, we assume the authorized users to be trustworthy. To protect the assets of the client systems against unauthorized users, different methods can be employed: Physical security measures can prevent unauthorized users from getting physical access to client machines. The security mechanisms of the clients operating system can ensure that only authorized users can log onto the machines directly or via network. Finally, data on the clients mass storage can be protected by hard disk encryption.

6.3   Network Data Sniffing

Interception of data exchanged by searchable encryption protocols could threaten the confidentiality of keywords as statistical properties of the trapdoor-keywords-associations can be exploited (for more detail, see Sect. 6.4). If general security flaws of the underlying scheme become known, these could also be exploited. Data sniffing on the network can however easily be prevented by encryption of network traffic between client and server (e.g. by using *Transport Layer Security*).

6.4   Attacks on the Server

In general, threats that originate from network data sniffing also exist on the server, as the entire communication of the scheme is observable. However, as the searchable encryption scheme has to be processed on the server (i.e. matching of trapdoors to documents), an additional layer of encryption is not an option. In addition, the server also has direct access to the encrypted index, which could make attacks targeting this data structure very efficient. As the server can also monitor the program execution, side-channel attacks are theoretically possible (e.g. timing attacks). In the following, we discuss the implications of these threats.

Attacks to the Encryption Scheme. The confidentiality of the keywords depends on the trust in the chosen underlying searchable encryption scheme. In the first place, it is desirable to use algorithms that are openly published and examined by cryptographic experts. In general, searchable encryption schemes are an active field of research, with many constructions from the recent past (see Sect. 2) that need more evaluation before they can be considered mature.

The Z-IDX scheme by Goh is among the oldest searchable schemes with no general attacks to the scheme published. The construction of the scheme is based on keyed hash functions, which are well examined and proved cryptographic tools (HMAC SHA-1 [21]). The scheme fulfills three security properties suggested by [4]: It supports *hidden queries* as the generated trapdoors do not reveal the keyword. Valid trapdoors cannot be generated without possession of the secret key (*controlled searching*). Both properties are ensured by using a keyed hash function. Finally, the scheme fulfills the property of *query isolation* which means that the server learns nothing more than the set of matching documents about a query.

The security properties of the scheme are formalized as the *IND-CKA* (Semantic Security Against Adaptive Chosen Keyword Attack) property: An adversary is given two documents D_0 and D_1 and an index which encodes the keywords of one of these documents. If the adversary cannot determine which documents keywords are encoded in the index with a probability significantly better than $\frac{1}{2}$ the index is considered *IND-CKA-secure*. To the best of our knowledge, no attacks that break IND-CKA-security of the Z-IDX scheme have been published to date. Our prototypical implementation of the Z-IDX scheme deliberately weakens this security guarantee by omitting the blinding of filters. The implications of this are discussed below.

Statistical Inference. Attacks using statistical inference are a possible against all searchable encryption schemes that follow the basic model outlined in this section. The threat of these attack is not based on weaknesses in the cryptographic constructions of searchable encryption schemes but is a direct consequence of the basic characteristics of such schemes. Under the same secret key K_{priv}, a keyword w is always mapped to the same trapdoor T_w. This allows the server to observe tuples $(w, \{D_1^w, ..., D_m^w\})$, i.e. combinations of encrypted queries and the set of matching documents, which leak statistical information: The sever can learn the frequency of certain queries as they occur over time and learn about the occurrence and frequency of distinct keywords in the document collection. While statistical information does not directly reveal keywords, it can be exploited to infer the semantics or plaintext of keyword using background knowledge about the data exchanged in the system. When handling medical data for example, very accurate assumptions about the prevalence of a specific medical condition among a population can be made using public sources of information. If this prevalence is expressed using a keyword and no other keyword in the document set possesses the same frequency, it is easy to infer the meaning of this keyword. While the given example might be trivial, statistical attack can pose a serious threat to the confidentiality of keywords. We review two practical attacks that have been published and discuss the implications of omitting filter blinding.

Search Pattern Leakage in Searchable Encryption: Attacks and New Constructions. [30] propose an attack based on the frequency of search patterns. The salient feature of the approach is that the frequency f_q at which a keyword q occurs is sampled over time, resulting in a frequency vector $V_q = \{V_q^1, ..., V_q^p\}$ for a specific keyword. Background knowledge for a dictionary of keywords $D = \{w_1, ..., w_m\}$ is drawn from external sources (the authors propose *Google Trends*) and represented as frequency vectors $V = \{V_{w_1}, ..., V_{w_m}\}$. To infer the plaintext of a keyword, a distance measuring function $Dist(V, V_{w_i})$ is used to determine the vector $\in V$ with the smallest distance to V_q – the corresponding keyword is then assumed to be q. The attack is amended by an active approach, where the background knowledge is adapted to a specific scenario (e.g. healthcare) to improve accuracy. To test the accuracy of their attack, they use frequency vectors obtained from Google Trends for the 52 weeks of the year 2011 and add varying levels of gaussian noise to simulate user queries. They show that under certain circumstances (e.g. keyword dictionary size of 1000, limited level of noise) it is easy to guess the keyword with a very high accuracy. They also present mitigation strategies, which are based on inserting random keywords along with every query, but do not consider the actual document matching on the server.

Access Pattern disclosure on Searchable Encryption: Ramification, Attack and Mitigation. [25] propose a statistical attack which is based on the frequency at which keywords appear in the document set. As background knowledge, information about the probability of two keywords occurring in the same document is assumed. This information can be obtained by scanning public document sources for a dictionary keywords $k_1, ..., k_m$. It is represented by a $m \times m$ matrix M, where $M_{i,j}$ contains the probability of keywords k_i and k_j occurring in the same document. The attacker then tries to find an order of encrypted queries $q_1, ..., q_m$ whose results set produce another matrix which is similar to M. This sequence that produces the matrix most similar to M is considered the result of the attack and reveals keywords by aligning the vectors of queries and keywords so that q_x corresponds to m_x. The problem can be formalized by expressing the closeness between matrices as an arithmetic distance. The authors use simulated annealing to determine a keyword sequence that minimizes this distance. The quality of the attack is the percentage of keywords that are guessed correctly. This percentage is improved if the background knowledge also includes a set of known query-trapdoor associations – this is however not required. With 15 % known queries of 150 observed queries, their attack was able to infer close to 100 % of a set of 500 keywords correctly. To counteract the presented attack, they also suggest the insertion of noise to hide statistical properties of the query-document associations. Encrypted index structures are considered $(\alpha, 0)$-secure if for every keyword there are $\alpha - 1$ keywords that appear in the same set of documents - limiting an attackers probability of correctly inferring a keyword to $\frac{1}{\alpha}$ at best.

Omission of Filter Blinding. In Sect. 4.3, we presented a prototypical implementation of Z-IDX, which omits the step of filter blinding in favor of improved performance (see also Sect. 5.1). This deviation from the specification of the Z-IDX scheme enables inference attacks under conditions where the number of keywords in a document allows to draw conclusions on the content of keywords or documents. If such conclusions are possible using background knowledge in the application scenario, the addition of blinding bits to the filters as described in [1] can be used to effectively thwart this attack at the expense of performance.

6.5   Implications for Practical Use

The threat model in Sect. 6.1 shows that attacks on the confidentiality are possible in every part of the system. However, as shown in the previous sections, attacks by unauthorized users on the client and the network can effectively miti-gated by access control and encryption. The most relevant threat is the possibil-ity of inferring keywords by exploiting statistical properties that can be observed by monitoring queries. The threat posed by statistical inference attacks depends strongly on the set of keywords and their distribution in the document set. Statis-tical inference attacks are only a minor concern if the individual keywords exhibit very similar statistical properties, e.g. serial numbers that are evenly distributed across documents. However, attributes with statistical properties that could be available as background knowledge (e.g. medical diagnoses) to an attacker need to be treated with great caution and might require noise insertion.

7   Conclusion

In this paper, we investigated the practical usability of searchable encryption schemes to provide search capability over encrypted data archives in the cloud. As a practical example, we presented a prototypical implementation of the Z-IDX scheme embedded in the document-oriented database MongoDB. Benchmarks on this prototype revealed a that under realistic conditions, the performance impact for encrypted queries is little for insert operations. Encrypted search operations however are considerably slower due to the linear complexity of the Z-IDX scheme. However, we also note that execution time can be vastly improved by parallel execution of the search operation.

To evaluate the security aspects of searchable encrypted, we gave a qualitative analysis of threats to keyword confidentiality as an attack-defense-tree model. We found the most relevant threat to be attacks using statistical inference, which exploits statistical properties of keywords that are leaked in most searchable encryption schemes. Depending on the use case and the statistical properties of keywords, noise insertion can be employed to counter such attacks. We present different attacks from literature and their mitigation strategies.

Further research could investigate the performance more recent constructions of searchable encryption schemes with constant search complexity (e.g. [16]) and schemes that provide extended search capabilities, such as range queries (see e.g. [13,17]).

References

1. Goh, E.-J., et al.: Secure indexes. IACR Cryptology ePrint Archive, 2003:216 (2003)
2. Bajaj, S., Sion, R.: TrustedDB: a trusted hardware based database with privacy and data confidentiality. In: Proceedings of SIGMOD 2011 International Confer-ence on Management of Data, pp. 205–216. ACM (2011)
3. Arasu, A., Blanas, S., Eguro, K., Joglekar, M., Kaushik, R., Kossmann, D., Rama-murthy, R., Upadhyaya, P., Venkatesan, R.: Secure database-as-a-service with cipherbase. In: Proceedings of SIGMOD 2013 International Conference on Man-agement of Data, pp. 1033–1036. ACM (2013)

4. Song, D.X., Wagner, D., Perrig, A.: Practical techniques for searches on encrypted data. In: Proceedings of the 2000 IEEE Symposium on Security and Privacy, S&P 2000, pp. 44–55. IEEE (2000)
5. Yang, Z., Zhong, S., Wright, R.N.: Privacy-preserving queries on encrypted data. In: Gollmann, D., Meier, J., Sabelfeld, A. (eds.) ESORICS 2006. LNCS, vol. 4189, pp. 479–495. Springer, Heidelberg (2006)
6. Popa, R.A., Redfield, C.M.S., Zeldovich, N., Balakrishnan, H.: CryptDB: protecting confidentiality with encrypted query processing. In: Proceedings of the Twenty-Third ACM Symposium on Operating Systems Principles, SOSP 2011, pp. 85–100. ACM (2011)
7. Agrawal, R., Kiernan, J., Srikant, R., Xu, Y.: Order preserving encryption for numeric data. In: Proceedings of SIGMOD 2004 International Conference on Management of Data, pp. 563–574. ACM (2004)
8. Rivest, R.L., Adleman, L., Dertouzos, M.L.: On data banks and privacy homomorphisms. Found. Secure Comput. **32**(4), 169–178 (1978)
9. Gentry, C.: Fully homomorphic encryption using ideal lattices. In: Proceedings of the 41st Annual ACM Symposium on Theory of Computing, pp. 169–178. ACM (2009)
10. van Dijk, M., Gentry, C., Halevi, S., Vaikuntanathan, V.: Fully homomorphic encryption over the integers. In: Gilbert, H. (ed.) EUROCRYPT 2010. LNCS, vol. 6110, pp. 24–43. Springer, Heidelberg (2010)
11. Shmueli, E., Waisenberg, R., Elovici, Y., Gudes, E.: Designing secure indexes for encrypted databases. In: Proceedings of the 19th Annual IFIP WG 11.3 Working Conference on Data and Applications Security, DBSec 2005, pp. 54–68 (2005)
12. Hore, B., Mehrotra, S., Tsudik, G.: A privacy-preserving index for range queries. In: Proceedings of the 13th International Conference on Very Large Data Bases, VLDB 2004, pp. 720–731 (2004)
13. El Abbadi, A., Agrawal, D., Wang, S.: A comprehensive framework for secure query processing on relational data in the cloud. In: Jonker, W., Petković, M. (eds.) SDM 2011. LNCS, vol. 6933, pp. 52–69. Springer, Heidelberg (2011)
14. Lauter, K., Kamara, S.: Cryptographic cloud storage. In: Sion, R., Curtmola, R., Dietrich, S., Kiayias, A., Miret, J.M., Sako, K., Sebé, F. (eds.) RLCPS, WECSR, and WLC 2010. LNCS, vol. 6054, pp. 136–149. Springer, Heidelberg (2010)
15. Curtmola, R., Garay, J., Kamara, S., Ostrovsky, R.: Searchable symmetric encryption: improved definitions and efficient constructions. In: Proceedings of the 13th ACM Conference on Computer and Communications Security, pp. 79–88. ACM (2006)
16. Kamara, S., Papamanthou, C., Roeder, T.: Dynamic searchable symmetric encryption. In: Proceedings of the 2012 ACM Conference on Computer and Communications Security, pp. 965–976. ACM (2012)
17. Ostrovsky, R., Di Crescenzo, G., Persiano, G., Boneh, D.: Public key encryption with keyword search. In: Cachin, C., Camenisch, J.L. (eds.) EUROCRYPT 2004. LNCS, vol. 3027, pp. 506–522. Springer, Heidelberg (2004)
18. Kiltz, E., et al.: Searchable encryption revisited: consistency properties, relation to anonymous IBE, and extensions. In: Shoup, V. (ed.) CRYPTO 2005. LNCS, vol. 3621, pp. 205–222. Springer, Heidelberg (2005)
19. Byun, J.W., Rhee, H.S., Park, H.-A., Lee, D.-H.: Off-line keyword guessing attacks on recent keyword search schemes over encrypted data. In: Jonker, W., Petković, M. (eds.) SDM 2006. LNCS, vol. 4165, pp. 75–83. Springer, Heidelberg (2006)
20. Bloom, B.H.: Space/time trade-offs in hash coding with allowable errors. Commun. ACM **13**(7), 422–426 (1970)

21. Krawczyk, H., Bellare, M., Canetti, R.: HMAC: Keyed-Hashing for Message Authentication. RFC 2104 (Informational). Updated by RFC 6151 (1997)
22. Floratou, A., Teletia, N., DeWitt, D.J., Patel, J.M., Zhang, D.: Can the elephants handle the NoSQL onslaught? Proc. VLDB Endow. **5**, 1712–1723 (2012)
23. ITSEC: Information technology security evaluation criteria (ITSEC): Preliminary harmonised criteria. Technical report, Commission of the European Communities (1991)
24. Avizienis, A., Laprie, J.-C., Randell, B., Landwehr, C.: Basic concepts and taxonomy of dependable and secure computing. IEEE Trans. Dependable Secure Comput. **1**(1), 11–33 (2004)
25. Islam, M., Kuzu, M., Kantarcioglu, M.: Access pattern disclosure on searchable encryption: ramification, attack and mitigation. In: Network and Distributed System Security Symposium (NDSS 2012) (2012)
26. Pinkas, B., Smart, N.P., Lindell, Y.: Implementing two-party computation efficiently with security against malicious adversaries. In: Ostrovsky, R., De Prisco, R., Visconti, I. (eds.) SCN 2008. LNCS, vol. 5229, pp. 2–20. Springer, Heidelberg (2008)
27. Kordy, B., Mauw, S., Radomirovic, S., Schweitzer, P.: Attack-defense trees. J. Logic Comput. (2012)
28. Bagnato, A., Kordy, B., Meland, P.H., Schweitzer, P.: Attribute decoration of attack-defense trees. Int. J. Secure Softw. Eng. (IJSSE) **3**(2), 1–35 (2012)
29. Schneier, B.: Attack trees. Dr. Dobb's J. **24**(12), 21–29 (1999)
30. Liu, C., Zhu, L., Wang, M., Tan, Y.: Search pattern leakage in searchable encryption: Attacks and new constructions. Cryptology ePrint Archive, Report 2013/163 (2013)

High Level Model Checker
Based Testing of Electronic Contracts

Ellis Solaiman[1]([✉]), Ioannis Sfyrakis[1], and Carlos Molina-Jimenez[2]

[1] School of Computing Science, Newcastle University, Newcastle upon Tyne, UK
{ellis.solaiman,i.sfyrakis}@ncl.ac.uk
[2] Computer Laboratory, University of Cambridge, Cambridge, UK
carlos.molina@cl.cam.ac.uk

Abstract. Within cloud and Internet-based collaborative settings, a business contract (service agreement) is a specification that describes permissible interactions between partners. Specifically, a business contract stipulates what operations the business partners have the rights, obligations or prohibitions to execute; it also specifies when the operations are to be executed and in which order. The main purpose of an electronic contract is to regulate (monitor and/or enforce) electronic service exchanges between the contracted parties, making sure that participants adhere to the service agreement in place. Because of the dynamic nature of Internet and cloud-based relationships, the rapidity at which electronic contracts are constructed, verified for correctness, tested, and deployed is an extremely important factor. This paper describes a model checker based framework for supporting automated testing and deployment of electronic contracts. The central components of the framework are a contract monitoring service called the *Contract Compliance Checker (CCC)*, the *SPIN* model checker coupled with *EPROMELA*, a high-level language developed specifically for modeling electronic contracts, and the *LTL Manager*; a graphical tool developed in order to aid with the specification of correctness properties in *Linear Temporal Logic (LTL)*. We describe how the *LTL Manager* can used to create a repository of common contract related LTL templates, which then can be easily selected and parameterized by the contract designer. We also describe how *SPIN* can be used to automatically generate execution sequences from an *EPROMELA* model of a contract, and how such sequences can then be used to test the correctness of the model equivalent electronic contract deployed to the *CCC*.

Keywords: Service agreement · Electronic contract · Service monitoring · Model checking · Automated testing · Service oriented computing · Cloud computing

1 Introduction

The context of this paper is Internet and cloud-based interactions conducted between two or more business partners. Such relationships are normally preceded

© Springer International Publishing Switzerland 2016
M. Helfert et al. (Eds.): CLOSER 2015, CCIS 581, pp. 193–215, 2016.
DOI: 10.1007/978-3-319-29582-4_11

by the negotiation and signing of business contracts also known as legal service agreements (SA). Legal agreements, explicitly define the permissible actions of the interacting parties, thus providing a legal basis for the resolution of any disputes. A Legal agreement can also be used as a guide for developing an electronic contract [1].

An electronic contract is an executable version of the service agreement, and its main purpose is to regulate (monitor and/or enforce) electronic service exchanges between the contracted parties, checking that business participants adhere to the SA in place, and that performed actions comply with various message timing and sequencing constraints. Electronic contracts are not confined to the business domain, and can also be used for example to monitor/enforce SAs between the components of distributed systems in the cloud and/or the "Internet of Things".

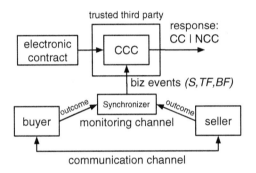

Fig. 1. The CCC deployed as a contract monitor.

Constructing an electronic contract that is correct (free from conflicts, and which correctly represents the requirements of the original legal document), is a challenging and time-consuming task. Cloud-based business relationships can be both complex and of a highly dynamic nature [2]. Therefore, it is important that the process of converting a legal document into an electronic contract that is correct is automated. Previous work towards this goal has been extensive and has covered problems such as electronic contract representation and modeling [3], and contract verification [4,5]. Naturally, ensuring that a model of an electronic contract is correct, does not guarantee that the electronic contract itself is also correct. In this paper, we focus on the challenge of testing that an electronic contract acts correctly at run-time, and that modifications and/or corrections that need to be made to the rule base of the electronic contract can be applied quickly. To this end, we develop a high-level model checker based framework to support automatic electronic contract deployment and testing.

The central component of our framework is the *contract compliance checker (CCC)* (Fig. 1) [6,7], which together with the deployed electronic contract is our System Under Test (SUT). The CCC is an independent contract monitoring service that when provided with an executable specification of a contract, can be deployed by the contracted parties or by a third party. The CCC is able to observe and log relevant interaction events, which it processes to determine whether the actions of the business partners are consistent with respect to the rights, obligations, and prohibitions declared in the original legal contract. Namely, the CCC declares interaction events as either contract compliant (*CC*) or non contract compliant (*NCC*). As can be seen in Fig. 1, business partners use a communication channel for exchanging their business messages. In addition, they use a monitoring channel for notifying events of interest to the CCC. Notably, the figure shows that the CCC can cope with exceptions and failures, observing events that have been declared by the interacting parties as either *S (successful), TF (technical failure),* or *BF (business failure).*

The ability of the CCC to correctly declare interaction events as (*CC*) or (*NCC*) relies on an executable contract that has been specified correctly. Our goal is to provide a framework that enables; rapid testing of a deployed executable contract, and rapid update of the contract rules when testing detects errors. To do so, one must be able to exhaustively supply the CCC with execution sequences that it would be expected to observe during runtime. Our approach is to resort to model checker based testing. Previous research [8] describes the basic idea: construct a behavioral model of the SUT and validate the behavior using a model checker. Such a validated model can then be used for generating executable test cases for the SUT.

The model checking tool we use is SPIN [9], a tool originally designed for the verification of communication protocols. SPIN's input language, Promela, provides constructs for modeling communication concepts such as messages, channels, and basic data types that include bit, bye, arrays, etc. Using these basic constructs alone for modeling electronic contracts, at a sufficiently high level of abstraction and in any consistently standard fashion, is almost impossible. This in turn makes the process of generating accurate execution sequences required for testing the CCC difficult. Another difficulty is that specifying the contract correctness requirements is not easy. The contract designer needs to master both Promela, the input language of SPIN, and LTL (Linear Temporal Logic), the language for expressing correctness properties [10]. It is widely acknowledged that LTL is a powerful language for expressing correctness properties. Yet it has proven to be hard to master for non–experts in temporal logic. For instance, the LTL syntax traditionally accepted by SPIN is low level and based on the basic temporal logic operators (!, [], <>, etc.), which results in LTL formula that are not easy to read or write. In addition, the semantics of LTL formula are very subtle; thus writing an LTL formula that captures the intended correctness requirement within a Promela model is particularly challenging and error prone.

To address these challenges, we explore the development of a high level modeling and deployment framework. A fundamental component of our testing framework is *EPROMELA*, a high level language developed specifically for modeling electronic contracts [5]. *EPROMELA* extends Promela with constructs for expressing core electronic contract concepts contained in the CCC, thus enabling the construction of a contract model at a level of abstraction that is equivalent to the actual electronic contract. In addition, we have developed the *LTL Manager* [11], a graphical tool and a repository that can be populated by LTL experts with LTL templates (LTL formula with abstract variables) of typical correctness properties required for electronic contracts, together with their English language descriptions. These LTL templates can then be selected and parameterized by contract designers in order to produce LTLs that are specific to their requirements. The LTL properties are then mechanically included in the *EPROMELA* models and presented to SPIN for verification.

The overall contribution of this paper is to describe how *SPIN, EPROMELA*, and the *LTL Manager* can be instrumented with the aid of appropriate automation and message parsing tools, to automatically produce business events that can accurately test the executable electronic contract deployed within the CCC service.

The remainder of the paper is structured as follows: In Sect. 2 we describe key electronic contracting concepts with the aid of a simple example. Section 3 is dedicated to presenting our model checker based testing framework and its constituent tools. In Sect. 4 we present research work that is related to ours. Conclusions and future directions are discussed in Sect. 5.

2   Background

In order to elaborate key electronic contracting concepts, we present a simple scenario. Let us assume that Fig. 1 describes a relationship where two organisations, a Buyer and a Seller (a store), agree to a business contract. Below are some of its clauses:

1. *The buyer can place a **buy request** with the store to buy an item.*
2. *The store is obliged to respond with either **buy confirmation** or **buy rejection** within 3 days of receiving the buy request.*
   (a) *No response from the store within 3 days will be treated as a buy rejection.*
3. *The buyer can either **pay** or **cancel** the buy request within 7 days of receiving a confirmation.*
   (a) *No response from the buyer within 7 days will be treated as a cancellation.*

The clauses of such a legal agreement should take into consideration all relevant business operations (shown in bold in the contract text). A business contract specifies a well defined list of business operations. A business operation is a business activity which the participants are able to perform under certain conditions. In the CCC, business operations are used to formally define the vocabulary (alphabet) of the interaction. We use $B = \{bo_1, \ldots, bo_n\}$ to represent all the valid business operations in the contract. The buyer and seller are regarded as role players interested in executing the operations is a shared fashion. The set of valid role players is represented by $RP = \{rp_1, \ldots, rp_n\}$.

The execution of each business process generates an individual outcome event which is passed to the synchronizer shown in Fig. 1 through the monitor channel. The synchronizer integrates the pair of individual outcomes from each side into a single business event. This business event is sent to the CCC. As a monitor, the responsibility of the CCC is to determine whether a given event presented to it represents the notification of a contract compliant operation CC, or a none contract compliant operation NCC. To be able to make this determination, the CCC keeps track of the state of interaction as a *Finite State Machine (FSM)* with states being determined by enabling and disabling the current rights, obligations and prohibitions of the role players in force.

2.1 ROP Ontology

A contract distinguishes operations as *Rights*, *Obligations*, and *Prohibitions* (the *ROP* set). A *Right* is an operation that a party is allowed to perform under certain conditions, an *Obligation* is an operation that a party is expected to do under certain conditions, and a *Prohibition* is an operation that a party is not allowed to do under certain conditions.

We define an individual right r_i, obligation o_i or prohibition p_i as a set of operations where: $r_i \subseteq B$, $o_i \subseteq B$, and $p_i \subseteq B$. For a particular role player RP; $R_{rp} = \{r_1,\ldots,r_n\}$; $O_{rp} = \{o_1,\ldots,o_n\}$; and $P_{rp} = \{p_1,\ldots,p_n\}$, represent the sets of rights, obligations, and prohibitions currently assigned to the role player RP respectively. The sets of rights, obligations, and prohibitions of an RP are represented as ROP_{rp}.

2.2 Choreography of Interaction

To support our discussion, we will use a graphical representation of the contract written in *BPMN (Business Process Management Notation)* choreography language [12] (see Fig. 2). The figure involves five activities, each resulting in a message (*BuyReq, BuyRej, BuyConf, BuyPay, BuyCanc*) being sent from a sender (shown as a white label in each activity), to a receiver (shown as a shaded label). These messages correspond to the five business operations (buy request, buy reject, buy confirmation, buy payment, buy cancellation) shown in bold in the English text of the contract. The diamonds in the figure are gateways. The figure includes two exclusive fork gateways (G1 and G2) and a single exclusive merge gateway (G3).

The choreography specification describes, from a global perspective, all permissible message sequences that can be exchanged between the partners, and is used by the interacting parties for two purposes: (i) designing and implementing their individual parts of the business process; and (ii) it is also very useful as a guide for developing the electronic contract.

2.3 Electronic Contracts

The electronic contract designer is able to use the legal contract and choreography in order to accurately identify and extract the ROP set attributed to the business partners, and to specify the rules which operate on the ROP set [13].

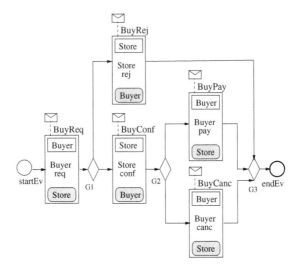

Fig. 2. Correct choreography of contract example.

Rule implementation requires an appropriate specification language; contract rules written for the CCC monitoring service are currently realized using the Drools Rule Language [14].

An example of a rule that deals with receipt of a *buy request* event by the CCC, written using Drools can be seen below. Line 5 checks that the *buyRequest* operation is a right that the buyer is currently allowed to perform. If so then *buyRequest* is declared by the CCC as contract compliant (line 13). This operation is also removed from the buyer's ROP set (line 8), meaning that the buyer no longer has a right to perform this operation. At lines 10 and 11, the seller is given an obligation to perform one of 2 operations: *buyConfirm*, or *buyReject*.

```
1 rule "Buy Request Received"
2 //Verify type of event, originator, and responder
3 when
4 $e: Event(type=="BUYREQ", originator=="buyer",
    responder=="store", status=="success")
5 eval(ropBuyer.matchesRights(buyRequest))
6 then
7 //Remove buyer's right to place other Buy Requests
8 ropBuyer.removeRight(buyRequest, seller);
9 //Add seller's obligation to either accept or reject order
10 BusinessOperation[] bos = {buyConfirm, buyReject};
11 ropSeller.addObligation("React To Buy Request", bos, buyer,
    60,2);
12 System.out.println("* Buy Request Received rule triggered");
13 responder.setContractCompliant(true)
14 end
```

Each of the activities declared in the choreography of Fig. 2 has a rule such as the one shown above. Typically, for each activity in a choreography, each business partner can have several rights, obligations, and prohibitions in force.

Once an electronic contract specification has been completed, it can be loaded into the CCC for deployment. As operations are executed, and events are received by the CCC; rights, obligations, and prohibitions are granted to and revoked as specified by the rules. Therefore within the CCC, a right, obligation or prohibition can be in one of two states only: *inactive* or *active*.

Drools as a language for specifying electronic contracts is verbose, and not as declarative and readable as would be ideal. A much more suitable tool is *EROP* a language that we developed precisely for the specification of electronic contracts. *EROP (for Events, Rights, Obligations, and Prohibitions)* was first introduced in [6], and we have just completed a tool for automatically translating EROP to Drools. The *EROP to Drools Translator* has been developed using Java, and *ANTLR* [15]. The translator takes as input an *EROP* file and outputs a Drools file containing the contract rules. An example of an *EROP* to Drools conversion is shown in Fig. 3. A detailed description of the EROP language can be found in [6].

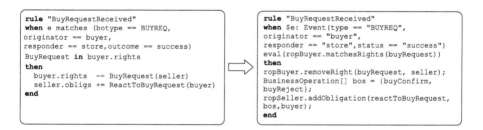

Fig. 3. EROP to Drools conversion.

2.4 Contract Compliance Within the CCC Monitor

The overall architecture of the CCC is described in detail in [11]. The CCC processes each event to determine if it is contract compliant *(CC)* or none contract compliant *(NCC)*. A business event is received by the CCC as an XML document that includes the names of the participants, the business operation, and its outcome from the set: *(Success, BizFail, TecFail)*:

```
<event>
  <originator>buyer</originator>
  <responder>seller</responder>
  <type>BuyReq</type>
  <status>success</status>
</event>
```

The event shown here is produced as a result of the implementation of a conversation synchronization protocol between the interacting parties. The protocol guarantees mutually agreed conversation outcomes. It is the responsibility of the interacting partners to apply the protocol. A detailed discussed can be found in [16]. The CCC inserts the response into an outcome queue, which can be accessed by the contracted parties. The response is of the format:

```
<result>
  <contractcompliant>true|false</contractcompliant>
</result>
```

The execution of a business operation (observed from the outcome event) is said to be CC if it satisfies the following three conditions and is said to be NCC if it does not:

(1) $bo_i \in BO$; the business operation matches an operation within the set of business operations expected by the CCC,
(2) $bo_i \vdash ROP_{rp}$; the business operation matches the ROP set of its role player (meaning, the role player that performed the operation has a right/obligation/prohibition to perform that particular operation). By "match", we mean that for a valid business operation bo_i, and a particular role player's ROP set; ROP_{rp} where: $R_{rp} = \{r_1, \dots, r_m\}$, $O_{rp} = \{o_1, \dots, o_m\}$, $P_{rp} = \{p_1, \dots, p_m\}$, and $m \geq 1$, their relationship should be that: $bo_i \in r_j$ or $bo_i \in o_j$ or $bo_i \in p_j$, where $1 \leq j \leq m$.
(3) the business operation must also satisfy the constraints stipulated in the contractual clauses. An example of a constraint is the seven day deadline in clause 3 of the contract discussed earlier.

We also consider that the execution of a given sequence of operations is NCC if it includes one or more operations that are flagged by the CCC as NCC. A sequence of operations is also known as an *execution sequence* or *execution trace* and drives the choreography from its initial state to a final state.

2.5   Exception Handling

The legal contract example and corresponding choreography of Fig. 2, deal with successful outcome events only. However, a contract monitoring service such as the CCC should also be able to observe outcome events that include exceptional circumstances [17]. Therefore, following the ebXML standard [18], we assume that at the end of a business conversation, each party independently declares an execution outcome event from the set {*Success(S)*, *BizFail(BF)*, *TecFail(TF)*} as shown in Fig. 1. *Success* events model successful execution outcomes. *TecFail* models protocol related failures detected at the middleware level, such as a late, or a syntactically incorrect message. *BizFail* models semantic errors in a message detected at the business level, e.g., the credit card details extracted from the received payment document are incorrect.

Adding exceptional outcome events to the CCC's set of observable events, naturally means that the CCC has to monitor a much larger number of execution sequences. The task of generating these in order to test the CCC effectively is extremely challenging, and strengthens the case for needing to automate the testing process.

3   Model Checker Based Testing Framework

To be able to claim that an electronic contract within the CCC is correct and conflict free, we need to test that it can correctly identify contract compliant and non-contract compliant executions of sequences and their constituent business operations. To this end, one needs to be able produce sequences of operations that are known to be contract compliant, and also produce sequences that include both contract compliant and non contract compliant operations. The challenge here is the production of such sequences.

Figure 4 shows the main elements of our testing framework. Squares with smooth corners represent humans involved in the design process. Tools are represented by solid squares with sharp corners, and dashed squares represent data. The framework has been updated with 2 new tools since our work in [19] with the addition of the *LTL Manager*, and the *EROP to Drools Translator*.

Electronic contract models are constructed using EPROMELA, a modeling language we developed specifically for modeling electronic contracts [5]. EPROMELA is essentially a high-level tool that extends SPIN's modeling language Promela with constructs for expressing core electronic contract concepts contained in the CCC. Correctness properties that an EPROMELA model is expected to satisfy, can be expressed by the model designer using Linear Temporal Logic (LTL), which is not an easy task. The *LTL Manager* is a tool we have developed in order to help the contract designer with expressing correctness properties using LTL. When provided with a model of the contract and appropriate LTL properties, SPIN is able to verify the correctness of the model with respect to those properties. With the aid of tools for message parsing and automation, SPIN also can be instrumented to generate message sequences that can be used to test the ability of the CCC to detect contract compliant and non contract compliant message sequences, a process that we will describe next. Model checker based sequence generation follows these steps:

1. The designer constructs an abstract model of the System Under Test (SUT) using EPROMELA, and verifies that the model is correct in that it satisfies the correctness properties of interest.
2. The verified abstract model is used for generating execution sequences. This is done by presenting the verification tool with the verified abstract model, together with a negated correctness requirement in LTL (a trap property), and then challenging the verification tool to find and produce counter examples that violate the LTL.
3. Each counter example contains an execution sequence that can be extracted with the aid of a message parsing tool.

3.1   EPROMELA Interaction Model

An abstract view of EPROMELA components is shown in Fig. 5, which essentially models the system depicted in Fig. 1. The Business Event Generator (BEG)

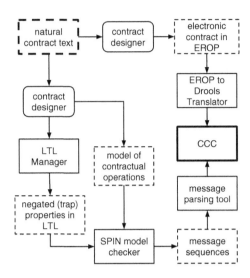

Fig. 4. Model Checker based testing framework.

generates events that are simulations of events generated by the interacting parties; for example a payment event placed by the buyer. The Contract Rules Manager (CRM) together with the ROP sets and the ECA rules (rule base) represent the CCC. The CRM is responsible for including rules as needed. The BEG and CMR communicate by two uni-directional channels (BEG2R and R2BEG). The contract rules are composed in a separate file. The ROP sets contain information about the rights, obligations, and prohibitions currently in force. For a full description, see [5]. The rule base contains a rule for each business event representing the outcome of an operation execution. So for a business operation such as "submit purchase order" there will be a rule for the operation terminating successfully (S), and optionally (depending on whether the contact has clauses dealing with failure outcomes) a rule for the operation terminating in a technical failure (TF) and one for the operation terminating in a business failure (BF).

The execution behavior of the interaction model shown in Fig. 5 is as follows: (1) BEG generates event be_i and sends it through the BEG2R channel; (2) CRM reads be_i from the BEG2R channel; (3) CMR includes the contract rule R_i corresponding to be_i; (4) R_i checks be_i against the ROP sets, and executes the coded action if the associated conditions are satisfied; (5) R_i sends its decision about be_i (either contract compliant or non–contract–compliant) through the R2BEG channel; (6) BEG extracts the decision from the R2BEG channel and resumes its event generation process.

3.2   Model Construction and Verification

Below is an example of a rule within of our EPROMELA contract model. The rule deals with the *BUYRREQ* operation of Fig. 2. Each of the operations for

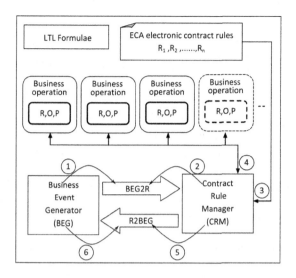

Fig. 5. EPROMELA interaction model.

the choreography in Fig. 2 has a rule which updates the status of the ROP set belonging the participants as they transition from state to state. Notice that we include within the rule, print statements that produce XML events. These are XML events that will eventually be extracted and used to automatically test the electronic contract deployed in the CCC. The end of each execution sequence is marked using a *reset* message.

```
1  RULE(BUYREQ)
2  {
3  WHEN::EVENT(BUYREQ,
       IS_R(BUYREQ,BUYER),SC(BUYREQ))->{
4  SET_X(BUYREQ,BUYER);
5  atomic{
6  printf("<originator>buyer</originator>");
7  printf("<responder>store</responder>");
8  printf("<type>BUYREQ</type>");
9  printf("<status>success</status>");
10 }
11 SET_R(BUYREQ,0);
12 SET_O(BUYREJ,1);
13 SET_O(BUYCONF,1);
14 RD(BUYREQ,BUYER,CCR,CO);
15 }
16 END(BUYREQ);
```

Line 3 of the model deals with receiving a successful buy request event SC(BUYREQ). IS_R(BUYREQ,BUYER) is a guard that checks if the *BUYER* has a right to perform the *BUYREQ* operation. If so, then SET_X(BUYREQ,BUYER) declares that this operation has been executed, and the buyer's right to execute *BUYREQ* is removed at line 11. The rule then sets an obligation to the Store to execute either *BUYREJ* or *BUYCONF* (lines 12–13). At line 6 we introduce the print statements required for parsing the generated execution sequences. The print statements produce XML events in the format expected by the CCC. Each of the operations *BUYREQ, BUYREJ, BUYCONF, BUYPAR, BUYCANC*, has a rule such as the one above.

When the entire EPROMELA model has been constructed, SPIN can be used to verify that the model is free from any inconsistencies. Common correctness properties such as absence of deadlocks and reachability of states, can easily be checked using SPIN's configuration options. Checking for contract specific correctness properties however, requires the application of Linear Temporal Logic (LTL) formula. Typical correctness properties of the electronic contracting domain are those that express mutual exclusion of rights, obligations, and prohibitions; for example the requirement that the execution of a given operation (such as making a purchase order) is never simultaneously obliged and prohibited. Thanks to the contract constructs offered by EPROMELA, this correctness requirement can be elegantly and intuitively expressed in LTL as follows: `[]!(IS_O(BUYREQ, BUYER) && IS_P(BUYREQ, BUYER))` where `[]` is the LTL always operator. `!` is the universal not, `IS_O(BUYREQ, BUYER)` returns true if the `BUYREQ` operation is currently obliged and `IS_P(BUYREQ, BUYER)` returns true if the `BUYREQ` operation is currently prohibited. Instructing SPIN to run through the EPROMELA model using this LTL, will drive SPIN to find any examples that violate this property. If such an example is found, then it is presented as a counter example to the designer, who must then correct the model.

3.3   The LTL Manager

As discussed earlier, *Linear Temporal Logic (LTL)*, which we use for specifying contract correctness requirements, is not easy to master. In order to deal with this challenge, we have developed the *LTL manager*, a graphical interface that can be used by contract designers to include correctness properties within their EPROMELA models. The *LTL manager* offers the capability of editing LTL templates (LTL formula with abstract variables), and stores them in a database. The database is a repository of typical contract LTL formula that can be populated by LTL experts. Once the LTL repository has been populated, a contract designer can retrieve an LTL template of interest, parameterize, and include it in an EPROMELA model. The SPIN model checker is invoked from the *LTL manager* by the designer. It takes EPROMELA models augmented with LTL correctness properties and verifies whether the LTLs are satisfied or violated. Details of how to download the LTL Manager can be found in [19].

Using the tool (see Fig. 6): (a) the LTL expert specifies and adds to the template repository, common LTL templates that are of interest to contract designers. This needs to be done in natural language (*Description* box), and in LTL syntax (*Formula* box). (b) the contract designer can then load the LTLs from the database, select, and parameterize those templates of interest. As can be seen in Fig. 6, the @V1@ @V2@ @V3@ @V4@ variables are LTL propositional symbols that can be parameterized. The tool offers a drop–down list that has all six operations (*BuyReq,*

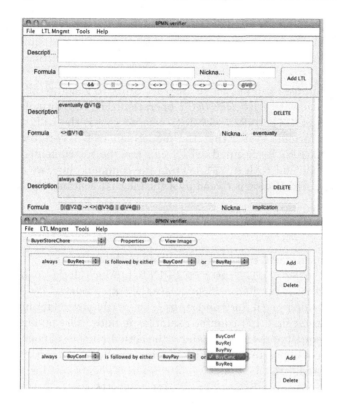

Fig. 6. Using the LTL Manager to (a) create LTL templates and (b) parametrize them.

BuyRej, BuyConf, BuyPay, BuyCan) included in the choreography of Fig. 2. The designer selects the desired parameters as shown in Fig. 6, and the *LTL Manager* automatically creates the correct LTLs. After the LTL pattern has been parameterized in the previous step, the designer can now simply validate the model by pressing the *Add* button, and then the *Validate button* on the next screen (not shown here). The results of the validation are then displayed to the designer. In this case, both LTLs are satisfied by the validation model; consequently, SPIN displays *errors: 0.* If on the other hand, the designer adds an LTL property that cannot be satisfied by the model; for example (<> BuyPay) (all execution paths must eventually result in BuyPay to be executed), SPIN signals that the formula is violated, and displays *errors: 1.* In addition, SPIN creates a trail file in the working folder that can be used by the designer to trace the source of the error within the model.

3.4 Generating the Test Sequences

Once the contract model has been verified for required correctness properties, it can be used as an oracle for producing sequences that can test the electronic contract. Test sequence generation is very similar to verification in that we make use of LTL properties. We can instruct SPIN to find undesirable examples of sequences that violate a desirable property. But we also need to be able to instruct SPIN to find desirable sequences that violate a non-desirable property. The latter is done by negating a desirable LTL property converting it into a *trap* property.

As a very simple example, let us instruct SPIN to generate all sequences of messages that end with a *BUYREJECT* operation. The LTL formula required for this task is: !<>IS_X(BUYREJ,STORE) where < > is the LTL eventually operator. The formula states that the model will not eventually reach a state where BUYREJ is executed. SPIN can now be instrumented to show all sequences that do end with BUYREJ. From the command line, we apply the following steps (*CorrectChore* is the name if the file that contains the EPROMELA model):

1. % spin -a CorrectChore is used for generating the verifier source code in C.
2. % cc -o pan pan.c is used for compiling the verifier.
3. % ./pan -a -e -c100 instructs SPIN to produce all the counter examples (trail files) that it can find, which violate the trap property. By default, SPIN produces the first one it finds and stops. The -c100 parameter instructs SPIN to generate the first 100 counter examples it finds. The number of counter examples requested needs to be above the actual number of counter examples that SPIN could possibly find. This number can be determine by the designer using trial and error.
4. spin -tN -s -r -B CorrectChore converts the Nth trail file into a text file that includes the XML messages involved in the execution sequence.

Given the potentially large number of trail files that can be produced by SPIN, it is advisable to mechanize the process. We use a simple shell script for this purpose. The following text represents the contents of one of the trail files produced by the Linux shell script. To ease readability, we have removed some irrelevant lines.

```
2: proc 0 (Buyer) line 35 "CorrectChore" Sent BuyReq,1
3: proc 1 (Store) line 71 "CorrectChore" Recv BuyReq,1

<originator>buyer</originator>
<responder>store</responder>
<type>BUYREQ</type>
<status>success</status>

5: proc 1 (Store) line 114 "CorrectChore" Sent BuyRej,1
6: proc 0 (Buyer) line 049 "CorrectChore" Recv BuyRej,1

<originator>store</originator>
<responder>buyer</responder>
<type>BUYREJ</type>
<status>success</status>

<originator>reset</originator>
<responder>reset</responder>
<type>reset</type>
<status>reset</status>
```

The execution sequence shown above includes a *BUYREQ* message sent from the buyer to the store, followed by *BUYREJ* sent by the store to the buyer. The status element indicates the outcome of the execution of the operation. The status in this example accounts only for successful execution outcomes (No exceptional circumstances such as technical failures are assumed), consequently, the content of this element is always *success*. The last message is the *reset* message, which we artificially include to mark the end of the sequence. As can be appreciated from this example, the files produced by SPIN and the shell script need parsing to extract the XML tagged messages.

3.5   Sequence Parsing

Our parser is built using Python. It extracts all the XML tagged messages from a given sequence and stores each message as an individual XML file. The parser achieves this by creating a recursive grammar that describes the precise structure of the business events inside a sequence. As seen in the code segment below in lines 2–5, we first define the XML tags we want to find.

```
1 #define grammar for sequence file
2 tagOriginator = pyp.Literal("<originator>") +
    pyp.Word(pyp.alphas) + pyp.Literal("</originator>")
3 tagResponder = pyp.Literal("<responder>") +
    pyp.Word(pyp.alphas) + pyp.Literal("</responder>")
4 tagType = pyp.Literal("<type>") + pyp.Word(pyp.alphas) +
    pyp.Literal("</type>")
5 tagStatus = pyp.Literal("<status>") + pyp.Word(pyp.alphas) +
    pyp.Literal("</status>")
6 lineString = tagOriginator | tagResponder | tagType |
    tagStatus
```

The parser reads a file containing a message sequence, and searches for matches against each line according to the following rule in line 6: *If there is a line that includes a tag definition of either the originator, responder, type, or status, then the match is successful.* If the parser finds a match, then it performs the following actions: (i) the parser creates a new folder with the name of the sequence, (ii) it extracts the XML part that is matched according to the above rule, (iii) a new XML file is created that includes the extracted business event. Thus, the folder *ExeSeq1–xml* for the sequence shown above will contain three XML files because the sequences contain three messages, namely *BUYREQ* → *BUYREJ* → *reset*.

3.6   Testing the Electronic Contract

After loading and initializing the CCC with the rules that encode the electronic contract, we can proceed with sending each of the execution sequences to the *BEvent queue*. Responses are collected from the *outcome queue* (see Fig. 1). The following lines show the results of testing the execution sequence *BUYREQ* → *BUYREJ* → *reset*:

```
1 filename: event1.xml
2 -Begin Request to CCC service-
3 BusinessEvent [originator=buyer, responder=store, type=BUYREQ,
    status=success]
4 -End Request to CCC service-
5
6 -Begin Response from CCC service-
7 <result>
8 <contractCompliant>true</contractCompliant>
9 </result>
10-End Response from CCC service-
11
12 filename: event2.xml
13 -Begin Request to CCC service-
14 BusinessEvent [originator=store, responder=buyer,
    type=BUYREJ, status=success]
15 -End Request to CCC service-
16
17 -Begin Response from CCC service-
18 <result>
19 <contractCompliant>true</contractCompliant>
20 </result>
21 -End Response from CCC service-
22
23 filename: event3.xml
24 -Begin Request to CCC service-
25 BusinessEvent [originator=reset, responder=reset, type=reset,
    status=reset]
26 -End Request to CCC service-
27 -Begin Response from CCC service-
28 <result>
29 <contractCompliant>true</contractCompliant>
30 </result>
31 -End Response from CCC service-
```

The operations (*BUYREQ* and *BUYREJ*) included in the sequence, are declared
contract compliant by the CCC indicating that the contract rules have been coded
correctly with respect to the LTL property in Sect. 3.4. The first operation is sent
to the CCC in line 3, and its response <contractCompliant>true is shown at
line 8. Similarly, *BUYREJ* operation is sent to the CCC at line 14, and its response
<contractCompliant>true can be seen at line 19.

3.7   Testing None Compliant Events

A model that has been verified will by default generate test sequences with events
corresponding to the execution of contract compliant (CC) operations only. An
EPROMELA model can be tuned to generate sequences which include unknown
and none contract compliant (NCC) business events using the EPROMELA
Event Generator module mentioned under Sect. 3.1. Thus, we can alter the
EPROMELA model to follow any variation of the choreography shown in Fig. 2.
For example, the modified choreography of Fig. 7 does not correctly reflect the
original text contract.

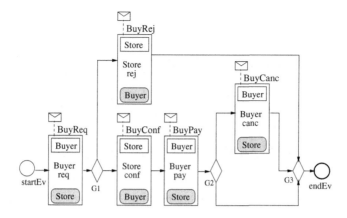

Fig. 7. Incorrect choreography of contract example.

The particularity of this diagram is that it produces CC sequences such as $BuyReq \rightarrow BuyRej$. In addition, it produces NCC sequences, for instance it allows for cancellation after payment which is not stipulated in the original contract. Consequently, the execution of $BuyCanc$ within the sequence $BuyReq \rightarrow BuyConf \rightarrow BuyPay \rightarrow BuyCanc$ should be declared NCC by the CCC. The following text shows the results of the execution of the NCC sequence discussed above. The first 2 events $BUYREQ, BUYCONF$, were declared CC by the CCC as expected. To save space we only show the outcome of the 2 events of relevance in this example ($BUYPAY$ followed by $BUYCANC$):

```
1  filename: event3.xml
2  -Begin Request to CCC service-
3  BusinessEvent [originator=buyer, responder=store, type=BUYPAY,
       status=success]
4  -End Request to CCC service-
5
6  -Begin Response from CCC service-
7  <result>
8  <contractCompliant> true </contractCompliant>
9  </result>
10 -End Response from CCC service-
11
12 filename: event4.xml
13 -Begin Request to CCC service-
14 BusinessEvent [originator=buyer, responder=store,
     type=BUYCANC, status=success]
15 -End Request to CCC service-
16
17 -Begin Response from CCC service-
18 <result>
19 <contractCompliant> false </contractCompliant>
20 </result>
21 -End Response from CCC service-
```

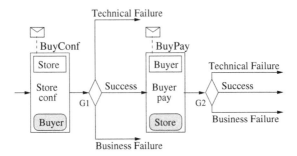

Fig. 8. Execution model with success and failures.

The process *BUYPAY* is CC (lines 3 and 8). The execution of *BUYCANC* at line 14 and the corresponding response received at line 19 indicates that the CCC has declared *BUYCANC* NCC. This is the desired behavior from the CCC, as it has detected that this sequence of events is not consistent with the contract.

3.8   Accounting for Exceptional Outcome Events

The contract example we have used so far assumes that the execution of operations always succeeds; it does not account for potential failures. More realistic examples would include the execution of activities as shown in Fig. 8, which account for successful and failed outcomes. As discussed in Sect. 2, and following the ebXML standard [18], we would like to be able to detect two types of failures; business failures, and technical failures. To this end, the EPROMELA modeling language has been designed with the ability to deal with these 2 types of failures. As an example of an electronic contract that can handle exceptional outcomes, we add the following clause to our original contract to account for potential semantic errors (*business failures*) in the execution of any operation:

4. *Failure handling: if after 2 attempts, an operation is not performed correctly, then the contractual interaction shall be declared terminated.*

Below we show how an exception such as a business failure of the *BUYREQ* operation can be intuitively and naturally modeled using EPROMELA. The rule for *BUYREQ* described in Sect. 3.2 can be easily enhanced as follows:

```
1 /*handle failure outcome event*/
2 ::EVENT(BUYREQ,IS_R(BUYREQ,BUYER),BF(BUYREQ))->{
3 atomic{
4 printf("<originator>buyer</originator>");
5 printf("<responder>store</responder>");
6 printf("<type>BUYREQ</type>");
7 printf("<status>bizfail</status>");
8 }
9 if /*1st notification of BF*/
10 ::(ReqFailBefore==NO)->ReqFailBefore=YES;
11 printf("First BUYREQ-BF");
12 RD(BUYREQ,BUYER,CCR,CO);
13 /*2nd notification of BF*/
14 ::(ReqFailBefore==YES)->abncoend=TRUE;
15 printf("Last BUYREQ-BF");
16 SET_R(BUYREQ,0);
17 atomic{
19 printf("<originator>reset</originator>");
20 printf("<responder>reset</responder>");
21 printf("<type>reset</type>");
22 printf("<status>reset</status>");
23 RD(BUYREQ,BUYER,NCCR,CND); /*abnormal contract end*/
```

The model can now also handle *BUYREQ* events that result in *BF* outcomes (line 2). If a failed event is received, then the rule checks if a failure of this kind has happened before. If not (line 10), then this first failure is registered, and contract execution is allowed to continue (line 12). On the other hand, if this is the second time *BUYREQ* has been received with a *BF* outcome then the rule terminates contract interaction at line 23. The EPROMELA model includes rules like the one described above for dealing with each of the 5 business events shown in bold in our contract example. After the model has been verified using SPIN, the electronic contract deployed to the CCC can be tested, in combination with the testing framework described previously, using much more realistic execution sequences that include exceptions. A detailed description of how exceptions are handled in the CCC can be found in [17].

4 Related Work

Research work on the monitoring of cross-organizational interactions between parties was pioneered by Minsky [20] with work on Law Governed Interaction (LGI). The notion of rights, obligations, and prohibitions was introduced in [21]. A useful summary of various issues involved in contract management is provided in [22].

Linear Temporal Logic (LTL) is a powerful tool for specifying correctness properties in a model whether it is for verifying the correctness of the model, or for the generation of test sequences. However, not all correctness properties can be expressed using LTL; for example it is not possible to specify that a particular property will hold for every 3rd or 4th state of the system. Such limitations are discussed in [23], where extensions to LTL are suggested.

Naturally, building a model of the SUT and describing the required LTL properties relies heavily on the skills of the technical person who must also be intimately familiar with the SUT. Also, it is difficult to ensure complete coverage of all possible system behaviors during testing with manually specified LTL properties. Therefore, it is desirable to be able to systematically create complete test suites according to some test objective [24]. Research work in [25] proposes to automate the task of specifying LTL properties by means of a graphical language (DecSerFlow) that is then mapped into LTL formulas. Using this language, the designer can specify a set of common or frequent correctness requirements, as can be done using our *LTL Manager*.

The advantages and disadvantages of model checker based testing are discussed in [26] where the author provides a practical guide. Although model checker based testing techniques have been studied widely in the software engineering community [27–29], their use in the testing of a contract monitoring service has received little attention. The principles of model checker based testing of electronic contracts are investigated previously by us in [8], however contract models in this work are built using Promela, the basic input language of SPIN. Attempting to predict how a designer would use basic Promela to model a contract in any standard manner is almost an impossible task, which makes developing tools for automating the testing process extremely difficult. An important contribution of this paper is that we highlight the benefits of developing a tool based framework that can leverage the capabilities of a domain specific modeling language such as *EPROMELA*, which was developed specifically for modeling electronic contracts.

5   Conclusion and Future Work

Cloud and Internet based interactions between business partners can be extremely complex, and this is especially true when exceptional outcome events from these interactions are taken into consideration. Reproducing such complex exchanges in order to test the correct functionality of a service such as the *Contract Compliance Checker (CCC)* is difficult and cannot be achieved manually. We have presented a model checker based framework that includes tools to automate the testing process. By using the SPIN model checker in combination with EPROMELA, a high level modeling language designed specifically for modeling electronic contracts, we can build verified models that accurately resemble the System Under Test (SUT) with relative ease. By using appropriate LTL formula within an EPROMELA model, we can instrument SPIN to automatically produce contract compliant, and none contract compliant execution sequences that are capable of exhaustively testing the correct operation of the CCC.

The *LTL Manager* presented in Sect. 3.3, enables the creation and description of common contract related correctness requirements as LTL templates, which are stored in an *LTL repository*. The choreography designer can use the *LTL manager* to augment an EPROMELA model with LTL correctness properties that result from the parameterization of the LTL templates. The EPROMELA model can then be presented to the SPIN model checker for verification and for generating test sequences.

There are a number of future research directions which we are currently exploring. We would like to enhance the CCC, which currently acts as a passive monitor, with the capability to act as a contract enforcer. The aim of a contract enforcement service would be to ensure that an operation is executed only if it is contract compliant. Also an important item for future work is to conduct experiments to determine how the presented testing framework performs as the number of possible events increases.

An issue that requires further exploration, is the development of mechanisms to aid with establishing conformance between electronic contracts and business choreographies [13]. Additional research work is required to extend such mechanisms to business functions involving more than two parties [30].

In addition to the *EROP* to Drools translator presented in Sect. 2.3, we would also like to create a translation tool that can produce an EPROMELA model from an electronic contract specification written in EROP automatically. This would reduce the risk of introducing unwanted errors into the contract model during construction. We believe that this goal is achievable because of the semantic similarities between EPROMELA and the electronic contracting concepts within the CCC.

References

1. Molina-Jimenez, C., Shrivastava, S., Solaiman, E., Warne, J.: Contract representation for run-time monitoring and enforcement. In: 2003 IEEE International Conference on E-Commerce (CEC 2003). IEEE (2003)
2. Molina-Jimenez, C., Shrivastava, S., Wheater, S.: An architecture for negotiation and enforcement of resource usage policies. In: IEEE International Conference on Service Oriented Computing and Applications (SOCA). IEEE (2011)
3. Strano, M., Molina-Jimenez, C., Shrivastava, S.: A rule-based notation to specify executable electronic contracts. In: Bassiliades, N., Governatori, G., Paschke, A. (eds.) RuleML 2008. LNCS, vol. 5321, pp. 81–88. Springer, Heidelberg (2008)
4. Solaiman, E., Molina-Jiménez, C., Shrivastav, S.: Model checking correctness properties of electronic contracts. In: Orlowska, M.E., Weerawarana, S., Papazoglou, M.P., Yang, J. (eds.) ICSOC 2003. LNCS, vol. 2910, pp. 303–318. Springer, Heidelberg (2003)
5. Abdelsadiq, A., Molina-Jimenez, C., Shrivastava, S.: A high level model checking tool for verifying service agreements. In: The 6th IEEE International Symposium on Service-Oriented System Engineering (SOSE 2011). IEEE (2011)
6. Strano, M., Molina-Jimenez, C., Shrivastava, S.: Implementing a rule-based contract compliance checker. In: Godart, C., Gronau, N., Sharma, S., Canals, G. (eds.) I3E 2009. IFIP AICT, vol. 305, pp. 96–111. Springer, Heidelberg (2009)
7. Molina-Jimenez, C., Shrivastava, S., Strano, M.: A model for checking contractual compliance of business interactions. IEEE Trans. Serv. Comput. 5(2), 276–289 (2012)
8. Abdelsadiq, A., Molina-Jimenez, C., Shrivastava, S.: On model checker based testing of electronic contracting systems. In: IEEE International Conference on Commerce and Enterprise Computing (CEC 2010). IEEE (2010)

9. Holzmann, G.J.: The Spin Model Checker: Primer and Reference Manual. Addison Wesley Professional, Boston (2003)

10. Pnueli, A.: The temporal logic of programs. In: Proceedings of 18th Annual Symposium on Foundations of Computer Science (FOCS 1977), pp. 46–57 (1977)

11. Solaiman, E., Sun, W., Molina-Jimenez, C.: A tool for the automatic verification of bpmn choreographies. In: IEEE 12th International Conference on Services Computing (SCC). IEEE (2015)

12. OMG: Documents associated with business process model and notation (bpmn) version 2.0 (2011). http://www.omg.org/spec/BPMN/2.0/

13. Molina-Jimenez, C., Shrivastava, S.: Establishing conformance between contracts and choreographies. In: 15th IEEE Conference on Business Informatics (CBI), IEEE Computer Society, Vienna, Austria. IEEE (2013)

14. RedHat: Drools (2013). http://www.drools.org/

15. Parr, T.: The Definitive ANTLR 4 Reference, January 2013

16. Molina-Jimenez, C., Shrivastava, S., Cook, N.: Implementing business conversations with consistency guarantees using message-oriented middleware. In: IEEE 11th International Enterprise Computing Conference (EDOC 2007), pp. 51–62 (2007)

17. Molina-Jimenez, C., Shrivastava, S., Strano, M.: Exception handling in electronic contracting. In: IEEE Conference on Commerce and Enterprise Computing (CEC). IEEE, Vienna, Austria (2009)

18. OASIS: ebXML Business Process Specification Schema Technical Specification v2.0.4. http://docs.oasis-open.org/ebxml-bp/2.0.4/OS/spec/ebxmlbp-v2.0.4-Spec-os-en.pdf (2006)

19. Solaiman, E., Sfyrakis, I., Molina-Jimenez, C.: Dynamic testing and deployment of a contract monitoring service. In: 5th International Conference on Cloud Computing and Services Science. SCITEPRESS (2015)

20. Ungureanu, V., Minsky, N.H.: Establishing business rules for inter-enterprise electronic commerce. In: Herlihy, M.P. (ed.) DISC 2000. LNCS, vol. 1914, pp. 179–193. Springer, Heidelberg (2000)

21. Ludwig, H., Stolze, M.: Simple obligation and right model (SORM) - for the runtime management of electronic service contracts. In: Bussler, C.J., Fensel, D., Orlowska, M.E., Yang, J. (eds.) WES 2003. LNCS, vol. 3095, pp. 62–76. Springer, Heidelberg (2004)

22. Hvitved, T.: A survey of formal languages for contracts. In: Fourth Workshop on Formal Languages and Analysis of Contract-Oriented Software (FLACOS 2010) (2010)

23. Galton, A.: Temporal Logics and Computer Science: an Overview. Academic Press, Cambridge (1987). Chap. 1

24. Fraser, G., Wotawa, F., Ammann, P.: Testing with model checkers: a survey, pp. 215–261. Verification and Reliability, Software Testing (2009)

25. van der Aalst, W.M.P., Pesic, M.: DecSerFlow: towards a truly declarative service flow language. In: Bravetti, M., Núñez, M., Zavattaro, G. (eds.) WS-FM 2006. LNCS, vol. 4184, pp. 1–23. Springer, Heidelberg (2006)

26. El-Far, I.K.: Enjoying the perks of model-based testing. In: Proceedings of the Software Testing, Analysis, and Review Conference (STARWEST 2001) (2001)

27. Utting, M., Legeard, B.: Practical Model-Based Testing: a Tools Approach. Morgan-Kaufmann, Burlington (2006)

28. Pezze, M., Young, M.: Software Testing and Analysis: Process. Wiley, Principles and Techniques, New York (2008)

29. Torsel, A.M.: A testing tool for web applications using a domain-specific modelling language and the nusmv model checker. In: IEEE Sixth International Conference on Software Testing, Verification and Validation (2013)
30. Shrivastava, S., Little, M.: Designing atomic business functions with distributed control. In: 17th IEEE Conference on Business Informatics (CBI 2015). IEEE (2015)

Streamlining APIfication by Generating APIs for Diverse Executables Using Any2API

Johannes Wettinger$^{(\boxtimes)}$, Uwe Breitenbücher, and Frank Leymann

Institute of Architecture of Application Systems, University of Stuttgart,
Universitätsstr. 38, Stuttgart, Germany
{wettinger,breitenbuecher,leymann}@iaas.uni-stuttgart.de

Abstract. For many of today's systems, diverse application and management functionality is exposed by APIs to be used for integration and orchestration purposes. One important use case is the implementation of fully automated deployment processes that are utilized to create instances of Web applications or back-ends for mobile apps. Not all functionality that needs to be integrated in this context is exposed through APIs natively: such processes typically require a multitude of other heterogeneous technologies such as scripting languages and deployment automation tooling. This makes it hard to seamlessly and efficiently combine and integrate different kinds of building blocks such as scripts and configuration definitions that are required. Therefore, in this paper, we present a generic approach to automatically generate API implementations for arbitrary executables such as scripts and compiled programs, which are not natively exposed as APIs. This *APIfication* enables the uniform invocation of various heterogeneous building blocks, but aims to avoid the costly and manual wrapping of existing executables. In addition, we present the modular and extensible open-source framework ANY2API that implements the previously introduced APIfication approach. We evaluate the APIfication approach as well as the ANY2API framework by measuring the overhead of generating and using API implementations. Moreover, a detailed case study is conducted to confirm the technical feasibility of the presented approach.

Keywords: API · APIfication · Service · Web · REST · DevOps · Deployment · Cloud computing

1 Introduction

Many of today's applications provide *application programming interfaces* (APIs) [1] to be used for various purposes. This is especially the case for many Web applications as well as back-end systems and platforms for mobile apps. An API aims to provide a well-defined and documented interface, which is exposed to access and utilize application functionality in a programmatic manner. Technically, APIs hide and abstract from implementation-specific details such as invocation mechanisms and data models inherited from the underlying technology stack.

© Springer International Publishing Switzerland 2016
M. Helfert et al. (Eds.): CLOSER 2015, CCIS 581, pp. 216–238, 2016.
DOI: 10.1007/978-3-319-29582-4_12

This forms the foundation for integrating and orchestrating diverse applications and application components, enabling the systematic development and reliable operations of various kinds of distributed systems. APIs are also used to integrate applications with business partners, suppliers, and customers [2]. Moreover, devices are interconnected to enable the *Web of things* [3]. APIs are exposed and utilized in different forms. Both (i) libraries that are bound to a particular programming language and (ii) language-agnostic Web services such as Web-based RESTful APIs [1,4] or WSDL/SOAP-based services [5] are widespread forms of providing and using APIs. Many popular providers such as Twitter, GitHub, Facebook, and Google offer such libraries[1] and Web services[2]. In the context of this paper, we consider a *Web API* as one particular kind of *API*, which may be preferred in many environments because of its platform-independent and language-agnostic characteristics. Therefore, the use cases, examples, and implementations discussed in this paper often focus on Web APIs. However, the concepts and methods are suitably generic to be applied to other kinds of APIs, too.

The API directory *Programmable Web*[3] lists more than 12000 APIs and the number of publicly available Web APIs is constantly growing[4]. Popular providers such as Google, Facebook, and Twitter are serving billions of API calls per day[5]. These statistics underpin the importance and relevance of APIs. Available frameworks such as Hapi[6] (Node.js) and Jersey[7] (Java) as well as existing literature [1,4] provide holistic support, best practices, and templates for building Web APIs. This is state of the art for building Web applications and backends for mobile apps. Additionally, Web APIs as a platform-independent and language-agnostic means for integration and orchestration purposes are heavily utilized for automating the deployment and management of Cloud applications [6,7], which leads to significant cost reductions and enables applications to scale: Cloud providers offer management APIs that can be utilized programmatically in a self-service manner to provision virtual servers, deploy applications using platform services, or to configure scaling and network properties.

Such management APIs typically provide basic functionality only. Therefore, they need to be used in conjunction with further configuration management systems to enable the deployment of non-trivial deployment processes: a huge number of reusable artifacts such as scripts (e.g., Chef cookbooks [8], Juju charms[8], Unix shell scripts) and templates like Docker container images [9] are provided by open-source communities to be reused in conjunction with provider-supplied service offerings. Typically, existing APIs can be orchestrated without too many

---

[1] Google APIs Client Libraries: http://developers.google.com/api-client-library.

[2] Google Compute Engine API: http://cloud.google.com/compute/docs/reference/latest.

[3] ProgrammableWeb: http://www.programmableweb.com.

[4] ProgrammableWeb statistics: http://goo.gl/2eQ01o.

[5] ProgrammableWeb calls per day: http://goo.gl/yhgyyW.

[6] Hapi: http://hapijs.com.

[7] Jersey: http://jersey.java.net.

[8] Juju charms: https://manage.jujucharms.com/charms.

obstacles due to well-known and common protocols such as HTTP. However, the technical integration with diverse artifacts and heterogeneous management systems is an error-prone, time-consuming, and complex challenge [7]. Thus, it is of utmost importance to handle the invocation of different artifacts, technologies, and service providers in a technically uniform manner to focus on the orchestration level, neglecting lower-level technical differences when building, deploying, and managing non-trivial systems.

Unfortunately, a significant amount of these individual artifacts are *executables* that cannot be utilized through an API without a central and monolithic middleware component [7] such as a service bus that (a) maps generic API calls into executable-specific invocations, (b) translates inputs and results of the invocation, and (c) makes them available through an API endpoint. However, such a monolithic middleware approach owns major drawbacks: (i) the individual artifacts are not packaged with their API to be utilized at runtime, so they are not self-contained; (ii) in order to utilize the executables through an API, a monolithic middleware component is inevitably required in addition to the individual artifacts to be invoked which results in additional costs and maintenance effort; (iii) in case a new kind of executable needs to be supported or an existing one requires an update, the monolithic middleware has to be adapted, extended, and redeployed accordingly with potential risks such as downtime, functional failures, and unintended side effects. The major goal of our work is to overcome these drawbacks by introducing an automated approach to *generate API implementations (APIfication)* that are packaged including the corresponding artifacts such as the executable and all its dependencies in a portable manner. This approach makes them truly self-contained without depending on a monolithic middleware. The generated API implementations simplify the orchestration of different kinds of artifacts and their integration with existing provider-hosted APIs. In this context, we present the major contributions of our work:

- We present an automated *APIfication method,* respecting the requirements we derived from a use case and motivating scenario in the field of Cloud computing and deployment automation.
- We introduce an *APIfication framework* to implement the method we presented before and provide a prototype implementation to demonstrate the feasibility.
- We *validate* the proposed APIfication approach using a prototype implementation and perform an *evaluation* to analyze the efficiency of our approach.
- We conduct a *case study* in the field of deployment automation and discuss further use cases of the APIfication approach in other fields such as e-science.
- We outline and discuss further use cases to apply the presented APIfication approach.

This paper is an extended and refined revision of our previously published work entitled *Any2API – Automated APIfication* [10] at the 5th International Conference on Cloud Computing and Services Science (CLOSER 2015). The remainder of this paper is structured as follows: Sect. 2 describes the problem statement and outlines a use case and motivating scenario in the field of deployment automation. Based on the generic APIfication method presented in Sect. 3, we propose and discuss an APIfication framework in Sect. 4. Our prototype implementation ANY2API as well as its validation and evaluation are discussed in Sect. 5. Moreover, we present a case study in that section. Section 6 outlines further use cases to apply our APIfication approach. Finally, Sects. 7 and 8 conclude the paper, including the discussion of related work and future work.

2   Problem Statement and Use Case

As discussed in Sect. 1, APIs serve as a platform-independent and language-agnostic means for integration and orchestration purposes. There are several frameworks based on different programming languages and technology stacks established to develop APIs, especially Web APIs. However, an individual API still needs to be implemented manually using these development frameworks. While this is state of the art for creating new applications such as Web applications or back-ends for mobile apps, for some use cases the individual development of an API is not feasible or even impossible. This is due to scaling issues (e.g., creating APIs for a huge amount of individual executables) or missing expertise, meaning the person, who needs to utilize certain functionality is not able to develop a corresponding API. In the following we discuss an important use case that requires API implementations to be generated in an automated manner.

2.1   Use Case: Deployment Automation

A major use case originates in the DevOps community [11], proposing the implementation of fully automated deployment processes to enable continuous delivery of software [12,13]. This is the foundation for rapidly putting changes, new features, and bug fixes into production. Especially users and customers of Cloud-based Web applications and mobile apps expect fast responses to their changing and growing requirements. Thus, it is a competitive advantage to implement automated processes to enable fast and frequent releases [11]. As an example, Flickr performs more than 10 deployments per day[9]; HubSpot with 200 to 300 deployments per day goes even further[10]. This is impossible to achieve without highly automated deployment processes. The constantly growing DevOps community supports the implementation of automated processes by providing a huge variety of individual approaches such as tools and artifacts to implement holistic deployment automation. Reusable executables such as scripts, configuration definitions, and templates are publicly available to be used for deployment automation. Juju charms and Chef cookbooks are examples for these [8,14]. Such executables usually depend on certain tools. For instance, Chef cookbooks require a Chef runtime, whereas Juju charms need a Juju environment. This

---

[9] Flickr deployments per day: http://goo.gl/VEmVqE.
[10] HubSpot deployments per day: http://goo.gl/4AQy1h.

makes it challenging to reuse different kinds of heterogeneous artifacts in combination with others. Especially when systems have to be deployed that consist of various types of components, typically multiple tools have to be combined because they focus on different kinds of middleware and application components. Thus, there is a variety of solutions and orchestrating the best of them requires to integrate the corresponding tools, e.g., by writing scripts that handle the underlying lower-level invocations, parameter passing, etc. However, this is a difficult, costly, and error-prone task as many of the executables cannot be utilized through an API without relying on a central middleware component. Consequently, all artifact- and tooling-specific details (invocation mechanism, rendering input and output, etc.) have to be known and considered when integrating and orchestrating different kinds of executables. We tackle these issues with our work presented in this paper by generating APIs for individual executables. The generated APIs hide and abstract from artifact- and tooling-specific details, thereby significantly simplifying the integration and orchestration of very different kinds of artifacts.

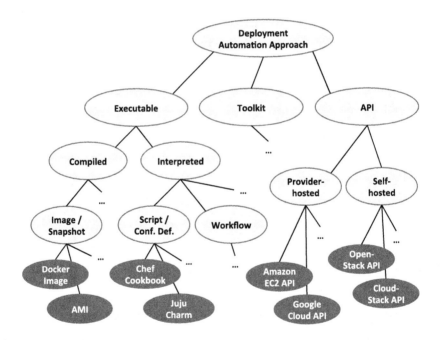

Fig. 1. Deployment automation classification.

Figure 1 shows an initial classification of deployment automation approaches. Executables are categorized in *compiled* and *interpreted* artifacts. Examples for compiled executables are pre-built virtual machine snapshots and container images such as Amazon machine images (AMI)[11] or Docker container images[12]. In contrast to those, scripts and configuration definitions such as Chef cookbooks and Juju charms are interpreted at runtime. Beside executables, existing *APIs* can be utilized in two flavors: (i) provider-hosted APIs are offered by Cloud providers to provision virtual servers, storage, and other resources; (ii) self-hosted APIs are offered, e.g., by open-source Cloud management platforms such as OpenStack [15]. Our work focuses on transforming existing individual executables into self-hosted APIs by generating corresponding API implementations. As a result, full deployment automation can be achieved by integrating and orchestrating provider-hosted and self-hosted APIs without considering the tooling- and artifact-specific details of different kinds of executables. Moreover, this approach broadens the potential variety of tools and artifacts because their implementation-specific differences are completely hidden by using the generated API implementations.

Technically, the integration and orchestration of generated and existing APIs can be implemented using arbitrary scripting languages such as JavaScript, Ruby, or Python; alternatively, service composition languages such as BPMN [16] or BPEL [17] may be used. For scripting languages, provider-independent and provider-specific *toolkits* are available to implement deployment plans that orchestrate and integrate different APIs. Examples are fog[13] and Google's API libraries[14]. Furthermore, general-purpose libraries to interact with different kinds of Web APIs are available for all major scripting languages: restler (JavaScript)[15], node-soap (JavaScript)[16], rest-client (Ruby)[17], Savon (Ruby)[18], etc.

2.2   Motivating Scenario: Facebook App

Considering the deployment automation use case discussed before, this section presents a comprehensive example as motivating scenario: the automated deployment of a Cloud-based Facebook application. The structure and parts of the application are shown in Fig. 2. A *canvas frame*[19] is used to create and embed a corresponding application on the Facebook platform. The *canvas URL* points to an externally hosted Web application that is run based on a PHP runtime environment. It provides both the user interface and the underlying application logic. The PHP runtime itself is provided by an Apache HTTP server in conjunction with a PHP module. Both are deployed on a virtual machine, running Ubuntu 14.04 as operating system, which itself runs in the Cloud, hosted on

---

[11] Amazon Machine Images (AMI): http://goo.gl/S1Zx8Q.
[12] Docker Hub Registry: https://registry.hub.docker.com.
[13] fog: http://fog.io.
[14] Google APIs Client Libraries: http://developers.google.com/api-client-library.
[15] restler: https://github.com/danwrong/restler.
[16] node-soap: https://github.com/vpulim/node-soap.
[17] rest-client: https://github.com/rest-client/rest-client.
[18] Savon: http://savonrb.com.
[19] Facebook canvas frame: http://goo.gl/5guKas.

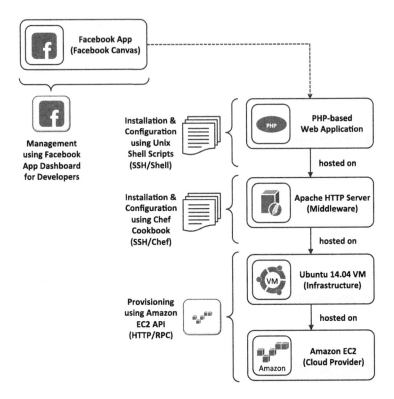

Fig. 2. Facebook application stack.

Amazon's public infrastructure (EC2[20]). The scenario covers a typical setting used to deploy and run Web-based social applications as it employs and combines modern social media platforms such as Facebook as well as Cloud infrastructures such as Amazon EC2. It could be further refined, e.g., by connecting the Web application to a database that is provided by a database-as-a-service offering hosted on a different Cloud infrastructure.

To provision the complete application stack in an automated manner, different types of interfaces and invocation mechanisms have to be integrated. The virtual machine with its operating system is acquired by using the HTTP/RPC API provided by Amazon EC2. A Chef cookbook is executed on the virtual machine through an SSH connection to install the middleware of the application stack (Apache HTTP server). Furthermore, SSH is used to run custom Unix shell scripts to install and configure the actual Web application. However, remotely running executables such as Chef cookbooks and Unix shell scripts is not as straightforward as calling a well-defined API endpoint: (i) an executable needs to be placed on the virtual machine, e.g., using file transport protocols such as FTP and SCP. Moreover, (ii) the executable may require a particular runtime

---

[20] Amazon EC2: http://aws.amazon.com/ec2.

environment to be installed on the virtual machine such as a Chef runtime for Chef cookbooks. An SSH connection can be used to drive the installation. Afterward, (iii) the execution of the scripts needs to be parameterized, which may be done by setting environment variables or storing configuration files. The final challenge is (iv) retrieving the results of the invocation, e.g., by reading, parsing, and potentially transforming the console output or files that were written to disk. In comparison to a simple API call, these steps are more complex and error-prone because lower-level implementation details such as different transport protocols and invocation mechanisms have to be considered and combined with each other. The overarching provisioning logic orchestrating all API calls as well as the preparation and invocation of the executables could be implemented by a script using a general-purpose scripting language such as Ruby or Python. However, such a script would be polluted with lower-level implementation details such as establishing SSH connections and placing files on the virtual machine. Furthermore, service composition languages such as BPEL or BPMN cannot be used without manually creating wrapping logic for the different executables involved. This is due to their focus on Web service orchestration. Consequently, the implementation details of the underlying APIs and executables directly influence which orchestration approaches can be used. This clearly contradicts with the idea of loose coupling, i.e., selecting an orchestration approach and implementing the orchestration logic without considering the implementation details of the underlying, lower-level technologies.

To tackle these challenges we propose an automated approach to generate APIs for arbitrary executables. The approach is based on the *APIfication method* we present in Sect. 3. In the context of our motivating scenario discussed in this section, the approach can be used to completely wrap the script invocation by generating an API that hides the (i) placement, (ii) installation of required runtime environments, (iii) parameterization and execution of the executable, as well as (iv) transforming and returning the results. Consequently, the orchestration logic deals with API calls only, without getting polluted, error-prone, or unnecessarily complex because of implementation details of the underlying executables.

3   APIfication Method

The APIfication approach presented in this section is based on the assumption that each executable has some metadata associated with it. These metadata are either natively attached and/or they are explicitly specified and additionally attached to the executable. Metadata indicate which input parameters are expected, where results are put, which dependencies have to be resolved before the invocation, etc. The main purpose of a generated API implementation is to enable the invocation of the corresponding executable through a well-defined interface, independent from the underlying technology stack. Furthermore, a generated API implementation enables the invocation of the corresponding executable not only locally in the same environment (e.g., same server), but enables the execution using remote access mechanisms such as SSH and PowerShell in remote environments. This is to decouple the environment of an API implementation instance from the environment of the actual executable that is exposed by the API. Distributed environments as they are, for instance, used in the field of Cloud computing are thereby supported. An API call could be made from a workstation (running a script that orchestrates multiple APIs) to an API implementation instance that is hosted on premises (e.g., a local server); the actual executable (e.g., a Chef cookbook to install a middleware component) runs on a Cloud infrastructure. However, one could also run all parts on a single machine, e.g., a developer's laptop.

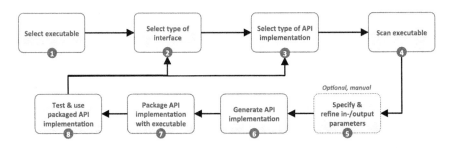

Fig. 3. APIfication method.

Figure 3 shows an overview of the *APIfication method*, outlining the individual steps and their ordering to generate API implementations in an automated manner. In the **first step,** the executable targeted for the APIfication is selected. Then, the interface type (e.g., RESTful API) and the API implementation type (e.g., Node.js or Java) is selected **(steps 2 and 3).** The type of interface including the communication protocol (HTTP, WebSocket, etc.) and the communication paradigm (RPC, REST, etc.) can be chosen when generating an API implementation. This choice may be driven by existing expertise, alignment with existing APIs, or personal preferences. Similarly motivated, the type of the underlying implementation (Java, Node.js, etc.) for the generated API can be chosen when generating an API implementation. A generated API should be language-agnostic to allow the usage of arbitrary languages (scripting languages, programming languages, service composition languages, etc.) to orchestrate and integrate different APIs. Thus, Web APIs are the preferred and universal type of APIs because they can be utilized in nearly any kind of language.

After the selection part, the executable including its metadata is scanned to discover input and output parameters **(step 4).** If the scan did not discover all parameters, the following (optional) step can be used to refine the input and output parameters for the generated API **(step 5).** However, this is not required if the metadata associated with the executable are sufficient as this is, e.g., the case for many open-source deployment automation artifacts such as Chef cookbooks and Juju charms. Consequently, the method can be applied to a huge amount

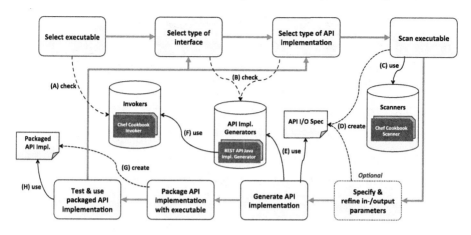

Fig. 4. APIfication framework with technical examples.

and variety of such artifacts in an automated manner. Then, the API implementation is generated **(step 6)**. To enable an API implementation to be hosted in different environments, it must be packaged in a portable manner **(step 7)**. Thus, the implementation must be self-contained without depending on central middleware components, which dynamically provide data format transformations, parameter mappings, etc. at runtime. All these and related functionality are incorporated in the API implementation when it is generated at build time. The portability aspect is key for automated deployment processes because they need to run in very different environments (development, test, production, etc.). These environments may be hosted on different infrastructures (developer laptop, test cloud, etc.), so portability of the generated API implementations is key in this context. Technically, containerization technology [9,18] may be utilized for this purpose: each API implementation gets packaged as a portable container image that can be instantiated in different environments.

Later, the generated implementation may be refined or updated by going back to the selection steps for the interface type and the API implementation type. The APIfication method presented in this section addresses the challenges we identified in Sect. 2, including the deployment automation use case and the motivating scenario. However, the method itself is still abstract and can be implemented in various ways. The following section presents a modular and extensible framework to implement the APIfication method.

4 APIfication Framework

In order to implement the APIfication method introduced in Sect. 3, we present a modular, plugin-based, and extensible framework in this chapter to support the individual steps of the method. Figure 4 shows several artifacts organized in multiple registries that are linked to the steps of the method, associated with

Invoker	Executable Type
Cookbook Invoker	Chef Cookbook
Charm Invoker	Juju Charm
Docker Invoker	Docker Image
	Dockerfile
...	

Fig. 5. Invoker registry.

Generator	Interface Type	Implementation Type
REST API Generator	HTTP+REST	Java
	HTTP+REST	Node.js
	HTTP+REST	Ruby
SOAP/WSDL API Gen.	HTTP+WSDL+SOAP	Java
	HTTP+WSDL+SOAP	Node.js
JSON-RPC API Gen.	HTTP+JSONRPC	Java
Node.js JSON-RPC API Gen.	HTTP+JSONRPC	Node.js
...		

Fig. 6. Generator registry.

certain actions (check, use, create). When selecting an executable for its API-fication, the available *invokers* are checked (**action A**) if there is at least one invoker available that is capable of running the given type of executable (e.g., a Chef cookbook). Figure 5 outlines the registry, in which the invokers are stored: each invoker supports at least one *executable type*. For instance, the *Cookbook Invoker* can be used to run Chef cookbooks. The generator registry (Fig. 6) is checked (**action B**) when selecting the interface type and the API implementation type. As an example, a Chef cookbook may be selected in conjunction with HTTP+REST as interface type and Node.js as implementation type. In this case all checks would succeed because the *Cookbook Invoker* is available and the *REST API Generator* can be used to generate an HTTP+REST interface; this is possible because the chosen generator can deal with Node.js as implementation type. Consequently, the generator uses the invoker to provide an API implementation that can run the given Chef cookbook.

Next, the given executable with its metadata is analyzed by a corresponding *scanner* (**action C**) from the scanner registry (Fig. 7) to create an *API I/O specification* (**action D**). A scanner is a specialized module in the framework that is able to scan executables of a certain type such as a *Chef cookbook scanner* to scan cookbooks. Figure 8 shows an example for a specification (produced by a scanner) for a MySQL cookbook: it contains the input and output *parameter names*, their *data types*, and the *mapping information* to properly map between

Scanner	Executable Type
Cookbook Scanner	Chef Cookbook
Charm Scanner	Juju Charm
Docker Scanner	Docker Image
	Dockerfile
...	

Fig. 7. Scanner registry.

Param. Name	Mode	Data Type	Default	Param. Mapping
version	in	string	"5.1"	CHEF_ATTR:mysql/version
port	in	number	3306	CHEF_ATTR:mysql/port
logs	out	string	–	STDOUT
...				
invoker_config	in	object	–	ENV:INVOKER_CONFIG

Fig. 8. API I/O spec for MySQL cookbook.

API parameters to the executable parameters at runtime. The *mode* of a parameter indicates whether this parameter is used as input or it is used to return some output of an invocation. Optionally, a *default value* can be associated with a parameter, which is used in case no value is defined at runtime for the corresponding parameter. In case the data type is object, a schema definition, e.g., XML schema [19] or JSON schema [20] can be attached to the parameter. This is to specify the expected data structure for values (objects) of a particular parameter in more detail. The mapping of parameters specifies the target for input parameters and the source for output parameters at runtime. To refer to Fig. 8: the API parameter version is mapped to the Chef attribute mysql/version, whereas the console output of the executable (STDOUT) is mapped to the API parameter logs. Optionally, the specification can be refined manually in the following step, which is not required if the executable's metadata is sufficient. The invoker_config parameter (mapped to the environment variable INVOKER_CONFIG) is a special one, provided by the framework; it cannot be modified or deleted during the (optional) manual refinement step. The parameter is used to configure the underlying invoker itself when using the generated API to run the executable. This is, for instance, needed to support remote access mechanisms, enabling the execution in remote environments. As an example the invoker_config parameter can hold the following JSON object to use SSH to run the executable remotely:

```
{
  "remote_access": "ssh",
  "remote_host": "173.194.44.88",
  "ssh_user": "ubuntu",
  "ssh_key": "-----BEGIN RSA PRIVATE KEY ..."
}
```

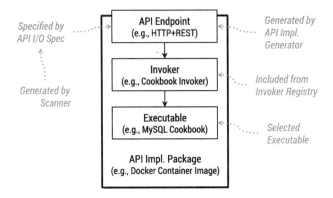

Fig. 9. Generated API implementation package.

This sample configuration (given at runtime and transparently forwarded to the invoker) triggers the invocation of the underlying executable on the machine associated with the given IP address (`remote_host`) through SSH. Beside the special `invoker_config` parameter, the API I/O specification tells the corresponding *generator* how to create a proper API implementation (**action E**). A generator is a specialized module that performs the actual work to generate an API implementation. One part of the generation process is to put the corresponding invoker into the generated API implementation. The invoker is provided by the invoker registry to run the given executable (**action F**). Finally, the API implementation is packaged with the executable in a self-contained manner (**action G**). With this, the APIfication procedure for the given executable is finished, so the generated and packaged API implementation can be tested and used (**action H**). Figure 9 outlines the structure of a generated and packaged API implementation: the invoker (e.g., the cookbook invoker) is retrieved from the invoker registry to invoke the selected executable such as the MySQL cookbook at runtime. The API endpoint is specified by the API I/O specification, which itself is generated by a scanner module provided by the framework. A generator module uses the specification to generate the implementation of the API endpoint. Finally, all parts are packaged in a self-contained manner, e.g., in a Docker container image. The following Sect. 5 presents the validation and evaluation of the APIfication method and framework we discussed in Sect. 3 and this section, based on a prototype implementation we provide.

5   Validation and Evaluation

In order to evaluate our APIfication method and framework, we developed ANY2API[21] as a prototype implementation. The following Sect. 5.1 presents and discusses the implementation. In addition, the generated API implementations

---

[21] ANY2API: http://any2api.org.

include simple tests to validate the correctness of the generated implementation (Sect. 5.2). In order to evaluate our framework and the ANY2API implementation, we performed experiments to measure the overhead both at build time and runtime (Sect. 5.3). Finally, Sect. 5.4 presents a comprehensive case study in the field of deployment automation.

5.1 Any2API Implementation

ANY2API is a modular and extensible implementation of the APIfication framework presented in Sect. 4. Technically, it is based on Node.js, so most parts of it are implemented in JavaScript. Therefore, we use the Node Package Manager (NPM)[22] and the associated NPM registry to manage and publish Node.js modules. However, this does not imply that all parts of the framework have to be implemented in JavaScript. As an example, *invoker modules* expose several scripts that can (but do not have to) be implemented in JavaScript. Technically, these are specified as *NPM scripts*[23] in the `package.json` file of a module:

```
"scripts": {
  "prepare-executable": "node ./prep-exec.js",
  "prepare-runtime": "sh ./prep-runtime.sh",
  "start": "java -jar ./invoke.jar",
  ...
}
```

Such a script can then be called using the `npm run` command, e.g., to trigger an invocation of an executable that is packaged with a generated API implementation: `npm run start`. This command is executed by the generated API implementation, which itself can be of an arbitrary implementation type such as a JAR file (Java) or a Node.js module (JavaScript). Moreover, the API implementation needs to set predefined environment variables before running the script such as `PARAMETERS` to parameterize the invocation accordingly. These environment variables contain JSON objects that are parsed and processed by the invoker. As an example, the input parameters for invoking a MySQL cookbook may be rendered as follows:

```
{
  "version": "5.1",
  "port": 3306,
  ...
}
```

The `prepare-executable` script is triggered at build time, i.e., when generating an API implementation to prepare the packaged executable. Such preparations may include resolving all dependencies of a particular executable to package

---

[22] NPM: https://www.npmjs.org.
[23] NPM scripts: http://docs.npmjs.com/misc/scripts.

the executable in a truly self-contained manner. At runtime (i.e., when an invocation of the executable is triggered) the `prepare-executable` script is executed before the `start` script to install prerequisites required for the invoker to run such as a Java runtime environment.

Generators and *scanners* are implemented as Node.js modules, too. Each *generator module* exposes a `generate` function to produce an API implementation based on the given API I/O specification. Each *scanner module* exposes a `scan` function, which analyzes the given executable to generate an API I/O specification. This specification (after optional, manual refinement) can then be used in conjunction with a generator to produce an API implementation. In addition, we implemented the `any2api-core`[24] module, which provides simple registries as discussed in Sect. 4 for *scanner modules, generator modules,* and *invoker modules.* To actually use and interact with the framework, the `any2api-cli`[25] module provides a command-line interface (CLI) to scan executables as well as to generate packaged API implementations:

```
# any2api -o ./mysql_spec scan ./mysql_cookbook
# any2api -o ./api_impl gen ./mysql_spec
```

The first command scans an existing Chef cookbook, generating an API I/O specification. Based on this specification, the second command generates a corresponding API implementation. By default, a Node.js-based API implementation exposing a RESTful interface is generated. A `Dockerfile`[26] (build plan to create a self-contained and portable container image) is included in each generated API implementation. Consequently, Docker can be used to create API implementation packages. Moreover, public and private Docker registries[27] can be utilized to store, manage, and retrieve potentially different versions of pre-built API implementations. Following this approach, a huge variety of existing tools that are part of the Docker ecosystem can be used to manage instances of generated API implementations. As an example, CoreOS[28] may be utilized to host API implementations in a managed cluster of Docker containers.

Currently, two *scanner modules* are implemented for analyzing Chef cookbooks and Juju charms. The *Chef invoker module* enables the invocation of Chef cookbooks, both in local and remote environments using SSH transparently. Using the *REST generator module,* Node.js-based RESTful API implementations can be generated. Further modules are currently being developed such as a Juju invoker, a Docker invoker, a Docker scanner, as well as alternative generators to support different type of interfaces (SOAP/WSDL, JSON-RPC, XML-RPC, etc.) and alternative implementation types (Java, Ruby, etc.).

---

[24] `any2api-core`: https://github.com/any2api/any2api-core.

[25] `any2api-cli`: https://github.com/any2api/any2api-cli.

[26] `Dockerfile` reference: http://docs.docker.com/reference/builder.

[27] Docker registry: http://github.com/docker/docker-registry.

[28] CoreOS: https://coreos.com.

5.2   Tests

The previous Sect. 5.1 presented ANY2API, the prototype implementation of our APIfication framework discussed in Sect. 4. In order to validate the correctness of the generated API implementations, each of them includes a test script. By running the test script (using the command npm run test), an API call is made to the generated API implementation, triggering the invocation of the packaged executable with its default parameters. This is a simple, but auto-generated 'smoke test' to validate that the generated API implementations works. We generated an API implementation for a selection of the most downloaded Chef cookbooks[29], covering the automated installation and configuration of very common and widely used middleware components, including mysql, apache2, java, nginx, zabbix, glassfish, postgresql, and php. As an example, apache2 and php are required for the automated deployment of the Facebook application we outlined in the motivating scenario (Sect. 2.2). We documented the required commands in a test script[30] that we executed on a Ubuntu 14.04 server system (64-bit) for each cookbook to generate and test the corresponding Node.js-based RESTful API implementation. All API implementations are generated fully automatically without any manual refinement. Of course, additional test cases with different parameter settings can be implemented manually to perform further validation of a generated API implementation.

5.3   Measurements

In order to evaluate the efficiency of our approach compared to the plain usage of the corresponding executable, we measured the overhead of the APIfication. Therefore, we selected some of the most downloaded Chef cookbooks, which we were using for our tests before (Sect. 5.2). First, we measured the overall duration it takes to scan the executable (Chef cookbook) and to generate a corresponding API implementation (Node.js-based RESTful API). Second, we check the additional size of the generated API implementation without the corresponding executable. This is to estimate the disk space that is additionally required at runtime when using an instance of an API implementation. Third, we measured the execution duration and memory usage for running the corresponding executable both *with* and *without* using the generated API implementation. The evaluation was run on a clean virtual machine (4 virtual CPUs clocked at 2.8 GHz, 64-bit, 4 GB of memory) on top of the VirtualBox hypervisor, running a minimalist Linux system including Docker. The processing and invocation of a particular Chef cookbook was done in a clean Docker-based Ubuntu 14.04 container, with exactly one container running on the virtual machine at a time. We did all measurements at container level to completely focus on the workload that is linked to the executable and the API implementation.

Table 1 shows the results of our evaluation. The measured average duration to scan and generate an API implementation is in the range from 7 to 90 s. This

---

[29] Most downloaded cookbooks: http://goo.gl/8xZUCT.
[30] Test script: http://goo.gl/g847Ws.

Table 1. Measurements regarding generated API implementations for Chef cookbooks.

	mysql	apache2	java	nginx	zabbix	glassfish	postgresql	php ...
Avg. duration to scan and generate API impl.	13s	14s	7s	25s	90s	17s	16s	29s
Add. size of generated API implementation	25M	25M	25M	25M	25M	25M	25M	25M
Avg. execution duration with API impl.	54s	48s	84s	45s	47s	153s	60s	123s
Avg. execution duration without API impl.	54s	39s	82s	39s	42s	140s	59s	110s
Max. memory usage with API impl.	556M	471M	507M	461M	429M	674M	510M	614M
Max. memory usage without API impl.	343M	258M	402M	270M	212M	456M	310M	426M

duration is the overhead at build time, including the retrieval of the executable and all its dependencies. The additional size of the generated API implementation leads to slightly more disk space usage at runtime. Moreover, there is a minor overhead in terms of execution duration and memory consumption at runtime. In most of today's environments this overhead should be acceptable, considering the significant simplification of using the generated APIs compared to the plain executables. In addition, when using the plain executables directly, much of the complexity hidden by the generated API implementation has to be covered at the orchestration level. So, the overall consumption of resources may be the same or even worse, depending on the selected means for orchestration. Furthermore, instances of API implementations can be reused to run an executable multiple times and potentially in different remote environments. Through this reuse, the overhead can be quickly compensated in large-scale environments.

5.4 Deployment Automation Case Study

We used the presented APIfication approach to ease implementing and generating workflows for the deployment of Cloud applications based on the Open-TOSCA ecosystem [21, 22]. This ecosystem is based on the TOSCA standard [23], which enables describing Cloud applications and their management in a portable fashion. To define management tasks imperatively, e.g., to migrate application components, the ecosystem employs management plans based on the workflow language BPEL [17]. Therefore, the orchestration of management scripts, APIs, and other executables is a major challenge. The presented APIfication approach eases developing management workflows significantly as it reduces the required effort and complexity of integrating different technologies. Using our approach, modeling management workflows requires the orchestration of APIs only, which is much more straightforward compared to the former integration of various heterogeneous technologies. Combined with the generated APIs for Chef cookbooks as discussed in Sect. 5.3, the integration of both the ecosystem and our APIfication approach provides a powerful means to enable a fast development of management workflows for Cloud applications.

6   Further Use Cases

Beside the deployment automation use case (Sect. 2) we were focusing so far, we identified further use cases to apply our APIfication approach presented in this paper. These use cases are outlined and described in the following sections.

6.1   Cyberinfrastructure and e-Science

In the cyberinfrastructure and e-Science community [24], scientific applications are utilized, orchestrated, and run in Grid and Cloud environments to perform complex and CPU-intensive calculations such as scientific simulations and other experiments. These applications are implemented in arbitrary programming or scripting languages; they are usually run as executables directly. Consequently, they cannot be directly utilized through APIs. Existing works focus on the usage of scientific applications through Web APIs [25,26] to ease their integration and orchestration for more sophisticated experiments, where multiple scientific applications are involved. As an example, Opal [27] is a framework for wrapping scientific applications, so they can be used through a Web API, abstracting from the application-specific details and differences such as invocation mechanisms and parameter passing. We tackle these challenges with our work by generating API implementations and packaging them together with the actual scientific application, i.e., the executable. This eases the integration and orchestration of different scientific application through Web APIs, without having to create API wrappers manually from scratch. As a result, running complex experiments that involve several scientific applications becomes easier.

6.2   Treat API Endpoints as Executables

In the previously described use cases of deployment automation (Sect. 2) and e-science (Sect. 6.1), we implicitly assumed an executable to be an individual file or a collection of files (scripts, compiled executables, scientific applications, etc.). However, existing API endpoints as they are, e.g., exposed by provider-hosted Cloud APIs and social media APIs (Facebook[31], Twitter[32], etc.) can be considered as executables, too. This is motivated by the need for wrapping existing API endpoints to make them available through different communication protocols (e.g., wrap WebSocket by HTTP) or communication paradigms (e.g., wrap RPC by REST). As an example, Twitter provides the *users/show* endpoint[33]

---

[31] Facebook Graph API: http://goo.gl/HKGpZG.

[32] Twitter REST API: https://dev.twitter.com/rest.

[33] Twitter *users/show* API endpoint: http://goo.gl/dmsJ22.

to retrieve a variety of information about a particular Twitter user. If this API endpoint needs to be utilized in a deployment workflow implemented in BPEL, a wrapper has to be implemented to make the endpoint accessible through a WSDL/SOAP-based interface [7]. By treating API endpoints as executables, API implementations could potentially be generated for existing endpoints to make them accessible through different protocols and communication paradigms, without relying on central middleware components such as a service bus.

6.3 API Libraries

So far, we were focusing on APIs, which expose functionality through network-based endpoints. Prominent examples are various types of Web APIs (SOAP, JSON-RPC, REST, etc.) as well as messaging APIs. Other kinds of APIs expose functionality through 'native' libraries and modules, which can be used immediately in the context of a certain technology stack or programming language. Examples are Java libraries packaged as JAR files, Node.js modules shipped as NPM packages, and Python modules. On the one hand, such APIs are typically not language-agnostic in contrast to endpoint-based APIs; on the other hand, they enable a much easier integration and usage within the context of a particular programming language or technology stack. As an example, a Java method that is offered by a Java-based API library can be directly invoked instead of using a general-purpose HTTP client library to interact with a RESTful Web API. Endpoint APIs and API libraries can also be used complementary: API libraries can effectively wrap endpoint APIs to ease the usage and integration of their functionality in various contexts. Therefore, API libraries add an additional layer of abstraction to seamlessly integrate with the programming model of the corresponding language or stack.

6.4 Microservice Architectures

With microservices [28] becoming increasingly popular as an architecture paradigm, the APIfication approach we present in this paper can be used to build systems that follow this paradigm. The basic idea of this emerging paradigm is to develop highly specialized and scoped components, which are independently maintained and deployable; they expose functionality as microservices (APIs) that make up a complex system by combining and integrating them. This is in contrast to building monolithic systems that are typically hard to scale, change, and maintain in the long term. To ease the development of certain microservices, the core functionality (e.g., business logic) can be initially implemented as executables, without dealing with API implementations to make the functionality available to other components. Then, the APIfication approach can be utilized to generate API implementations, which are independently deployable entities in the sense of microservices. This enables clear separation of concerns when developing and maintaining microservices.

7   Related Work

As discussed in Sects. 1 and 2, using and creating APIs is of utmost importance today [2]. Consequently, a huge variety of approaches is available to simplify the creation and development of APIs. Beside API development frameworks to create API implementations manually (e.g., Hapi[34] and LoopBack[35]), there are solutions to semi-automatically create Web APIs. As an example, API specifications defined using the *RESTful API Modeling Language (RAML)*[36] can be utilized to generate an API implementation skeleton based on Jersey[37], a Java framework to develop RESTful APIs [1,4]. These generated skeletons have to be refined by adding application-specific logic. Consequently, such approaches can be immediately used to develop *generator modules* for our APIfication framework: the generator produces a skeleton, which is then automatically refined by adding the logic to call a corresponding invoker to run the selected executable. Moreover, solutions such as Kimono[38] and Import.io[39] can be used to generate Web APIs for existing Web sites. These approaches provide interactive ways to extract content from HTML pages (e.g., using CSS selectors) to make them available in more machine-readable formats such as JSON. Thus, such Web page-centric approaches focus on extracting and re-formatting content, whereas our approach tackles the issue of managing the invocation of arbitrary executables. In contrast to service providers such as Kimono, our approach aims to generate self-contained, portable, and packaged API implementations that can be hosted anywhere, so they do not depend on specific provider offerings.

RPC frameworks such as Apache Thrift[40] and Google's Protocol Buffers[41] aim to ease the integration of application logic and executables that are implemented based on different technology stacks. For efficiency reasons, they typically do not rely on Web APIs but use lower-level TCP connection-based protocols. Such RPC frameworks can be perfectly combined with our APIfication approach by implementing *generator modules*. In this case, a module generates an API implementation, e.g., exposing a Thrift interface instead of an HTTP-based RESTful interface. Some of these frameworks offer support to generate code skeletons based on interface descriptions. This functionality can be reused to ease the implementation of a corresponding *generator module*. However, by sticking to such non-standard communication protocols there are limitations on the orchestration level, meaning the same framework has to be used instead of interacting with a standards-based interface such as HTTP/REST. This is a trade-off between efficiency and interoperability that needs to be made individually based on concrete use cases. Since our framework supports both approaches,

---

[34] Hapi: http://hapijs.com.
[35] LoopBack: http://loopback.io.
[36] RAML: http://raml.org.
[37] RAML to JAX-RS (Jersey): http://goo.gl/E39jun.
[38] Kimono: https://www.kimonolabs.com.
[39] Import.io: https://import.io.
[40] Apache Thrift: http://thrift.apache.org.
[41] Protocol Buffers: http://developers.google.com/protocol-buffers.

different API implementations (e.g., Thrift-based and HTTP/REST-based) can be generated and exchanged for a particular executable as needed. In the field of Web APIs, approaches such as websockify[42] and websocketd[43] can be used to expose the functionality of executables through the standards-based WebSocket protocol [29]. Corresponding *generator modules* can be implemented to reuse these approaches in the context of our APIfication framework.

8   Conclusion

The automated APIfication approach, which eases the integration and orchestration of diverse executables represents the core contribution of this paper. In order to justify the need for such an approach, we systematically derived relevant requirements from the deployment automation use case and the motivating scenario. A generic APIfication method was presented in conjunction with a corresponding framework to fulfill the identified requirements. These two building blocks (method and framework) eventually allow to automatically generate API implementations. To confirm the practical feasibility of the presented method and framework, we developed ANY2API as a modular, extensible, and open-source implementation of the framework. Moreover, we validated the correctness of generated API implementations using simple but auto-generated test scripts ('smoke tests') that invoke the packaged executable with its default parameters. In terms of quantitative evaluation of the APIfication approach, we analyzed the efficiency of our approach by conducting comprehensive measurements. These measurements show a small overhead when following the APIfication approach, which is acceptable for most environments, considering the significant simplification and convenience, which the presented approach provides. In addition, we did a case study in the field of deployment automation to confirm the actual applicability of our approach in practice. Finally, we outlined additional use cases in different fields to apply the proposed APIfication approach.

In ongoing and future work, we aim to extend the APIfication framework to support an additional but optional step to refine the parameter mapping, e.g., aggregating, splitting, or transforming parameter values. We intend to enable this feature by allowing the definition of JavaScript functions that are executed in a sandboxed environment at runtime. Furthermore, we plan to extend and refine the ANY2API implementation. Existing scanners, generators, and invokers will be refined, and additional ones will be implemented. As an example, such a refinement may include authentication and authorization mechanisms for generated API implementations. The currently implemented generators can be used to create API implementations that expose Web APIs such as HTTP/REST. In future, we plan to implement generators in conjunction with alternative packaging formats to generate API libraries that can be directly used in conjunction with different programming and scripting languages such as Java and Python.

---

[42] websockify: https://github.com/kanaka/websockify.
[43] websocketd: https://github.com/joewalnes/websocketd.

Finally, to improve the user experience of the framework, a graphical user interface as well as a RESTful API are planned to be implemented. These are meant to be used as an alternative to the command-line interface in order to interact with the framework.

Acknowledgement. This work was partially funded by the BMWi project *CloudCycle* (01MD11023) and the DFG project *SitOPT* (610872).

References

1. Richardson, L., Amundsen, M., Ruby, S.: RESTful Web APIs. O'Reilly Media Inc., Sebastopol (2013)
2. Rudrakshi, C., Varshney, A., Yadla, B., Kanneganti, R., Somalwar, K.: APIfication - core building block of the digital enterprise. Technical report, HCL Technologies (2014)
3. Guinard, D., Trifa, V., Wilde, E.: A resource oriented architecture for the web of things. In: Internet of Things (IOT), 2010. IEEE (2010)
4. Masse, M.: REST API Design Rulebook. O'Reilly Media Inc., Sebastopol (2011)
5. W3C: SOAP Specification, Version 1.2 (2007)
6. Mell, P., Grance, T.: The NIST Definition of Cloud Computing. National Institute of Standards and Technology (2011)
7. Wettinger, J., Binz, T., Breitenbücher, U., Kopp, O., Leymann, F., Zimmermann, M.: Unified invocation of scripts and services for provisioning, deployment, and management of cloud applications based on TOSCA. In: Proceedings of the 4th International Conference on Cloud Computing and Services Science. SciTePress (2014)
8. Nelson-Smith, S.: Test-Driven Infrastructure with Chef. O'Reilly Media Inc., Sebastopol (2013)
9. Turnbull, J.: The Docker Book. Lulu.com (2014)
10. Wettinger, J., Breitenbücher, U., Leymann, F.: Any2API - Automated APIfication. In: Proceedings of the 5th International Conference on Cloud Computing and Services Science. SciTePress (2015)
11. Hüttermann, M.: DevOps for Developers. Apress, Berkeley (2012)
12. Humble, J., Farley, D.: Continuous Delivery: Reliable Software Releases Through Build, Test, and Deployment Automation. Addison-Wesley Professional, Boston (2010)
13. Wettinger, J., Breitenbücher, U., Leymann, F.: Standards-based DevOps automation and integration using TOSCA. In: Proceedings of the 7th International Conference on Utility and Cloud Computing (UCC) (2014)
14. Sabharwal, N., Wadhwa, M.: Automation through Chef Opscode: A Hands-on Approach to Chef. Apress, Berkeley (2014)
15. Pepple, K.: Deploying OpenStack. O'Reilly Media, Sebastopol (2011)
16. OMG: Business Process Model and Notation (BPMN) Version 2.0 (2011)
17. OASIS: Web Services Business Process Execution Language (BPEL) Version 2.0 (2007)
18. Scheepers, M.J.: Virtualization and Containerization of Application Infrastructure: A Comparison (2014)
19. World Wide Web Consortium (W3C): XML Schema (2012)

20. Internet Engineering Task Force: JSON Schema (2013)
21. Binz, T., Breitenbücher, U., Haupt, F., Kopp, O., Leymann, F., Nowak, A., Wagner, S.: OpenTOSCA – a runtime for TOSCA-based cloud applications. In: Basu, S., Pautasso, C., Zhang, L., Fu, X. (eds.) ICSOC 2013. LNCS, vol. 8274, pp. 692–695. Springer, Heidelberg (2013)
22. Kopp, O., Binz, T., Breitenbücher, U., Leymann, F.: Winery – a modeling tool for TOSCA-based cloud applications. In: Basu, S., Pautasso, C., Zhang, L., Fu, X. (eds.) ICSOC 2013. LNCS, vol. 8274, pp. 700–704. Springer, Heidelberg (2013)
23. Binz, T., Breitenbücher, U., Kopp, O., Leymann, F.: TOSCA: portable automated deployment and management of cloud applications. In: Bouguettaya, A., Sheng, Q.Z., Daniel, F. (eds.) Advanced Web Services, pp. 527–549. Springer, New York (2014)
24. Yang, X., Wang, L., Jie, W.: Guide to e-Science. Springer, London (2011)
25. Afanasiev, A., Sukhoroslov, O., Voloshinov, V.: MathCloud: publication and reuse of scientific applications as RESTful web services. In: Malyshkin, V. (ed.) PaCT 2013. LNCS, vol. 7979, pp. 394–408. Springer, Heidelberg (2013)
26. Sukhoroslov, O., Afanasiev, A.: Everest: a cloud platform for computational web services. In: Proceedings of the 4th International Conference on Cloud Computing and Services Science. SciTePress (2014)
27. Krishnan, S., Clementi, L., Ren, J., Papadopoulos, P., Li, W.: Design and evaluation of Opal2: a toolkit for scientific software as a service. In: World Conference on Services I. IEEE (2009)
28. Newman, S.: Building Microservices. O'Reilly Media, Sebastopol (2015)
29. IETF: The WebSocket Protocol (2011)

Hybrid TOSCA Provisioning Plans: Integrating Declarative and Imperative Cloud Application Provisioning Technologies

Uwe Breitenbücher[1]([✉]), Tobias Binz[1], Oliver Kopp[2], Kálmán Képes[1],
Frank Leymann[1], and Johannes Wettinger[1]

[1] Institute of Architecture of Application Systems, University of Stuttgart,
Stuttgart, Germany
{breitenbuecher,binz,kepes,leymann,wettinger}@informatik.uni-stuttgart.de
[2] Institute for Parallel and Distributed Systems, University of Stuttgart,
Stuttgart, Germany
kopp@informatik.uni-stuttgart.de

Abstract. The efficient provisioning of complex applications is one of the most challenging issues in Cloud Computing. Therefore, various provisioning and configuration management technologies have been developed that can be categorized as follows: imperative approaches enable a precise specification of the low-level tasks to be executed whereas declarative approaches focus on describing the desired goals and constraints. Since complex applications employ a plethora of heterogeneous components that must be wired and configured, typically multiple of these technologies have to be integrated to automate the entire provisioning process. In a former work, we presented a workflow modelling concept that enables the seamless integration of imperative and declarative technologies. This paper is an extension of that work to integrate the modelling concept with the Cloud standard TOSCA. In particular, we show how Hybrid Provisioning Plans can be created that retrieve all required information about the desired provisioning directly from the corresponding TOSCA model. We validate the practical feasibility of the concept by extending the OpenTOSCA runtime environment and the workflow language BPEL.

Keywords: Cloud application provisioning · TOSCA · Hybrid plans · Automation · Declarative modelling · Imperative modelling · Integration

1 Introduction

With the growing adoption of Cloud Computing in enterprises, the rapid and reliable provisioning of Cloud applications becomes an increasingly important issue. Consequently, strategic aspects such as time to market, high availability, mobile computing, and continuous delivery mainly dominate strategic IT development, provisioning, and maintenance. Especially the increasing number of available

© Springer International Publishing Switzerland 2016
M. Helfert et al. (Eds.): CLOSER 2015, CCIS 581, pp. 239–262, 2016.
DOI: 10.1007/978-3-319-29582-4_13

services offered by Cloud providers, e. g., Amazon and Google, provide powerful Cloud properties such as automatic elasticity, self-service, and pay-per-use features that are provided entirely by the autonomous management systems of Cloud environments [23]. Due to this trend, more and more business applications are outsourced to the Cloud [2]. As a result, Cloud-based applications become (i) increasingly complex and (ii) employ a plethora of heterogeneous software, middleware, and XaaS components offered by different providers including non-trivial dependencies among each other. Unfortunately, automating the provisioning of such applications becomes a serious management challenge: different kinds of Cloud offerings (IaaS, PaaS, SaaS, etc.) must be provisioned and complex configurations are required to setup and wire the involved components. This typically requires the combination of multiple management technologies, especially if the application components are distributed across multiple Clouds [9]. However, combining (i) proprietary APIs, (ii) non-standardized configuration management tools, and (iii) different virtualization technologies in a single automated provisioning process is a complex modelling and integration challenge using traditional approaches such as workflows. This complexity results from the different management paradigms that have to be integrated: there are *declarative technologies*, such as Chef [26,31] or Puppet [33], which only describe the desired state of application components without specifying the actual tasks that have to be executed to reach this state. *Imperative technologies*, e. g., scripts or workflows, explicitly specify each step to be executed in detail. While there are approaches for orchestrating imperative technologies homogeneously [19], combining different declarative and imperative technologies requires implementing huge amounts of wrapper code as the two flavors are hardly interoperable with each other.

In this paper, which is an extended version of our former work [10] that we have presented at the *5th International Conference on Cloud Computing and Services Science (CLOSER)*, we tackle these issues. The paper presents a workflow modelling concept to integrate declarative and imperative management technologies seamlessly. We introduce the concept of *Declarative Provisioning Activities* that enables modelling declarative goals directly in an imperative workflow model. Using this modelling concept, developers are able to create *Hybrid Provisioning Plans*, which specify not only imperative statements but declarative statements as well—without polluting the workflow model with technical integration logic. The new contribution of this extended version of the original paper [10] is an extension of the modelling concept to support the Cloud standard TOSCA [28,29]: We show how executable Hybrid Provisioning Plans can be linked with TOSCA models to retrieve all required information about the desired provisioning. The technical feasibility of the approach is validated by a prototypical implementation, which is integrated with the standards-based Cloud management ecosystem Open-TOSCA [5,7,20] and the workflow language BPEL [27]. We evaluate the approach by several criteria and discuss its limitations.

The remainder is structured as follows. For a better comprehension, we repeat the original contributions of our previous work [10] in Sects. 2, 3, and 4: Sect. 2 presents an analysis of declarative and imperative provisioning technologies and discusses combination concepts. Sections 3 and 4 present the original modelling approach. In Sect. 5, we present the new contribution of this extended version that integrates the Cloud standard TOSCA. The extended validation is presented in Sects. 6 and 7 presents the original evaluation. Section 8 concludes the paper and gives an outlook on future work.

2   State of the Art Analysis

In this section, we conduct a state of the art analysis of declarative and imperative provisioning approaches and existing technologies including a critical evaluation. Afterwards, we discuss related work that attempts to combine the two flavors.

2.1   The Declarative Flavor

Declarative approaches can be used to describe the provisioning of an application by modelling its desired goal state, which is enforced by a declarative provisioning system. They typically employ domain-specific languages (DSLs) [14] to describe goals in a declarative way, i. e., only the *what* is described without providing any details about the technical *how*. For example, a declarative specification may describe that a Webserver has to be installed on a virtual machine, but without specifying the technical tasks that have to be performed to reach this goal. The main strength of declarative approaches is that the technical provisioning logic, i. e., the technical tasks to be performed, is inferred automatically by the provisioning system, which eases modelling provisionings as the technical execution details are hidden [16]. One of the most prominent examples of declarative provisioning description languages is Amazon CloudFormation[1]. This JSON-based language enables to describe the desired application deployment using Amazon's Cloud services including their configuration in a declarative model, which is consumed to fully automatically setup the application. In contrast to provider-specific languages, which quickly lead to vendor lock-in, also provider-independent configuration management technologies have been developed, e. g., Puppet [33].

Due to the automatic inference of provisioning logic, declarative systems have to understand the declared statements. This restricts declarative provisioning capabilities to standard component types and predefined semantics that are known by the runtime [11]. Thus, individual customizations for the provisioning of complex application structures cannot be realized arbitrarily

---

[1] http://aws.amazon.com/cloudformation/.

and have to comply with the general, overall provisioning logic. As a consequence, the declarative approach is rather suited for applications that consist of common components and configurations, but is limited in terms of deploying big, complex business applications that require specific configurations with nontrivial component dependencies. Even mechanisms to integrate script executions, API calls, or service invocations at certain points in their deployment lifecycle, as supported by many declarative approaches, do often not provide the required flexibility as the overall logic cannot be changed arbitrarily. As the integration of other technologies is often not supported natively, models get polluted by glue and wrapper code, which results in complex models including low-level technical integration details [36]. Nevertheless, the declarative flavor is very important due to (i) native support by Cloud providers, (ii) huge communities providing reusable artifacts and (iii) the simplicity of specifying application deployments.

2.2   The Imperative Flavor

In contrast to the declarative flavor, the imperative provisioning approach enables developers to specify each technical detail about the provisioning execution by creating an explicit process model that can be executed fully automatically by a runtime. Imperative models define (i) the control flow of activities, (ii) the data flow between them, as well as (iii) all technical details required to execute these activities. Thus, compared to declarative approaches, they describe not only *what* has to be done, but also *how* the provisioning tasks have to be executed. Imperative processes are typically implemented using (i) programming languages such as Java, (ii) scripting languages, e. g., Bash or Python, and (iii) workflow languages such as BPEL [27] or BPMN [30]. However, programming and scripting languages are not suited to orchestrate other provisioning technologies as they are not able to provide the robust and reliable execution features that are supported by the workflow technology [16,24]. Since general-purpose workflow languages do not natively support modeling features for application provisioning, we developed BPMN4TOSCA [19], which is a BPMN extension that supports API calls, script-executions, and service invocations based on the TOSCA standard [29] (a standard to describe Cloud applications). This language can be used to seamlessly integrate such tasks as it provides a separate activity type for each of them. However, BPMN4TOSCA lacks support for the direct integration of declarative provisioning technologies, which need to be wrapped for their invocation. Thus, similar to general-purpose technologies, seamlessly integrating domain-specific technologies in one process model is not possible. To wrap management technologies, we presented a management bus that provides a unified API for the invocation of arbitrary technologies [36]. However, invoking the bus obfuscates the actual technical statements, which impedes maintaining and understanding models.

Imperative approaches are suited to model complex provisionings that employ a plethora of heterogeneous components, especially for multi-cloud applications [32]. As they provide full control over the tasks to be executed, imperative models are able to automate exactly the manual steps that would be executed by a human administrator who provisions the application manually. Thus, while declarative approaches are rather suited for standard provisionings, imperative approaches enable developers to define arbitrary provisioning logic. The main drawback of the imperative approaches results from the huge amount of statements that must be specified since the runtime infers no logic by itself. Consequently, manual process authoring is a labor-intensive, time-consuming, and error-prone task that requires a lot of low-level, technical expertise in different fields [9, 11]: heterogeneous services need to be orchestrated (e. g., SOAP-based and RESTful provider APIs), low-level tools must be integrated, and, especially, declarative technologies must be wrapped. As currently no technology supports the seamless integration of both flavors, their orchestration results in large, polluted, technically complex processes that require multiple different wrappers to support the various invocation mechanisms and protocols [36]. These wrappers decrease the transparency as only simplified interfaces are exposed to the orchestrating process while the technical details, which are in many cases of vital importance to avoid errors when modelling multiple steps that depend on each other, are abstracted completely. In addition, wrappers significantly impede maintaining process models as not simply the orchestration process has to be adapted, but often wrapper code needs to be modified and built again, too.

2.3   Combination Approaches

Since non-trivial Cloud applications get more and more distributed across multiple different Cloud providers[2] [34] and employ various Cloud services on different conceptual levels (IaaS, PaaS, SaaS, etc.) possibly offered by heterogeneous providers, multiple of these approaches have to be combined and integrated to achieve a fully automated end-to-end deployment and management process for non-trivial applications. Therefore, in this section, we present related work that attempts to combine both flavors. There are several general purpose concepts that attempt to bridge the gap between imperative provisioning logic and declarative models which generate provisioning workflows by analyzing the declarative specifications [6, 11–13, 16, 18, 22, 25]. These approaches are able to interpret declarative specifications modelled using a domain-specific modelling language for generating provisioning plans, which can be executed fully automatically. The advantage of these approaches is the full control over the executed provisioning steps as the resulting workflows can be adapted and configured arbitrarily. However, the complexity, lack of transparency, and the polluted control and data flows of the resulting workflows are still problems that impede extending the

---

[2] Reasons for using multiple Cloud providers are differences in pricing, quality of service, offered service types, and features or when building hybrid Cloud applications that combine private and public Clouds [9, 34].

plans if customization is required. Thus, the approach we present in this paper may be applied to these technologies for improving the quality of the generated processes. Andrzejak et al. [1] sketch an approach to specify declarative goals in a workflow section, which are automatically transformed into a partial order of activities to reach these goals by a planner. However, they do not support directly integrating domain-specific languages of declarative management technologies into the workflow model. Thus, to integrate other technologies, also wrappers are required. As a result, to ensure the correct operation and to ease the creation of complex provisioning processes for non-trivial applications, a hybrid modelling approach is required to seamlessly integrate both kinds of technologies.

3   A Hybrid Modelling Concept

In this section, we present an approach that enables integrating declarative and imperative provisioning models seamlessly into the control and data flow of an imperative workflow model. In Sect. 3.1, we introduce the abstract concept of the approach in a technology-independent manner and define an internal data handling concepts in Sect. 3.2. In Sect. 4, we apply the approach to the workflow language BPEL in order to show how the concept can be realized using a concrete standardized workflow language.

3.1   Declarative Provisioning Activities

The general modelling approach is shown in Fig. 1 and based on extending standardized, imperative workflow languages such as BPMN or BPEL by the concept of *Declarative Provisioning Activities*. These activities enable to specify declarative provisioning goals directly in the control flow of a workflow model that describes the tasks to provision a certain application. To present the conceptual contribution independently from a concrete workflow language, we first introduce the general concept in an abstract way and show its applicability to the standardized workflow language BPEL afterwards. Therefore, in this section, we distinguish only between (i) Imperative Provisioning Activities and (ii) Declarative Provisioning Activities that abstract from concrete realizations of provisioning tasks in different workflow languages. Of course, other control and data flow constructs, such as events and gateways, are also required to model executable provisioning workflows. However, these constructs are language-specific and do not influence the presented modelling concept in general.

An *Imperative Provisioning Activity (IPA)* describes a technically detailed execution of a provisioning task as a sequence of one or more imperative statements. This can be, for example, a script implemented in Python or a simple HTTP-POST request that specifies a URL and data to be sent. Thus, the term is an

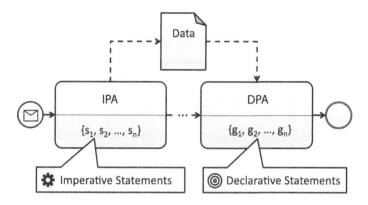

Fig. 1. Concept of the hybrid modelling approach.

abstraction of several existing imperative approaches such as scripts and programs that implement a workflow activity or the invocation of an API etc. The modeling and execution of such Imperative Provisioning Activities is supported natively by many workflow languages through general-purpose concepts or by domain-specific extensions, respectively. For example, BPMN natively supports the execution of script tasks [30], the BPEL extension BPEL4REST [15] enables sending arbitrary HTTP requests, and BPMN4TOSCA natively supports orchestrating provisioning operations based on the TOSCA-standard—especially the execution of configuration scripts on a target VM [5,36]. This enables orchestrating arbitrary imperative provisioning tasks using workflows that describe the technical details required for the automated provisioning of complex applications.

In contrast to this, we introduce the new concept of *Declarative Provisioning Activities (DPA)* in this paper that enables specifying desired provisioning goals in a declarative manner. A DPA consists of a set of declarative statements that describe *what* has to be achieved, e. g., a desired configuration of a certain application component, but without specifying any technical details about *how* to achieve the declared goals. Similar to other activity constructs of workflow languages, Declarative Provisioning Activities are modelled directly in the control and data flow of the process model the same way as IPAs. This enables combining Imperative and Declarative Provisioning Activities intuitively while preserving a clear understanding about the overall flow. The operational semantics of Declarative Provisioning Activities are defined as follows: if the control flow reaches the activity, the declarative statements, i. e., the modelled goals, are enforced by the runtime that executes the workflow. The activity is executed until all goals are achieved and all affected application components are in the desired state specified by the DPA. Then, the activity completes and the control flow continues following the links to the next activities. Process models that contain both provisioning activity types are called *Hybrid Provisioning Plans*.

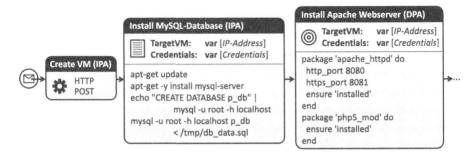

Fig. 2. Simplified example of a Hybrid Provisioning Plan that (i) instantiates a virtual machine, (ii) installs a database, and (iii) installs a Webserver on the virtual machine.

Figure 2 shows an example of a Hybrid Provisioning Plan that contains two Imperative Provisioning Activities and one Declarative Provisioning Activity, which (i) instantiate a virtual machine, (ii) install a MySQL-database, and (iii) install a Webserver on the virtual machine. The first IPA is an HTTP request to an API of a Cloud provider or an infrastructure virtualization technology that triggers the instantiation of the virtual machine. The activity specifies the request including all required configuration parameters and invokes the API correspondingly. After waiting for the successful instantiation, the IP-address and SSH credentials of the VM, which can be polled at the API, are stored in two variables of the workflow model: "IP-Address" and "Credentials". As these are standard tasks, we omit details in the figure for reasons of space.

The second IPA installs a MySQL database on the VM: the shown activity uses a low-level Bash script that imperatively specifies statements to be executed to install the database and to import a referenced SQL-file, which is uploaded to the VM by a previous IPA (omitted in the figure). To copy and execute this script on the VM, the process variables that contain the IP-Address and SSH credentials of the target VM are used by the IPA to access the virtual machine via SSH and to execute the imperatively specified statements. To model the installation and configuration of the Apache Webserver on the virtual machine, the DSL of the configuration management technology Chef [31] is used to declaratively specify the configuration of the desired installation. Consequently, a Declarative Provisioning Activity is used that specifies the desired goals by declaratively describing the state and configuration of the Webserver that has to be enforced when executing the activity. Similarly to the second script-based IPA, the activity references the same process variables to access the virtual machine.

This example shows that the direct integration of declarative and imperative languages and technologies in one orchestration process provides a powerful modelling approach as the corresponding imperative programming or scripting-languages, respectively, as well as the domain-specific languages of declarative approaches can be used seamlessly in one process model. Therefore, there is no need to write complex integration code or to invoke services wrapping these technologies that pollute the process model. Thus, the approach enables using the *right* technology for the *right* task while ensuring full-control over their orchestration without polluting the workflow model.

3.2 Internal Data Handling

Both types of activities exchange data within the workflow. Therefore, we define three concepts including their operational semantics that enable describing the internal data flow between provisioning activities in a Hybrid Provisioning Plan: (i) input parameters, (ii) output parameters, and (iii) content injection. Again, we abstract from data storage concepts and constructs of workflow languages by simply referring to "process variables" and show in the next section how these concepts can be realized using the standardized workflow language BPEL.

As shown in Fig. 2, the imperative script-activity and the declarative Chef-activity reference process variables ("IP-Address" and "Credentials") that are assigned to a "TargetVM" and a "Credentials" attribute of the activities. These attributes represent predefined, activity-specific *input parameters* of the activity implementation. When the control flow reaches the activity, the runtime copies the content of the referenced process variables "by value" and takes them as input parameters for invoking the activity's implementation.

To exchange data between DPAs and IPAs, both may specify *output parameters* that contain the results of their execution. Each output parameter is represented as a pair of (i) *activity-internal data reference* and (ii) process variable. An activity-internal data reference is a reference to a data container in the language of the activity. For example, an environment variable of a script. When the execution of the statements is finished, the referenced data is copied by the activity implementation to the specified process variables "by value".

Content injection enables using process variables directly in the declarative or imperative language of a provisioning activity. These serve as placeholders that are replaced by the current content of the referenced variable when the execution of the activity starts. For example, a script may use the variable "IP-Address" to write the IP-address of the virtual machine into a set of firewall rules to enable accessing the Webserver from the outside, i.e., by external clients.

4 Realization Using BPEL

In this section, we prove that the presented approach is practically feasible by applying the hybrid modelling concept to the workflow standard BPEL. We (i) show how Imperative Provisioning Activities can be realized using existing constructs and extensions of BPEL and how (ii) Declarative Provisioning Activities can be modelled and executed using BPEL extension activities [27]. The result of this section is a standards-based, hybrid provisioning modelling language that supports the direct integration of imperative and declarative languages.

```
1  <extensionActivity>
2     <REST:POST ResponseVar="VMCreationResponse"
3              URL="https://ec2.amazonaws.com/
4                   ?Action=RunInstances
5                   &ImageId=ami-31814f58
6                   &InstanceType=m1.small&..." />
7  </extensionActivity>
8     ...
9  <extensionActivity>
10    <DPA:Chef TargetVM="$bpelvar[IP-Address]"
11             Credentials="$bpelvar[Credentials]">
12
13          package 'apache_httpd' do
14                http_port $bpelvar[HTTPPort]
15                https_port 8081
16                ...
17                ensure 'installed'
18          end
19          ...
20    </DPA:Chef>
21  </extensionActivity>
```

Listing 1.1. Simplified snippet of a BPEL model that employs an HTTP-Request as IPA and a DPA that declares Chef statements.

In general, we realize DPAs by applying the BPEL concept of extension activities that enables implementing custom activity types using programming languages such as Java [21]. BPEL workflow runtimes support registering multiple different types of extension activities including their implementations. If the control flow of a workflow reaches an extension activity-element, its implementation is executed by the workflow engine and the whole XML-content of the extension activity-element in the BPEL model is passed to the implementation of the extension activity as input. Thus, the concept enables modelling arbitrary XML-definitions which are parsed and interpreted by the extension activity implementation. To select the right implementation, the element name of the extension activity-element's first child serves as lookup key for the workflow engine. Hence, we can realize arbitrary types of DPAs by implementing small programs that are executed when the control flow reaches one of these activities.

We show how IPAs and DPAs can be realized using extension activities by conducting an example. A modeller, e. g., developers or operations personnel [17], manually models a Hybrid Provisioning Plan that consists of Declarative as well as Imperative Provisioning Activities where suitable. The XML shown in Listing 1.1 is an excerpt of a BPEL model that instantiates a virtual machine on the Cloud-offering Amazon EC2 and installs an Apache Webserver on it. The instantiation of the VM is modelled as activity that sends an HTTP-POST request to the management API of Amazon[3] (lines 1–7). We employ here the BPEL4REST extension activity approach [15], which supports specifying output parameters: the Amazon API synchronously returns the instance ID of the virtual machine in the HTTP response. As the provisioning of a virtual machine takes some time, the ID can be used to poll the status of the VM instantiation. Therefore, we store the response in a process variable called "VMCreationResponse" (line 2). The implementation of the extension activity reads this mapping and writes the content of the HTTP response as value to the VMCreationResponse variable. This variable can be used by other activities to monitor the current VM status and to retrieve the IP-address of the running virtual machine when the instantiation finished using similar API calls (omitted in Listing 1.1).

After the virtual machine is provisioned, a Chef-DPA installs the Webserver on it (lines 9–21). This Declarative Provisioning Activity specifies the attributes used in our previous example with identical semantics. Similar to the HTTP extension activity, the extension activity implementation of the Chef-DPA reads its XML fragment, extracts the relevant information, and enforces the declared goals by accessing the virtual machine using SSH, installing a Chef agent, and sending the declarative statements to this agent that enforces them. In this example, the input parameter concept is used to specify the target VM on which the Webserver has to be installed and to specify the credentials to access the virtual machine (lines 10 & 11). The referenced BPEL variables of the workflow model are replaced by the extension activity implementation for execution. In addition, also the content injection concept is used: in line 14, a BPEL variable is specified as configuration for the HTTP-port of the Webserver. Thus, when executing the Declarative Provisioning Activity, its implementation retrieves the value of the "HTTPPort" workflow variable and replaces the placeholder before enforcing the declared configuration—similarly to input parameters.

5   Accessing External Data Based on TOSCA

In this section, we extend our previous work [10] by a concept that systematically enables accessing required data from an external source, i.e., data that is not produced by activities within the workflow. In particular, we show how information about the application to be provisioned can be retrieved in a standardized manner by employing the *Topology and Orchestration Specification for Cloud Applications (TOSCA)* [28,29]. Before we present the new contribution of this paper, we first explain the main concepts of TOSCA in the next subsection.

5.1   An Overview of TOSCA

TOSCA is an OASIS standard that enables modelling Cloud applications and their management processes in a portable way. In this section, we describe the

---

[3] http://docs.aws.amazon.com/AWSEC2/latest/APIReference/API_RunInstances.html.

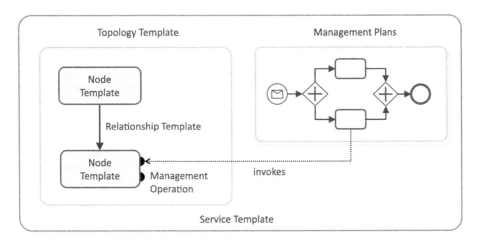

Fig. 3. TOSCA concept: Topology Template (left) and plans (right) (adapted from [3]).

important concepts of TOSCA required to understand the presented approach. For details, we refer interested readers to the TOSCA Specification [29] and the TOSCA Primer [28]. A compact overview of TOSCA is given by Binz et al. [3,4].

TOSCA defines a language for modelling (i) the application's structure in the form of a *Topology Template* and (ii) management processes in the form of executable *plans*. Figure 3 shows an overview. A Topology Template is a graph consisting of nodes, which represent the application's components, and edges, which describe their relationships. For example, PHP applications, databases, and SQL-connections. Components are modelled as *Node Templates*, relationships as *Relationship Templates*. Node as well as Relationship Templates are typed by *Node Types* and *Relationship Types*. The open type system enables defining arbitrary types of components and relations. Therefore, TOSCA can be used to model deployments on any infrastructure and platform service. The Topology Template, Node and Relationship Types, and other TOSCA elements are contained in a *Service Template*, which also specifies a unique identifier for the application.

Figure 4 shows a simplified TOSCA Service Template of a Webshop application. We use this topology model in the following to explain the presented approach. The model is rendered using VINO4TOSCA [8][4]: Node Templates are depicted as rounded rectangles, Relationship Templates as arrows. Node and Relationship Types are enclosed by parentheses. The application consists of a Web-based frontend implemented in PHP, which is hosted on an Apache Webserver. The Webserver employs the PHP module to run the frontend component. This is described directly by the Node Template's type. Of course, the PHP module could be modelled as separate component, too. The Webserver is hosted on a virtual machine that runs on Amazon's public Cloud offering EC2. On the same VM,

---

[4] VINO4TOSCA is supported, for example, by the TOSCA modelling tool *Winery* [20].

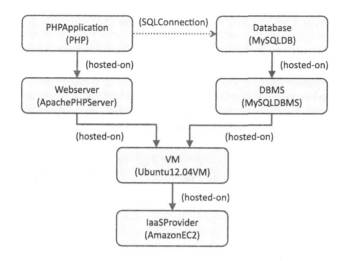

Fig. 4. Simplified TOSCA Topology Template of a Webshop application.

a MySQL database management system and a corresponding database are hosted that contains the Webshop's data. The frontend and the database are linked by an Relationship Template of type "SQLConnection". To provision this application, artifacts implementing the business logic are required, e. g., the PHP files of the Webshop's frontend and the database schema. In TOSCA, these artifacts are modelled as *Deployment Artifacts*, which typically consist of meta information and an URL that references the respective file. In addition, Node and Relationship Types may specify management operations that are implemented by *Implementation Artifacts*, for example, a Node Type "ApachePHPServer" provides an operation to deploy PHP applications.

Management plans describe management processes in the form of executable workflow models. These workflows invoke and orchestrate the management operations provided by Node and Relationship Templates to implement a more sophisticated management functionality, e. g., to model the provisioning of the Webshop application or to describe how the application can be automatically scaled. To describe these workflows, TOSCA supports using arbitrary languages, for example, the standardized workflow modelling languages BPEL [27] or BPMN [30]. Beside complex management plans that are typically authored by hand, provisioning plans can be automatically generated based on the topology model [11]. Moreover, TOSCA standardizes a package format called *Cloud Service Archive (CSAR)*, which contains all required models and files, i. e., the Service Template, all plans, as well as the required artifacts, e. g., application files or installation scripts.

5.2 Referencing Properties in Hybrid TOSCA Provisioning Plans

Both kinds of types, Node Types and Relationship Types, specify properties for the corresponding templates that have to be considered by the runtime when deploying the application, e. g., a Node Template of type "ApachePHPServer" specifies the property "HTTPPort", which has to be used for accessing the Webserver via HTTP. After deploying the application, the properties defined by types describe runtime information or the current state of the respective component or relationship, respectively, e. g., the IP-address of the virtual machine the Webserver is deployed on or the current workload of the Webserver. Thus, these properties are (i) read when initially deploying a new component or establishing a new relationship to configure this step, (ii) required to retrieve information about already provisioned entities, and (iii) used to update information about entities, e. g., when a management task changes the HTTP port of the Webserver on runtime, the corresponding property should be updated in the instance model.

Properties of Node and Relationship Templates can be retrieved by an API provided by the employed TOSCA runtime, e. g., *OpenTOSCA* [5] provides an REST-API to access properties of Node and Relationship Templates. This API does not distinguish between the original values specified in the TOSCA Service Template and the current runtime values and just returns the current value of the property. Therefore, in general, properties can be accessed by plans to get the current information about an entity. Thus, based on the topology model, information about the components and relations can be used to dynamically configure the provisioning plan. For example, instead of specifying port numbers directly in the plan, retrieving this information from the corresponding property of the Webserver Node Template would enable creating flexible plans. However, writing and reading properties using native constructs of the workflow language requires additional activities that pollute the workflow model. Therefore, we extend the concepts of internal data handling introduced in Sect. 3.2 by a concept to directly access these properties. To enable this in a structured manner, we allow referencing properties of Node and Relationship Templates for input parameters, output parameters, and content injection. Such a property reference is a triple consisting of (i) the identifier of the Service Template, (ii) the identifier of the Node or Relationship Template, and (iii) the name of the property that has to be accessed, e. g., (*Webshop,Webserver,IP-Address*). As the TOSCA standard allows defining type hierarchies, the triple refers to the property that results after applying all inheritance rules specified by the standard [29]. For example, the value of the "HTTP-Port" property of an "ApachePHPServer" Node Type overrides the property with the same name of its super Node Type "Webserver".

5.3 Illustration of the Concept

Figure 5 illustrates the concept to access properties contained in TOSCA models as described in the previous paragraph. On the left, an excerpt of a Hybrid

Provisioning Plan is shown, which contains a Declarative Provisioning Activity. On the right, an excerpt of the TOSCA Service Template is depicted that describes the PHP stack of the Webshop application introduced in Sect. 5.1. The Declarative Provisioning Activity on the left employs the concept of specifying TOSCA properties to reference external data. For example, the desired HTTP- and HTTPS-Ports of the Webserver are retrieved from the topology model and used to inject the respective content directly into the declarative statements as illustrated by the arrows. This information is typically specified during design time and, therefore, static. In addition, to install the Webserver on the virtual machine, dynamic runtime information is required, such as the IP-address of the virtual machine and its credentials. Therefore, the input variable of the Declarative Provisioning Activity references this property of the virtual machine Node Template in the Service Template. When executing this DPA, for example, the value of the IP-address has been set by a previous activity in the provisioning plan that instantiated the virtual machine. Thus, this information is dynamic and represents current runtime information of the respective template. As a result, the shown Declarative Provisioning Activity illustrates the benefits of combining the internal data handling concept presented in the original paper and the external data handling concept introduced in this extended version.

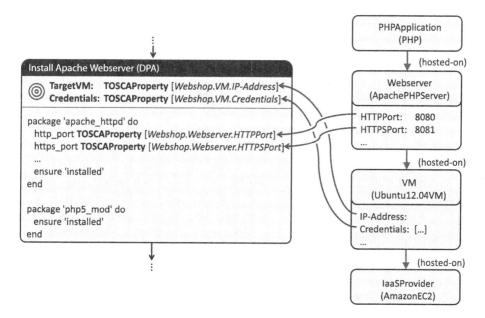

Fig. 5. Illustration of the extended data handling concept: Declarative Provisioning Activity (left) and the PHP stack of the Webshop's TOSCA Topology Template (right).

5.4   Extending BPEL by TOSCA Property References

In this section, we extend our BPEL realization presented in Sect. 4 by the introduced concept to reference TOSCA properties. We define the BPEL syntax to reference TOSCA properties similarly to the internal data handling concept: in addition to *bpelvar*, we introduce a new keyword named *TOSCAProperty* that expects one value that points to the desired property. We encode the triple consisting of Service Template identifier, Node Template identifier, and property name as concatenation separated by dots. The operational semantics are defined as follows: the extension activity's implementation is responsible for replacing the placeholder, i. e., reading and writing the referenced properties of the respective template by accessing the API provided by the employed TOSCA runtime.

```
1  <extensionActivity>
2    <DPA:Chef TargetVM="$TOSCAProperty[Webshop.VM.IP-Address]"
3          Credentials="$TOSCAProperty[Webshop.VM.Credentials]">
4      package 'apache_httpd' do
5        http_port $TOSCAProperty[Webshop.Webserver.HTTPPort]
6        https_port $TOSCAProperty[Webshop.Webserver.HTTPSPort]
7        ...
8        ensure 'installed'
9      end
10       ...
11   </DPA:Chef>
12 </extensionActivity>
```

Listing 1.2. Simplified BPEL model of a DPA that references TOSCA properties.

Listing 1.2 gives an example. The shown Declarative Provisioning Activity originates from the example shown in Listing 1.1 between lines 9 and 21. We exchanged the internal data reference by an external reference to the Webserver of the Webshop, in particular to its HTTP- and HTTPS properties: the *TOSCAProperty* keyword is used to specify the Service Template, the Node Template, and the desired property, in this case "Webshop", "Webserver", and "HTTPPort". When the control flow reaches this DPA, the extension activity accesses the API of the runtime to read the values specified for the referenced property and replaces the placeholder by this value. Similarly, we reference TOSCA properties of the virtual machine to specify the input parameters (lines 2 and 3). This concept enables specifying the configuration of a Hybrid Provisioning Plan directly in the respective topology by using a standardized metamodel. Thus, if this kind of information has to be adjusted for other deployments, not the plan has to be adapted but simply the TOSCA model. This separation of concerns enables avoiding complex data flows within a provisioning workflow that have to be modelled every time output data of former activities has to be used as input for other activities. As a result, if the provisioning plan has to be adapted, applying this external data reference concept significantly eases maintenance tasks because the coupling of activities is significantly reduced regarding the data flow.

6 Standards-Based Prototype

To prove the technical feasibility of the presented approach, we implemented a prototype based on the two standards TOSCA and BPEL. We applied the presented concept to an open-source Cloud application management ecosystem, which consists of the modelling tool *Winery* [20], the *OpenTOSCA runtime environment* [5], and the self-service portal *Vinothek* [7]. As explained in Sect. 5, TOSCA enables describing the application structure including all required artifacts in the form of a CSAR. These archives can be modelled using Winery. A CSAR is consumed by the OpenTOSCA runtime, which deploys the management workflows contained therein. Therefore, the runtime employs a workflow engine (WSO2 BPS)[5] to execute BPEL workflows. Using the self-service portal Vinothek, their execution can be triggered by a simple graphical user interface.

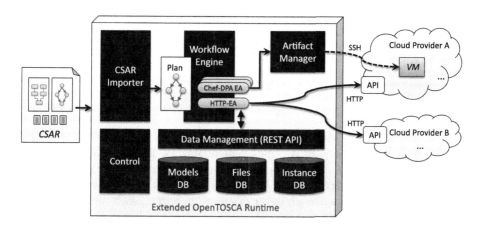

Fig. 6. Prototypical implementation based on the OpenTOSCA runtime.

Figure 6 shows a simplified architecture of the OpenTOSCA runtime environment including our prototypical extension of the hybrid modelling concept including the concepts for external data handling introduced in this paper. The *CSAR Importer* is responsible for consuming CSARs and processing the contained data, e. g., by storing the models and all associated files in local databases. The *Control* then triggers the local deployment of all management plans so that they can be invoked by the Vinothek to provision a new application instance or to manage a running instance. The concept presented in this paper

---

[5] http://wso2.com/products/.

is realized by implementing extension activity-plugins for the workflow engine. The HTTP-extension activity, for example, can be used in BPEL workflows to invoke management APIs of providers to instantiate or manage virtual machines. As described in the previous sections, DPAs can then use process variables to access these virtual machines in order to install or configure software etc. To implement these extension activities, e. g., the Chef-DPA, we delegate executing the declaratively described goals to a component called *Artifact Manager*. This plugin-based manager is able to execute various configuration management technologies such as Chef and imperative scripts, e. g., Bash scripts [35,36]. Thus, implementing IPAs and DPAs is eased by invoking this manager. Of course, arbitrary technologies can be integrated without using the artifact manager, too.

To realize the external data handling concept, we use the *Data Management* component, which provides access to databases that store (i) all models and (ii) artifacts of deployed CSARs as well as (iii) runtime information about deployed application instances. The component provides a REST-based API, which can be used by the implementation of DPAs and IPAs, i. e., extension activities, to retrieve information from the models or to write information back if the provisioning activity updates property values, respectively. For modelling Hybrid TOSCA Provisioning Plans, we employ the modelling tool *BPEL Designer*[6]. Since the prototype extension is based on TOSCA and BPEL, it provides an end-to-end, standards-based Cloud application management platform that enables integrating various provisioning, configuration, and management technologies.

7 Evaluation

In this section, we evaluate the presented approach by comparing it with the plain declarative and imperative management flavors. For the comparison, we reuse the management feature criteria for comparing service-centric and script-centric management technologies [9] and additionally add criteria that are derived from the features of each flavor discussed in Sect. 2. As a result, the criteria represent requirements that must be fulfilled to fully automatically provision the kind of complex composite Cloud applications described in the introduction (cf. Sect. 1). An "x" in Table 1 denotes that the corresponding approach fully supports the criterion. An "x" in parentheses denotes partial support.

Full control means that the provisioning may be customized arbitrarily by the workflow modeller in each technical detail. As declarative approaches infer the details about the execution by themselves, the general provisioning logic cannot be changed easily. In contrast to this, imperative approaches explicitly model each step to be performed and can be, therefore, customized arbitrarily. Because the hybrid approach supports both, it fulfills this criterion completely.

Complex deployments denotes that real, non-trivial business applications that employ various heterogeneous components and services can be deployed using

---

[6] https://eclipse.org/bpel/.

a technology of the flavor. Declarative approaches reach their limits at a certain point of required customizability: as the provisioning logic is inferred by a general-purpose provisioning system, only known declarative statements can be understood and processed (cf. Sect. 2). Thus, if a very specific, arbitrarily customized application structure or configuration has to be deployed, declarative approaches are often not able to fulfill these rare and very special requirements completely. The integration of low-level execution code such as scripts partially solves this problem. In contrast to this, based on the full control criterion, in general arbitrary complex provisionings can be described using imperative approaches such as scripts or workflows. However, the technical complexity of the resulting processes hard to manage and to maintain since the integration of technologies, as explained in Sect. 2, leads to a lot of glue and wrapper code, which results in many lines of process implementation code. Thus, plain imperative approaches are not ideal for handling such cases completely and are, therefore, only partially suited. Our integration approach solves these issues as the optimal technology can be chosen without polluting plans.

Table 1. Criteria evaluation.

Feature	Declarative	Imperative	Integrated approach
Full control		x	x
Complex deployments	(x)	(x)	x
Hybrid and multi-cloud applications	(x)	x	x
Seamless integration			x
Component wiring	(x)	x	x
XaaS integration	(x)	x	x
Full automation	x	x	x
Straightforwardness	x		x
Extensibility	(x)	x	x
Flexibility		(x)	(x)

The *hybrid and multi-Cloud applications* criteria evaluate the support for applications that are either hosted on (i) a combination of private and public Cloud services or (ii) Cloud services offered by different providers. Since many declarative approaches, such as Amazon CloudFormation, employ proprietary, non-standardized domain-specific languages, many of these technologies are not able to provision a distributed application as described above. General purpose technologies such as TOSCA [29] allow to provision hybrid as well as multi-Cloud applications, for example, by using the TOSCA plan generator [11]. However, if multiple providers are involved, typically their proprietary languages have to be used as the declarative general-purpose technologies are not able to support all individual technical features. Based on the criteria *full control* and *complex deployments*, the imperative as well as the proposed approach fulfill this criterion.

Seamless integration evaluates the capability to employ arbitrary management technologies without (i) polluting the model or (ii) leading to abstracted wrapper calls (cf. Sect. 2). As extensively discussed in the previous sections, neither declarative nor imperative approaches natively support all required integration concepts. In contrast, the presented approach fulfills this criterion due to the introduced concepts of Imperative and Declarative Provisioning Activities.

The *component wiring* criterion means that multiple application components can be wired. Declarative approaches support this partially as unknown components or complex wiring tasks cannot be described in a fully customizable manner. The imperative as well as the integrated approach solve this issue as any task to wire such components can be orchestrated arbitrarily.

XaaS integration means the ability to orchestrate various kinds of Cloud services that represent application components. Generic declarative approaches support this only partially as complex configuration tasks are hard to model. Proprietary approaches, such as Amazon CloudFormation, are bound to a certain provider and, therefore, require glue code to integrate other services. The imperative and the presented approach fully support this requirement following the argumentation of *component wiring*.

The *full automation* criterion is fulfilled by all kinds of approaches, as all of them enable a fully automated provisioning of the described applications.

Straightforwardness evaluates whether describing the provisioning of an application can be done in an efficient manner requiring appropriate effort. The declarative approaches are typically easy to learn, as technical complexity is shifted to the provisioning systems and only the desired goals have to be specified. Imperative approaches, such as scripts or workflows, quickly become huge and complex due to the directly visible low-level details about the control flow and the data flow. In addition, in many cases, trivial steps have to be modelled explicitly. The presented integration approach fulfills this criterion completely as the optimal technology can be selected for a certain provisioning task. Even a single DPA may be modelled that declares all provisioning goals.

The *extensibility* criterion means the ability to involve other management technologies. Declarative approaches allow this by using glue code at certain points in the inferred logic. Due to the *full control* criterion, imperative approaches are able to include arbitrary implementations at any point in the process. Thus, the presented hybrid approach supports this feature.

The declarative approaches do not support *flexibility* due to the *full control* criterion. However, also using imperative approaches are limited in terms of flexibility: if a complex application leads to a huge provisioning process, adapting this process is a challenging task. Therefore, imperative as well as the presented approach fulfill this criterion only partially. To tackle these issues, we conduct research on modelling situation-aware processes to increase the flexibility.

To summarize the evaluation, the presented approach profits from all benefits of the two provisioning flavors while solving drawbacks by the strengths of each other. Whereas complex application provisionings can be modelled in a flexible manner preserving the full control over the provisioning, standard tasks can be modelled easily using declarative specifications in a straightforward manner. Even distributed application structures, for example, hybrid and multi-Cloud applications can be provisioned using the integrated approach described in this paper. One of the most important criteria, the seamless integration of provisioning technologies, is solved by the concept of Declarative Provisioning Activities while imperative technologies are typically integrated already in existing languages. Thus, while the resulting process models are implemented in a standards-compliant manner, intuitive provisioning modelling helps developing and maintaining Hybrid Provisioning Plans—even for complex applications.

7.1   Limitations

In this section, we discuss the limitations of the presented approach. A drawback is the tight coupling of Hybrid Provisioning Plans to the structure of the application to be provisioned. Imperative orchestrations to provision the components of a certain application structure are sensitive to structural changes: different combinations of components lead to different workflow models that must be created and maintained separately [6,12,13]. Thus, as the concept of Hybrid Provisioning Plans is based on imperatively orchestrating the two kinds of provisioning activities, this applies also for the approach presented in this paper. As a result, Hybrid Provisioning Plans for new applications often have to be created from scratch while maintaining existing processes results in complex and time-consuming adaptations [11]. The concept presented in this paper extension decreases this coupling as configuration properties, such as desired ports, can be retrieved from the TOSCA model. Thus, if such kind information must be changed, only the Service Template has to be adapted not the workflow model. To reduce the coupling further, we plan to combine the approach in this paper with our previous work on generic management process fragments [6,9].

8   Conclusion

In this paper, we presented a hybrid provisioning modelling concept that enables the seamless integration of imperative and declarative provisioning models and the corresponding technologies. The introduced concepts of Declarative Provisioning Activities and Hybrid Provisioning Plans enable intuitive provisioning modelling without handling technical integration issues regarding different provisioning and configuration management technologies. Thus, the modelling concept avoids polluting the control and data flow of the overall workflow model. To prove the technical feasibility of the approach, we extended our original work by an integration with the Cloud standard TOSCA and implemented a prototype that extends the OpenTOSCA runtime environment based on the standardized workflow language BPEL. Our evaluation shows that the presented approach enables benefiting from the strengths of both flavors: declarative models can be used to specify desired goals and constraints without providing technical execution logic whereas imperative models enable modelling complex cross-cutting configuration and wiring tasks on a very low technical level. Thereby, Hybrid TOSCA Provisioning Plans can be created that employ the *right* technology for the *right* job. In future work, we plan to employ the concept also for application management. In addition, we are working on an abstraction layer for Declarative Provisioning Activities that enables declaratively specifying high-level tasks to be executed without the need to understand the low-level technical details.

Acknowledgements. This work was partially funded by the projects SitOPT (Research Grant 610872, DFG) and NEMAR (Research Grant 03ET40188, BMWi).

References

1. Andrzejak, A., Hermann, U., Sahai, A.: Feedbackflow - an adaptive workflow generator for systems management. In: ICAC 2005, pp. 335–336, June 2005
2. Binz, T., Breitenbücher, U., Kopp, O., Leymann, F.: Migration of enterprise applications to the cloud. It - Inf. Technol. Spec. Issue Architect. Web Appl. **56**(3), 106–111 (2014)
3. Binz, T., Breitenbücher, U., Kopp, O., Leymann, F.: TOSCA: portable automated deployment and management of cloud applications. In: Bouguettaya, A., Sheng, Q.Z., Daniel, F. (eds.) Advanced Web Services, pp. 527–549. Springer, Heidelberg (2014)
4. Binz, T., Breiter, G., Leymann, F., Spatzier, T.: Portable cloud services using TOSCA. IEEE Internet Comput. **16**(03), 80–85 (2012)
5. Binz, T., Breitenbücher, U., Haupt, F., Kopp, O., Leymann, F., Nowak, A., Wagner, S.: OpenTOSCA – a runtime for TOSCA-based cloud applications. In: Basu, S., Pautasso, C., Zhang, L., Fu, X. (eds.) ICSOC 2013. LNCS, vol. 8274, pp. 692–695. Springer, Heidelberg (2013)
6. Breitenbücher, U., Binz, T., Kopp, O., Leymann, F.: Pattern-based runtime management of composite cloud applications. In: CLOSER 2013, pp. 475–482. SciTePress, May 2013
7. Breitenbücher, U., Binz, T., Kopp, O., Leymann, F.: Vinothek - a self-service portal for TOSCA. In: ZEUS 2014. CEUR Workshop Proceedings, vol. 1140, pp. 69–72. CEUR-WS.org, March 2014
8. Breitenbücher, U., Binz, T., Kopp, O., Leymann, F., Schumm, D.: Vino4TOSCA: a visual notation for application topologies based on TOSCA. In: Meersman, R., Panetto, H., Dillon, T., Rinderle-Ma, S., Dadam, P., Zhou, X., Pearson, S., Ferscha, A., Bergamaschi, S., Cruz, I.F. (eds.) OTM 2012, Part I. LNCS, vol. 7565, pp. 416–424. Springer, Heidelberg (2012)
9. Breitenbücher, U., Binz, T., Kopp, O., Leymann, F., Wettinger, J.: Integrated cloud application provisioning: interconnecting service-centric and script-centric management technologies. In: Meersman, R., Panetto, H., Dillon, T., Eder, J., Bellahsene, Z., Ritter, N., Leenheer, P., Dou, D. (eds.) ODBASE 2013. LNCS, vol. 8185, pp. 130–148. Springer, Heidelberg (2013)
10. Breitenbücher, U., Binz, T., Kopp, O., Leymann, F., Wettinger, J.: A modelling concept to integrate declarative and imperative cloud application provisioning technologies. In: CLOSER 2015. SciTePress (2015)
11. Breitenbücher, U., et al.: Combining declarative and imperative cloud application provisioning based on TOSCA. In: IC2E 2014, pp. 87–96. IEEE, March 2014

12. Eilam, T., Elder, M., Konstantinou, A., Snible, E.: Pattern-based composite application deployment. In: IM 2011, pp. 217–224. IEEE, May 2011
13. El Maghraoui, K., Meghranjani, A., Eilam, T., Kalantar, M., Konstantinou, A.V.: Model driven provisioning: bridging the gap between declarative object models and procedural provisioning tools. In: Steen, M., Henning, M. (eds.) Middleware 2006. LNCS, vol. 4290, pp. 404–423. Springer, Heidelberg (2006)
14. Günther, S., Haupt, M., Splieth, M.: Utilizing internal domain-specific languages for deployment and maintenance of IT infrastructures. Very Large Business Applications Lab Magdeburg, Otto von Guericke University Magdeburg, Technical report (2010)
15. Haupt, F., Fischer, M., Karastoyanova, D., Leymann, F., Vukojevic-Haupt, K.: Service composition for REST. In: EDOC 2014. IEEE, September 2014
16. Herry, H., Anderson, P., Wickler, G.: Automated planning for configuration changes. In: LISA 2011. USENIX (2011)
17. Hüttermann, M.: DevOps for Developers. Apress, New York (2012)
18. Keller, A., Hellerstein, J.L., Wolf, J.L., Wu, K.L., Krishnan, V.: The CHAMPS system: change management with planning and scheduling. In: Network Operations and Management Symposium, pp. 395–408, April 2004
19. Kopp, O., Binz, T., Breitenbücher, U., Leymann, F.: BPMN4TOSCA: a domain-specific language to model management plans for composite applications. In: Mendling, J., Weidlich, M. (eds.) BPMN 2012. LNBIP, vol. 125, pp. 38–52. Springer, Heidelberg (2012)
20. Kopp, O., Binz, T., Breitenbücher, U., Leymann, F.: Winery – a modeling tool for TOSCA-based cloud applications. In: Basu, S., Pautasso, C., Zhang, L., Fu, X. (eds.) ICSOC 2013. LNCS, vol. 8274, pp. 700–704. Springer, Heidelberg (2013)
21. Kopp, O.: A classification of BPEL extensions. J. Syst. Integr. 2(4), 2–28 (2011)
22. Levanti, K., Ranganathan, A.: Planning-based configuration and management of distributed systems. In: IM 2009, pp. 65–72, June 2009
23. Leymann, F.: Cloud computing: the next revolution in IT. In: Proceedings of the 52th Photogrammetric Week, pp. 3–12, September 2009
24. Leymann, F., Roller, D.: Production Workflow: Concepts and Techniques. Prentice Hall PTR, Upper Saddle River (2000)
25. Mietzner, R.: A method and implementation to define and provision variable composite applications, and its usage in cloud computing. Dissertation, University of Stuttgart, Germany, August 2010
26. Nelson-Smith, S.: Test-Driven Infrastructure with Chef. O'Reilly Media, Inc., Sebastopol (2013)
27. OASIS: Web Services Business Process Execution Language (WS-BPEL) Version 2.0. OASIS, April 2007
28. OASIS: Topology and Orchestration Specification for Cloud Applications Primer Version 1.0. OASIS, January 2013
29. OASIS: Topology and Orchestration Specification for Cloud Applications Version 1.0, May 2013
30. OMG: Business Process Model and Notation (BPMN), Version 2.0, January 2011
31. Opscode, Inc.: Chef official site (2015). http://www.opscode.com/chef
32. Petcu, D.: Consuming resources and services from multiple clouds. J. Grid Comput. 12(2), 321–345 (2014)
33. Puppet Labs, Inc.: Puppet official site (2015). http://puppetlabs.com/puppet/what-is-puppet

34. Smit, M., Shtern, M., Simmons, B., Litoiu, M.: Partitioning applications for hybrid and federated clouds. In: Proceedings of the 2012 Conference of the Center for Advanced Studies on Collaborative Research, CASCON 2012, pp. 27–41. IBM Corp. (2012)
35. Wettinger, J., Binz, T., Breitenbücher, U., Kopp, O., Leymann, F.: Streamlining cloud management automation by unifying the invocation of scripts and services based on TOSCA. Int. J. Organ. Collective Intell. (IJOCI) 4(2), 45–63 (2014)
36. Wettinger, J., et al.: Unified invocation of scripts and services for provisioning, deployment, and management of cloud applications based on TOSCA. In: CLOSER 2014, pp. 559–568. SciTePress, April 2014

An Analysis of Power Consumption in Mobile Cloud Computing

Abdelmounaam Rezgui[1](✉) and Zaki Malik[2]

[1] Department of Computer Science and Engineering, New Mexico Tech,
Socorro, NM, USA
rezgui@cs.nmt.edu
http://www.cs.nmt.edu/~rezgui
[2] Department of Computer Science, Wayne State University, Detroit, MI, USA
zaki@wayne.edu
http://www.cs.wayne.edu/~zaki

Abstract. With the rapid proliferation of mobile devices, mobile cloud computing is emerging as an increasingly omnipresent paradigm enabling users to use battery-powered mobile devices to access a wide range of compute-intensive applications hosted on the clouds. Often, the assumption is that mobile devices consume less power when they access an application run on the cloud than when the application is run on the device itself. This, however, is increasingly questionable with the significant recent progress in improving power efficiency of mobile devices (e.g., using ultra low power GPUs). This paper aims at analyzing and comparing the benefits of these two alternatives using *mobile cloud gaming* as an example. Our evaluation shows that, despite the recent advances towards reducing power consumption in mobile devices, mobile cloud computing remains the best of the two alternatives in a wide range of scenarios.

Keywords: Mobile cloud gaming · GPUs · NICs · Power consumption · Visualization as a Service (VaaS) · Offloading

1 Introduction

Mobile devices (mobile phones, tablets, and ultra mobile PCs) are driving a phenomenal market shift. A Gartner report (Table 1) predicts that, by 2017, device shipments will reach more than 2.9 billion units, out of which 90 % will be mobile devices [18]. The growth is particularly strong in mobile phones. A June 2015 Ericsson report indicates that the total number of mobile subscriptions worldwide in Q1 2015 was 7.2 billion, 40 % of which are associated with smartphones. The report also predicts that, by 2016, the number of smartphone subscriptions will surpass those of basic phones, and the number of smartphones will reach 6.1 billion by 2020 [4]. This growth is accompanied by an equally phenomenal boom in mobile applications. According to the research firm MarketsandMarkets, the total global mobile applications market is expected to be worth $25 billion by 2015 (up from about $6.8 billion in 2010) [17]. A 2012 study by the Application

© Springer International Publishing Switzerland 2016
M. Helfert et al. (Eds.): CLOSER 2015, CCIS 581, pp. 263–278, 2016.
DOI: 10.1007/978-3-319-29582-4_14

Table 1. Worldwide device shipments by segment (thousands of units) [18].

Device type	2012	2013	2014	2017
PC (Desk-based and notebook)	341,263	315,229	302,315	271,612
Ultramobile	9,822	23,592	38,687	96,350
Tablet	116,113	197,202	265,731	467,951
Mobile phone	1,746,176	1,875,774	1,949,722	2,128,871
Total	2,213,373	2,411,796	2,556,455	2,964,783

Developers Alliance found that 62 % of the U. S. online population owned *app-capable* devices and that 74 % of those device owners use mobile applications. A March 2015 ReportLinker study estimated that there were more than 3.17 million applications available on various app stores [25].

As the rendering capabilities of mobile devices improves, mobile applications are becoming increasingly graphics-intensive. This requires intensive computations that quickly drain the device's battery. Several solutions are being developed to reduce power consumption in graphics-intensive mobile applications. Some solutions are to be used at development time while others are to be used when the application is running. The former focus on tools that help developers estimate power consumption at development time. For example, in [30], the authors present SPOT (System Power Optimization Tool), which is a model-driven tool that automates power consumption emulation code generation. In [7], the authors use program analysis during development time to estimate mobile application energy consumption. The latter type of solutions focus on reducing power consumption of hardware components such as the GPU or NIC at runtime. Examples include the *racing to sleep* technique (that sends data at the highest possible rate), wide channels, and multiple RF chains [6].

A third alternative is application offloading, the process of running compute-intensive tasks on servers (often in the cloud) and delivering the results of these computations to mobile devices through their wireless interfaces. However, these wireless interfaces also may consume substantial amounts of power when receiving large amounts of data as is typical in many modern, interactive, graphics-intensive mobile applications. It is therefore important to understand the power consumption implications of the two alternatives: running the graphics-intensive application on the cloud or on the mobile device itself.

In this paper, we use *mobile cloud gaming* as an example to analyze and compare these two alternatives in terms of power consumption. We show through actual hardware specifications that, despite the recent introduction of ultra low power GPUs for mobile devices, it remains far more power efficient to offload graphics-intensive tasks to cloud servers. To make our discussion concrete, we focus on two cases of mobile devices: (i) notebooks and (ii) smartphones. In both cases, we only consider gaming using the device's WiFi interface (not its cellular interface.) The reason for this is that the high latency and high cost make mobile cloud gaming using cellular networks (UMTS, LTE, etc.) an impractical alternative for most consumers. We will elaborate on this in Sect. 4.

1.1 Paper Organization

This paper is organized as follows. We first discuss some current approaches that aim at reducing power consumption in mobile cloud computing. In Sect. 3, we give an overview of mobile cloud gaming. In Sect. 4, we contrast cellular-based and WiFi-based mobile cloud gaming from the perspectives of power consumption, throughput, latency, and cost. In Sects. 5 and 6, we present power consumption trends in modern mobile GPUs and 802.11 network cards. In Sect. 7, we quantitatively evaluate and compare power consumption of a gaming session in the two previously mentioned scenarios in the context of notebooks. We repeat the same analysis for smartphones in Sect. 8. We summarize the conclusions from our study in Sect. 9.

2 Current Approaches for Power Saving in Mobile Cloud Computing

Research approaches for reducing power consumption in mobile cloud computing environments have focused on one (or both) of the two following directions: (i) adding hardware/software layers in the vicinity of the mobile devices, e.g., cloudlets and (ii) context-aware offloading.

2.1 Cloudlets

The term "cloudlet" was first introduced by M. Satyanarayanan and his team at Carnegie Mellon University [1]. A cloudlet "represents the middle tier of a 3-tier hierarchy: mobile device — cloudlet — cloud" [27]. It serves as a "data center in a box" with the goal of bringing the cloud closer to the mobile device. Several researchers have used the idea of cloudlets to develop offloading approaches. A promising direction is to offload compute-intensive processing to the cloudlet instead of offloading to the cloud. An example of work that used the idea of cloudlets is [16] where the authors propose an architecture for mobile cloud computing that includes a middle layer composed of cloudlets between mobile devices and the cloud infrastructure. Cloudlets are deployed next to IEEE 802.11 access points and are used as a "service point" that improves the performance of mobile cloud services accessed by nearby mobile devices. The authors also propose an offloading algorithm that decides whether or not to offload. The algorithm takes into consideration the energy consumption for task execution and the network status while satisfying constraints related to task response time. To further improve performance, the authors introduce a data caching mechanism deployed at cloudlets.

2.2   Context-Aware Offloading

In this approach, the current "context" of the mobile device is taken into account when making decision as to whether or not to offload to the clouds. The term "context" may mean different things. For example, in [32], the authors consider a mobile cloud computing architecture with multiple resources (e.g., mobile ad-hoc network, cloudlet, and public clouds.) They propose a context-aware offloading system that takes into account these resources to provide code offloading decisions that help in selecting the wireless medium and the potential cloud resources to be used as the offloading location based on the device's context. In [3], the authors present an algorithm called MAO (Mobile Application's Offloading) triggered by a "context" that consists of the current CPU load and state of charge (SoC) of the battery. The algorithm also differentiates between interactive and delay tolerant mobile applications. When the algorithm cannot satisfy a user's quality of experience (QoE) and/or energy efficiency requirements, it rejects the job.

In [14], the authors consider the case of multiple tasks that dynamically arrive at the nodes of a mobile ad hoc network-based cloud computing environment. They propose a set of online and batch scheduling heuristics that aim at improving performance and reducing energy consumption by offloading compute-intensive applications. Their experimental evaluation focused on both user-centric and system-centric metrics such as the average makespan, the average waiting time, the average slowdown and the average utilization.

3   Mobile Cloud Gaming

Mobile cloud computing (MCC) is the process of offloading compute-intensive tasks from mobile devices to cloud servers [28, 29]. The purpose is often to save power on the mobile device and/or access servers with much higher computing power. A prime example of MCC is *mobile cloud gaming* which is the process of providing video games on-demand to consumers through the use of cloud technologies. One benefit is that the cloud, instead of the user's device, carries out most of the computations necessary to play the game, e.g., complex graphical calculations. This is obviously a tremendous advantage in case the player uses a battery-powered, mobile device. Even when power is not a critical issue for the user's device, cloud gaming still provides other cloud services, e.g., storage. Cloud gaming enables power savings also on the cloud itself as it makes it possible that several players simultaneously share cloud GPUs. For example, Nvidia's VGX Hypervisor manages GPU resources to allow multiple users to share GPU hardware while improving user density and the utilization of GPU cycles [22]. To illustrate, a single cloud gaming-capable Nvidia VGX K2 unit requires 38 W per cloud user [24], whereas a comparable single-user Nvidia GTX 690 consumer unit requires 300 W to operate [23]. In this case, cloud gaming can reduce the overall graphics-related power consumption by 87 %.

4 Cellular-Based vs. WiFi-Based Mobile Cloud Gaming

Mobile cloud gaming may be achieved using cellular connections or WiFi connections. While both options are technically possible and relatively comparable in terms of power consumption, the WiFi option seems much more attractive when we consider throughput, latency and cost. In this section, we present results from recent studies analyzing power consumption, throughput, latency, and cost in both scenarios:

4.1 Power Consumption and Throughput

In [2], the authors analyze power consumption of smartphones. In particular, they studied power consumption of the two main networking components of the device: WiFi and GPRS (provided by the GSM subsystem). The test consisted of downloading a simple file via HTTP using `wget`. The files contained random data, and were 15 MiB for WiFi, and 50 KiB for GPRS. While the test was not a gaming session, it still gave valuable insights. The experiments showed that WiFi achieved a throughput of 660.1 ± 36.8 KiB/s, and GPRS 3.8 ± 1.0 KiB/s. However, they both show *comparable* power consumption far exceeding the contribution of the RAM and CPU (Fig. 1). The experiments also showed that, with the increase in throughput possible using WiFi, CPU and RAM power consumption also increases reflecting the increase in the cost of processing data with a higher throughput.

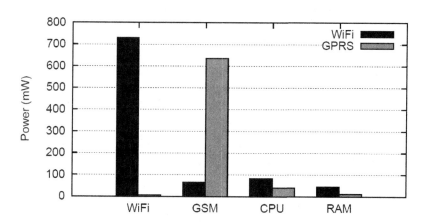

Fig. 1. Power consumption of WiFi and GSM modems, CPU, and RAM [2].

4.2 Latency

In the context of mobile cloud gaming, latency refers to the timespan between a user's action and the corresponding reaction [12], e.g., time between the action of pressing a button and seeing a character in the game move as a result of that action. High latency is a real challenge in mobile cloud gaming. Wireless connections (WiFi and cellular) and even wired residential end host round trip times (RTTs) can exceed 100 ms [13]. To many gamers, this is the point when a game's responsiveness becomes unacceptable. A recent effort to reduce latency in mobile cloud gaming is Outatime, a speculative execution system for mobile cloud gaming that is able to mask up to 250 ms of network latency [13]. It produces speculative rendered frames of future possible outcomes, delivering them to the client one entire RTT ahead of time.

While latency is an issue in both cellular-based and WiFi-based mobile gaming, WiFi connections typically have much less latency than cellular connections [12].

4.3 Cost

Cost is also a major factor in favor of WiFi-based mobile cloud gaming. For example, in [12], the authors give an analytical assessment that shows that the cost (from cellular data transfer) of a gaming session of one hour would be about 2.36 Euros without including the likely additional usage fee to be paid to the cloud gaming provider.

As we may conclude from the previous discussion, WiFi-based mobile cloud gaming is currently more practical than cellular-based mobile cloud gaming. We, therefore, limit our discussion to this option in the remainder of this paper.

5   Power Consumption Trends in Modern Mobile GPUs

It is currently generally true that GPUs offering a good rendering capability consume much power for operation and cooling. To illustrate the current power consumption trends of mobile GPUs, we list in Table 2 some modern notebook GPUs and their respective power consumptions. The table suggests that playing a game on a notebook equipped with one of the listed GPUs may not be a viable option. For example, the Dell Precision M6700 mobile workstation (which Dell touted as the "world's most powerful 17.3" mobile workstation") is equipped with the Nvidia Quadro K5000M GPU. The configuration can pull 98W of power when running on battery under a heavy CPU or GPU load. This means that it would be possible to drain the system battery in about an hour [20]. Even with this limited ability to support long running, compute-intensive applications, this configuration costs more than $2K. Better battery life may be possible but with much more expensive configurations. Efforts are underway to develop mobile devices with power efficient computing components (e.g., multicore CPUs and ultra low power GPUs) and batteries that can run compute-intensive applications (e.g., games and other graphics-intensive applications) for many hours. For example, Nvidia is introducing Tegra 4, a mobile GeForce GPU with up to 72 custom cores, a quad-core ARM Cortex-A15 processor with a fifth Companion Core that further improves performance and battery life. According to Nvidia, a battery of a capacity of 38 watt-hours would be sufficient to operate a Tegra

Table 2. Energy consumption of some modern notebook GPUs.

GPU card	Power consumption (Watts)
NVIDIA GeForce GTX 680M SLI	2×100
AMD Radeon HD 7970M Crossfire	2×100
NVIDIA GeForce GTX 680MX	122
NVIDIA GeForce GTX 675M SLI	2×100
GeForce GTX 680M	100
Quadro K5000M	100
AMD Radeon HD 7970M	100

4 mobile device running a gaming application between 5 and 10 h. This corresponds to a power consumption (for the entire device) of 4 to 8 W [9]. However, it is expected that mobile devices with these high-end configurations will remain beyond the reach of average users for the foreseeable future.

6   Power Consumption Trends in Modern Notebook NICs

The original 1997 release of the IEEE 802.11 standard operated in the 2.4 GHz frequency band and provided a data bit rate of 1 to 2 Mb/s. The standard release approved in February 2014 (known as 802.11ad) operates in the 2.4/5/60 GHz frequency bands and provides a data bit rate of up to 6.75 Gbit/s. While higher bit rates often translate into higher power consumption, this is less true in recent ultra-low power 802.11 standards. For example, today's fastest 3 antenna 802.11n device can achieve 450 Mbps. A single antenna 802.11ac device can achieve a similar bit rate with similar power consumption. This means that a typical tablet with single antenna 802.11n 150 Mbps WiFi can now support 450 Mbps with 802.11ac without any increase in power consumption or decrease in battery life [19].

7   Graphics-Intensive Applications: GPUs vs. NICs

To assess the benefits of using a mobile GPU versus offloading to the cloud, we consider gaming as it is a typical example of graphics-intensive mobile applications. Specifically, we consider four modern games that rely heavily on GPUs. We compare two scenarios in terms of power consumption. In the first scenario, the game is run entirely on the mobile device and uses only its GPU. In the second scenario, we consider an execution where the game is run on a cloud server and the mobile device only receives and renders sequences of frames produced by the server. We analytically evaluate power consumption in these two scenarios and show that, with modern wireless technology, offloading is a far better alternative to running graphics-intensive applications using the device's GPU. To make the comparison even more in favor of the GPU-based alternative,

Table 3. Average frame rate of some combinations of GPU cards, games, and resolutions.

GPU card	GRID autosport	Watch dogs	Titanfall	Thief
	L|M|H|U	L|M|H|U	L|M|H|U	L|M|H|U
GeForce GTX 770M (75 W)	199.6|130.3|92.6|46.5	80.7|66.1|27.7|19.8	60|60|59.3|48.3	57.1|51.3|46.8|26.6
GeForce GTX 860M (60 W)	192.15|109.65|88|47.2	71.2|60.7|27.7|18.9	60|60|59.5|42.4	60.5|52.7|44|23.95
GeForce GTX 850M (40–45 W)	166.65|99.33|68.3|34.7	61.8|52.3|20.75|14.7	60|59.7|53.25|34.3	46.45|39.6|36.65|18.2
GeForce GTX 765M (50–75 W)	191.9|130.7|74.1|34.8	81.3|56.9|21.1|	60|59.7|54.3|35.6	58.2|43.1|37|19.1

we ignore the power consumption of the device's disk. We assume that, when a graphics-intensive application is run on a mobile device, most of the power is consumed by the device's GPU. This is becoming increasingly true with the wide availability of mobile devices with solid-state disk drives.

To compare power consumption in the two scenarios, we first present a simple model that captures the interactions between the player and the gaming application. We will assume that, during a given gaming session of duration t, the player takes an action after every r seconds on average. We call r the *reactivity* of the player. To respond to the player's action, the application generates a video stream of length v seconds.[1] So, during the entire session, the application generates t/r video sequences whose length is v seconds each. In total, the application generates tv/r seconds of video during the given gaming session.

7.1   Scenario 1: Gaming Using the Mobile Device's GPU

To assess the power consumed by a notebook's GPU in a gaming session, we used the benchmark presented in [21]. The benchmark has a large number of notebook GPUs and a number of popular games. For each combination of game and GPU card, the benchmark gives the average number of frames per second (fps) that the GPU card achieves with four different resolution levels: Low (L), Medium (M), High (H), and Ultra (U). The benchmark considers that a frame rate of 25 fps is sufficient for fluent gaming. For the purpose of this study, we considered four GPU cards and four 2014 games, namely GRID Autosport, Watch Dogs, Titanfall, and Thief. Table 3 gives the frame rates obtained in the given combinations[2]. The resolutions in the table are as follows: Low (1024 × 768), Medium (1366 × 768), High (1920 × 1080 for the first two games and 1366 × 768 for the last two games), and Ultra (1920 × 1080). Table 3 also gives power consumption for the four GPU cards.

As an example, consider a mobile device equipped with a GPU of type Nvidia GeForce GTX 850M. As shown in Table 3, this GPU card will consume between 40 and 45 W in one hour. We will show that offloading to the cloud (Scenario 2) brings an order of magnitude reduction in terms of the power consumed by the mobile device.

---

[1] This is to simplify our discussion. In practice, the application likely generates two video sequences of different lengths in response to two different actions.

[2] The missing value in the last row corresponds to a test that could not be run because the GPU card could not support a sufficiently acceptable frame rate.

7.2   Scenario 2: Mobile Cloud Gaming

We now evaluate the required data bit rate that the NIC card of a notebook would have to support to achieve the same game fluency (i.e., 25 fps) for one of the four GPU cards of Table 3. As an example, consider again the Nvidia GeForce GTX 850M (which is the best of the four GPUs in terms of power consumption.) For the game GRID Autosport and for low resolution, the Nvidia GeForce GTX 850M is able to support 166.65 fps which is: $166.65 \times 1024 \times 768 \times 8 = 1048471142.4$ bits/s (assuming a color depth of 8 bits/pixel). Thus the NIC card would have to operate at a bit rate of about 1.05 Gb/s. A similar computation for the Ultra high resolution level gives us a bit rate of: $34.7 \times 1920 \times 1080 \times 8 = 575631360$ bits/s. Thus, to support the same gaming fluency at the Ultra-high resolution level, the NIC would have to operate at 575 Mb/s. Note that the required bit rate at the Ultra-high resolution level is almost half of that of the required bit rate at the low resolution level because the GPU supports a lower frame rate at the Ultra-high resolution level. To support these bit rates, the mobile device's NIC would have to be 802.11ad compliant. The 802.11ad standard is able to support bit rates up to 6.77 Gbit/s.

To evaluate the power consumed by the device's wireless networking card during the considered gaming session, we will assume a model of a wireless networking card that consumes ρ_{tx} watts when in transmit mode and ρ_{rx} watts when in receive mode. With single-antenna 802.11 devices, the devices cannot send and receive simultaneously. This normally implies that one has also to take into account the cost of frequently switching the device's radio between the transmit and the receive mode. However, this is changing as mobile devices are now increasingly being equipped with MIMO (multiple-input and multiple-output) technology enabling the use of multiple antennas at both the transmitter and receiver. In fact, Mobile Experts predicts that the use of MIMO technology will reach 500 million PCs, tablets, and smartphones by 2016 [15]. As a result, we will only take into account power consumption due to transmission, reception, and idling. We will note the power consumption of the radio during idling by ρ_{id}.

Let μ_t and μ_r be the transmission and reception rates respectively. Let l be the length of the packet sent to the application when the player takes an action. The time needed to transmit this packet is then: l/μ_t. Let t be the length of the entire gaming session (in seconds). During the time t, the device transmits t/r times where r is the player's reactivity (defined earlier). The total time during which the device transmits is therefore:

$$\frac{tl}{r\mu_t}\text{secs.} \tag{1}$$

The corresponding power consumption during the period of time t is:

$$P_{tx} = \frac{\rho_{tx}tl}{r\mu_t} \tag{2}$$

To evaluate the power consumed by the device's receiver, recall that our model assumes that, to respond to each player's action, the application generates

Table 4. Power consumption for the Intel Dual Band Wireless-AC 7260 802.11ac, 2×2 Wi-Fi Adapter [8].

Mode	Power (mWatts)
Transmit	2000
Receive	1600
Idle (WLAN associated)	250
Idle (WLAN unassociated)	100
Radio off	75

a video stream of length v seconds. The devices spends v/μ_r seconds to receive each of these video streams. Since we have t/r of these video streams during the considered time period of length t, the device's NIC receives video streams during:

$$\frac{tv}{r\mu_r}\text{secs.} \tag{3}$$

Let P_{rx} be the power that the device's NIC consumes to receive the t/r video sequences. P_{rx} can be given by:

$$P_{rx} = \frac{\rho_{rx}tv}{r\mu_r} \tag{4}$$

The device's NIC is in the idle mode when it is not transmitting and not receiving. This occurs during:

$$t - \frac{tl}{r\mu_t} - \frac{tv}{r\mu_r}\text{secs.} \tag{5}$$

The power consumed by the device's NIC while idling is therefore:

$$P_{id} = \rho_{id}t(1 - \frac{l}{r\mu_t} - \frac{v}{r\mu_r}) \tag{6}$$

Let $P_{NIC}(t)$ be the power consumed by the wireless NIC during the t-second gaming session. $P_{NIC}(t)$ is then:

$$P_{NIC}(t) = P_{tx} + P_{rx} + P_{id}$$
$$= \frac{\rho_{tx}tl}{r\mu_t} + \frac{\rho_{rx}tv}{r\mu_r} + \rho_{id}t(1 - \frac{l}{r\mu_t} - \frac{v}{r\mu_r})$$

In practice, one must consider values for ρ_{rx} that accommodate high reception rates (for high definition gaming) and values for ρ_{tx} that correspond to low transmission rates since the user's actions usually translate into short packets.

To illustrate, we consider the case of an HP EliteBook Folio 1040 G1 Notebook PC. This notebook is equipped with the Intel Dual Band Wireless-AC 7260 802.11ac Wi-Fi Adapter whose power consumption is given in Table 4 [8].

Assume that the NIC card is 80 % of the time in reception mode, 10 % of the time in transmit mode, and is idle (but associated) 10 % of the time. If we apply our power model to this WiFi adapter, power consumption in one hour would be (approximately):

$$P_{NIC}(t) = P_{tx} + P_{rx} + P_{idle}$$
$$= 0.1 \times 2000 + 0.8 \times 1600 + 0.1 \times 250$$
$$= 1505 \text{ mW}$$

assuming the highest Rx and Tx power levels.

Considering the example of a notebook equipped with a GPU of type Nvidia GeForce GTX 850M (Sect. 7.1), we can estimate that, in one hour, the GPU card will consume about between 0.8×40 W and 0.8×45 W, i.e., between 32 W and 36 W, assuming a GPU utilization of 80 % similar to our assumption of the NIC card being in the Rx mode 80 % of the time.

From the results obtained in the two scenarios, it is clear that using the wireless networking interface in a gaming session consumes much less power than using a modern GPU card installed on the same device. Specifically, the power consumed using the wireless card would be around $(1505/34000) \times 100$, i.e., around 4.42 % of the power consumed by the on-device GPU.

8 Mobile Cloud Gaming Using Smartphones

We now compare power consumption between GPU-based gaming and cloud-based gaming on smartphones.

8.1 Power Consumption of GPU-Based Gaming on Smartphones

In [10], the authors measured power consumption of a Qualcomm Adreno 320 GPU in a Google Nexus 4 smartphone. They used two games in their tests: Angry Birds (2D game) and Droid Invaders (3D game). The authors report results for a gaming session that lasted 560 s for Angry Birds and 505 s for Droid Invaders. Throughout the two gaming sessions, power consumption remained approximately at around 1750 mW for Angry Birds and at around 2000 mW for Droid Invaders. We will use the average of these two numbers (1875 mW) as an estimate of the average power consumption of both 2D and 3D games.

8.2 Power Consumption of Cloud-Based Gaming on Smartphones

To compare power consumption of cloud-based gaming with GPU-based gaming, we first need to evaluate the NIC bit rate that would be necessary to provide a gaming experience comparable to the one achieved through GPU-based gaming. For this, we used results from the GFXBench 3.0 benchmark, a cross-platform OpenGL ES 3 benchmark designed for measuring graphics performance, render quality and power consumption on several types of devices including smartphones. In particular, the benchmark has battery and stability tests that measure

274   A. Rezgui and Z. Malik

Table 5. Frame rates for the Adreno 320 GPU on a Google Nexus 4 and on a Samsung Galaxy S4 using the Manhattan benchmark [5].

Smartphone model	GPU	Resolution	Frame rate
Google Nexus 4 (LG E960)	Adreno 320	1196 × 768	9.2
Google Nexus 5	Adreno 330	1794 × 1080	10.1
Samsung GT-I9507 Galaxy S4	Adreno 320	1920 × 1080	5.4
Samsung GT-I9515 Galaxy S4 Value Edition	Adreno 320	1920 × 1080	5.1
Samsung Galaxy S4 Active (GT-I9295, SGH-I537)	Adreno 320	1920 × 1080	5.1
Samsung Galaxy S4 (GT-I9505, GT-I9508, SC-04E, SCH-I545, SCH-R970, SGH-I337, SGH-M919, SPH-L720)	Adreno 320	1920 × 1080	5.1

the devices battery life and performance stability by logging frames-per-second (fps) performance and expected battery running time while running sustained game-like animations [5]. We focused on results for the Adreno 320 GPU on a Google Nexus 4, which is the same configuration used in the GPU-based scenario of the previous section.

Table 5 shows the frame rate for several tests using the Manhattan benchmark [5]. Row 1 of the table shows that the Adreno 320 GPU on a Google Nexus 4 achieved a frame rate of 9.2 fps. Considering this frame rate and the given resolution (1196 × 768), the NIC bit rate that would be necessary to achieve a similar gaming experience can be derived as: 9.2 × 1196 × 768 × 24 (bits/pixel) = 202810982.4 bps ≈ 203 Mbps.

We now turn to evaluating the power needed on the NIC to sustain this bit rate. For this, we use the results from [26] where the authors experiment with a variety of smartphones supporting different subsets of 802.11n/ac features. In particular, the authors measured throughput and power consumption in a Galaxy S4 using different configurations. Based on their findings for the Galaxy S4 used in the experiment, only 802.11ac offers Rx throughput levels sufficient for the considered gaming bit rate (of 203 Mbps).

Figure 2 (reproduced from [26]) shows that the best Rx throughput with 802.11ac was about 250 Mbps. Power consumption in this case was about 1100 mW.

The authors did not provide measurements for the throughput and power consumption in transmit mode with 802.11ac. They, however, measured throughput and power consumption in transmit mode with 802.11n. Figure 3 shows their results. In particular, the results show that it is possible to achieve a Tx throughpout of more than 40 Mbps with as little power as 800 mW. Note that, in a cloud-based gaming session, a Tx throughout of 40 Mbps is typically sufficient. The authors also measured power consumption of the Galaxy S4 when it is in non-communication modes, i.e., power saving mode (PSM) or idle. Their results (Table 6) show that the highest 802.11ac power consumption in PSM was 31 mW

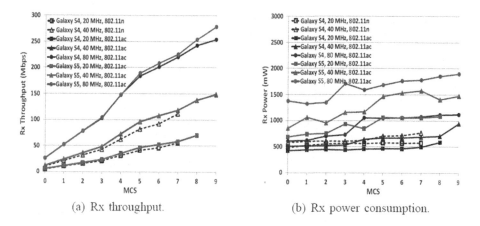

(a) Rx throughput.   (b) Rx power consumption.

Fig. 2. 802.11ac throughput and power comparison for Galaxy S4 and Galaxy S5 with a channel width of 20/40/80 MHz and FA on [26].

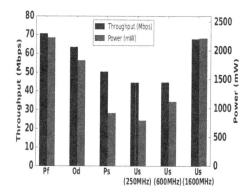

Fig. 3. Comparison of different CPU Governors/Frequencies for Galaxy S4 (802.11n) [26].

Table 6. Power consumption (in mW) in non-communicating modes [26].

Configuration	PSM	Idle
802.11n, 20 MHz, SS	24 ± 16	398 ± 7
802.11n, 40 MHz, SS	25 ± 5	413 ± 2
802.11ac, 20 MHz, SS	22 ± 9	374 ± 7
802.11ac, 40 MHz, SS	20 ± 9	425 ± 3
802.11ac, 80 MHz, SS	19 ± 10	529 ± 11

and that the highest 802.11ac power consumption when idle was 540 mW. The relatively high idle mode power consumption of larger channel widths (80 MHz) has also been observed by other studies (e.g., [31]).

Based on all the previous results from [26] and assuming that, in a cloud-based gaming session, the device's 802.11 adapter spends 80 % of the time receiving, 10 % of the time transmitting, and 10 % of the time idle, the total power consumed in one hour by the 802.11 adapter would be:

$$
\begin{aligned}
P_{NIC}(t) &= P_{tx} + P_{rx} + P_{idle} \\
&= 0.1 \times 800 + 0.8 \times 1100 + 0.1 \times 540 \\
&= 1014 \text{ mW}
\end{aligned}
$$

Comparing power consumption in the two scenarios: using GPU-based gaming (which is 1875 mW as derived in Sect. 8.1 and cloud-based gaming (which is 1014 mW as derived in this section), we conclude that, in the considered smartphone configuration, cloud-based gaming can potentially result into a power saving of about 46 %.

9   Conclusion

Reducing power consumption in mobile devices is crucial. Mobile cloud computing is one alternative that has been increasingly used to reduce power consumption on mobile devices. While offloading is generally accepted to be effective, little research has been conducted to quantify the exact difference in terms of power consumption between scenarios where mobile devices access applications run on the clouds and scenarios where those same applications are run on the mobile devices themselves. In this paper, we used mobile cloud gaming as a case study to analyze and compare power consumption in the two scenarios. Our study shows that substantial savings in power consumption may be achieved when graphics-intensive applications are run on the clouds instead of mobile devices. We call the computing model that enables mobile devices to access advanced cloud-based visualization capabilities Visualization-as-a-Service (VaaS). Based on our analysis, we posit that VaaS is a viable computing model despite the recent advances in terms of low power hardware for mobile devices.

In a survey of computation offloading for mobile systems [11], the authors predict that "mobile computing speeds will not grow as fast as the growth in data and the computational requirements of applications." As a result, offloading will remain a natural solution to the problem of improving performance while reducing energy consumption of mobile devices. We concur with this prediction and believe that more work is needed in the area of mobile cloud computing both in terms of new architectures and in terms of new offloading techniques.

References

1. Elijah: Cloudlet-based Mobile Computing. http://elijah.cs.cmu.edu
2. Carroll, A., Heiser, G.: An analysis of power consumption in a smartphone. In: Proceedings of the 2010 USENIX Conference on USENIX Annual Technical Conference, USENIXATC 2010, pp. 21–21. USENIX Association, Berkeley (2010). http://dl.acm.org/citation.cfm?id=1855840.1855861
3. Ellouze, A., Gagnaire, M., Haddad, A.: A mobile application offloading algorithm for mobile cloud computing. In: 2015 3rd IEEE International Conference on Mobile Cloud Computing, Services, and Engineering (MobileCloud), pp. 34–40, March 2015
4. Ericsson: Ericsson mobility report: on the pulse of the networked society. Technical report, Ericsson, June 2015
5. GFXBench: Gfxbench 3.0 directx (2015). http://www.gfxbench.com
6. Halperin, D., Greenstein, B., Sheth, A., Wetherall, D.: Demystifying 802.11n power consumption. In: Proceedings of the International Conference on Power-Aware Computing and Systems. HotPower, Vancouver (2010)
7. Hao, S., Li, D., Halfond, W.G.J., Govindan, R.: Estimating mobile application energy consumption using program analysis. In: Proceedings of the the the International Conference on Software Engineering (ICSE), San Francisco, California, May 2013
8. Hewlett Packard: HP EliteBook Folio 1040 G1 Notebook PC. Technical report (2013)
9. Hruska, J.: Nvidia's Tegra 4 Demystified: 28nm, 72-core GPU, Integrated LTE, and Questionable Power Consumption (2013). http://www.extremetech.com
10. Kim, Y.G., Kim, M., et al.: A novel GPU power model for accurate smartphone power breakdown. ETRI J. **37**(1), 157–164 (2015)
11. Kumar, K., Liu, J., Lu, Y.H., Bhargava, B.: A survey of computation offloading for mobile systems. Mob. Netw. Appl. **18**(1), 129–140 (2013)
12. Lampe, U., Hans, R., Steinmetz, R.: Will mobile cloud gaming work? findings on latency, energy, and cost. In: Proceedings of the 2013 IEEE Second International Conference on Mobile Services, MS 2013, pp. 103–104. IEEE Computer Society, Washington (2013). http://dx.doi.org/10.1109/MS.2013.21
13. Lee, K., Chu, D., Cuervo, E., Kopf, J., Grizan, S., Wolman, A., Flinn, J.: DeLorean: using speculation to enable low-latency continuous interaction for mobile cloud gaming. Technical report, Microsoft Research, August 2014
14. Li, B., Pei, Y., Wu, H., Shen, B.: Heuristics to allocate high-performance cloudlets for computation offloading in mobile ad hoc clouds. J. Supercomput. **71**(8), 3009–3036 (2015)
15. Madden, J.: MIMO adoption in mobile communications forecast: devices by operating system and user type, worldwide, 2010–2017, 1Q13 Update. Technical report, Mobile Experts, June 2011
16. Magurawalage, C.M.S., Yang, K., Hu, L., Zhang, J.: Energy-efficient and network-aware offloading algorithm for mobile cloud computing. Comput. Netw. **74**, 22–33 (2014)
17. MarketsandMarkets: World Mobile Applications Market - Advanced Technologies, Global Forecast (2010–2015). Technical report, MarketsandMarkets (2010)
18. Milanesi, C., Tay, L., Cozza, R., Atwal, R., Nguyen, T.H., Tsai, T., Zimmermann, A., Lu, C.K.: Forecast: devices by operating system and user type, worldwide, 2010–2017, 1Q13 Update. Technical report, Gartner, 28 March 2013

19. Netgear: Next Generation Gigabit WiFi - 802.11ac. Technical report (2012)
20. Notebook Review: Dell Precision M6700 Owner's Review (2015). http://forum. notebookreview.com/dell-latitude-vostro-precision/679326-dell-precision-m6700-owners-review.html
21. NoteBookCheck: Computer Games on Laptop Graphic Cards (2014). http://www. notebookcheck.net/Computer-Games-on-Laptop-Graphic-Cards.13849.0.html
22. Nvidia: Building Cloud Gaming Servers (2015). http://www.nvidia.com/object/ cloud-gaming-benefits.html
23. Nvidia: GeForce GTX 690 Specifications (2015). http://www.geforce.com/ hardware/desktop-gpus/geforce-gtx-690/specifications
24. Nvidia: Grid GPUs (2015). http://www.nvidia.com/object/grid-boards.html
25. ReportLinker: Global Mobile Application Market 2015–2019. Technical report, ReportLinker, March 2015
26. Saha, S.K., Deshpande, P., Inamdar, P.P., Sheshadri, R.K., Koutsonikolas, D.: Power-throughput tradeoffs of 802.11n/ac in smartphones. In: Proceedings of the 34th IEEE International Conference on Computer Communications (INFOCOM), Hong Long, Spain, 26 April–1 May 2015
27. Satyanarayanan, M., Chen, Z., Ha, K., Hu, W., Richter, W., Pillai, P.: Cloudlets: at the leading edge of mobile-cloud convergence. In: 2014 6th International Conference on Mobile Computing, Applications and Services (MobiCASE), pp. 1–9, November 2014
28. Shiraz, M., Gani, A., Khokhar, R., Buyya, R.: A review on distributed application processing frameworks in smart mobile devices for mobile cloud computing. IEEE Commun. Surv. Tutorials **15**(3), 1294–1313 (2013)
29. Soliman, O., Rezgui, A., Soliman, H., Manea, N.: Mobile cloud gaming: issues and challenges. In: Daniel, F., Papadopoulos, G.A., Thiran, P. (eds.) MobiWIS 2013. LNCS, vol. 8093, pp. 121–128. Springer, Heidelberg (2013). http://dx.doi.org/10.1007/978-3-642-40276-0_10
30. Thompson, C., Schmidt, D.C., Turner, H.A., White, J.: Analyzing mobile application software power consumption via model-driven engineering. In: Benavente-Peces, C., Filipe, J. (eds.) PECCS, pp. 101–113. SciTePress (2011)
31. Zeng, Y., Pathak, P.H., Mohapatra, P.: A first look at 802.11ac in action: energy efficiency and interference characterization. In: Proceedings of the 13th IFIP International Conferences on Networking, Trondheim, Norway, 2–4 June 2014
32. Zhou, B., Dastjerdi, A.V., Calheiros, R.N., Srirama, S.N., Buyya, R.: A context sensitive offloading scheme for mobile cloud computing service. In: 2015 IEEE 8th International Conference on Cloud Computing (CLOUD), pp. 869–876, June 2015

Using Satellite Execution to Reduce Latency for Mobile/Cloud Applications

Robert Pettersen[✉], Steffen Viken Valvåg, Åge Kvalnes, and Dag Johansen

Department of Computer Science, University of Tromsø,
The Arctic University of Norway, Tromsø, Norway
{robert,steffenv,aage,dag}@cs.uit.no
http://www.cs.uit.no

Abstract. We demonstrate a practical way to reduce latency for mobile .NET applications that interact with cloud services, without disrupting application architectures. We provide a programming abstraction for location-independent code, which has the potential to execute either locally or at a satellite execution environment in the cloud, where other cloud services can be accessed with low latency. This maintains a simple deployment model, but gives applications the option to offload latency-sensitive code to the cloud. Services like cloud databases can still be accessed programmatically, but with less concern for the aggregated latency of consecutively-issued requests. Our evaluation shows that this approach can significantly improve the response time for applications that execute dependent database queries, and that the required cloud-side resources are modest.

Keywords: Mobile · Cloud · Performance · Latency · Satellite execution · Code offloading · Cloud databases

1 Introduction

Use of cloud-provided services is integral to the operation of modern distributed and mobile applications. For example, cloud databases simplify application logic by serving as highly available repositories for critical state. For improved scalability and availability these databases are commonly NoSQL, with limited support for tabular relations and transactions and with a more relaxed consistency model than a conventional relational database. Queries are issued through a programmatic interface, rather than a domain-specific, high-level query language.

This promotes a usage pattern where multiple, consecutively-issued queries implement a single logical transaction. For example, an atomic update can be implemented as a read of the old value, followed by a conditional write of the new value, with the predicate that the old value remains unchanged. Or a collection of related records can be retrieved in multiple steps, by manually following foreign key references, rather than using higher-level features like joins and subqueries.

© Springer International Publishing Switzerland 2016
M. Helfert et al. (Eds.): CLOSER 2015, CCIS 581, pp. 279–298, 2016.
DOI: 10.1007/978-3-319-29582-4_15

When the database is hosted in the cloud, issuing a sequence of dependent queries entails multiple round-trips of communication, and network latency becomes an important concern. For example, we have measured a latency of 50 ms–350 ms for accessing the Amazon DynamoDB [1] cloud database from a mobile device [2], whereas a study covering 260 global vantage points reports an average round-trip time (RTT) of 74 ms for accessing Amazon EC2 instances [3]. Issuing a sequence of queries to the cloud can result in unwanted delays that are perceptible by users.

One way to alleviate this problem is to move the execution of queries to a middle tier that is closer to the cloud database. If the entire sequence of queries can be moved as a unit, this can eliminate many round-trips between the client and the cloud, substituting them with shorter round-trips between the middle tier and the database. If an application experiences high latency, or needs to issue a long sequence of database queries, the queries can be offloaded to the cloud and executed in close proximity to the database service.

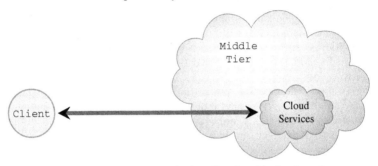

(a) Baseline; client communicating directly with cloud services.

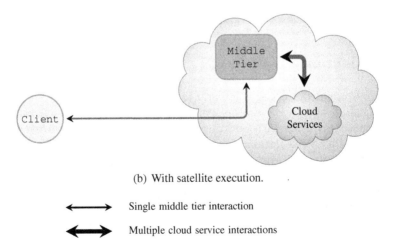

(b) With satellite execution.

→ Single middle tier interaction

↔ Multiple cloud service interactions

Fig. 1. How *satellite execution* is applied to eliminate extraneous round-trips of communication between a client and the cloud—by moving code to a middle tier close to cloud services—reducing overall latency.

In this paper, we refine and generalize this idea, to reduce latency for any mobile/cloud application that issues a sequence of dependent requests to the cloud. By moving the code that accesses cloud services to a middle tier, positioned in close proximity to the cloud, the code can execute in an environment with lower latency. We refer to this concept as *satellite execution*, and illustrate it in Fig. 1. Figure 1(a) shows the baseline scenario, where a client must send multiple requests over a high latency mobile network to the cloud in order to complete a task. These can be replaced with a single round-trip as in Fig. 1(b), where code is moved to the middle tier before multiple requests with intracloud latency are issued to the cloud service.

By implementing general-purpose offloading of code, and not just specializing on relaying of database queries, we preserve the programmatic style of database access, and its associated advantages. For example, offloaded code can perform computations, transformations, cryptographic operations, and any other manipulations of parameters and intermediate results that may be required when performing a sequence of queries. The increased flexibility also widens the applicability of satellite execution as a general concept.

To illustrate the benefits of our approach, we quantify latency savings when cloud database queries are executed from the middle tier rather than at the client-side device. We also examine communication traces of popular phone applications to determine the practicality of our approach, to see if real applications exhibit access patterns that are conducive to latency savings through satellite execution.

We implement satellite execution in a system called Dapper, which significantly extends and integrates the functionality of two previous systems: Rusta [4] and Jovaku [2]. Rusta is a platform for developing cloud applications that can utilize client-side storage and processing capacity, while the Jovaku system provides a distributed infrastructure for caching of cloud database values through the ubiquitous DNS service.

A goal with Rusta was to express computations in a location-independent way, allowing for opportune execution in the cloud or at client-side devices. This was accomplished by expressing computations in the Scala programming language and using built-in closure features to create transferable execution contexts. In Dapper we take a similar approach, but target the .NET platform, so that code in any of the .NET languages can be made transferable. Jovaku's architecture includes a cloud-side relay-node that bridges the DNS protocol with the database API. Dapper extends this component to include a middle-tier platform for hosting and safely executing offloaded code.

The rest of this paper is structured as follows. Section 2 elaborates on the background and context of our work, motivating our general approach. Section 3 describes the design and implementation of Dapper, and its programming abstractions for satellite execution. Section 4 contains a performance evaluation that focuses on the cloud database use-case, with measurements of typical reductions in latency, and the maximum query processing throughput that can be achieved in various configurations. Section 5 discusses related work, and Sect. 6 concludes.

2   Background

The desire to reduce latency for mobile/cloud applications tends to encourage a split application architecture, where parts of the application logic executes on the device, and other parts execute in the cloud. Higher-level operations such as submitting a comment or generating a news feed are delegated as a whole to the cloud, to avoid multiple round-trips of communication.

The split between frontend and backend also has a tangential benefit: it allows a variety of frontends, often tailored for different devices, to access the same backend service. For example, an on-line chess service will typically offer both a web-based frontend, as well as clients for various mobile devices and platforms. Users should be able to switch seamlessly between client devices, e.g. moving from their laptop to their phone, so the state of on-going games must be maintained by the backend. This requires frequent communication with the cloud to retrieve and update application state.

Many frameworks and platforms aim to ease the development of mobile applications that are factored into separate backend and frontend components. One example is Parse [5], which provides a backend-as-a-service solution that offers backend cloud storage, as well as the ability to deploy application modules that execute in the cloud, close to the data. One common downside of these approaches is that the device-specific and cloud-specific parts of the application are deployed independently, through different channels. This increases the risk of breakage, when old versions deployed on devices interact with the newest version deployed in the cloud.

We approach the problem differently; rather than explicitly deploying parts of applications in the cloud, we empower applications to offload latency-sensitive code on demand, in a dynamic manner. Offloaded code will execute in close proximity to the backend storage service, where latency is low. Thus, we address the main motivating concern—improving application responsiveness as experienced by users—without dictating a static deployment model for applications.

A key idea underlying this work is to move computations closer to the data that they touch, which is a well-known technique that finds diverse applications. When processing streams of data, the demand for network bandwidth can be reduced by filtering streams closer to the source, pushing computations upstream. When processing stored data, similar gains can be made by scheduling computations to execute locally on the storage nodes, using functional programming models like MapReduce [6] for location independence.

Our experience from mobile agents [7–9] and MapReduce-style distributed data processing have inspired some key aspects of this work. As in Cogset [10], we promote a functional programming model using the visitor pattern, where latency-sensitive code has the ability to *visit* the backend storage service as desired. In this case, a visitor also resembles a mobile agent; although restricted to moves back and forth between a client device and the cloud, it retains the defining ability to carry state.

3   Dapper

Instead of statically partitioning mobile/cloud applications into client-side and cloud-side components, satellite execution enables individual objects to move dynamically between the client and the cloud. The decision to deploy an object for satellite execution is taken at run-time. Deployment to the cloud involves moving an object's code (i.e., its class) and its current state. Incurred state changes while executing remotely are included when the object is moved back to the client. Objects can move repeatedly between the client and the cloud, for example in response to changes in application environment or state.

Jovaku's application-transparent interfacing with cloud databases through DNS was in part made possible by a cloud-side relay-node. The relay-node bridges the DNS infrastructure with the underlying cloud database service by turning DNS requests into database queries. The relay-node was placed in close proximity to the cloud database service to avoid extra latency when performing the translations. Since we have similar requirements for the middle tier in our satellite execution concept, integrating this functionality into Dapper was an intuitive solution. To realize the satellite execution concept, we therefore extended the relay-node with capabilities for hosting and executing offloaded .NET code. Two main components were identified as necessities for this extension:

An Execution Environment: that is capable of hosting multiple securely isolated *sandboxes*. Each of these sandboxes must be capable of loading and executing code on behalf of clients, without interfering with each other, or compromising the integrity of the surrounding execution environment.

A Message Processor: that will receive and process messages sent from clients and demultiplex and pass messages on to the execution environment. There are several feasible approaches to implementing an efficient message processor. The Windows Communication Foundation (WCF) offers one convenient framework, but we decided to use an asynchronous socket-based server with a customized communication protocol, because this gave slightly better throughput.

An overview of the extended architecture with the new components can be seen in Fig. 2. The Name Server is a BIND [11] server with a custom DLZ [12] driver that resolves DNS queries by accessing a cloud database service. As noted, this functionality stems from the original Jovaku system and complements the satellite execution capabilities of Dapper.

In addition to these new relay-node components, we saw the need to create a programming abstraction for execution of offloaded code. To this end, we defined the IMobileFunction interface, seen in Code Listing 1, which clients use to specify offloadable code. Implementations of this interface are called *mobile functions*, as they can be serialized and moved for remote execution on a relay-node. The entry point of a mobile function is its Execute method, which may be invoked asynchronously using .NET's task-based asynchronous pattern.

Mobile functions contain user-defined code, and are black boxes to Dapper. Being implemented in C# or another .NET language, they enjoy the expressive

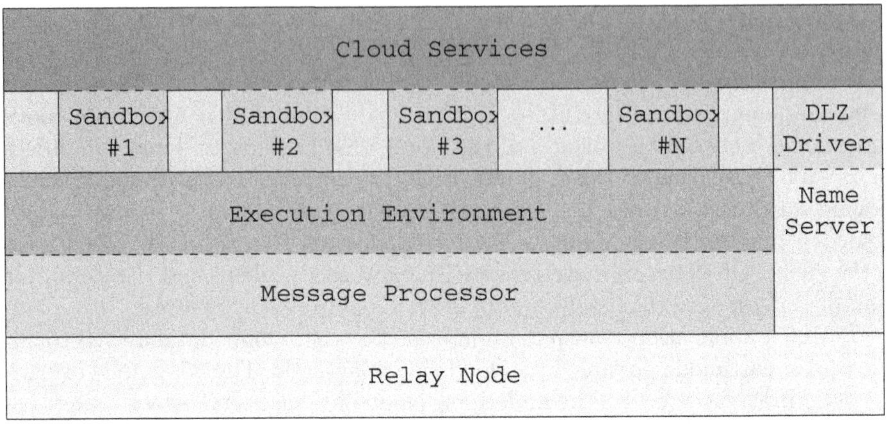

Fig. 2. An overview of the extended architecture where the message processor and execution environment have been integrated into the relay-node. The execution environment is capable of hosting multiple isolated sandboxes for loading and executing offloaded client code.

Code Listing 1. Interface to be implemented by mobile functions.

```
public interface IMobileFunction
{
    Task Execute(IContext ctx);
}
```

Code Listing 2. Interface for accessing cloud-side resources from a mobile function.

```
public interface IContext
{
    Task<object> Get(string key);

    Task<List<object>> GetMany(string key);

    Task<bool> Put(string key, object value);
}
```

power of a general-purpose programming language. However, this power must be checked in order to provide a reasonable balance between flexibility and safety. Dapper will only invoke mobile functions from sandboxes that are intended to isolate the environment from unwanted side effects, restricting the mobile

Code Listing 3. Interface for requesting remote execution of a mobile function.

```
public interface IDapper
{
    Task<object> ExecuteAt(IMobileFunction function,
        Uri location = null);
}
```

function's capabilities for actions like file and network i/o. To compensate, Dapper will let mobile functions access *safe* implementations of selected operations through the IContext interface, shown in Code Listing 2. These operations can involve i/o, but they are implemented by Dapper, with rigorous validation of arguments to minimize the potential for abuse.

Since we have selected cloud database services as a use case to focus on, our IContext interface provides basic key/value operations that can be supported by any common NoSQL database. When applying satellite execution in other

Code Listing 4. Creating a new application domain, with minimal permissions and a set of trusted assemblies.

```
private Sandbox CreateSandbox(string name)
{
    var pSet = new PermissionSet(PermissionState.None);
    pSet.AddPermission(new SecurityPermission(Execution));

    var fullTrustAssemblies = new Assembly[]
    {
        typeof(Sandbox).Assembly,
        typeof(SecureContext).Assembly,
        typeof(Amazon.DynamoDBClient).Assembly,
    };

    var newAppDomain = AppDomain.CreateDomain(name, pSet,
        fullTrustAssemblies);

    var instance = Activator.CreateInstanceFrom(newAppDomain,
        typeof(Sandbox).Assembly.ManifestModule.FullyQualifiedName,
        typeof(Sandbox).FullName);

    return (Sandbox)instance.Unwrap();
}
```

contexts, the interface would be extended correspondingly, to expose the relevant cloud service functionality.

The indirection created by the IContext interface also serves to separate application logic from the particulars of the cloud services that are accessed, and adds flexibility to deployments. For example, an application can be tested and run as a fully client-side process by providing a context object that binds to a local database.

3.1   Implementation

Our current implementation targets Amazon's DynamoDB, which is a popular NoSQL cloud database service. The relay-node is manifested as an instance in the EC2 computing cluster, where DynamoDB can be accessed with very low network latency. In addition to the BIND process that serves DNS traffic, a separate server process—written in C#—implements the message processor and execution environment. Incoming messages either contain serialized mobile functions that should be deserialized and executed, or .NET assemblies that contain the compiled code for mobile functions. Received assemblies are cached by Dapper. Deserialization of a mobile function can fail, if its assembly is missing. In that case, the client is asked to first send the missing assembly, before retrying. This will be a rare event in practical use, because mobile functions can be parameterized, reusing the same code across many instances, and because one assembly can contain the code for multiple mobile functions.

From the client application's perspective, mobile functions are regular objects that may, upon request, be executed remotely. The ExecuteAt method in Code Listing 3 implements this abstraction by sending the object, in a serialized state, to a relay-node, where the object is deserialized and its Execute method is invoked. When the Execute method completes, the object is again serialized and moved back to the client. As such, mobile functions can simply store any relevant results of their cloud service interactions internally, and clients will be able to observe the corresponding state changes when ExecuteAt has completed.

In the relay-node, we sandbox the execution of mobile functions using .NET application domains [13], which provide an isolation boundary for security, reliability, and versioning, and for loading assemblies. Application domains are typically created by runtime hosts—which are responsible for bootstrapping the common language runtime before an application is run—but a process can create any number of application domains within the process to further separate and isolate execution of code. Dapper creates a new application domain for each mobile function assembly.

Each of these application domains is configured with a minimal set of permissions that will ensure that execution of code cannot compromise or access code or data running in other domains. The minimal set will also ensure that the code received from clients cannot do potentially malicious operations like accessing the file system, or participating in bot-nets that deplete network resources. Code Listing 4 shows the code to instantiate new application domains. Aside from the minimal permission set, which only includes the most basic Execution ability,

Code Listing 5. The IContext implementation used in the isolated application domains.

```csharp
class SecureContext : IContext
{
    private Amazon.DynamoDBClient _client;

    [SocketPermission(Assert, Unrestricted = true)]
    [ReflectionPermission(Assert, Unrestricted = true)]
    [WebPermission(Assert, Unrestricted = true)]
    public Task<string> Get(string key) { ... }

    [SocketPermission(Assert, Unrestricted = true)]
    [ReflectionPermission(Assert, Unrestricted = true)]
    [WebPermission(Assert, Unrestricted = true)]
    public async Task<List<string>> GetMany(string key) { ... }

    [SocketPermission(Assert, Unrestricted = true)]
    [ReflectionPermission(Assert, Unrestricted = true)]
    [WebPermission(Assert, Unrestricted = true)]
    public Task<bool> Put(string key, object value) { ... }
}
```

the code specifies a list of assemblies containing code that will be fully trusted by the sandbox. This includes Dapper's own assemblies, and the official DynamoDB API from Amazon.

When mobile functions execute, they can use the IContext interface to access cloud services. Dapper implements this interface in the SecureContext class shown in Code Listing 5. The various database operations that can be performed are implemented using Amazon's API, which requires certain additional permissions to work correctly. Socket and web permissions are needed to create sockets and sending web requests, and the API uses reflection to access protected methods in the .NET library, to add custom headers to web requests. Since the assembly that implements SecureContext is fully trusted, these permissions can be elevated selectively by marking the relevant methods with special security attributes. So the only way for a mobile function to access the network, for example, is through one of the methods of the IContext interface.

The CreateSandbox method returns a proxy object that can be used to communicate with the new application domain. Calls to the proxy object are implicitly converted into remote cross-domain calls. The Sandbox class in Code Listing 6 implements the internal execution environment of a sandbox, with methods to inject serialized assemblies and mobile functions into the sandbox. The sandbox will load the assemblies and put them into the AssemblyCache indexed on the full name of the assembly. The full name includes versioning information, so different versions of an assembly can be loaded at the same time, without issue.

Code Listing 6. The sandbox, isolating loading of untrusted assemblies, and execution of code.

```
class Sandbox : MarshalByRefObject
{
    private IContext Context;

    private Dictionary<string, Assembly> AssemblyCache;

    private Assembly AssemblyResolve(
        object sender, ResolveEventArgs args) { ... }

    public bool AddAssembly(byte[] rawBytes) { ... }

    public byte[] ExecuteFunction(byte[] obj) { ... }

    [SecurityPermission(Assert, Flags = SerializationFormatter)]
    private IMobileFunction DeserializeFunction(byte[] data) { ... }

    [SecurityPermission(Assert, Flags = SerializationFormatter)]
    private byte[] SerializeFunction(object graph) { ... }
}
```

Upon receiving serialized objects through the `ExecuteFunction` method, the sandbox will attempt to deserialize the byte array using the private method `DeserializeFunction`. This method is marked with a `SecurityPermission` attribute to allow deserialization of objects. We have restricted this permission to specific methods instead of allowing it for all client code, as the private data members of an object can potentially be retrieved by serializing it.

The sandbox also registers as a handler for the `AssemblyResolve` event, which is triggered whenever a new assembly must be resolved. Notably, this may happen during deserialization of mobile functions. The `ResolveEventArgs` will then contain the full name of the type that is being deserialized, and the sandbox can make lookups in the assembly cache to find the correct assembly. If the sandbox is unable to resolve the assembly required to deserialize the object, an exception will be thrown to the governing satellite execution environment, which in turn will inform the client of the missing assembly.

When an object has been deserialized successfully, the sandbox will typecast it to `IMobileFunction` and invoke its `Execute` method. When the `Execute` method completes, the mobile function is again serialized into a byte array, using `SerializeFunction`, and passed back to the client.

Code Listing 7 shows an example of a mobile function that implements a bag-of-queries abstraction. Database queries are added to the bag by invoking `AddQuery`; the queries are aggregated in the `_queryList` field. The `Execute`

Code Listing 7. Implementation of a bag-of-queries abstraction as a mobile function that can execute remotely in the cloud via satellite execution.

```
[Serializable]
public class QueryBag : IMobileFunction
{
    private List<string> _responseList;
    private List<string> _queryList;

    public async Task Execute(IContext ctx)
    {
        foreach (var query in _queryList)
        {
            var queryResponse = await ctx.GetMany(query);
            if (_responseList == null)
                _responseList = new List<string>();

            _responseList.AddRange(queryResponse);
        }
    }

    public void AddQuery(string query)
    {
        if (_queryList == null)
            _queryList = new List<string>();

        _queryList.Add(query);
    }

    public List<string> GetResponses()
    {
        return _responseList;
    }
}
```

method issues the aggregated queries via the context object and stores results in the _responseList field. After executing the mobile function, the client can observe the results of the queries by invoking GetResponses.

A potential optimization for the bag-of-queries example would be to reset the list of queries to null once it is no longer needed. This would reduce the amount of serialized data to return from the relay-node to the client. In general, mobile functions are free to implement their own serialization mechanisms via the ISerializable interface, but they can always fall back to the default serialization protocol, for convenience.

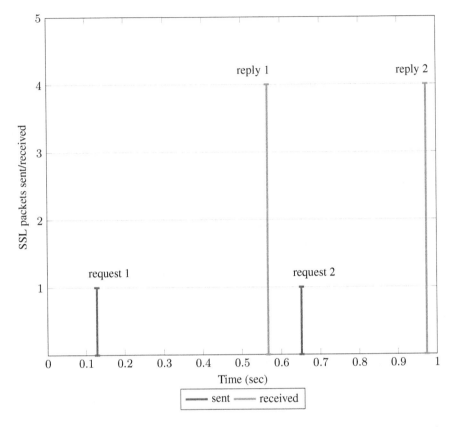

Fig. 3. Example communication pattern between mobile device and cloud assumed to be of a request/reply type.

4   Evaluation

Dapper runs on a variety of Microsoft Windows platforms, including phone, store, and desktop. We used two different client-side platforms in our experiments: (1) a phone with 2 GB memory and a quad-core QualComm Snapdragon 800 2.2 GHz CPU and (2) a desktop machine with 64 GB memory and a quad-core Intel Xeon E5-1620 3.7 GHz CPU. The phone ran Windows Phone 8.1 and communicated over 4 G, whereas the desktop machine ran Windows 10 and was connected to a LAN.

The relay-node was hosted on two types of Amazon EC2 instances. The first type was t1.micro, equipped with 613 MB memory and a single-core 64-bit vCPU operating at 1.85 GHz. The second type was t2.medium, equipped with 4 GB memory and a dual-core vCPU operating at 2.50 GHz. Both types of instances were running Microsoft Windows Server 2012 R2. We used Amazon's DynamoDB as the cloud-side database, instantiated in the same availability zone as our relay-node.

Table 1. Summary of cloud interactions during phone application startup.

Application	# request/reply	# connections
Social networking	1	1
	2	1
Instant messaging	1	4
	2	3
	7	1
Short messaging	1	7
	2	3
	4	1
	6	1
Picture exchange	1	1
	2	2

We first report on a black-box examination of the cloud communication patterns of some popular mobile applications. Here we sought to discover patterns consistent with sequences of dependent requests, with the motivation that satellite execution could be used in place of such interactions. We configured our phone platform to communicate through an access point instrumented to capture all ingress and egress network packets. We then inspected the encrypted TCP streams and dissected them into SSL packets, looking for what appeared as consecutive request/reply cloud interactions without intervening user actions. The particular pattern we looked for is exemplified in Fig. 3, which shows two interactions assumed to be of a request/reply type.

Our findings for cloud interactions during startup of four popular applications are summarized in Table 1. We observed that the applications communicate over a number of separate network connections, ranging from 2 for the social networking application to 12 for the short messaging application. Most of these connections are to different services within the same cloud, but some are external, typically in support of content distribution such as Akamai [14]. The number of assumed request/reply interactions varied across applications and connections, with the instant- and short messaging applications respectively having as many as 7 and 6 consecutive interactions. These findings suggest satellite execution could be effective if applied in these popular applications.

We continue with an experiment that quantifies latency when a client issues cloud database queries directly and when using satellite execution. For this we used the bag-of-queries implementation outlined in Code Listing 7 to issue queries to the cloud database. Latency when the bag contained between 1 and 5 queries is shown in Fig. 4. Results are averaged over 1000 runs, for both phone and desktop, with the relay-node hosted on a t1.micro instance. As shown, there are significant latency savings when the bag contains more than one query. This is because latency between the relay-node and the database is low, and the round-trip latency between the client and the cloud—approximately 64 ms for desktop and 105 ms for phone—overshadows the low cost of serializing and transferring the query bag.

The DynamoDB library uses the HTTP 100-continue feature when interacting with the cloud database. Use of this feature adds a communication round-trip to database interaction, needlessly inflating latency [2]. We therefore used platform interfaces to disable this HTTP feature on desktop. Similar interfaces do not exist on Windows Phone, however. The results in Fig. 4 consequently include one additional round-trip latency for phone, compared to desktop. To better convey the latency difference between phone and desktop, the figure also includes results where one round-trip latency has been subtracted from phone. Even after this normalization, phone has significantly higher latency than desktop, demonstrating the relative importance of our satellite execution technique for the mobile platform.

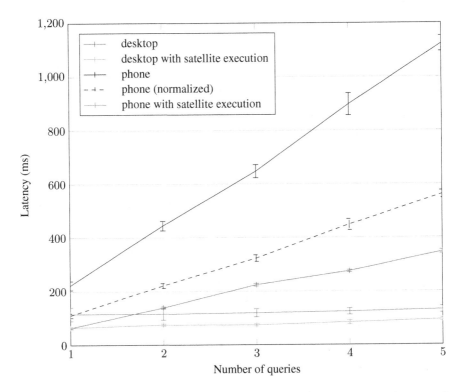

Fig. 4. Observed latency when executing a varying number of cloud database queries with and without satellite execution. Error bars show standard deviation.

The data on popular applications in Table 1 only indicates that latency savings are possible; determining the degree to which the interaction could exploit satellite execution would require access to application source code. To approximate the savings that could be experienced in a deployed application we reconstruct a scenario where a friend connection is established in the MSRBook, a social networking application based on Deuteronomy [15]. The addition of a friend in this network involves friend and news feed updates for both concerned parties, for a total of 4 queries. Equivalent queries were placed in our bag-of-queries and we ran the friend-add action 1000 times on both the desktop and the mobile platform, with and without satellite execution. Figure 5 illustrates latency savings. Savings due to satellite execution are pronounced; on desktop latency drops from around 265 ms to approximately 100 ms, while it drops on mobile from around 450 ms to approximately 125 ms.

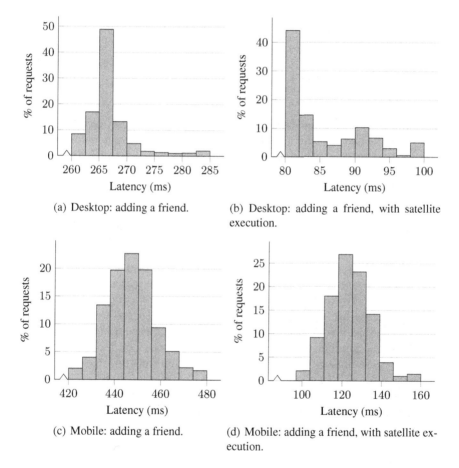

(a) Desktop: adding a friend.

(b) Desktop: adding a friend, with satellite execution.

(c) Mobile: adding a friend.

(d) Mobile: adding a friend, with satellite execution.

Fig. 5. Latencies when adding a friend to a social network, with and without satellite execution.

On a mobile device such as a smartphone, a person uses around 24 different applications every month [16]. Even the modest resource allocations available to

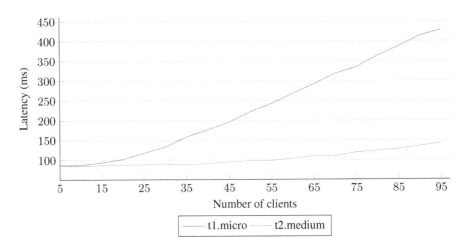

Fig. 6. Latency per bag-of-queries when increasing the number of clients that concurrently submit mobile functions to a relay-node.

the Amazon t1.micro instance used in our experiments are likely to be ample for a relay-node dedicated to a single mobile device. But if the relay-node functionality was a service offered by the cloud database provider, in a fashion similar to the Parse application module service [5], the relay-node would likely be shared among many mobile devices and its capacity would be a potential issue. We therefore last consider an experiment where the relay-node serves an increasing number of clients.

In the experiment, we configured each client to repeatedly submit mobile functions to the relay-node, in a closed loop. Each mobile function was a bag of 4 queries. We then increased the number of clients, ensuring high contention for relay-node resources, in an attempt to reveal the capacity for executing mobile functions. We repeated the experiment both for t1.micro and t2.medium instances. Results are shown in Figs. 6 and 7. We observe that the t1.micro instance is capable of completing around 250 bags per second before throughput levels off. As the number of clients continues to increase, each of them observes higher latency, as illustrated in Fig. 6. The t2.medium instance peaks at around 700 bags per second. In Fig. 7, we see a close correlation between throughput and CPU consumption for both instance types. This indicates that CPU is the likely bottleneck that causes throughput to peak.

The experiment does not expose any scalability issues in our relay-node implementation, with regards to concurrently serving an increasing number of clients. Throughput levels off and remains stable after it peaks. A single relay-node can thus be shared among multiple mobile devices, and also across different applications.

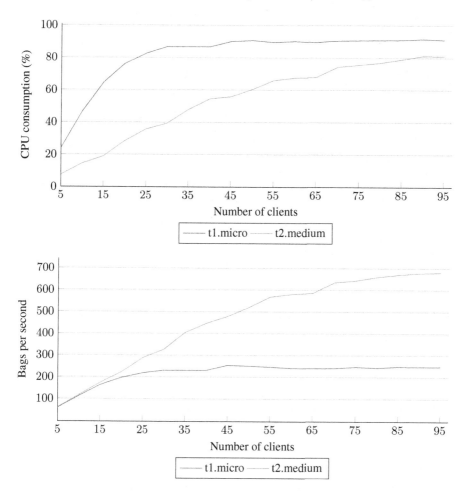

Fig. 7. CPU consumption and throughput at a relay-node when increasing the number of concurrent clients that submit mobile functions.

5   Related Work

The complexity of developing and deploying applications that span a variety of mobile devices, personal computers, and cloud services, has been recognized as a new challenge. Users expect applications and their state to follow them across devices, and to realize this functionality, one or more cloud service must usually be involved in the background. Sapphire [17] is a recent and comprehensive system that approaches this problem by making deployment more configurable and customizable, separating the deployment logic from the application logic. The aim is to allow deployment decisions to be changed, without major associated code changes. Applications are factored into collections of location-independent objects, communicating through remote procedure calls. Fabric [18] is another distributed system that aims to securely share objects among heterogeneous network nodes, and supports both data-shipping and function-shipping styles of execution.

Like these systems, Dapper provides a location-independent programming abstraction, but preserves a monolithic application structure, which allows the application to be installed in its entirety on a single device through a regular distribution channel like an app store. Code is then transferred on demand from the device to the cloud, as objects move to the cloud to enjoy low-latency execution. The decision to visit the cloud or stay on the local device can be made dynamically, at run time.

With Dapper, we introduce relay-nodes in the cloud as an architectural tier between the cloud and mobile devices. Similar middle tiers have been proposed for example with Cloudlets [19], and are implemented in code-offloading systems like COMET [20], MAUI [21], and CloneCloud [22]. However, the goal of these systems is often to augment mobile devices with additional computing power, or to conserve energy [23], so the added tier may be located close to the devices, on local server machines, or wherever cheap computing power is available. In contrast, our motivation is not to offload work, but to reduce the latency of accessing cloud services, and thus the new tier sits as close to the cloud services as possible.

Concretely, Dapper reduces latency by eliminating extraneous round-trips of communication to the cloud. An alternative way to achieve that is by having cloud databases support more expressive query languages, so that more sophisticated transactions can be submitted as a single operation. Indeed, relational databases with full SQL support are part of the offerings of major cloud providers like Amazon. However, the ability to access the database via a general-purpose programming language remains appealing for its generality and flexibility. This is a lesson learned from programming models like MapReduce [6], Oivos [24], and Cogset [10], where data is accessed programmatically through user-defined visitor functions that can integrate easily with legacy code and libraries. The programming model in Dapper follows a similar philosophy, with the difference that user-defined functions are visiting a database in the cloud rather than a partition of data in a cluster.

6   Conclusion

This work focuses on the general issue of latency as a concern for applications that interact with the cloud, and looks specifically at scenarios where multiple consecutive queries are issued to a database in the cloud. Intuitively, latency can be reduced by shortening communication distances, so our idea is to move the location where queries are issued closer to the database. Since cloud databases commonly have programmatic interfaces, we implement a general mechanism for code-offloading to support this pattern.

Having a relay-node in the cloud, located in close proximity to the database service, has already proven to be a useful technique for caching, and beneficial for read-mostly database workloads [2]. Here, we extend the relay-node with functionality for *satellite execution*, allowing code that has moved temporarily from a mobile device to execute in an environment with low-latency access to cloud services. This gives benefits for additional workloads, which may include database updates.

The key characteristic that a workload must exhibit to benefit from our approach is dependencies between requests. For example, if the results from one database query are used to shape the next query, there is a dependency between the two. If there is no need for user interaction in-between requests, a whole sequence of dependent requests can be offloaded to the cloud. By eliminating extraneous round-trips of communication, this improves response times.

To estimate the potential for improvement in real applications, our evaluation examines the communication patterns of some popular applications through a black-box technique. This has yielded some indications that dependent requests occur in practice, since sequences of up to 7 requests were observed back-to-back over the same connection on startup. Looking at a concrete implementation of a social networking application from [15], we found specific examples. For example, a friend request results in 4 dependent database queries; when offloaded to the cloud from a phone, the completion time of a friend request dropped from 450 ms to approximately 125 ms.

Our implementation handles the practicalities of transferring assemblies of .NET code, serializing and deserializing objects, and sandboxing code that executes on the relay-node. Our evaluation gives some data points on performance: a single Amazon t1.micro instance can serve hundreds of queries per second. One such instance can thus easily handle load imposed by a large number of applications. So, we can dramatically reduce latency without disrupting application architectures and with minimal requirements for resources in the cloud.

Acknowledgements. This work is part of the Information Access Disruptions (iAD) project, supported in part by the Research Council of Norway through the National Center for Research-based Innovation program. We thank our iAD colleagues for valuable feedback.

References

1. DeCandia, G., Hastorun, D., Jampani, M., Kakulapati, G., Lakshman, A., Pilchin, A., Sivasubramanian, S., Vosshall, P., Vogels, W.: Dynamo: amazon's highly available key-value store. SIGOPS Oper. Syst. Rev. **41**, 205–220 (2007)
2. Pettersen, R., Valvåg, S. V., Kvalnes, A., Johansen, D.: Jovaku: globally distributed caching for cloud database services using DNS. In: IEEE International Conference on Mobile Cloud Computing, Services, and Engineering, pp. 127–135 (2014)
3. Li, A., Yang, X., Kandula, S., Zhang, M.: CloudCmp: comparing public cloud providers. In: ACM SIGCOMM, pp. 1–14 (2010)
4. Valvåg, S.V., Johansen, D., Kvalnes, A.: Position paper: elastic processing and storage at the edge of the cloud. In: Proceedings of the 2013 International Workshop on Hot Topics in Cloud Services, HotTopiCS 2013, pp. 43–50. ACM, New York (2013)

5. Parse (2015). http://www.parse.com
6. Dean, J., Ghemawat, S.: MapReduce: simplified data processing on large clusters. In: Proceedings of the 6th Symposium on Operating Systems Design and Implementation, OSDI 2004, pp. 137–150. USENIX Association (2004)
7. Johansen, D., Lauvset, K.J., van Renesse, R., Schneider, F.B., Sudmann, N.P., Jacobsen, K.: A TACOMA retrospective. Softw. - Pract. Exp. **32**, 605–619 (2001)
8. Johansen, D., Marzullo, K., Lauvset, K. J.: An approach towards an agent computing environment. In: ICDCS 1999 Workshop on Middleware (1999)
9. Johansen, D.: Mobile agents: right concept, wrong approach. In: In 5th IEEE International Conference on Mobile Data Management (MDM 2004), pp. 300–301. IEEE Computer Society (2004)
10. Valvåg, S.V., Johansen, D., Kvalnes, A.: Cogset: a high performance MapReduce engine. Concurr. Comput.: Pract. Exp. **25**, 2–23 (2013)
11. (ISC Bind). https://www.isc.org/downloads/bind/
12. (Bind DLZ). http://bind-dlz.sourceforge.net/
13. Application Domains (2015). http://msdn.microsoft.com/en-us/library/cxk374d9%28v=vs.90%29.aspx
14. Nygren, E., Sitaraman, R.K., Sun, J.: The Akamai network: A platform for high-performance internet applications. SIGOPS Oper. Syst. Rev. **44**, 2–19 (2010)
15. Levandoski, J.J., Lomet, D.B., Mokbel, M.F., Zhao, K.: Deuteronomy: transaction support for cloud data. In: CIDR, pp. 123–133 (2011)
16. Nielsen (2014). http://www.nielsen.com/us/en/insights/news/2014/smartphones-so-many-apps–so-much-time.html
17. Zhang, I., Szekeres, A., Aken, D.V., Ackerman, I., Gribble, S.D., Krishnamurthy, A., Levy, H.M.: Customizable and extensible deployment for mobile/cloud applications. In: 11th USENIX Symposium on Operating Systems Design and Implementation (OSDI 2014), Broomfield, CO, pp. 97–112. USENIX Association (2014)
18. Liu, J., George, M.D., Vikram, K., Qi, X., Waye, L., Myers, A.C.: Fabric: A platform for secure distributed computation and storage. In: Proceedings of the ACM SIGOPS 22nd Symposium on Operating Systems Principles, SOSP 2009, pp. 321–334. ACM, New York (2009)
19. Satyanarayanan, M.: Cloudlets: at the leading edge of cloud-mobile convergence. In: Proceedings of the 9th International ACM SIGSOFT Conference on Quality of Software Architectures, pp. 1–2. ACM (2013)
20. Gordon, M.S., Jamshidi, D.A., Mahlke, S., Mao, Z.M., Chen, X.: Comet: code offload by migrating execution transparently. In: Proceedings of the 10th USENIX Conference on Operating Systems Design and Implementation, OSDI 2012, pp. 93–106. USENIX Association, Berkeley (2012)
21. Cuervo, E., Balasubramanian, A., Cho, D.K., Wolman, A., Saroiu, S., Chandra, R., Bahl, P.: Maui: making smartphones last longer with code offload. In: Proceedings of the 8th International Conference on Mobile Systems, Applications, and Services, MobiSys 2010, pp. 49–62. ACM, New York (2010)
22. Chun, B.G., Ihm, S., Maniatis, P., Naik, M., Patti, A.: Clonecloud: elastic execution between mobile device and cloud. In: Proceedings of the 6th Conference on Computer Systems, EuroSys 2011, pp. 301–314. ACM, New York (2011)
23. Tilevich, E., Kwon, Y.W.: Cloud-based execution to improve mobile application energy efficiency. Computer **47**, 75–77 (2014)
24. Valvåg, S.V., Johansen, D.: Oivos: simple and efficient distributed data processing. In: Proceedings of the 10th IEEE International Conference on High Performance Computing and Communications, HPCC 2008, pp. 113–122. IEEE Computer Society (2008)

Author Index

Andrikopoulos, Vasilios 153
Angulo, Julio 38

Barbhuiya, Sakil 135
Binz, Tobias 239
Bittencourt, Luiz F. 3
Breitenbücher, Uwe 216, 239

Cruzes, Daniela S. 38

Feinbube, Frank 171
Fischer-Hübner, Simone 38
Fortes, Renata 115

Gómez Sáez, Santiago 153

Hadji, Makhlouf 15
Hahn, Michael 153
Hasham, Khawar 74

Jaatun, Martin Gilje 38
Janusz, Daniel 171
Johansen, Dag 279

Karastoyanova, Dimka 153
Képes, Kálmán 239
Kilpatrick, Peter 135
Kopp, Oliver 239
Kvalnes, Åge 279

Leymann, Frank 153, 216, 239
Liang, Yongzheng 58
Lucrédio, Daniel 115

Malik, Zaki 263
McClatchey, Richard 74
Molina-Jimenez, Carlos 193
Moreira, Ana 115
Munir, Kamran 74

Neuhaus, Christian 171
Nikolopoulos, Dimitrios S. 135
Nogueira, Elias 115

Papazachos, Zafeirios 135
Petri, Ioan 3
Pettersen, Robert 279
Polze, Andreas 171
Pulls, Tobias 95

Rana, Omer 3
Reich, Christoph 95
Rezgui, Abdelmounaam 263
Rübsamen, Thomas 95

Sfyrakis, Ioannis 193
Shamdasani, Jetendr 74
Skouradaki, Marigianna 153
Solaiman, Ellis 193

Valvåg, Steffen Viken 279
Vukojevic-Haupt, Karolina 153

Wettinger, Johannes 216, 239

Printed in the United States
By Bookmasters